THE
MEMORY PALACE
OF
MATTEO RICCI

ff

THE MEMORY PALACE OF MATTEO RICCI

Jonathan D. Spence

faber and faber

LONDON · BOSTON

First published in the USA in 1984
by Viking Penguin Inc., New York
Published simultaneously in Canada
First published in Great Britain in 1985
by Faber and Faber Limited
3 Queen Square London WC1N 3AU
This paperback edition first published in 1988

Printed in Great Britain by
Cox & Wyman Ltd, Reading, Berkshire
All rights reserved

Copyright © The Jonathan D. Spence Children's Trust, 1983, 1984, 1985

Maps by David Lindroth
Calligraphy by Wang Fang-yu and Wang Sum Wai

A portion of this book appeared originally in the *Yale Review*
under the title "Ricci".

British Library Cataloguing in Publication Data

Spence, Jonathan D.
The memory palace of Matteo Ricci.
1. Ricci, Matteo   2. Missionaries—
China—Biography   3. Missionaries—
Italy—Biography
266'2'0924   BV3427.R46
ISBN 0-571-13959-0

FOR HELEN

CONTENTS

vii

CONTENTS

Illustrations appear on pages 25, 61, 94, 129, 163, 202, 263, 264.
Maps appear on pages xv and xvi.

viii

ACKNOWLEDGEMENTS

I owe thanks to many people for helping me with this book. I badgered numerous members of the Yale history department, at some time or other, with requests for information, and they all responded cheerfully and helpfully. Without my naming them all individually, I hope they will accept this collective mention of gratitude. The same was true for those in the Whitney Humanities Center at Yale, where the first draft was written. I would like to thank all the fellows there for their guidance and encouragement.

Among the scores of people from other departments at Yale who also helped with advice, I am especially grateful to Herbert Marks, Wayne Meeks and Thomas Greene for making what turned out to be crucial suggestions at the right times. For helping me track down Ricci's four prints, I am grateful to Egbert Haverkamp-Begemann and Jennifer Kilian, as well as to the staff of the Department of Prints and Photographs at the Metropolitan Museum of Art in New York, under whose guidance I at last held two of the originals in my hands. Leo Steinberg gave help with interpretations. Charles Boxer, at a memorable luncheon, charted my course for Goa and Macao.

I would also like to acknowledge the constant help of the staff in the Beinecke Rare Book Library, the Divinity School Library, the Art Library, and the Sterling Memorial Library, all at Yale. My thanks, too, to those who provided copies of rare materials from Berkeley, Chicago, Cornell, and Harvard, from Cambridge University Library, and from the Biblioteca Comunale at Macerata, where Aldo Adversi and Piero Corradini were of key assistance.

At the China Jesuit History Project in Los Gatos, where I spent a valuable week early in 1983, kind hospitality was offered by the rector, Father Joseph Costa, S.J., and the librarian, Father Carrol O'Sullivan, S.J. Theodore Foss and Brother Michael Grace in Chicago, as well as the Jesuit fathers George Ganss, Christopher Spalatin, Peter Hu, and William Spohn all gave me useful advice, and so—repeatedly and graciously—did Father Edward Malatesta, S.J.

For help with translations from Portuguese, Italian, Latin and Chinese, I particularly thank Carla Freccero, Claudia Brodsky, Cheng Peikai, K'ang Le, Ch'en Jo-shui, Sylvia Yü and Yü Ying-shih. Those who struggled in turn to decipher my opaque and troubled drafts were many, but my special thanks to the typists who suffered the most and the longest, Katrin van der Vaart with the first draft and Elna Godburn with the second.

The calligraphy for Ricci's four memory images was written expressly for this book by Chang Ch'ung-ho, and my thanks to her for her skill and sensitivity. Time to work out the basic scheme of the book and undertake the initial research was provided by a John Simon Guggenheim Memorial Fellowship, for which I thank the trustees. Helpful readings of the first draft were offered by Michael Cooke, Father Malatesta, S.J., and Jeanne Bloom, and of the second by Harold Bloom, Robert Fitzgerald, Hans Frei, and John Hollander, to all of whom my thanks. Elisabeth Sifton, as twice before, provided the careful reading of everything at all stages which encouraged me to keep trying. I am happy to have the book appear under her imprint.

Grateful acknowledgment is made to the following for permission to reprint copyright material:

Columbia University Press: selections from *Dictionary of Ming Biography*, eds. L. C. Goodrich and C. Y. Fan. Copyright © 1976 by Columbia University Press

Harvard University Press: excerpts from *Institutio Oratoria* by Quintilian, trs. H. E. Butler, vol. IV, 1936; *Ad Herennium*, anon., trs. Harry Caplan, 1968; *Epitome of Roman History* by Lucius Annaeus Florus, trs. E. S. Forster, 1929

Loyola University Press: excerpts from *The Spiritual Exercises* by Ignatius of Loyola, trs. Louis J. Puhl, S. J., Loyola University Press, 1951

Penguin Books Ltd: excerpt from *Gargantua and Pantagruel* by Rabelais, trs. J. M. Cohen, Penguin Classics, 1955, p. 658. Copyright 1955 by J. M. Cohen

Random House, Inc.: extract from the *Aeneid* by Virgil, trs. Robert Fitzgerald. Translation copyright © 1980, 1982, 1983 by Robert Fitzgerald

Universität Salzburg, Institut für Englische Sprache und Literatur: excerpt from *The Vita Christi of Ludolph of Saxony* by Charles Albert Conway, from *Analecta Cartusiana*, 34, ed. Dr James Hogg, University of Salzburg, 1976.

MATTEO RICCI:
A CHRONOLOGY

1552, October 6	Born in Macerata, Italy, in the papal domain.
1561	Becomes pupil in Jesuit school, Macerata.
1568	To Rome, to study law.
1571, August 15	Enters St. Andrew's Quirinale in Rome, as novice in the Society of Jesus.
1572–1573	Studies at Jesuit college, Florence.
1573, September–1577, May	Studies at Jesuit college in Rome.
1577, Summer	To Coimbra, Portugal. Studies Portuguese.
1578, March	Audience with King Sebastian.
——, March 24	Leaves Lisbon on the *St. Louis*.
——, September 13	Reaches Goa. Studies theology, teaches Latin and Greek.
1580	Lives in Cochin. Ordained priest, late July.
1581	Returns to Goa.
1582, April 26	Departs Goa by sea.
——, June	In Malacca.
——, August 7	Arrives in Macao.

1583, September 10	Settles in Zhaoqing, China, with Michele Ruggieri.
1584, October	Unauthorized copies of his world map are printed in Zhaoqing.
1589, August 3	Expelled from Zhaoqing by hostile mandarins.
——, August 26	Settles in Shaozhou.
1591, December	Begins draft translation of Chinese classical *Four Books*.
1592, July	Shaozhou residence attacked. Ricci injures foot.
1594, November	Jesuits change to Chinese literati dress.
1595, April 18	Leaves Shaozhou for Nanjing.
——, mid-May	Shipwreck and drowning of Barradas.
——, June 28	Settles in Nanchang.
——, November	Composes *Treatise on Friendship*.
1596, Spring	Composes draft of *Treatise on Mnemonic Arts*.
1597, August	Named superior of China mission.
1598, September 7–November 5	First trip to Peking; residence not permitted.
1599, February 6	Settles in Nanjing.
1600, November	Eunuch Ma Tang seizes crucifix.
1601, January 24	Enters Peking for second time.
——, February	Composes eight songs for emperor's court.
——, May 28	Peking residence permitted.
1602, August	Publishes revised version of world map.
1603, Autumn–Winter	Publishes *True Meaning of the Lord of Heaven*.
1604, mid-August	Plantin polyglot Bible reaches Peking.
1606, January	Gives four prints and commentaries to ink-maker Cheng Dayue.
1607, May	Publishes translation of first six books of Euclid's *Elements of Geometry*.
1608, January–February	Publishes *Ten Discourses by a Paradoxical Man*.
——, Autumn–Winter	Starts to write his *Historia*.
1609, September 8	First Marian sodality founded in Peking.
1610, May 11	Dies in Peking.

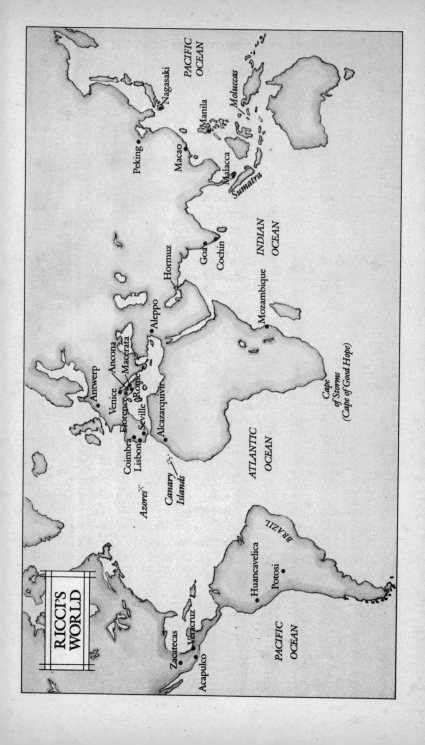

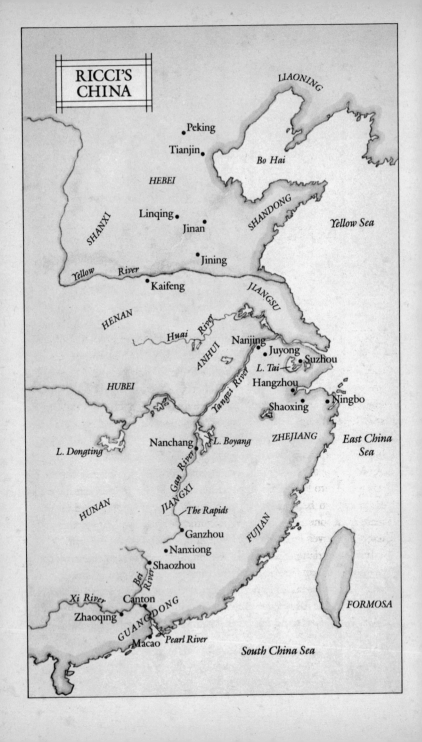

ONE

BUILDING THE PALACE

I n 1596 Matteo Ricci taught the Chinese how to build a memory palace. He told them that the size of the palace would depend on how much they wanted to remember: the most ambitious construction would consist of several hundred buildings of all shapes and sizes; "the more there are the better it will be," said Ricci, though he added that one did not have to build on a grandiose scale right away. One could create modest palaces, or one could build less dramatic structures such as a temple compound, a cluster of government offices, a public hostel, or a merchants' meeting lodge. If one wished to begin on a still smaller scale, then one could erect a simple reception hall, a pavilion, or a studio. And if one wanted an intimate space one could use just the corner of a pavilion, or an altar in a temple, or even such a homely object as a wardrobe or a divan.[1]

In summarizing this memory system, he explained that these palaces, pavilions, divans were mental structures to be kept in one's head, not solid objects to be literally constructed out of "real" materials. Ricci suggested that there were three main options for such memory locations. First, they could be drawn from reality—that is, from buildings that one had been in or from objects that one had seen with one's own eyes and recalled in one's memory. Second, they could be totally fictive, products of the imagination conjured up in any shape or size. Or third, they could be half real and half fictive, as in the case of a building one knew well and through the back wall of which one broke an imaginary door as a shortcut to new spaces, or in the middle of which one created a mental staircase that would lead one up to higher floors that had not existed before.

The real purpose of all these mental constructs was to provide storage spaces for the myriad concepts that make up the sum of our human knowledge. To everything that we wish to remember, wrote Ricci, we should give an image; and to every one of these images we should assign a position where it can repose peacefully until we are ready to reclaim it by an act of memory. Since this entire memory system can work only if the images stay in the assigned positions and if we can instantly remember where we stored them, obviously it would seem easiest to rely on real locations which we know so well that we cannot ever forget them. But that would be a mistake, thought Ricci. For it is by expanding the number of locations and the corresponding number of images that can be stored in them that we increase and strengthen our memory. Therefore the Chinese should struggle with the difficult task of creating fictive places, or mixing the fictive with the real, fixing them permanently in their minds by constant practice and review so that at last the fictive spaces become "as if real, and can never be erased."[2]

How on earth had such a system first evolved, the Chinese might well have asked, and Ricci anticipated the question by summarizing the ancient Western tradition that ascribed the idea of memory training through precise placement to the Greek poet Simonides. As Ricci explained (giving the nearest approximation he could provide in Chinese for the poet's name):

Long ago a Western poet, the noble Xi-mo-ni-de, was gathered with his relatives and friends for a drinking party at the palace, among a dense crowd of guests. When he left the crowd for a moment to step outside, the great hall came tumbling down in a sudden mighty wind. All the other revelers were crushed to death, their bodies were mangled and torn apart, not even their own families could recognize them. Xi-mo-ni-de, however, could remember the exact order in which his relatives and friends had been sitting, and as he recalled them one by one their bodies could be identified. From this we can see the birth of the mnemonic method that was transmitted to later ages.[3]

It was this general facility for remembering the order of things that had been elaborated into a system over the succeeding centuries; by Ricci's time it had become a way for ordering all one's knowledge of secular and religious subjects, and since he himself was a Catholic missionary Ricci hoped that once the Chinese learned to value his mnemonic powers they would be drawn to ask him about the religion that made such wonders possible.

Matteo Ricci had traveled a long road in order to win this chance to present his mnemonics to a scholarly Chinese audience. An Italian, born in the hill town of Macerata in 1552, Ricci became a novice in the Jesuit order in Rome in 1571 and, after extensive training in theology, humanities, and science, followed by a five-year apprenticeship in India and Macao, entered China in 1583 to undertake mission work. In 1595, by which time he had become fluent in the Chinese language, he took up residence in the prosperous administrative and commercial center of Nanchang, in the eastern province of Jiangxi.[4] At the very end of 1595 he gave expression to his newfound confidence in his own language skills by writing out, in Chinese ideographs, a book of maxims on friendship drawn from various classical authors and from the church fathers. He presented this manuscript to a prince of the Ming ruling house who was living in Nanchang and had frequently invited him to his palace for drinking parties.[5] At the same time he was beginning to discuss his theories on memory with local Chinese scholars and to give lessons in mnemonic techniques.[6] His description of the memory palace can be found in a short book on the art of memory which he wrote out in Chinese the following year and gave as a present to the governor of Jiangxi, Lu Wangai, and to Governor Lu's three sons.[7]

The family that Ricci was seeking to instruct in mnemonic skills stood at the apex of Chinese society. Governor Lu himself was an intelligent and wealthy scholar who had served in a wide variety of posts in the Ming dynasty bureaucracy. He knew the country well, for he had been stationed at various times in the far southwest, on the east coast, and in the north, and he had performed with distinction in each of the main areas of Chinese administration: the judicial, the financial, and the military. Now he had reached the peak of his career, as a provincial governor, and was preparing his three sons for the advanced government examinations; he himself had passed these exams with distinction twenty-eight years before, and knew along with all his contemporaries that success in the exams was the surest route to fame and fortune in the imperial Chinese state.[8] Thus we can be almost certain that Ricci was offering to teach the governor's sons advanced memory techniques so that they would have a better chance to pass the exams, and would then in gratitude use their newly won prestige to advance the cause of the Catholic church.

In the event, however, though the governor's children did extremely well in the exams, this does not seem to have been because of Ricci's mnemonic methods but rather because of diligent study along traditional Chinese lines of repetition and recitation, aided perhaps by the mnemonic poems and rhyming jingles that were part of current Chinese memory practice.[9] As Ricci wrote later that same year to the general of the Jesuit order, Claudio Acquaviva, the governor's eldest son had read the memory book with care, but had remarked to one of his confidants that "though the precepts are the true rules of memory, one has to have a remarkably fine memory to make any use of them."[10] And in a letter to a friend in Italy with whom he had first written out the rules for building memory palaces, Ricci observed that, although the Chinese in Nanchang "all admired the subtlety of the system, not all of them were willing to take the trouble to learn how to use it."[11]

Ricci himself saw nothing odd or particularly difficult in building memory palaces. He had grown up with them, together with a whole range of other techniques for fixing the subjects of one's schooling in the memory. Moreover, these skills were a fundamental part of the curriculum that Ricci had studied in his classes on rhetoric and ethics at the Jesuit College in Rome. Ricci was probably introduced to the idea of memory palaces by way of the scholar Cypriano Soarez, whose textbook on the basic lessons of rhetoric and grammar, the *De Arte Rhetorica*, was required reading for Jesuit students in the 1570s.[12] After leading his readers through the fundamentals of classical usage and sentence structure, and giving them examples of tropes and metaphors, metonymy, onomatopoeia, and metalepsis, allegory, irony, and hyperbole, Soarez introduced them to the art of memory placement, which he ascribed to Simonides and called the root of all eloquence, the *"thesaurus eloquantiae."* He noted how the system held words in order as well as things, and could be used for an "infinite progression" of terms. The students should practice creating dramatic images of various kinds, and designing locations for them: palatial buildings or spacious churches would be among the best.[13]

But such vague suggestions would hardly give one the full range of memory techniques, or even the principles behind them. Ricci would have learned the details from several other authors. One would have been Pliny, whose *Natural History* Ricci also read in school, and whose passage on the great memory experts of the past he translated into Chinese in his 1596 memory book.[14] Others would have been several writers of the first century B.C. and the first century A.D., such as the author of a Latin work on rhetoric called *Ad Herennium,* or Quintilian, who wrote about memory in his handbooks on oratory. These books gave detailed information on how to construct memory buildings and the images one would place in them. As the author of *Ad Herennium* explained:

We ought, then, to set up images of a kind that can adhere longest in the memory. And we shall do so if we establish likenesses as striking as possible; if we set up images that are not many or vague, but doing

5

something; if we assign to them exceptional beauty or singular ugliness; if we dress some of them with crowns or purple cloaks, for example, so that the likeness may be more distinct to us; or if we somehow disfigure them, as by introducing one stained with blood or soiled with mud or smeared with red paint, so that its form is more striking, or by assigning certain comic effects to our images, for that, too, will ensure our remembering them more readily.[15]

Such a description carried particular force, since throughout the Middle Ages the author of *Ad Herennium* was believed to be the revered Cicero himself.

Quintilian elaborated on the same topic by explaining what sort of places one would use to store the images one had chosen:

The first thought is placed, as it were, in the forecourt; the second, let us say, in the living room: the remainder are placed in due order all round the *impluvium* and entrusted not merely to bedrooms and parlours, but even to the care of statues and the like. This done, as soon as the memory of the facts requires to be revived, all these places are visited in turn and the various deposits are demanded from their custodians, as the sight of each recalls the respective details. Consequently, however large the number of these which it is required to remember, all are linked one to the other like dancers hand in hand, and there can be no mistake since they join what precedes to what follows, no trouble being required except the preliminary labour of committing the various points to memory. What I have spoken of as being done in a house, can equally well be done in connection with public buildings, a long journey, the ramparts of a city, or even pictures. Or we may even imagine such places to ourselves.[16]

Despite these attempts at explanation, the system sounds elusive and abstract to readers today. But if we digress a moment to provide a modern focus and context, perhaps we can sharpen our view of how Ricci sought to interest the Chinese in his memory theories by creating combinations of images, fixed in place, which through an association of ideas or a specific mnemonic rule would in turn yield, instantly, a required piece of information. Let us imagine a modern medical student facing an oral examination that reviews her work on bones, cells, and nerves. The student has in her head a whole memory city, neatly laid out in wards, streets, lanes, houses, containing all the knowledge she has acquired so far in her schooling; but facing the examiners she pays no attention to the wards of history, geology, poetry, chemistry, and mechanics. Her energy is concentrated on the three-story Physiology House in Body Lane, where, in separate rooms, the disparate, powerful, evocative images she has been creating in each evening of study are in place—around the walls, between the windows, on chairs, beds, tables. Three questions are fired at her: she must name the bones of the upper limbs, the stages of cell division in meiosis, and the order of nerves passing through the superior orbital tissue in the skull. Her mind races to the Upper Body Bone Room, at the top of the stairs on the second floor, where, in the third position from the door, a Canadian Mountie in a brilliant scarlet jacket sits on his horse with a manacled, distraught figure tied to the horse's crupper: from there it takes her only a fraction of a second to glide to the Cell Room in the basement where, near the furnace, a magnificent but savagely scarred African warrior is standing, a look of ineffable boredom on his face, despite the fact that he grasps with each huge hand the upper arm of a beautiful African girl; and as swiftly the student's thoughts wing to the top floor Skull Room where, reclining on a bedspread patterned on the stripes and colors of the flag of France, a voluptuous naked woman reclines, her little fist clutching a crumpled stack of dollar bills. The student's answers to the three questions come quickly. The image of the Mountie and his captive has at once given her the sentence *Some Criminals Have Underestimated Royal Canadian Mounted Police*, the first letter of each word yielding the correct list of scapula, clavicle, humerus, ulna, radius, carpals, metacarpals, and phalanges. The second image, of the *Lazy Zulu Pursuing Dark Damosels*, gives the student the stages of cell division in meiosis as leptotene, zygotene, pachytene, diplotene, and diakinesis. The third

7

image, the *Lazy French Tart Lying Naked In Anticipation*, yields the order of nerves in the skull's upper orbital tissues, to wit, the lacrimal, frontal, trochlear, lateral, nasociliary, internal, and abducens.[17]

In a medieval or late Renaissance world similar techniques would have had a different focus, and the images would have been appropriate to the times. As early as the fifth century A.D. one finds the philosopher Martianus Capella writing that Psyche, at her birth, had been given the most lovely presents, including "a vehicle with swift wheels"—the gift was Mercury's idea—"in which she could travel at an astonishing speed, although Memory bound it and weighed it down with golden chains." These were the chains of memory that stood for the stabilizing force of intellect and imagination on the human soul; they were not meant to be a metaphor for any idea of stasis.[18] And how sharp still, more than a millennium later, must have been for Ricci and his contemporaries the memory image of Rhetoric as Capella painted her, that woman with "so rich a wealth of diction, so vast a store of memory and recollection," who held memory in her domain. Here was fifth-century Rhetoric:

> A woman of the tallest stature and abounding self-confidence, a woman of outstanding beauty; she wore a helmet, and her head was wreathed with royal grandeur; in her hands the weapons which she used either to defend herself or to wound her enemies, shone with the brightness of lightning. The garment under her arms was covered by a robe wound about her shoulders in the Latin fashion; this robe was adorned with the light of all kinds of devices and showed the figures of them all, while she had a belt under her breast adorned with the rarest colors of jewels.

Each decoration of her robe—light, devices, figures, colors, jewels—referred to aspects of rhetorical ornament and would be retained forever by the student who kept her in his head.[19] And how perfect was the contrast between this glowing figure of Rhetoric and the terrible figure of Idolatry, given *her* lineaments by the fifth-century theologian and mythologist Fulgentius and then updated into a Latin mnemonic jingle by the fourteenth-century monk Ridevall. For Idolatry was depicted as a prostitute, a trumpet blaring above her head to give notice to all of her condition. Summoning up this figure from her resting place when the topic of idolatry had to be broached, one would at once recall the salient points of theological argument: she was a harlot because the unfaithful have abandoned God and fornicated with idols; she was blind and deaf because Fulgentius had taught that the first idol had been a dead son's likeness made by slaves to lessen the grief of the child's father, and she was blind and deaf to the true belief that should have banished such superstitions.[20]

How many such images could one or did one seek to retain in the memory palaces of one's mind? Ricci wrote quite casually in 1595 of running through a list of four to five hundred random Chinese ideograms and then repeating the list in reverse order, while Chinese friends described him as being able to recite volumes of the Chinese classics after scanning them only once.[21] But such feats were not particularly startling: Francesco Panigarola, an older contemporary who may have taught Ricci memory arts either in Rome or in Macerata—the manuscript draft of Panigarola's little tract on memory method still reposes in the Macerata library—was described by acquaintances in Florence as being able to roam across a hundred thousand memory images, each in its own fixed space.[22] As Ricci, echoing the past books on memory, told Governor Lu Wangai, it was the order and sequence of the places ready for images inside each building that were crucial to the mnemonic art:

Once your places are all fixed in order, then you can walk through the door and make your start. Turn to the right and proceed from there. As with the practice of calligraphy, in which you move from the beginning to the end, as with fish who swim along in ordered schools, so is everything arranged in your brain, and all the images are ready for whatever you seek to remember. If you are going to use a great many [images], then let the buildings be hundreds or thousands of units in

9

extent; if you only want a few, then take a single reception hall and just divide it up by its corners.[23]

In her wonderfully erudite and comprehensive work on medieval and Renaissance mnemonic theory, *The Art of Memory,* Frances Yates mused over "what a Christianized artificial memory might have been like" and regretted the fact that "an *Ars memorativa* treatise, though it will always give the rules, rarely gives any concrete application of the rules, that is to say it rarely sets out a system of mnemonic images on their places."[24] Matteo Ricci's Chinese version of a memory system cannot totally fill these lacunae, but it does give us a sense of how the traditional memory system could be adhered to on the far side of the globe.

Furthermore, Ricci has left us, in his Chinese book on memory, one explicit group of images, each fixed in its own place and described in sequence. The first image was two warriors grappling, the second a tribeswoman from the west, the third a peasant cutting grain, the fourth a maidservant holding a child in her arms. True to his own injunctions about a simple way to begin a memory system, Ricci chose to place these images in the four corners of one specific room. This room was a reception hall, a fairly large formal space supported by pillars, which I take to be the entry way to the memory palace proper. Governor Lu or any beginner who was reading Ricci could follow him without difficulty on this first mental memory stroll; we can see them walking together to the door, entering the hall, and, turning to their right, perusing the images one by one.[25]

Once one grew familiar with the methodology, however, one did not have the sole choice of building ever larger and larger clusters of rooms and chambers. One could increase the content of given structures by placing ever more images within them. The only danger here was that the space might become too cluttered for the mind to seize easily on all the images it contained. But with that one caution one could introduce articles of furniture into the room, place small decorative objects of gold or jade upon occasional tables, and paint the walls themselves in glittering colors.[26] One could also use specific "pictures" to evoke the images, wrote Ricci, just as Quintilian had urged in the first century A.D., or as Ludovico Dolce had in mind in 1562 when he suggested as an example that certain works of Titian be remembered in all their intricate details by students interested in classical mythology.[27] Ricci clearly knew the mnemonic effect of vivid illustrations, and his letters show that he was not only aware of religious books like Jeronimo Nadal's *Commentaries on the Gospels,* copiously illustrated with woodcuts, which the Jesuits were publishing with the aim of making every important moment in Christ's life fresh and vivid in the viewer's mind, but he even had his own copy of Nadal with him in China and wrote to friends in Italy that he found it invaluable.[28]

Just as Ricci left four memory images for his reception hall, so he left four religious pictures, each with a caption in his calligraphy and three of them embellished with his own commentaries: these were of Christ and Peter at the Sea of Galilee, of Christ and the two disciples at Emmaus, of the men of Sodom falling blinded before the angel of the Lord, and of the Virgin Mary holding the Christ Child. That these pictures have been preserved is due to Ricci's friendship with the publisher and inkstone connoisseur Cheng Dayue, who was introduced to him by a mutual friend in Peking in 1605. Cheng, who was about to publish a collection of Chinese calligraphy and graphics under the title of "The Ink Garden," was eager to include samples of Western art and handwriting, and requested Ricci to contribute some. Though Ricci, elaborately self-deprecating, confessed to Cheng that only "one ten-thousandth part" of Western culture could be of any interest to the erudite Chinese, he nevertheless consented, with the result that the following year his four pictures appeared along with his commentaries in Cheng's elegant volume.[29] Such religious pictures could be confidently expected to fix in Chinese minds the details of dramatic passages from the Bible, whether these were from moments in Christ's life or from antecedents in the Book of Genesis. If arranged in rigorous sequence, like the memory images, they could be used to supplement the storage and retrieval mechanisms of the memory palace itself.

Despite Ricci's apparent self-confidence about the value of his memory system, such structures were beginning to be challenged in Europe well before he sailed to the East in 1578. In the 1530s Cornelius Agrippa, despite his interest in magic and in scientific alchemy, wrote in his book *Of the Vanitie and Uncertaintie of Artes and Sciences* that he felt the natural memory of men was dulled by the "monstrous images" concocted in mnemonic arts; the attempt to overload the mind with infinite pieces of information often "caused madness and frenzy instead of profound and sure memory." Agrippa saw a kind of puerile exhibitionism in this flaunting of knowledge. In the English translation of his work that appeared in 1569, this disgust comes through strongly: "It is a shameful thinge, and a shamelesse mannes propertie to set out in al mens sighte, the readings of many thinges, like as Marchantes do theire wares: whereas in the meane while the howse is emptie."[30] Religious thinkers like Erasmus and Melanchthon saw these memory systems as going back to an earlier age of monkish superstition and felt that the systems were of no practical use.[31] Rabelais, also in the 1530s, had used his marvelous powers of mockery further to discredit the memory arts. He described how Gargantua was taught by his tutor Holofernes to memorize the most abstruse grammatical works of his time, along with their full panoply of learned commentaries by such scholars as Bangbreeze, Scallywag, and Claptrap. The upshot, wrote Rabelais gravely, was that though Gargantua could indeed repeat the books he had learned "backwards by heart," and "became as wise as any man baked in an oven," when one wanted intelligent commentary from him "it was no more possible to draw a word from him than a fart from a dead donkey."[32] By the end of the century Francis Bacon, despite his fascination with the power of *natural* memory to organize and analyze data, had developed a definitive critique of the artificial memory devices. Though he acknowledged the surface impressiveness of feats

12

that could be attained with memory training, calling them "of ostentation prodigious," Bacon concluded that the systems were fundamentally "barren." "I make no more estimation of repeating a great number of names or words upon once hearing," he wrote, "than I do of the tricks of tumblers, funamboloes, baladines: the one being the same in the mind that the other is in the body, matters of strangeness without worthiness."[33]

But most Catholic theologians of Ricci's time, like Ricci himself, were not dissuaded by these dismissive arguments. They concentrated on the positive aspects of the system, ignoring the growing body of scholarship which proved that the key early text on memory systems, *Ad Herennium,* had in fact not been written by Cicero at all and continuing to make it a fundamental part of their curriculum.[34] It was Thomas Aquinas himself who had firmly implanted the idea that systems of memory were a part of ethics rather than merely an aspect of rhetoric, as they had usually been considered previously. In his commentaries on Aristotle, Aquinas described the importance of "corporeal similitudes"—or memory images in bodily form—in preventing "subtle and spiritual things" falling away from the soul. Oddly enough, Aquinas strengthened his arguments for use of memory-place systems by pointing out that Cicero in *Ad Herennium* had said we need "solicitude" for our memory images; Aquinas interpreted this as meaning we should "cleave with affection" to our memory images, and thus made it possible to apply mnemonic images to devotional and scriptural uses. The fact that *Ad Herennium* had said we need "solitude" to pick out our memory images, not "solicitude," was not noted for centuries. And Aquinas's slip—ironically, he had probably been quoting from memory in any case—led to the strengthening of a Christian mnemonic tradition that focused on memory arts as the means to marshal "spiritual intentions." Such an interpretation spread widely. For instance, the idea that memory systems were used to "remember Heaven and Hell" can explain much of the iconography of Giotto's paintings or the structure and detail of Dante's *Inferno,* and was commonplace in scores of books published in the sixteenth century.[35]

13

In the time of Aquinas, and in the following two centuries, there developed a whole tradition of texts that sought to sharpen Christian devotion through evoking the imagination of believers, some of the most important of which, like William of Paris's twelfth-century *Rhetorica Divina*, reached back to Quintilian for inspiration.[36] Ludolfus of Saxony, a fourteenth-century devotional writer whom Ignatius of Loyola was later to read with fascination, used language of exceptional force. Ludolfus compelled his Christian readers to be present at the Crucifixion, pounding his words into the reader's ears as the nails pounded through Christ: "After all the nerves and veins had been strained, and the bones and joints dislocated by the violent extension, he was fastened to the cross. His hands and feet were rudely pierced and wounded by coarse, heavy nails that injured skin and flesh, nerves and veins, and also the ligaments of the bones."[37] In such moods, where "gospel time is made to suffuse present time," Ludolfus could tell the believer to proceed "with a certain devout curiosity, feeling your way, [and] touching each of the wounds of your Saviour, who has thus died for you"—wounds of which, according to Bridget of Sweden, whose work Ludolfus drew on, there were 5,490.[38] Ludolfus, a monastic Carthusian, urged that the active imagination must at all times be applied to Christ, "in walking along and in standing still, in sitting down and in lying down, in eating and in drinking, in talking and in keeping silent, when alone and when with others."[39] By the middle of the fifteenth century, the author of a book of devotions for girls was urging them to give to characters in the Bible—not excluding Christ himself—the faces of friends and acquaintances, so that they would be fixed in their memories. He told his young audience to place these figures in their own mental Jerusalem, "taking for this purpose a city that is well-known to you." Thereafter, "alone and solitary" in her chamber, each girl could undertake her devotions, reliving the Bible story by "moving slowly from episode to episode."[40]

This vivid restructuring of memory was also a fundamental component of the edifice of discipline and religious training that the converted Spanish soldier Ignatius of Loyola developed for the members of the Society of Jesus, which he founded in 1540; he had been marshaling his arguments in writing the early drafts of the *Spiritual Exercises,* which was to be published in its final form eight years later. In order that his followers might live the biblical narrative in all its force, Ignatius instructed them to apply their five senses to those scriptural passages that they were contemplating. At the simplest level, those practicing the exercises would call to mind the physical setting in which a given event took place, or what Ignatius called "an imaginative representation" of the place:[41] for example, the road from Bethany to Jerusalem on which Christ traveled toward his passion, the room in which he held his last supper, the garden in which he was betrayed, the house in which Mary his mother waited after the Crucifixion.[42] Within these contexts, said Ignatius, one could then move to a sharper picture by adding the sense of hearing: "Listen to what is being said by the people on the earth's surface, talking to each other, swearing and blaspheming." Contrast with this the words of the three divine persons of the Trinity, and listen to them as they say, "Let us bring about the redemption of mankind." After seeing and listening, one can proceed to involve the rest of the five senses in the act of memory: "Smell the indescribable fragrance and taste the boundless sweetness of the divinity. Touch by kissing and clinging to the places where these persons walk or sit, always trying to profit thereby."[43] If the five senses evoke the past in its diversity and bring it—contextually primed, as it were—into the present, it is the three faculties of memory, reason, and will that have the burden of deepening the significance of what is being contemplated, especially when the subject matter is not something visible in a conventional sense, as in the case of an awareness of sin. Here, said Ignatius, the "picture will be the idea, produced by an effort of the imagination, that my soul is a prisoner in this corruptible body and that my whole self, body and soul, is condemned to live amongst animals on this earth, like someone in a foreign land." (Though this was not written expressly for missionaries, one can guess the force the passage must have gained for Ricci as he lived out his life in China, struggling for periods of leisure to reinforce his spiritual life.) As Ignatius

15

phrased it, each of the three faculties could be employed in turn, with memory leading the way:

> By an effort of my memory, I will recall the first sin, that of the angels; next, I will use my reason to think about it; then my will, striving to remember and think about all this in order to develop in myself a sense of utter shame, as I compare my numerous sins with the angels' one sin: that one sin brought them to Hell: how often have I deserved it for all my sins. The memory's part is to recall how the angels were created in grace, but refused to make the most of their free-will in honoring and obeying their Creator and Lord: they fell victims to pride, and their state of grace was perverted to one of evil will, as they were plunged from Heaven into hell. Using my reason in the same way, I will think about all this in greater detail: by my will I try to evoke the proper sentiments.[44]

As each person practicing the exercises reflected on his own sins by placing them in the most domestic and intimate of contexts—seeing himself in the houses where he had lived at different times, thinking of all his personal relations with others, and reflecting on the various positions of service or authority he had held—so he could move from the contemplation of the angels' first sin to a panoramic vision of the great spiritual battle that pitted Christ and his forces against the armies of the devil.[45]

The urgent calls of Ludolfus and Ignatius that the faithful Christian should incorporate these "memories" of an unlived past into the spiritual present echoed not only Thomas Aquinas but also the *Confessions* of Augustine, written eleven hundred years before Ricci was born, for it was Augustine who had said: "Perchance it might be properly said, 'there be three times; a present of things past, a present of things present, and a present of things future.' "[46] Yet Ignatius's own Catholic contemporaries worried that he or his followers might be going too far in their invocation of claims to special insight into the divine realm. The bishop of Valencia complained that the *Spiritual Exercises* was little better than "mystery mongering" and was written under the influence of Illuminist ideas prevalent at the time.[47] Six priests who claimed, in 1548, that through the exercises they could obtain a "direct" communication with God were called for examination by the Inquisition: the inquisitors were worried by the priests' claim that "the Holy Spirit might come upon them as he once did upon the apostles."[48] Some Dominicans, in 1553, went so far as to suggest that Ignatius was "notoriously a heretic," charges that prompted Ignatius's friend Nadal (author of the *Contemplations* that Ricci introduced to China) to insist that Ignatius drew his ideas from Scripture, not from direct channels.[49] Conscious of these controversies, Claudio Acquaviva, as general of the order during Ricci's China service, was to downplay Ignatius's views of the "application of the senses" and refer to them as a "very easy mode," not to be compared to more complex forms of contemplation and prayer.[50]

The precise line between religious experiences and so-called magical powers has always been a difficult one to draw. Some scholars have recently suggested that interconnections between religion and magic always lay in the words and incantations of the Mass itself, and in the music, the lights, the wine, the transformations that lie at its heart.[51] Ricci's experiences in China show that there was, in the public mind, a natural presupposition that his skills derived form magical sources. On October 13, 1596, he wrote from the city of Nanchang to General Acquaviva in Rome. After recounting briefly the difficult negotiations he had followed in order to get permission not only to reside in Nanchang but also to buy a house there, Ricci described the crowds of distinguished Chinese literati who were now flocking to his house to congratulate him. Ricci listed the three major motives that he believed the Chinese had for these visits: their conviction that the Jesuits could turn mercury into pure silver; their desire to study Western mathematics; and their eagerness to learn his mnemonic system.[52] The list is completely believable in the context of the European intellectual and religious life of Ricci's time, when memory systems were combined with numerological skills and the arcane semiscientific world of alchemy to give the adept a power over his fate that mirrored the power of con-

17

ventional religion. We must remember that if at one level Ricci's career makes sense only in the context of an aggressive Counter-Reformation Catholicism, as part of an "expansion of Europe" in the later sixteenth century that took place under the guns of Spanish and Portuguese men-of-war, it also makes sense only in a far older context, pre-Renaissance in many aspects, a context reaching back through the Middle Ages to classical antiquity, to worlds where the priests of the Christian religion shared the tasks of consoling mankind with the "cunning men" who dealt in magic, alchemy, cosmography, and astrology.[53]

The protracted and complex debates held by order of the Papacy at the Council of Trent between 1545 and 1563 may have solved some of the most difficult problems raised by the leaders of the Catholic church, who were responding both to their personal awareness of the church's internal decay and to the searching questions of their Protestant opponents, but these "solutions" reached only a fraction of the people. Others continued to hold their own idiosyncratic interpretations: thus God had emerged from a state of chaos in which the four elements of earth, water, fire, and air were already present, according to one North Italian miller questioned by the Inquisition in 1584. "Who moves the chaos?" the inquisitor asked, and the miller responded, "It moves by itself."[54] "My mind was lofty and wished for a new world," said the same miller, explaining that much of his disquiet came from the vision of other lands and peoples that he had absorbed from John Mandeville's tales of his travels in Africa and Cathay.[55] The miller can stand as one humble exemplar of all those men and women in the sixteenth century who continued to search for meanings on their own because neither Protestant nor Catholic reformers had succeeded in convincing them that they could explain either the ultimate mysteries of the world's origins or such localized yet baffling phenomena as intense mental depression, catastrophic sudden death of humans and animals, the loss of cherished possessions, or the failures of the harvest.[56]

And so the lines between aspects of magic and religion continued to be blurred. The miller developed his four-elements theory to the point where God became the air, Christ the earth, and the Holy Spirit the water, while the fire raged everywhere on its own.[57] His poorer contemporaries dreamed of a universe in which rivers were shored up with embankments of ricotta cheese while the heavens rained down ravioli and marzipan.[58] Ricci and his friends, even if they denied any magical force to the objects, tossed tiny talismans made of the wax from the paschal candles of Rome into the stormy seas as they rounded the Cape of Good Hope in 1578, and outside the walls of Peking in 1601 Ricci kept always with him some grains of soil from the Holy Land and a tiny cross made, he believed, from fragments of the true cross on which Christ had died.[59] And in ostensibly "reformed" England, so numerous were the magic practitioners that in one county during the reign of Queen Elizabeth it has been proved that no one lived more than ten miles away from some "cunning man."[60]

In a world used to looking carefully at the sky, each phase of planetary motion, each waxing of the moon, each stellar appearance was carefully tracked, and as carefully analyzed for possible significance on human fate. Educated men and women could be devout members of the Catholic church while still keeping room in their minds for what one historian has called the alternative systems of "undiscovered occult influences" that "pulsated" in their Neoplatonic universes.[61] Within many of these systems it was a truism that special strengths accrued to the individual who could fuse the forces of the cosmos with the mnemonic prowess of his own brain. Quite a strong level of memory, even among the poor and uneducated, was still taken for granted in a culture that remained largely oral. Montaigne, for instance, on his Italian journey of 1581, described a group of peasants in the fields near Florence, their girl friends at their sides, reciting lengthy passages of Ariosto as they strummed on their lutes.[62] Yet at the same time, possession of too strong a memory could swiftly lead one's neighbors to suspect one of having magical powers, as happened with Arnaud du Tilh in southern France during the midsixteenth century.[63] For Shakespeare's audiences it would still have been commonplace to know how

19

to use memory and how to strengthen it. When Ophelia, after Hamlet has killed her father, walks in front of her brother, Laertes, and cries, "There's rosemary, that's for remembrance; pray you, love, remember," she is not simply mad; she is also steeling Laertes for an act of vengeance by invoking the widely held belief, carried in many mnemonic treatises of the day, that rosemary was the sovereign herb for strengthening the memory.[64]

While Ricci was a schoolboy, several charges of practicing black magic were brought against the clergy of his hometown of Macerata, and these might have been connected to some misuse of mnemonic arts, though we don't have the details of what the practitioners were trying to accomplish.[65] What we do know is that all through the sixteenth century "astrologically centered mnemonic systems" were being constructed with extraordinary care in such cities as Venice and Naples and not only used at home but also exported by their eager creators to France and England, among other countries. These systems organized the forces of the universe into "memory theaters," concentric diagrams, or imaginary cities in such a way that those forces could be consulted directly and drawn upon, making the practitioner of the art a "solar magus" of potentially great power. The "theater" created by the remarkable Italian scholar Camillo in the 1540s suggests the range: in the foreground were piles of little boxes, intricately arranged and jammed with all the works of Cicero; rising away into the distance were arrays of cosmic images designed to show the "universe expanding from First Causes through the stages of creation," so that the theater master would be like a man gazing down upon a forest from a high hill, able at last to understand both the individual trees and the shape of the whole. As Camillo explained, "This high and incomparable placing not only performs the office of conserving for us the things, words and acts which we confide to it, so that we may find them at once whenever we need them, but also gives us true wisdom."[66]

Nor was such wisdom confined to the world of words or the stage. It ran on a score of trails throughout the theory and practice of Renaissance architecture, where the "hidden lines" that dictated the perfect spaces could give meaning to a building by expressing ideas of gravity or love, and where the perfect proportions of the human figure could be transposed with cosmic force into stone.[67] It lay at the heart of Renaissance music, which had inherited a process by which mnemonic strength, first manifested in the alphabet and rhyme, was fixed firmly in the melodic line and in which the two attributes of music—as number-mysticism and as science—could flow, in the minds of serious theorists, either into realms of sexual force and regeneration or into those of a specific international discourse. So Kepler, at the same time that he was making his remarkable discoveries on planetary orbits and immersing himself in the work of alchemists at Emperor Rudolph's court, could develop an interpretation that had the interval of the major third in a given piece of music representing male sexual fulfillment while the minor third stood for the receptive female;[68] whereas Nicolo Vicentino, in a treatise of 1555 on his new six-manual harpsichord, the *archicembalo,* could write that his new instrument would be able to produce the sounds of German, French, Spanish, Hungarian, and Turkish. "The inflections and intervals that all nations of the world use in their native speech do not proceed only in whole and half tones, but also in quarter tones and even smaller intervals, so that with the division of our harpsichord we can accommodate all the nations of the world."[69] Ricci, on first seeing Chinese ideographs in Macao in 1582, was to be similarly struck by their incredible potentiality for serving as universal forms that could transcend the differences in pronunciation that inhered in language.[70]

Disparate though these images and examples are, they can serve to underline the fundamental variety of thoughts about memory and its literal and transformative powers that coexisted in what is loosely called the Counter-Reformation period. They make it hard to believe that, as Ricci used his mnemonic methodologies alongside his Western scientific learning and his profound theological training to woo the Chinese people away from their amalgam of Confucianism, Buddhism,

21

and Taoism, he was unmindful of the powers over man and nature that his European contemporaries ascribed to mnemonic arts.

The four memory images that have survived in Ricci's treatise are but a tantalizing hint of the riches stored in his memory palace, just as his four religious pictures represent but a fraction of the Catholic iconography at the heart of the religion to which he tried to convert the Chinese. But since it is so astonishing that even this much has been preserved, and since Ricci chose with care the images and pictures that have come down to us, I have chosen in my turn to build this book around these eight distant fragments. Ricci told Cheng Dayue in 1606, "the whole point of writing something down is that your voice will then carry for thousands of miles, whereas in direct conversation it fades at a hundred paces." He was right, and it is through these accidental survivals that we can enter his past. We can be confident that Ricci would approve this procedure, for as he also said to Cheng Dayue:

> Those who will live one hundred generations after us are not yet born, and I cannot tell what sort of people they will be. Yet thanks to the existence of written culture even those living ten thousand generations hence will be able to enter into my mind as if we were contemporaries. As for those worthy figures who lived a hundred generations ago, although they too are gone, yet thanks to the books they left behind we who come after can hear their modes of discourse, observe their grand demeanor, and understand both the good order and the chaos of their times, exactly as if we were living among them.[71]

To late Renaissance humanists, the men who had lived in the great days of the Roman Empire were the models for this discourse and demeanor. Those were the days in which Quintilian had written his words on memory, and there is a gentle echo of that familiarity in the fact that Ricci's cycles of memory images began with two warriors grappling, while the pictorial cycle began with the sea of Galilee:

22

Quintilian had suggested war and the sea as the first two things one could remember, through the images of a spear and an anchor.[72]

As we travel with Matteo Ricci, we should remember one other link between his classical past and his Chinese present. The best-known Roman memory text stated that one must put certain marks in one's flow of images, signposts, as it were, at every fifth or tenth grouping, such as a golden hand to remind one of the number five or a friend with a name like Decimus to evoke the number ten.[73] Ricci was able to integrate this idea into the flow of his Chinese images and to combine it with his central Christian goal of conversion—to which all his intellectual ingenuity was directed—by a stroke of linguistic brilliance that was made possible only by the nature of the Chinese ideographic script. Instead of the golden hand or the man named Decimus, he proposed to the Chinese that at every tenth memory place they should simply insert a memory image of the Chinese ideograph for "ten."[74] The wonderful elegance of this idea came from the fact that the ideograph for ten, written 十 in Chinese, was used by the Chinese to express many other objects or places in which two lines were crossed, as with a wooden frame or a crossroads. For this reason the earliest Nestorian Christians, who had come to China in the seventh century, had taken "ten" as their word for the cross of Christ, a usage made official by the Mongol conquerors of China in the thirteenth century and adopted by Ricci and the sixteenth-century Jesuits in their turn.[75] Thus as the Chinese of the Ming dynasty followed Matteo Ricci through his reception hall, past his pictures, and on into the recesses of the memory palace, they were guided not only by the logic of the decimal system but also by the implacable symbolism of the sign of the cross itself.

TWO

THE FIRST IMAGE:
THE WARRIORS

For the first image in his memory palace, Ricci decides to build on the Chinese ideograph for war, pronounced *wu*. To present *wu* in the form of a memory image that the reader will remember, he first cuts the ideograph into two sections on a diagonal axis running from upper left to lower right. This dissection yields two separate ideographs, the upper one of which represents the word for spear, the lower a word with the sense of "to stop" or "to prevent." In dividing the ideograph in this fashion Ricci follows—whether wittingly or not—a tradition among Chinese scholars reaching back almost two millennia, a tradition that allowed one to see, buried inside the word for war, the possibilities, however frail, of peace.[1]

Ricci draws from these two ideas and recombines them into one interconnected image: A warrior, the very picture of martial vigor, holds a spear, poised to strike at his enemy; that second warrior grasps the first by the wrist, striving to stop the blow from falling.

Ricci describes to the Chinese, in his memory book, how such images should be formed, placed, and lighted if they are truly to help our human memory. In the rules for the images themselves, he explains

that they must be lively and not too static, that they must arouse strong emotions, that the figures must wear clothes or uniforms which clearly show their social station and the nature of their business or occupation. The differences between figures in a composite image must be exaggerated, their features distorted by joy or pain; they may even be ridiculous or laughable, if that seems advisable; and they must be kept separate and distinct.[2]

As for the location where a given image is to be stored, Ricci gives the Chinese a number of further rules. The place should be spacious, but not so crowded with images that a single one gets lost: a magistrate's yamen, a busy market, or a school jammed with students would all be unsuitable. The light must be clear and even, though not bright enough to dazzle. The spaces must be clean and dry, and kept covered lest the images be streaked with rain or dew. They should be at floor level or just above, not balanced on a beam or perched on the roof, which would make them inaccessible. The mental eye should be able to roam completely from one image to the next, so they should never be closer to their neighbor than three feet nor farther than six feet. They should be firmly planted, not fixed in unstable attitudes susceptible to sudden movement—for example, they should never be suspended from a pulley or balanced on a wheel.[3]

So Ricci constructs the reception hall of his memory palace along these lines and orients it so that it faces south, in deference to the Chinese tradition that gives greatest honor to that direction. He enters the door and turns at once to the right. It is here, in the southeast corner of the building, that he puts the two warriors. Once they are securely placed, he can forget about them for a while. The two men will stay there locked in combat, one striving to kill and the other not to be killed, for as long as he chooses to leave them.

Ricci's childhood world of Macerata was encircled by war and suffused with violence. In the narrow stone streets that he walked to school during the 1550s and 1560s the young men of the Alaleona and Pellicani families had been stalking each other for years, pursuing a feud that reached back to the 1520s: some had been stabbed in broad daylight, others cut down as they said Mass. And those two families had their bloody company, for other noblemen fell to masked killers, or fled to other cities after wreaking their acts of vengeance, there to wait or fight as soldiers until their long terms of exile were up.[4]

Ricci was three years old when three members of the Ciminella family gave a new dimension to this violence by killing Francesco Ciappardelli with a rain of pistol bullets; he was five when a Benedictine friar killed a member of the Floriani family in Macerata; and he was eleven at the time the city resounded to the story that a sixteen-year-old from the same Floriani clan had knifed a young man who had taken a bite out of his ear. In the spate of murders and fights, at least one man and one woman bearing the Ricci name lost their lives, though we do not know if they were close relatives of Matteo. Despite recurrent efforts of the clergy and the city fathers to end the violence, such murders were still commonplace when Matteo Ricci left Macerata in 1568 to study law in Rome.[5]

Outside the walls of Macerata the rural poor, refugees from the war-ravaged cities to the north, and deserters from the myriad mercenary armies that had been fighting on Italian soil coalesced into bandit groups that roamed the countryside almost with impunity. Every kind of bounty was offered to local troops who could kill or capture the bandits, and the Macerata city records show a steady increase in the need for jail space as well as for interrogation rooms where torture could be used to extract further information from the captives.[6] Yet these local initiatives were not enough, and general order was restored only after 1568, when the papal legates who had jurisdiction over the area hired armies to conduct sweeps of the countryside and house-to-house searches and registration drives.[7] (Macerata was within the belt of territory in central Italy that constituted the papal domain, and the

Vatican's legates shared power with Macerata's own government.)
Even so, for years after, travel in the Macerata countryside remained
unsafe, and despite the impressive speeds of the couriers claimed in
some sources, communication with Rome was slow and uncertain.[8]

The bleakness of the situation was compounded by military officers
of the Macerata commune who gave illicit sanctuary to robbers and
killers and provided storage bases for stolen goods. If, like Captain
Francesco De Vico in 1554, they were exposed, arrested, and condemned to death, they could regain their life, freedom, and even the
profits of their crimes by skillful use of a local statute offering freemen
of the city pardon in exchange for bandits they or their friends had
killed. So, wrote Macerata's historian, Libero Paci, could "De Vico become once again an honored citizen, living for the longest span of years
on the fruits of his rapine." Indeed, De Vico lived prosperously in Macerata for all the years of Ricci's upbringing there and finally died in
1584, by which time Ricci had been a year in China.[9]

Being a key city in the administration of the papal domain, Macerata
could not hope to stay free from papal politics, whether international
or local. There had been war scares in the city during 1555 when the
struggles between Pope Paul IV and the powerful Colonna family
threatened to spread to Macerata, but these faded to insignificance the
following year when Pope Paul's mounting troubles with the Spaniards, who controlled southern Italy from their base in the Kingdom of
Naples, brought the Spanish general the duke of Alva into papal territory. Macerata was assessed for military levies by Pope Paul, and the citizens rather belatedly saw to the town's defense, buying up one
hundred arquebuses to swell the armory, distributing pikes to local mi-
litia, converting an old mill tower on the nearby river into a fort, and
hiring a military architect to draw up a master plan for the city's fortifications.[10] Pope Paul sought to counter Spanish power through a
French alliance, and the Maceratans were ordered to prepare supplies
for the French army as well as to repair the roads over which the troops
would be traveling and to send draft animals and supplies to the front.
The French troops, under the command of the duke of Guise, reached

central Italy in March 1557 with an army consisting of twelve thousand infantry and six thousand cavalry. Guise was in Macerata during early April, and the visit was uneventful. More alarming was his return in May, after he had failed to capture the strategic Spanish-held fortress of Civitella, southeast of Rome, for now it was believed that Alva's Spanish troops were on his heels. But peace came in December, and Macerata was spared an attack by one of Philip II's greatest generals, whose reputation for military terror in the Netherlands two decades later was to be as great as the duke of Guise's for intolerance and duplicity in the religious wars of France.[11]

Enmeshed with these local manifestations of the current European drama lay the Muslim forces of the Ottoman Empire. Macerata, a town that looked for trade and economic life as much to the east through its nearby outlet to the sea, the rich Adriatic harbor of Ancona, as west to the markets of Rome, was constantly aware of the dangers of Turkish attack. During the 1540s the Maceratans had to provide money to strengthen Ancona's defenses as well as their own, and in 1551, the year before Ricci was born, new threats of Turkish coastal attacks led the papal legate to order a complete listing of those in Macerata aged eighteen to forty and eligible for military service, a list from which members of the clergy were not to be excluded.[12] Such musterings of Catholics against the Muslim menace call to mind the passions aroused by the Crusades four centuries before, even though in the midsixteenth century religious passions did not always transcend international diplomacy. Thus the French, campaigning against the Holy Roman Emperor Charles V in 1544, had not hesitated to offer the Ottomans the use of Toulon harbor for winter anchorage in exchange for the pressure the Turkish fleets could put on Spain; and similarly in 1556, faced with the threat of the duke of Alva to Rome and the Papal States, Pope Paul IV had sent secret emissaries to the French king asking his help in getting the Turkish fleet to disrupt Spain's military shipments in the Mediterranean.[13]

The vagaries of Maceratan life in this confused situation are shown well enough by events in the mid-1560s: by this time changes in the military politics of the Ottoman Empire had led to corresponding changes in diplomacy and had renewed the threat of Turkish attack in the Adriatic. The citizens of Macerata, desperate to rebuild their ineffective city walls, had done so by getting dispensation from the obligation to provide money to Ancona, even though Ancona's strong defense was essential to Macerata's own survival. But Turkish attacks on the coastal town of Gargano in the summer of 1566, even though some distance to the south, were still near enough to bring home the reality of the threat. Macerata became the base for an emergency force of four thousand infantry and cavalry, who filled all five inns in the town and had to be billeted also in the local monasteries, which profited financially from the extra guests. At other times citizens of Macerata took part in the defense of Malta or fought on the fields of Hungary against the Ottoman ruler Suleiman's forces; some served in the galleys of the Mediterranean fleets in response to papal orders that Macerata provide four rowers for each one hundred registered families; some who had campaigned on various fronts were captured by the Turks and became slaves—the more fortunate ones being ransomed by their families.[14]

In these years of Ricci's youth, military technology was changing swiftly, and these changes necessitated shifts in military tactics. Improved and lighter firearms altered the relationship between infantry and cavalry and gave dominance to the cohesive infantry square, where musketeers (protected during reloading by pikemen) could fight off any traditional cavalry charge. As a sixteenth-century English theorist of the art of war noted, "It is rarely seene in our dayes, that men come often to hand-blowes, as in old time they did: For now in this age the shot so employeth and busieth the field (being well backed with a resolute stand of pikes) that the most valiantest and skilfullest therein do commonly import the victorie, or the best, at the least wise, before men come to many hand-blowes."[15] While the number of "hand-blowes" thus decreased, the need for intensive drill and technical training brought greater rewards to those professional troops who would devote their lives to war, as opposed to rustic conscripts: the Spanish regular troops came to excel at this style of warfare, while the mercenaries of the German principalities and of Switzerland became the spines of a dozen armies, from the Netherlands to Africa and Italy. These mercenary troops fought for money and could be the scourges of any countryside they passed through: Macerata's first test of the usefulness of its new walls came, not in the face of the Turks, but when an army of 4,200 Swiss mercenaries, hired by the Spaniards in the Kingdom of Naples, passed by in the spring of 1566. The Swiss were intended to boost Naples's defenses against the Turks, but the Maceratans clearly feared they might attack the towns they passed en route, and they firmly closed their gates. From this panic-stricken reaction of the Maceratan commune it seems that these potential allies were as much feared as the enemy they would fight against.[16]

Faced by the mixture of threats against them, the Maceratans had turned to a military architect in the late 1550s, and here they were in tune with the spirit of the times. As cannon developed in range and accuracy, and siege warfare grew more complex, old fortifications yielded to a new design of smooth-walled pentagon-shaped fortresses with projecting redoubts at each of their five corners, which yielded maximum open fields of fire along two defensive axes. Italian military designers had the greatest prestige in Europe at this time, and major cities competed for the best of them: the elegant modern fortress not merely was sought for defensive reasons but had come to replace the cathedral as an index of a city's prestige.[17] But of course the designers responded to market demand by raising their prices, and the Maceratans were distressed to find that their choice, the Florentine expert Bastiano, required an expensive annual contract.[18]

Ricci was enough aware of these trends to join his contemporaries in viewing warfare as a scientific operation, and his longest passage of sustained reflection on war—written in 1607, when he had been in China for more than two decades—appears suitably enough in the introduction to one of his own most spectacular scholarly achievements, his translation into Chinese of Euclid's *Elements of Geometry*. There Ricci wrote that mathematical precision was even more important for the military officer than it was for the farmer, the statesman, the doctor, or the merchant. Without mathematical skills, the general would be unsuccessful, however great his knowledge and valor might be. As Ricci summarized it, the army required precise skills for three main reasons:

> First, the good general has to estimate the availability of food supplies for his troops and his horses, and calculate all the elements on his line of march—the distances involved, the type of terrain in terms of ease of movement, and the chances of his troops being safe from harm there. Second, he estimates the best way to deploy his military units: whether a circular formation to make his army look small, a horn formation to make it look numerous, or a crescent moon formation so as to encompass the enemy, or a wedge-shaped one to rout him utterly. Third, he checks the effectiveness of all weapons of attack and defense in varying circumstances, and explores every mode of improving them, adding new technique to new technique. For anyone who has carefully read the historical records of various countries knows that the man who develops new offensive weapons will have the means either for victory in battle or for a secure defense.[19]

But this particular passage makes Ricci seem more complacent and deterministic about war than he really was. The new technological developments of war in Europe—and perhaps to a somewhat similar extent in Asia, inasmuch as the Portuguese and Spaniards brought new levels of artillery and naval gunnery to the Far East—introduced new horrors that it was hard to avoid confronting. In one pessimistic passage Ricci wrote of that same quest for novelty in war, which he had praised in his Euclid introduction, as inevitably being destructive in itself. He expounded this view in the context of a philosophical dialogue on the course of human existence, initially written in 1601 at just about the same time he reached Peking and republished during 1608:

> Members of the human race bring destruction on each other: they make murderous instruments that can sever hands and feet and slice limbs from torsos. Most of those not killed by fate are killed by their fellow men, and since nowadays men disdain the old ways of war as

inadequate, they are constantly thinking up new techniques and dreaming of ways to increase the damage they cause. It has truly reached the point that in every stretch of countryside and in every town the killing never stops.[20]

It is difficult, perusing this passage, not to believe that Ricci had read some accounts of the terrible moment in Spain's siege of Antwerp in 1585 when the defenders, trying to dislodge the Spanish troops who had built a bridge of boats across the River Scheldt to block supplies from reaching the city, floated downstream a new type of mine designed by their consultant, the Italian engineer Frederico Giambelli. This "mine" was in fact a seventy-ton ship whose hold was lined with bricks and filled with an admixture of gunpowder and sal ammoniac, over which were placed layers of tombstones, marble shards, metal boat hooks, stones, and nails. The vast mass of explosives and projectiles was covered by a roof of heavy stone slabs so that the blast would be forced sideways and outward instead of upward. The vessel exploded when a carefully prepared fuse reached the hold, just at the moment the Spanish troops were trying to maneuver it out of the way. Though the casualties could not be counted because the bodies were so mutilated, between four and eight hundred men were killed in the one explosion, establishing some kind of new benchmark in the history of war.[21]

But the wars that touched Ricci more nearly were fought in traditional ways. They represented, indeed, the pinnacle of those very medieval modes that were at last being superseded by a higher technology. One was the battle of Lepanto, fought in 1571 in the Gulf of Corinth, where the Ottoman Turks were defeated by a "Holy League" formed by Spain, Venice, and the Papacy, this being the most decisive (but virtually the last) of all great encounters between fleets of armed Mediterranean galleys; the other was the battle of Alcazarquivir in North Africa, in 1578, in which King Sebastian of Portugal was routed by the Saadian ruler of Morocco after a brutal mélange of close-range cavalry charges and hand-to-hand fighting with sword and dagger.

Men from Macerata fought in the galleys at Lepanto, and priests from Macerata ministered to the troops, one of them at least being wounded in the battle.[22] But Ricci was far from the action, living as a novice at St. Andrew's Quirinale in Rome when, in October 1571, news was received of the Catholic commander in chief Don John of Austria's decisive victory over the Turks. In this gigantic naval engagement the Holy League assembled by Pope Pius V had mustered 208 galleys backed by 100 support vessels, and the Turks had around 250 war galleys. The outcome of the battle was decided by the boarding parties that fought through the day rather than by naval tactics or long-range fire power. Don John's forces suffered at least 20,000 casualties out of a total of 80,000 soldiers, sailors, and galley slaves; the Turkish dead (among whom was the Ottoman commander, Ali Pasha) were believed to number 30,000, and 8,000 more were taken prisoner.[23]

Though the victory at Lepanto came just after the loss of Cyprus to the Turks and was not followed up adequately, it was nevertheless correctly perceived by the Catholic forces as a major setback to Ottoman expansion and was celebrated with colossal pomp. Triumphal arches soared above the processions that filled European streets, bells rang out, Te Deums were sung in all the major churches, and a literature of self-congratulation sprang from scores of pens. Don John, the bastard son of the Emperor Charles V, became briefly the stuff of legend, as poets recorded his heroic exploits in battle and, more poignant than heroic, the moments he had sailed past his massed galleys, exhorting his troops in the face of the advancing Turkish fleet while the troops knelt in prayer. Francesco Panigarola wrote a brief passage in his book on memory techniques to teach his students how to recall—through punning images—Don John's two great victories, one at Lepanto and the other over the converted Muslims who had rebelled in Spain two years earlier.[24] Some artists, searching for models to encapsulate the victory, did not even bother to study the actual tactics or methodology of the battle but merely changed the labeling and some trifling details on heroic pictures of the Roman legions' defeat of Hannibal in the Second Punic War near Carthage in 202 B.C., so that bemused viewers around the world—versions of these prints, in exquisite detail, had reached Japan by the late sixteenth century—could see legionaries in short tunics carrying the insignia of ancient Rome, a few of them wearing Spanish ruffs or carrying muskets, hurling themselves against the elephants of the infidel.[25]

The Punic Wars were, in fact, a fine analogy for those in Counter-Reformation Rome who were striving to destroy the forces of Islam. The summary of ancient Roman history by the second-century A.D. scholar Lucius Florus, which—thanks to the precise mind of a long-forgotten recording clerk—we know that Ricci had in his luggage when he registered at the Jesuit novitiate in Rome in August 1571, caught in the confrontation of Hannibal and Scipio the echoes of Don John's battle with Ali Pasha:

> In the whole history of the Roman Empire there was no more notable occasion than when the two generals, greater than any before or since, the one the conqueror of Italy, the other of Spain, drew up their armies for a pitched battle. But first a conference was held between them about terms of peace, and they stood for a while motionless in mutual admiration. When, however, no agreement was reached about peace, the signal was given for battle. It is agreed from the admission of both sides that no armies could have been better arrayed and no battle more obstinately contested; Scipio acknowledged this about Hannibal's army and Hannibal about that of Scipio. But Hannibal had to yield, and Africa became the prize of victory; and the whole world soon followed the fate of Africa.[26]

It was a sunny day, December 4, 1571, when the victorious admiral of the papal contingent in the Lepanto fleet, the Roman Marcantonio Colonna, returned to his native city. He rode a white horse (a gift from the pope, Pius V) and wore a cloth-of-gold tunic, a black silk mantle lined with fur, and the decoration of the Order of the Golden Fleece; on his head was a black velvet cap, with a trailing white plume fastened to it by a pearl clasp.[27] Even if Ricci was kept at his lessons and did not see this exquisite figure of martial glory, he would have heard the artillery salvos and the trumpets that blared at the hero's return, and would have seen the triumphal arches of Constantine and Titus decked out with fresh inscriptions. The churches where he prayed were decorated with great tapestries of Scipio's victory over Hannibal, visually reinforcing those famous speeches which he knew by heart. Perhaps, too, he saw the ingenious mechanical statue of a Roman soldier, holding a sword in his right hand and the head of a Turk—gushing imitation blood—in its left, which some grateful citizens placed in the street. It would not have escaped him that the Virgin Mary was hailed as the Lady of Victory, and that in the subsequent paintings in her honor she was portrayed as standing on the crescent moon, symbol of the vanquished Turkish state.[28]

Even more moving for Ricci, however, must have been the outcome of the battle of Alcazarquivir and the death there of the Portuguese king Sebastian. From early in his reign Sebastian had been a backer of the Jesuit missionaries traveling to India and the East, giving them money for the journey, ordering airy cabins for them on the Portuguese ships that sailed annually from Lisbon to Goa, and even providing them with wine allowances and white flour for the voyage so they could supplement the dry ship biscuit with bread rolls.[29] Sebastian was a brooding young man, profoundly religious, deeply influenced by his Jesuit confessors, who encouraged him in his passionate commitment to break the power of the Muslims in North Africa. Fair-haired, blue-eyed, he was desperately self-conscious about his slightly deformed body, which he would never allow his valets to see naked and which he sought to strengthen by a Spartan regimen of constant fencing and jousting practice and protracted hunts on horseback.[30] Ricci met King Sebastian in March 1578 at the king's winter palace near Lisbon, when the twenty-four-year-old Sebastian gave an audience to the Jesuits preparing to leave for Goa. Ricci was so charmed by the young king's graciousness and bearing that he often spoke of him thereafter to his fellow missionaries.[31]

Even as Sebastian speeded the missionaries on their way with flattering words on their prowess, he was planning the great African campaign that he hoped would bring Morocco back under Portuguese control, reversing the pattern of foreign policy pursued by his father, who had chosen to concentrate on Portugal's newer possessions in Brazil and India. Despite lukewarm Spanish support, a shortage of trained troops, a depleted treasury, no clear plan of campaign, and the warnings of his senior military advisers, Sebastian sailed with a fleet of some eight hundred vessels from Lisbon in June 1578 in almost a carnival atmosphere and landed at Arzila, on the northwest African coast, in July. His leisurely approach to the campaign had given ample time for his adversary, Abd-al-Malik, to raise a formidable army that far outnumbered Sebastian's in cavalry and arquebusiers. Abd-al-Malik also knew the country intimately as Sebastian did not, and had the correct equipment for fighting in the blinding desert sun—Sebastian's armor grew so hot that he had to have water poured over his body under the metal plates, and the sufferings of his troops, who could not afford this luxury, must have been extraordinary.[32] Furthermore, Sebastian's army was slowed by the huge royal coaches he had insisted on bringing, by the lavish pavilions of the nobility that had to be stored and carried, by several portable chapels, and by thousands of camp followers whose ranks included, besides the papal delegate and two senior bishops, several hundred priests and crowds of page boys, musicians, black slaves, and prostitutes; this entire supernumerary entourage numbered perhaps ten thousand or more, or one for every active soldier in the regular line of march.[33]

Perhaps nothing so typifies one side of the Counter-Reformation at war as the crazed yet deadly battle that subsequently took place on August 4, 1578, at Alcazarquivir. Thousands of Portuguese nobles and conscripts died, as did the Walloon, German, Dutch, and English mercenaries who fought alongside them. After charging again and again on horseback into the Muslim ranks, King Sebastian lost his own life, though in the chaos of the fighting no one saw him die—all that his retainers found was his corpse, stripped naked and covered with wounds. Abd-al-Malik, who had been desperately ill before the battle began, died as he tried to mount his own horse to rally his dispirited troops. And al-Mutawakkil, to save whose throne King Sebastian had ostensibly gone to war, drowned while fleeing the fighting. Of the others left on the field of battle, an observer wrote that "the dead [were] on top of the living and the living on top of the dead, all cut to pieces, Christians and Moors locked in each other's arms, crying and dying, some on top of the artillery, others dragging limbs and entrails, caught under horses or mangled on top of them, and everything was much worse than I can describe to you now because the memory of what I went through grieves me so." Only a hundred people from the Portuguese host managed to avoid death or capture and to make their way back to the fleet anchored off the coast.[34]

Two specially commissioned vessels left Lisbon late that year to carry news of the catastrophe to Goa and the other Portuguese dominions in the East, for Sebastian had died unmarried, without an heir. This meant that one of the main claimants to the Portuguese crown would be King Philip II of Spain, and so the future of the Portuguese empire now lay in doubt. The news reached Goa in May 1579, and the Jesuits there joined in the solemn Masses for the dead king, Masses held with such pomp and genuine sorrow that those who had attended the other ceremonies considered those for Sebastian to be no less fine than the obsequies for the emperors Charles V, Ferdinand I, and Maximilian II.[35] Ricci's emotions at the receipt of the news are not recorded, but perhaps one can catch a hint of an epitaph for the dead king in the few lines that he wrote across northwest Africa on his world map (composed in Chinese around 1584) and appended to the area of the Atlas Mountains that circled the deadly battlefield to the south: "One cannot see the summit, and men call this the axis of the heavens. And the strange thing is that men sleep here without dreams."[36] A clearer sign of Ricci's sense of loss and homage can be gathered from the fact that when, in the early 1580s, he looked for Chinese ideographs that could serve to represent the first syllable "ma" of his Christian name Matteo, from among the many Chinese characters that could be so pronounced he chose the one which combined two simple and unambiguous components—a king and a horse.

One dangerous effect of King Sebastian's death, as various Jesuits noted in 1579, was that it decreased the prestige of the Europeans just at the time they were trying to shore up their community against the Muslim rulers of northern and western India.[37] From their base in Goa the comparatively small number of Portuguese sailors and soldiers had the prodigious task of protecting the coast and the sea lanes from Hormuz in the Persian Gulf down to Ceylon, and this in the face of consistent Muslim hostility and a monsoon pattern that left the Indian harbors unusable by deep-draught sailing vessels for almost half the year.

Goa—a city the size of Pisa at this time, as an Italian merchant observed—was at once a crisis center, an international trade mart, and a luxurious fleshpot, as one of Ricci's contemporaries there noted with becoming economy just after their arrival in the port:

> This is the place for merchants to fill their sacks, for this city is at the center and hither come all the goods from both north and south. Here one finds Jews and Gentiles, Moors, Persians, Arabs, Venetians (who come here overland through Turkey), Turks themselves and also Italians. There is no better place for soldiers because here armies are being formed every day to go to one area or another, by land or sea, and all military forces are based here. For those who are lazy or pleasure-loving life is so good here that it were better for them if it were not so good.[38]

Ricci echoed this praise in general terms, writing that India "has the best goods in the world: fine cloth, gold, silver, spices, scented roots, incense, medicines, and malachite, so at all seasons the merchants from the eastern and western oceans trade here." Ricci did not add that Goa was also a central market for the opium trade, conducted there on a gigantic scale—one contemporary merchant casually mentions investing 2,100 ducats in sixty parcels of Indian opium—which may have accounted for some of the indolence of the population, as well as for some of the Portuguese prosperity, since dues were collected on all major consignments.[39] Ricci wrote that he found the Goanese "soft," and in his earliest surviving letters to friends in Rome, written either from Goa or from Cochin to the south, though he did argue against those who said the Indians were incapable of absorbing advanced European education, he showed little sympathy or interest for the Indians themselves.[40] In this he was echoing the negative feelings of the formidable visitor of the Jesuit order in the East Indies, Alessandro Valignano, who had come to Goa in 1574.

Valignano was a remarkably talented and vigorous man whose views about foreign races and mission procedures were to have an immense effect on Matteo Ricci. He was born in 1539 to a wealthy family in the town of Chieti in the southern Italian Abruzzi. His parents were close friends of the local bishop, Gian Pietro Carafa, who later became pope as Paul IV; after Valignano had obtained a law degree, Pope Paul's favor brought him an abbacy at eighteen and ensconced him as a canon of the cathedral in Chieti by the age of twenty. Suddenly bereft of his patron by Paul's death in 1559, Valignano—a powerful man over six feet tall, who in 1577 was to walk across southern India from coast to coast—clearly got himself into youthful scrapes and spent a year or more in a Venetian prison on the oddly violent and hotly disputed charge of having wounded someone in the face with his sword. By 1566, he was apparently a reformed character, however, entered the Jesuit order, and became a student in the Roman college. There he studied mathematics under Clavius, along with physics, philosophy, and theology, and by 1571 he was appointed master of novices; in this role, during the autumn of that same year, he administered the first-year examinations to the young Matteo Ricci.[41] Valignano then served for a year as rector of the college in Macerata before the general of the Jesuit order, Everard Mercurian, summoned him in 1573 to be visitor to the missions in India, an assignment which, by the nature of the church's organization at the time, gave the thirty-four-year-old Valignano at one swoop powers equivalent to those of the general himself over all the Jesuit missions from the Cape of Good Hope to Japan.[42]

Valignano's mission was to reinfuse the Asian missions with spiritual ardor, to bring extra manpower so that some respite from field work and refreshing of spiritual resources would be made possible for the missionaries, and to handle the thorny problem of whether to establish separate mission bases in India north of the Ganges, in the Moluccas, in Malacca, and in Japan. He was biased before his departure toward the Japanese, whom he described in a letter to General Mercurian as "a gifted, reliable people, not given to many vices. They are poorly off and not intemperate in eating. After receiving baptism they are quite capable of appreciating spiritual things."[43] If he had a similar predisposition to be fair to the Indians, all trace of such leanings had vanished by the end of 1575, when he had completed an initial year's residence in Portuguese India. In a report of that year, Valignano described the future of India in the darkest terms: he described a government system so bad that the Jesuits hesitated to hear the confessions of the civil and military officials, and depicted a society of badly paid soldiers, poorly armed forts, shabby fleets, and a vilely unfair system of justice.[44]

Even though Valignano, despite his lack of affection for the Indians, developed language courses for the Jesuits and ordered instruction in the faith to begin in the local dialect in São Tomé, it is apparent that many missionaries were in fact reluctant to master an Indian language lest they be condemned to work forever among poor Indians in the countryside rather than among the Portuguese and never have a chance to transfer to the more exciting and promising field of Japan; so in the north, at Bassein, he was content to let the Jesuits work through interpreters.[45]

En route to, and in, Malacca in 1577, a year before Ricci arrived in Goa, Valignano wrote his most careful assessment of Indian realities. His experience of Indian heat, disease, vice, and lethargy led him to lump the peoples of India with those of Africa as little better than the "brute beasts." He added, "A trait common to all these peoples (I am not speaking now of the so-called white races of China or Japan) is a lack of distinction and talent. As Aristotle would say, they are born to serve rather than to command."[46] Yet only two years after this, in 1579,

Valignano began to realize that he had been misled by Jesuit reportage from the Far East and that the Japanese were not to be trusted either. He now claimed that the Japanese, whom he had previously praised as "white" and as "simple pious folk," were in fact "the most dissembling and insincere people to be found anywhere." With reference to further mission work in the East, Valignano felt himself to be "in a state of anxious uncertainty and at my wits' end, at a loss for an answer."[47] The Japanese mixture of cruelty, dignity, depravity, and hypocrisy was so complex that he despaired of analyzing it accurately: even after conversion they seemed "tepid" in the faith. Perhaps it were "better to have no Christians than Christians of that type!" Besides, a little Christian learning might prove to be a dangerous thing, as Valignano noted, speaking now as a leader in the Counter-Reformation: since many Japanese believed that by invoking the name of Amida Buddha they would be saved, one had to confront the melancholy fact that "their views of justification resembled those of the Lutherans." Thus tepid congregations led by poorly trained priests might lead to a situation in which Protestantism would begin to flourish.[48]

As Valignano began to grow disillusioned about the Japanese nature and character, he reflected back on the ten months he had spent among the Chinese in Macao during 1577 and 1578, and from his words we can see how a sequence was being repeated: in the mid-1570s euphoria for Japan had succeeded the disillusion with India; by the end of the decade China, unsullied by too much personal knowledge, was becoming the focus for euphoria as dejection about Japanese realities deepened. He noted in a report to the new general of the order, Claudio Acquaviva, the Chinese love of learning, their neat dress, their delicate eating habits, their banning of weapons in public places, the shyness of their women, their good government—contrasting every one of these attributes with negative images from Japan. Even if Acquaviva pointed out somewhat tartly that people insisted on being baffled by Japan in a way that they never were by Transylvania or Poland, though surely in those lands things were different enough also, he was impressed by the opportunities for evangelism offered by China and encouraged Valignano to bring more Jesuits—one of whom was Matteo Ricci—to Macao so that they could prepare there for China service.[49]

Ricci never visited Japan, and his few declarative statements on that country seem to echo Valignano's judgment, encapsulating the whole island nation with the phrases that the Japanese "revered force" and "liked war rather than civil culture."[50] He was inclined initially to present Chinese ways by means of simple contrasts, and a year after his 1583 posting to the town of Zhaoqing, not far from Canton, Ricci wrote about Chinese men to the Manila-based agent of the Spanish king in terms that seem designed to contrast them not only to the Japanese but even more to the rough-and-tumble men in the Macerata of his youth:

To tell you the truth, whatever else I might write to your Honor about the Chinese I would not say that they were men of war, because both in outward appearance and in their inner hearts they are just like women: if one shows them one's teeth they will humble themselves, and whoever makes them subject can put his foot on their necks. Each day the men take two hours to do their hair and to dress themselves meticulously, devoting to this all the sweet time they can. Flight among these men is not a matter of shame, nor are injuries and insults, as they would be to us; rather they show a womanly anger and pull each other's hair, and when they weary of that they become friends again. Rarely do they wound or kill each other, and even if they wanted to they don't have the means, because not only are there few soldiers, but most of them don't even have a knife in the house. In short, one has no more to fear from them than one would have from any large crowd of men; and though in truth they have plenty of fortresses, and their cities are all walled against the attacks of thieves, they are not walls built along geometrical principles, and they have neither traverses nor ditches.[51]

In this particular letter it is hard to sort out Ricci's personal views from the views commonly held about China by Europeans. Several of his points—such as those about the elaborate coiffures of Chinese men and their penchant for hair-pulling—had already been made in the earliest reports to be published on China, those by the Italian trader Galeote Pereira, published in Venice in 1565, and by the Dominican friar Gaspar da Cruz, published in Portugal during 1569, either or both of which Ricci had ample opportunity to read before he sailed to the East.[52] Ricci may also have been playing up to his audience here, for the Spaniards were particularly interested in China's military capabilities, and general discussion of the possibilities of conquering China—how long it would take, and how many men—was widespread among both the missionaries and those who saw themselves as descended from the conquistadors who had so swiftly conquered the vast territories of Mexico and Peru. Especially in Mexico and the Philippines, among churchmen of all the religious orders, Franciscan, Dominican, and Jesuit, a lively debate raged about the morality of an attack on China and whether such an attack could be viewed as a "just war" in the light of China's intransigence toward foreign missionaries, her continued resistance to opening ports for foreign trade, and the harshness with which her civil authorities often treated baptized Chinese Christians.[53]

But Ricci was not posing when he found the Chinese ambiguous about warfare, and he reflected on the particular paradoxes in Chinese views of physical violence for the rest of his life. In his account of his time in China, which he wrote between 1608 and 1610 and entitled *Historia,* Ricci found it praiseworthy that the Chinese almost never carried arms unless they were bodyguards in the entourage of a great mandarin, soldiers going to the training grounds, or travelers on a particularly dangerous journey, who might carry daggers. Once again, his comments seem almost expressly designed to contrast the China of his middle age with the hurly-burly Macerata of his youth: "Amongst us, it is held to be a fine thing to see an armed man, but to them it seems evil, and they have a fear of seeing anything so horrible. And so they have none of the factions and tumults that we always have, as we take our revenge for some insult with weapons and with death. They consider that the most honorable man is he who flees and does not wish to harm another."[54]

44

The Chinese regular army baffled him. At some levels he noticed dramatic efficiency, as "the military captains in each area, but especially on coasts and the borders, patrol in great numbers by day and night and guard the walls and gates, harbors and forts, as if they were at war, performing their drills in proper unison." He noted that army officers were excused from the rule applied to other bureaucrats that prohibited them from serving in their native provinces so as to avoid graft and influence peddling. Army officers, it was believed, would fight with extra ferocity to defend their own homes.[55] In the garrison town of Ganzhou, which had been made the central headquarters for a special zone to suppress banditry in the four major southeastern provinces, Ricci was astonished at the martial display put on in the spring of 1595 for a visiting mandarin in whose entourage he happened to be traveling: "The minister was received with great pomp, more than three thousand soldiers coming two or three miles out of the city to greet him, in their uniforms, with banners and arms; among them were stationed arquebusiers who fired off their arquebuses and muskets as he passed, and made a grand sight at their various stations on each bank of the river, among the leafy trees."[56] Equally imposing was the great armada of supply boats and war vessels he found filling the rivers and canals near Tianjin in the summer of 1598.[57] Yet the pomp and the display often seemed to be taken more seriously than active combat. For instance, Ricci believed that because the Chinese had considerable trouble breaking in horses they tended to use only geldings and that these geldings, whose hooves were never shod with iron, could not gallop over stony ground and tended to flee at the sound of an approaching enemy;[58] and he never got used to the paradoxical way that the Chinese loved to use gunpowder:

> Not so much for their arquebuses, of which they have few, nor for bombards and artillery which are also in short supply, but for their firework displays, which take place every year at their festivals with such ingenuity that none of us ever saw them without amazement. They created fantastic shows of flowers and fruit and battles all spinning through the air, every one made out of these same fireworks; and

45

one year when I was in Nanjing [1599] I estimated that in the month-long New Year celebrations they used up more saltpetre and gunpowder than we would need for a war lasting two or three years.[59]

The side of Ricci that admired martial display and had been impressed by the military prowess of European armies could never accept the ultimate fact that the elite Chinese civil bureaucrats seemed to despise both the military officers and their troops. The army was constantly watched, he noted, and was kept in subservience to civilian authorities, who doled out their pay and rations. Even the military examination system, allegedly established to parallel the one for civilian officials, was only a pale shadow of the other and never taken so seriously by youthful candidates seeking careers.[60] "Whereas amongst our people the noblest and bravest become soldiers, in China it is the vilest and most cowardly who attend to matters of war." Such men, wrote Ricci, were motivated neither by patriotism nor love of king nor search for glory, but sought only sustenance for themselves and their families. Treating soldiering as a job, as they did, it was not surprising they were treated without respect and had to work "in base occupations" as baggage carriers, muleteers, and servants. The result was that "no one of virile spirit chooses the army over civilian life."[61]

In writing this Ricci showed his ignorance of the extraordinary history of military success at suppressing bandits and pirates that had taken place in southeastern China two decades before he arrived, and of which the troops and pomp of the garrison center at Ganzhou which he had so delighted in were at once the legacy and the symbol. It is true that during the 1570s there had been some serious pirate raids on Zhaoqing, where Ricci first resided in China, in which hundreds of people were killed, and that in 1582, just one year before he arrived, a smaller group of water-borne bandits had attacked the area, only to be driven off by local villagers.[62] But these were minor disturbances in comparison with the scourge of massive Sino-Japanese pirate raids—often striking deep inland—that had ravaged China during the 1550s and 1560s as badly as Protestant corsairs had harried Spain in the Atlantic or the Muslim fleets disrupted Venetian shipping in the Mediterranean.[63] The Chinese generals responsible for ending these raids had forged remarkably disciplined armed forces out of a complex mix of aboriginal Dai and Miao tribesmen from the southwest, local peasants, released prisoners, displaced Buddhist monks, and salt smugglers; with such unlikely allies they had managed to reimpose order in the countryside and close key harbors and rivers to the pirates, mopping up their bases one by one.[64] They introduced new forms of military accounting and taxation to cope with the mounting price of war, which just as in Europe was beginning to rise precipitously owing to the high cost of firearms, fortifications, and wheeled vehicles, the larger numbers of troops on fixed pay, and the increasing circulation of silver bullion, which pushed the country into an inflationary spiral.[65] These same generals introduced new techniques for drilling troops, new defensive tactics against cavalry, and new weapons like complex multibladed spears, as well as instituting innovative gunnery techniques, signals, and information-gathering systems which—under brilliant leaders like Qi Jiguang—might have led to a new order in the Ming polity.[66]

Yet the fates of Qi and many other generals, who often ended their careers disgraced, imprisoned, or even executed, could only reinforce Ricci's sense that the Chinese army lacked respect and focus within the society, and that the civilian bureaucracy, through its factional and manipulative skills, if not for any superior learning, played havoc with the military officer's chances for success. A supervising censor found nothing ironic in describing General Qi as a man who "has given up literature for a military career, but understands syntax thoroughly,"[67] the implication being obviously that such officers were usually boorish louts. But beyond such mild slights, what Ricci noticed constantly was the tension between the alleged martial life of soldiers and the fact that they were subjected to humiliating beatings—on whim—by the civilian magistrates who had ultimate supervision over them. In this Ricci was elaborating on an earlier analysis by Valignano that, whereas the Japanese found satisfaction in killing with their swords, the Chinese preferred to beat people and watch the blood flow.[68] Ricci paralleled the moral effect of these beatings of the Chinese people by their mandarins to that of schoolboys by their teachers in European schools—that was not a random metaphor, but one he returned to several times, so that the trembling child and the victimized adult become as one in his accounts.[69]

At these levels of personalized physical violence the last veneers of mutual respect were stripped away. Though both Galeote Pereira and Gaspar da Cruz had offered vivid descriptions of Chinese beating procedures in their earlier works on China, Ricci's language moved beyond theirs and took on an astonishing precision as he described one such scene. The blows seem to thud out of the page as he writes:

> The victims are beaten in public audience, on the back of the thighs, lying stretched out on the ground; they are beaten with a pole of the hardest possible wood, the thickness of a finger, four fingers wide, long as one's two arms outstretched. The dispensers of the punishment hold the pole with both hands and use great force, giving now ten, now twenty, now thirty blows, showing great ruthlessness, such that with the first blow they often take away the skin, and with the other blows the flesh, piece by piece. From which many people die.[70]

The fact that such punishments were given to both soldiers and civilians more or less on a mandarin's whim—a magistrate might kill twenty or thirty people in such a way and receive only mild censure—seemed to Ricci a major reason for criticizing the Chinese state: "The poor subjects have such fear of this shameful and cruel punishment, and of the death to which it can lead, that they will give everything they have to free themselves from the mandarins' hands." The result, wrote Ricci, was that the Chinese lived constantly in fear of being falsely charged, so that "no one in China is master of his own property."[71] He was fully aware of the force of what he was saying and of the reasons for saying it. He had come within an inch of getting such a beating himself, in 1584, on the orders of an enraged mandarin in Zhaoqing, and never forgot the fear the possibility induced; on other occasions Chinese officials forced him to be present when others received similar beatings, and with his Jesuit colleague Michele Ruggieri, who was with him during his first years in China, he had nursed one criminal who had been subjected to eighty such blows, though the man died after a month despite their ministrations.[72]

More poignant still to Ricci must have been the news of Francesco Martines's death, which occurred in Canton in 1606. Ricci was not a witness, but he reconstructed the grim events in a heartfelt passage of his *Historia*. Francesco Martines was the baptismal name of a young Chinese, born Huang Mingshao in Macao and educated in Jesuit schools, who served his novitiate with Ricci in Shaozhou in 1590 and entered the Jesuit order the following year. The Portuguese name of this young Chinese Jesuit had been anything but randomly chosen, but was the same as the name of a Jesuit missionary known to Ricci whose tragic death at sea between Mozambique and Goa he had mourned in 1581. This Chinese Martines had served the church long and faithfully, partly as a Chinese-language instructor for other Western missionaries, but also as the nurse to the dying Father Almeida and as a formative influence in the final conversion of the alchemist and scholar Qu Ru-kuei.[73] Martines was arrested by the authorities in Canton, after celebrating Holy Week with the Chinese Christians there, on charges of being a spy from Macao in the pay of the Portuguese. Ricci described how Martines was dragged at night, with the youthful acolytes and the servants who had been with him, through streets filled with a hostile, jeering crowd, illuminated by the flickering light of torches, and thrown into prison. The marks of the tonsure under his long dark hair, and the Portuguese shirts and drawers in his luggage, were taken as evidence of guilt, a guilt confirmed when a Chinese acolyte confessed under torture that Martines dealt in guns and gunpowder and was planning to foment insurrection. First tortured by heavy bars on his legs, and then stripped and beaten on two successive days with heavy poles, in an attempt to make him confess, denied all water or any other nourishment, Martines died on March 31.[74]

Ricci noted that death came at 3:00 P.M. when Martines was thirty-three years old—a time and age that for Catholics would have at once recalled Mark's notation in his gospel that Christ's crucifixion occurred at 3:00 P.M. (Mark 15:25) when Christ—by received wisdom—was thirty-three. In making a slip here (Martines was thirty-eight at the time of his death) Ricci but underlined the scriptural context in which he placed such sufferings.[75] This scriptural context was reinforced by the acts of memory demanded of all Jesuits by Ignatius of Loyala in the *Spiritual Exercises*. Several exercises were designed to force the faithful back to presence at the acts of Christ's life and passion, so that they felt and saw every blow that the soldiers landed on Christ's body as they questioned him, saw his pitiful nakedness and felt its shame, flinched at the mockery, felt the cold air of winter in which the suffering took place, saw the blood soak through the thin clothing with which Christ sought to cover himself once again. So that the worshiper might draw closer to the mystery of God's purpose in enduring such suffering through his own son, Ludolfus of Saxony, from whose work Ignatius of Loyola drew so richly in his own meditations, urged the devotee to "turn away thine eyes for a while from His Godhead, and consider him simply as a man." No violent detail is to be avoided, said Ludolfus, no item of pain and humiliation glossed as the blows fall: "Piled on top of each other, repeated again and again, close together, stroke over stroke, bruise over bruise, wound over wound, blood over blood, till both his tormentors and the spectators are wearied out."[76]

The missionaries in China knew all about the crowds that pressed in upon them so constantly, surrounding their lodgings, peering through the doorways, both by day and by night, sometimes merely curious but more often mocking or hostile.[77] To be in China meant, for Westerners and for Chinese converts alike, to learn to be hated, and danger could spring from the mightiest clashes between nations or from petty clashes over a few coins. When in 1587 the Japanese general Hideyoshi Toyotomi announced his decision to conquer Korea and thereafter to crush the Chinese emperor himself, it was not surprising that any foreigners living in China were suspect to the Chinese bureaucrats. But the Catholic fathers fell under special suspicion because among the most feared of Hideyoshi's troops were more than fifteen thousand Japanese Christians led by the convert general Konishi Yukinaga, who fought major battles in Korea in 1592 and again in 1597 and 1598.[78] During these years, when alarms of war were constant and imperial edicts fulminated against foreigners, Ricci would find whole cities nervous at his coming, no one willing to give him lodging or to deliver the messages in which he protested his plight.[79]

The war scares continued into the seventeenth century, and Ricci wrote that the 1606 death of Francesco Martines was mainly due to the fact that troublemakers in Macao had spread a rumor that an alliance of Jesuits, Portuguese, Dutch, and Japanese was planning to use the city as a springboard for an invasion of China; before this invasion, they warned, all the Chinese living in Macao could be massacred. Many Chinese did indeed flee from Macao in 1606 since, unlikely as the nature of the threatened alliance of Western religions and nations now sounds, a massacre of Chinese had in fact occurred in the Philippines in 1603. In October of that year, after a protracted series of arguments over money and eunuch meddling in foreign policy, the Spanish authorities had panicked over the threat of a violent uprising by the Chinese congregated in Manila and, in a preemptive strike of appalling savagery, had killed close to twenty thousand Chinese settlers and merchants.[80]

The reality of the tens of thousands of corpses in Manila shows how far the Chinese in Macao were from paranoia when they brooded about Westerners' intentions toward them, and the fear naturally increased when other Westerners deliberately played on it. It seems to have been an Augustinian friar, Michele dos Santos—once a Jesuit himself before changing orders and rising to be the acting administrator of the church in Macao following the death of the bishop there—who spread the alarm to the Macao Chinese about his former mentors' martial intentions. Behind dos Santos's wild charges lay many years of complex struggles between the Jesuits and members of other religious orders. The dominant role played by the Jesuits in the late sixteenth and early seventeenth centuries should not let us forget that their forerunners in exploring China had been Augustinians, Dominicans, and Franciscans, and there was often little love lost between the groups. In one of his religious works Ricci praised the personal holiness of Francis of Assisi and his followers, but elsewhere he expressed no admiration for the brash mission tactics of the Franciscans themselves—indeed, he seems to have seen them almost as enemies, since their forceful approach to preaching to the poor so irritated the Chinese that the Jesuits inevitably felt the backlash.[81] As to Ricci's feelings concerning the Augustinians, they can be gauged by his depiction of dos Santos's peccadilloes. According to his *Historia,* it was a complicated story involving dos Santos's bitterness at his former confreres and at least two public disputes with the Jesuits, one over his decision to confiscate a large sum of silver being brought illegally into Macao from Japan, the other over a case of alleged clerical abuse by one of the Macao priests. These disputes had led the Westerners in Macao to fight each other with swords and guns in the streets, in what Ricci called "a great scandal to gentiles and New Christians alike."[82] With no knowledge of the ecclesiastical and financial bickerings that lay behind the charges, the Chinese authorities could only assess them at what seemed to be face value. As hundreds of Macao Chinese fled across the border, Canton armed forces were put on a wartime footing: the homes of the poor, huddled alongside the city walls, were destroyed to provide a clear field of fire; a ban on food sales to Macao was imposed; and all Portuguese trade was forbidden.[83]

It is not surprising that the Chinese authorities could not work out clearly which foreigners were enemies and which were friends, and there must have been a certain sourness in the bantering remark a senior Chinese official made to the Jesuit Cattaneo: "So have you already become king of China?"[84] Consider the three elements in dos Santos's equation. The Dutch Protestants, enemies of the Catholic Portuguese, were out to wreck Portugal's Far Eastern empire and seize control of the spice trade for themselves, determined in so doing to keep supplies limited and prices high, while at the same time they engaged in a calculated violence toward the Chinese inhabitants of Southeast Asia and the Pescadores as harsh as any perpetrated by the Spaniards or the Portuguese.[85] In contrast, the Japanese not only had made peace with China over Korea following Hideyoshi's death but had also indicated that they might soon extirpate Christianity from their domains altogether, if one could deduce this from their crucifixion of twenty-six Christians, both Japanese and Westerners, outside Nagasaki in 1597—a grim act that attained maximum publicity since the bodies were left hanging for months, forming an irresistible spectacle for contemporary visitors to the thriving harbor and a popular motif in the decoration of textiles in the ensuing decade.[86] Yet at the same time, because of the long years during which Japanese pirates had attacked China's coasts, the Cantonese still held the sentiment (and inscribed it in stone in their city) that "as long as the sun and moon give light, the Chinese and Japanese cannot live under the same sky or drink the same water."[87] Furthermore, Japanese Christians who had either fled the persecutions in their homeland or been brought earlier by the Jesuits to receive training in Macao, were now firmly though illegally ensconced on an island near the city, and showed a willingness to defend their "property" in the face of Chinese attempts to evict them.[88]

As for the Portuguese, the Chinese believed they had the Jesuits in their pockets. Ricci had experienced this in 1593, when he was living in Shaozhou and a group of local Chinese submitted a written affidavit stating that Ricci and his colleagues "came from Macao, and have had much dealings with foreign countries, contrary to China's laws. They have built here a house with walls, like a castle, where they shelter over forty people who have also come from Macao."[89] If the Chinese in Shaozhou had worried that the small new Jesuit house there was a fortified castle, it is not surprising what they thought of the spacious new stone church that the Jesuits built a decade later, at a cost of 700 ounces of silver, on a hill in Macao after their first church was destroyed by fire. The Chinese officials of Xiangshan county, who technically still had jurisdiction over Macao city, tried to prevent this construction: as Ricci analyzed their reasons, they did so "either because they fear it is a fortress disguised as a church or because they are trying to get as many *scudi** as they can before they grant permission."[90] The "sumptuous" church (the word is Ricci's), with its 160-by-84-foot dimensions, 50-foot columns and three naves, may indeed have been a religious structure, but the Chinese could hardly be expected to distinguish its functions from those of the equally substantial Jesuit college, which was the place that all the wealthy Portuguese used to shelter their silver plate and their families the moment they sighted Dutch sails.[91] In addition, the Portuguese had further defied Chinese bans by building what Ricci disarmingly called "a bit of a wall and a sort of a fortress" in response to the stepped-up danger of Dutch attacks in 1604.[92]

By the end of his life Ricci had learned enough to attempt a working definition of Chinese motives and attitudes, as he wrote in a letter to his former teacher Fabio de Fabii, whom he had last seen thirty years before:

> It remains hard for us to believe how such a huge kingdom with so many soldiers could live in continual fear of other states that are so much smaller, so that they fear some great disaster every year and spare no pains to protect themselves from their neighbors either with troops or with deceit and feigned friendship: the Chinese place absolutely no trust in any foreign country, and thus they allow no one at all to enter and reside here unless they undertake never again to return home, as is the case with us.[93]

In this life sentence to service, Ricci could only observe and wait, drawing what consolation he could from his order's founder, Ignatius of Loyola, whose metaphors in the supplement to the *Spiritual Exercises* as to how the devil might strike were couched in suitably military terms. The enemy of Christ, Ignatius wrote, acts "like a leader intent

---

* Ricci used "ducats" and *"scudi"* interchangeably in his writings. Each ducat was about twenty-nine grams, or approximately one ounce, of silver, which made it equivalent to the Chinese unit called a "tael." A *"giulio"* was 1/10 of a ducat, a *baiocco* and a *bolignino* were each 1/100 of a ducat. The basic gold:silver ratio in the 1570s in Europe was about 1:11. Full details of coins and exchange ratios for this period are given in Jean Delumeau, *Vie économique et sociale de Rome dans la seconde moitié du XVIe siècle,* 2/657–65.

upon seizing and plundering a position he desires. A commander and leader of an army will encamp, explore the fortifications and defenses of the stronghold, and attack at the weakest point."[94] Ricci might feel that the new theological formulations of the Council of Trent provided the "fortifications" that could brace and prepare one for such an assault. But the enemy was also "like a woman," wrote Ignatius, yielding if sure of being overwhelmed, but full of "anger, vindictiveness, and rage" if the man began to waver: "If one begins to be afraid and to lose courage in temptations, no wild animal on earth can be more fierce than the enemy of our human nature. He will carry out his perverse intentions with consummate malice."[95]

This battle could not but be more lonely and protracted than the major sieges launched during full-dress campaigns; one can only guess at the levels of endurance Ricci needed in this protracted war of spiritual attrition, when so often the Chinese en masse must have seemed the enemy. He tells us of how he watched as Chinese passengers and crew on a river boat joined together in throwing his baggage onto the shore because his travel papers were not in order;[96] of the sound of an endless rain of stones on the roof of his house in Zhaoqing, thrown by schoolboys from the commanding elevation of a nearby tower;[97] of the dejection felt after a Chinese crowd playing musical instruments and shouting their victory cries smashed his doors, windows, and furniture and tore down his newly erected garden fence.[98] Was it through such small harassments that the devil showed that "consummate malice" of which Ignatius spoke? If so, the challenge became to place one's own priorities within the context of the whole community, as Thomas Aquinas had argued with his usual good sense and sharply chosen metaphor in *The Perfection of Spiritual Life:* "The common good is, according to right reason, to be preferred to one's proper good. As a result, each member of the body is directed to the good of the whole by a natural instinct. An indication of this is that a person uses his hand to block a blow, in order to protect his heart or his head, on which his whole life may depend."[99]

That, too, was fine as long as natural instincts truly converged on a common goal that could be agreed to by all. It was the divisiveness and uncertainty that grew wearying, and though Ricci did not allow the language of quiet despair to mar the polished language of his *Historia*, it does break through in certain letters to his family, teachers, and friends. "This sterile land" (*questa sterilita*) he called China to Giulio Fuligatti; to other friends he described China as *"questa rocca"* or *"un deserto si lontano,"* and the Chinese as *"questa remotissima gente"* among whom he felt "abandoned" or "cast off" (*bottato*). The Chinese marveled, he told his brother Orazio, that he was white-haired and while "not yet advanced in age should already look so old." "They do not know," he added, "that it is they who are the cause of these white hairs."[100] In a letter of August 1595 to his superior in Macao, the Portuguese Edoardo de Sande, Ricci observed that God had chosen to give him twelve years of hardship and humiliation.[101]

Most of the language and images here had obvious scriptural overtones that all Ricci's correspondents would have caught. Ludolfus of Saxony had often written of Christians living in deserts or wastelands "cut off from home," and he held up the three central New Testament examples of flight or withdrawal—the Holy Family's to Egypt, John the Baptist's to the desert, and Christ's to the wilderness—as model subjects for contemplation that must be pursued with every element available for thought. The hardships had been bravely endured by Christ's "very tender and young mother" and by "the very old Joseph," through "a wooded way, dark, covered with bushes, uninhabited, and a way indeed very long."[102] The contemporary Christian could do no less. Gian Pietro Maffei, who taught rhetoric at the Roman college in the 1560s before moving to Lisbon so he could be at the heart of European seafaring life while he prepared his history of the Portuguese in India, wrote in a similar vein. In the introduction to his lengthy history, a draft of which he sent to Ricci, with whom he had been corresponding, Maffei wrote of the mission workers being lost among "sterile bushes and ravaged forests."[103] Ricci, who admired Maffei greatly, had no false modesty about drawing similar parallels, and in a letter to General Acquaviva he was brave enough to echo Paul's famous lament to the

Corinthians in referring to the hardships he had experienced in China: "In journeyings often, in perils of waters, in perils of robbers, in perils by mine own countrymen, in perils by the heathen, in perils in the city, in perils in the wilderness, in perils in the sea, in perils among false brethren."[104]

From overlapping accounts that appear both in his personal letters and in the *Historia,* we can detail one of the brief conjunctions, a few minutes in duration, that caught the overlays of violence in Ricci's Chinese life. Around midnight, in July 1592, some young men who had been gambling in the suburbs of Shaozhou, near the boat bridge that connected the main town to the rural area to the west where the Jesuits lived, decided to raid the Jesuit residence. They seem to have been incited to make this attack by the priests in a nearby Buddhist monastery, and the priests furnished them with rough and ready weapons, but the Buddhists need not take all the blame. The Shaozhou region had been full of rumor and dissatisfaction since bandit raids led by a self-styled "magician" had coincided with a bad drought in 1589, and the Jesuits might well have been seen as harbingers of a malevolent fate.[105] The gang of youths came over the bridge, gathered outside the walled compound of Ricci's house, and tossed ropes over the wall into the courtyard. A few of them climbed into the yard and opened the main gate from the inside, admitting some twenty companions. Most of the rowdies held staves; some carried unlighted torches; others had small axes. Two of Ricci's servants, going downstairs to investigate the noise, blundered into the group in the dark and were badly hurt. Father Francesco de Petris, hastening to their aid, was wounded on the head. As Ricci came out of his room the invaders lighted their torches, perhaps preparing to explore or loot the residence; in the light of the flames Ricci saw them surge through the outer doors of the house, which the servants and Petris had left ajar as they went to see what was happening. He called his own group back to the door of the inner house and tried to close it, but the attackers jammed their staves into the opening. Shouting, shoving at the crowd, Ricci held them back for a few moments until a blow from an axe caught him on the hand; then he ordered all the members of his group to retreat to their own private rooms and bar their doors. One of the servants clambered onto the roof and began to hurl tiles at the heads of the rowdies; Ricci barred his own door and jumped through the window into the garden to summon help. Twisting his ankle, he lay helpless on the ground, unable to move but still shouting for aid. The attackers, bruised by the tiles and believing from the shouts that Ricci had reached the road and was summoning aid, broke and fled. In their haste, they took nothing from the residence, and one of them left his hat lying in the courtyard.[106]

This hat was to be important later, a key piece of evidence against one of the young men who had instigated the attack on the Jesuit residence. As for Ricci, his hand healed quite rapidly but his foot never recovered completely; and though he made a special trip to Macao to see if the Portuguese doctors there could help him, they advised against any operations which might only make things worse. For the eighteen years remaining to him, whenever he had to walk long distances, the pain would return to haunt him, forcing him to limp.[107]

THREE

THE FIRST PICTURE:
THE APOSTLE IN THE WAVES

T he first of the pictures that Ricci gives to Cheng Dayue to publish in the "Ink Garden" is the apostle Peter floundering in the Sea of Galilee. In his mind, Ricci carries the passage from the Gospel according to Matthew, chapter 14, the passage that describes what occurs after Christ has fed the multitude from five loaves and two fish and has then retired alone into the mountains to pray, sending his disciples ahead by boat, across the sea:

When evening came, he was there alone, but the boat by this time was many furlongs distant from the land, beaten by the waves; for the wind was against them.

And in the fourth watch of the night he came to them, walking on the sea.

But when the disciples saw him walking on the sea, they were terrified, saying, "It is a ghost!" And they cried out for fear. But immediately he spoke to them, saying, "Take heart, it is I; have no fear."

And Peter answered him, "Lord, if it is you, bid me come to you on the water." He said, "Come." So Peter got out of the boat and walked on the water and came to Jesus, but when he saw the wind, he was afraid, and beginning to sink he cried out, "Lord, save me." Jesus immediately reached out his hand and caught him, saying to him, "O man of little faith, why did you doubt?" And when they got into the boat, the wind ceased. And those in the boat worshiped him, saying "Truly you are the Son of God."[1]

Within the bounds of discretion, Ricci is free to render this story as he chooses, for there is as yet no translation of the Bible into Chinese. Though many Chinese have asked him to undertake such a translation, he has constantly refused, pleading pressures of work, the difficulty of the task, and the need to secure papal approval before commencing.[2] But since Cheng Dayue wants a text written out in Chinese to go with each picture, Ricci starts off with the Bible story and adapts it to suit his own views of what will best appeal to Chinese ideas of morality and fate. (To render Peter's name he chooses the ideographs pronounced "Bo-do-lo," the nearest he can get to the sound of Pietro, Pedro, or Petrus.) Ricci entitles his brief essay "If you believe, you will walk on the sea, but once you doubt you will sink."

After the Lord of Heaven was born on earth, and had taken human form to spread his teaching to the world, he first shared his teachings with twelve holy followers. The first of these was called Bo-do-lo. One day Bo-do-lo was on a boat when he saw the distant outline of the Lord of Heaven standing on the seashore, so he said to him, "If you are the Lord, bid me walk on the water and not sink." The Lord so instructed him. But as he began to walk he saw the wild wind lashing up the waves, his heart filled with doubt, and he began to sink. The Lord reached out his hand to him, saying, "Your faith is small, why did you doubt?"

A man who has strong faith in the Way can walk on the yielding water as if on solid rock, but if he goes back to doubting, then the water will go back to its true nature, and how can he stay brave? When the wise man follows heaven's decrees, fire does not burn him, a sword does not cut him, water does not drown him. Why should wind or waves worry him? This first follower doubted so that we

Harner. de nos inuentes dubauith vitra schipsel II dinernis os forme inc. excudit.

might believe; one man's moment of doubt can serve to end the doubts of all those millions who come after him. If he had not been made to doubt, our faith would have been without foundation. Therefore we give thanks for his faith as we give thanks for his doubts.[3]

The second paragraph of this passage is entirely Ricci's creation. Ricci's "wise man" is here like the sages in China's own philosophical tradition who were so purified by their contemplation of the Way that they could withstand the forces of water and fire. But Ricci's use of this interpretation does not explain the differences between his first paragraph and the exact words of the gospel story. Ricci's Chinese Christ is "standing on the seashore" and "reaching out a hand" to Peter; the Christ in Matthew's gospel is "walking on the sea" and "catches" Peter as he sinks. In a universe embattled over subtle doctrinal distinctions this might seem to have interpretative significance, but for Ricci it is a matter not of interpretation but of necessity, caused by the demands of visual precision when using pictures for mnemonic purposes. If he had had the picture he most wanted at hand when Cheng Dayue gave him the chance to make his prints, he would not have had to make these changes. That picture was in Jeronimo Nadal's *Images from the Gospels,* a book that Ricci treasured and carried with him for many years in China. As he wrote in May 1605 to General Acquaviva's assistant, Alvarez, "This book is of even greater use than the Bible in the sense that while we are in the middle of talking we can also place right in front of their eyes things that with words alone we would not be able to make clear."[4] It was picture number 44 from Nadal that Ricci would have given to Cheng Dayue to illustrate Peter's story: it showed the frightened disciples, some straining at the oars, some tugging at the furled sails, others raising their hands or crying out in fear at the sight of the breaking waves and the Christ figure they believed to be a ghost. On the edge of the boat was Peter, prepared to step out, his robe hitched around his knees, and, in the foreground, Peter again, this time with frightened face sinking under the water. The figure of Christ dominated the picture, as he walked the waves with firm and level step; he was portrayed as gently grasping Peter's right wrist with his left hand, while holding his own right hand open and aloft in blessing.[5]

Unfortunately, when Cheng Dayue came to call, Ricci no longer had the Nadal volume. He had lent it to his Jesuit confrere Father Emmanuel Diaz, and Diaz had taken it to Nanchang to use in his mission work there. Ricci had made a deal with Diaz by which Ricci would keep a beautiful eight-volume Plantin polyglot Bible (which had just arrived in China) in his Peking residence while the Nadal went south. He soon repented this decision and sent a letter to Europe asking for replacement copies, but none were yet forthcoming.[6]

Confronted by Cheng's request, which is too valuable to be passed over, Ricci chooses to juggle the images. He has, in the Peking residence, a set of twenty-one wood engravings of the Passion of Christ, engraved by that same Anthony Wierix who did many of the Nadal prints. This second series of prints starts with Christ's entry into Jerusalem and ends with the Ascension; it does not illustrate earlier events in Christ's life such as the walking-on-water episode. But Ricci has noticed that number 19 in this series represents Christ appearing to his disciples after his resurrection, while they were fishing in the Sea of Galilee. In the gospel story of that event, found in the Gospel according to John, chapter 21, it is the apostle John who recognizes Christ but the ever-impetuous Peter who leaps into the water (first clothing himself, for he had been working stripped down) to hasten to his lord's side. Though Wierix's picture shows the waves rather small and the apostles hard at work over their nets rather than terrified at night on a stormy sea, Peter at least is in the water and Christ is reaching out his hand toward him. If the original text in Matthew is amended to have Christ on the shore rather than on the water—gesturing to Peter, perhaps, rather than holding him—then imagination can do the rest. And as for the fact that Wierix's original print clearly shows the nail holes of the stigmata in Christ's hands and feet, and the wound that a Roman soldier's spear made in his right side, that is swiftly remedied. Ricci has the Chinese artist who copies the print cover over the telltale signs that the Christ here portrayed had already suffered his crucifixion.[7]

So Ricci adjusts the gospel in order that the wrong picture may do the right work. When text and picture are together, as they will be on the outside of the expensive inkcakes that Cheng Dayue makes and sells to the wealthy literati of China, or in the book that Cheng will also print to generate more revenue, then they will reinforce each other. But when the picture is alone, evoking Chinese faith through memory, prior to the application of reason and will, the burden that falls upon it will be great. The visual image will have to conjure up the missing text, and every detail matters in this attempt. There is the city, from which the hungry came out to be fed. There is the mountain, where Christ retreated to pray. There is the fishing boat, with all the crew at work. Or rather all the crew save one, all save Bo-do-lo, who leaves the comparative safety of the vessel to struggle in his heavy robes among the waves and gazes up anxiously at the calm figure of Christ upon the shore.

Ricci's world was both riven and bonded by water. When he sailed from Portugal to India in 1578, the great days of early seaborne exploration by Columbus, Vasco da Gama, and Magellan lay more than seventy years in the past, and the new ocean routes from Seville to Veracruz, from Acapulco to Manila, and from Lisbon to Goa and Macao were accepted parts of global life. Yet knowledge of the sea remained uncertain, and most of it was uncharted; even in the revised version of his great world map, done in Peking in 1602, which drew on the latest geographical discoveries and the finest cartographical skills, Ricci showed the entire lower section of the Southern Hemisphere as one gigantic subcontinent. Those sailing even a few miles too far south of the Cape of Good Hope or in the Straits of Magellan could confidently expect to be dashed to pieces on the rocks of inhospitable and uninhabited shores. Ricci in fact never used the new euphemistic coinage "Cape of Good Hope" in his own writings; he preferred the more venerable and accurate "Cape of Storms."[8]

By Ricci's time habit and experience had led to certain common procedures for those traveling to India or the Far East. Since the world was still nominally divided according to the 1494 papal ruling at Tordesillas into two great zones, each controlled by one of the major Catholic maritime powers, those sailing west to Latin America, the Pacific, or the Philippines would take passage on Spanish vessels, while those traveling east to India, the Spice Islands of the Moluccas, to Macao, or to Japan would sail on Portuguese. (The naval forces of England, the Netherlands, and France were just beginning to contest these monopolies but had not as yet succeeded in breaking them in any fundamental way.) To have the best chance of obtaining favorable winds, the ships sailing for Goa tried to leave Lisbon in March (although anytime before Easter was considered fairly safe) and bore due south down the western coast of Africa before veering southwest past the coast of Brazil; on reaching the 30° southern latitudes they would bear east, passing by Tristan da Cunha and the Cape of Good Hope, whence southwest monsoon winds brought them to Goa by September. If they had hopes of returning within a year they had to leave Goa by Christmas to catch the northeast monsoons and round the Cape before the next May.[9]

There were long delays at any harbor, waiting for the correct month to commence each leg of the journey, with sailing dates naturally dictated by monsoons or prevailing trade winds. Some of the finest of the high-pooped Portuguese vessels—or "carracks," as they were termed—could reach 2,000 tons and mount twenty-eight guns, though most were more commonly around 400 tons with some twenty guns and a crew of 120; they were often built of Indian teak in the shipyards of Cochin and Goa, making up in part for the severe shortage of shipbuilding wood in southern Europe by the later sixteenth century.[10] But apart from changes in size there had been no great technological developments since the days of the early sixteenth-century explorers, and the bigger Portuguese carracks were less seaworthy than their smaller predecessors; science and seamanship were not yet linked with any precision, and no benefits from the exploration of the heavens opened up by Copernicus had yet been applied to the art of navigation. Timekeeping was uncertain at sea, and magnetic compasses were often erratic; latitudes could be gauged with precision, but assessing longitude was often little better than guesswork.[11] And though certain hardy merchants like the Italian Francesco Carletti were able to draw on their experiences and dream by the century's end of opening mercantile routes that would enable traders to span the globe in two years or less, Carletti himself took eight years (1594–1602) to complete his own journey from Seville to Zeeland in the Netherlands by way of Mexico and Nagasaki, and few would have been surprised at such a time span.[12]

The Jesuits in China knew enough of the sea's dangers to send each of their letters to Europe in two copies—one via Mexico on the Spanish galleons out of Manila, and one via Goa on the Portuguese carracks leaving Macao. Ricci's superior Valignano may have been startled that one of his letters to Rome took seventeen years in transit from Macao,[13] but Ricci accepted six to seven years as the norm for receiving an answer to a given letter. As he wrote from Shaozhou to a friend in 1594, this long time span meant not only that situations prompting the original letter changed drastically, "but also that people have moved from life on earth to another sphere: and often when I call to mind the number of lengthy letters that I have written about this place to those who were already dead, I lose the strength and the spirit to write any more."[14] In few cases was this more poignant for Ricci than in that of his own father, the wealthy Maceratan pharmacist Giovanni Battista Ricci. As Matteo wrote to his father in 1593, since he had heard nothing of his parents since one letter they had sent just after his departure from Lisbon five years before, "if it is not too much trouble it would cheer me up to know how the family are and if you are all alive."[15] Three years later Matteo heard from a close friend in Italy that his father had died, and he memorialized the event with a series of solemn

Masses.[16] Alerted at last in 1605 to the news that his father was not dead after all, Matteo wrote the only really warm family letter of his life (at least the only one that has come down to us), summarizing the main achievements of his career in China and ending, "I know not if this letter of mine will find you on earth or in heaven: in any event I wanted to write to you."[17] By the time the letter reached Macerata, however, Giovanni Battista was dead; and so was Matteo by the time the news—this time accurate—could have reached him.[18]

Matteo Ricci's general feelings of foreboding were not misplaced. Marine catastrophes were frequent throughout the period of his life in the East, and not just because of rocks, high seas, or sudden storms. Late departures because of bureaucratic or shipbuilding delays were legion, and ships frequently had to set sail with all the odds of wind and weather against them. Despite the justified fame of Portuguese seamanship, the crews were often untrained or inept, it being recorded that one captain found his crew—freshly recruited from the countryside—unable to tell which side of the ship was port and which starboard until he tied heads of garlic on one side and a string of onions on the other. The rosters of new sailors included "tailors, cobblers, lackeys, ploughmen and ignorant boys," according to one historian's portmanteau listing—and many senior officers were inexperienced gentry.[19] Food and water were in short supply from the start and soon became foul, the shortages made worse by the presence of stowaways or extra, semilegal passengers, including on occasion prostitutes bound for India or the mistresses of the ships' officers.[20] Then there were the diseases that raced through the vessels with horrible frequency, especially among the two or three thousand desperately poor Portuguese who traveled out each year, so that on some voyages, even when the weather remained fair, half the ship's complement might nevertheless perish. Men descending below decks often vomited or fainted at the fearsome stenches that rose from the refuse there, a noisomeness compounded by most passengers' unwillingness to use the common toilet facilities, jerry-rigged perches that hung unsteadily over the ships' sides and must have been terrifying enough in calm waters, let alone in a storm.

But most important as a cause of disaster was the insane overloading that characterized these infrequent sailings from which such mighty profits could be realized if all else went well: great mounds of goods were piled haphazardly over the decks, in teetering stacks, and crew and poorer passengers alike bartered their valuable cabin spaces for money and slept on deck among the goods, in fair weather and foul, adding to the chaos.[21] And as if all that were not enough, many ships were built of poorly seasoned wood and badly maintained, so that caulking and nails fell out of the softened timbers and the very keel wood could be split apart with a Bengal cane, as one disgusted Portuguese officer proved to his satisfaction after losing most of his possessions in a wreck. Some ships sailed these terrible seas held together by ropes slung hurriedly around bow and stern, tightened by a capstan.[22] Ricci noted in his *Historia* that when the Jesuits were threatened by hostile officials in 1587 with expulsion from China, he begged the Chinese for mercy with tears in his eyes, stating that there was "no way" they could once again pass over "all those seas that lay between China and their own homeland."[23] His friend Nicholas Spinola, safe ashore at Goa with Ricci in September 1578, wrote to his superiors at Rome: "Those desirous of traveling to India should not be too tied to life but ever ready to die, having great faith in Our Lord and a great desire for suffering, ready to mortify all their senses, for here one learns to know oneself by experience, not by theoretical reflection."[24]

Privateers provided a different kind of hazard, and one no less dangerous. The fleet in which Ricci and his fellow Jesuits sailed out of Lisbon harbor on March 24, 1578, was shadowed for days by two well-armed French vessels (possibly Huguenot ships allied to dissident Dutch Protestant forces), trying to pick up any stragglers from among the smaller merchant vessels. These latter, bound mainly for Brazil, sailed close to the three large carracks of the India fleet for this part of the journey to the Canary Islands. The carracks' captains ordered the guns run out, while the Jesuits (though suffering grievously from seasickness) stood on deck, clasping their crucifixes and ready to exhort the crews into battle. Unwilling to risk a gunfight with three such well-armed ships,

68

the French finally sailed away with a specious story that they were not French but Flemish grain ships that had strayed from their route.[25]

Other ships were often less lucky, and by the late sixteenth century both English and Dutch privateers had joined the French, adding the bitterness of religious war to their daring raids on points as distant as Havana, Mozambique, and Macao. On many occasions the Portuguese especially fought off their attackers with incredible courage, taking heavy casualties, and even letting their carracks go to the bottom with most of the hands and all of the cargo rather than surrender anything to Protestant or Japanese foes.[26] But inevitably the highly maneuverable and heavily gunned privateers scored some signal successes: the British seized the huge Spanish treasure galleon *St. Ana* off Acapulco in 1587, and the Dutch took two Portuguese carracks in the space of a few weeks at Malacca and Macao during 1603, to mention only the two grandest coups. These brought prize money estimated at five hundred thousand crowns in the first case and in excess of three and a half million guilders in the second.[27]

It was the nature of sixteenth-century naval practice to devolve extraordinary responsibility upon the lone figure of the pilot; in the case of Spanish and Portuguese vessels, royal regulations gave the pilot sole charge over the ship's course. Thus armed with whatever experience they had of winds and currents, fish movements and birds' flight, carrying simple maps and the narratives of previous voyagers when these existed, with compass, astrolabe, and quadrant, the pilots took responsibility for vessels of a thousand tons or more, with more than a thousand passengers and crew jammed aboard.[28] The pilots were given the blame for anything that went wrong on a given voyage and were pilloried in contemporary accounts. Thomas Aquinas, in his famous analysis of four kinds of causality, which was standard reading for any educated Catholic churchman, had observed: "Nor is it impossible for the same thing to be the cause of contrary effects. For instance, a pilot may be the cause of saving or sinking a ship: of the former by his presence, of the latter by his absence."[29] But that was written in the thirteenth century, before the advent of long-range sea voyages, and most of Ricci's contemporaries would have amended Aquinas to add a third cause, the pilot who sinks the ship by virtue of his presence. The mild English Jesuit Thomas Stevens, generally so appreciative of people's skills, and grateful for having reached Goa unscathed in 1579, could not resist blaming the pilot for his only near disaster, which occurred as he rounded the Cape of Good Hope, with its terrible reputation for storms:

> But we there found no tempest, only immense waves, where our pilot was guilty of an oversight; for, whereas commonly all navigators do never come within sight of land, but, contenting themselves with signs and finding the bottom, go their course safe and sure, he, thinking to have the winds at will, shot nigh the land; when the wind, changing into the south, with the assistance of the mountainous waves, rolled us so near the land that we were in less than fourteen fathoms, only six miles from *Capo das Agulias,* and there we looked to be utterly lost. Under us were huge rocks, so sharp and cutting that no anchor could possibly hold the ship, and the shore was so excessively bad that nothing could take the land, which besides is full of *tigers* and savage people, who put all strangers to death, so that we had no hope or comfort, but only in God and a good conscience.[30]

True to his general theme, it was to God rather than to the pilot that Stevens ascribed the ship's survival and the safe conclusion of his journey.

Many travelers had more dramatic tales than this to tell, and accounts by survivors of spectacular naval disasters were ever-popular items in the late sixteenth century, being published in pamphlet or book form after each new catastrophe. Ricci and the Jesuits at the college of Coimbra, waiting for ten long months in 1577 and early 1578 as the latest fleet was assembled for the Goa run, could have read in detail the pilot's role in the fate of the *St. Paul,* published in Lisbon in 1565. The *St. Paul* had left Lisbon for Goa near the end of April in 1560, with a complement of five hundred people—among whom were listed one hundred crew members, thirty-three women, thirty boys under twelve years of age, two Jesuit fathers, the rest being ship's officers, various male passengers, and miscellaneous slaves. The sailing date was too late for safety, as the crew and passengers must have known from the experiences of others, and though the *St. Paul* was one of the ships built in India, "very strong and like a firm rock in all the winds that blew," in the words of the chronicler of her fate, the pharmacist Henrique Dias who sailed on her for Goa with his full medicine chest, "she was an ill sailor when close-hauled, and difficult and hard to steer."[31] First hit by a savage storm, then misdirected by the pilot, who "was a novice in this India voyage," the ship was becalmed for two months of desperate tacking off the Guinea coast of Africa; crew and passengers fell sick with delirium and swollen groins, with no medical help for their pain but bleeding, for Henrique Dias's drugs were soon exhausted. The rigging rotted in the incessant rains, and at one time three hundred fifty out of the five hundred aboard lay ill.[32]

Only in late July did the ship cross the equator and reach Salvador after four months of horror; there it was refitted. But with the company further depleted by the loss of a hundred men who went to seek Brazilian gold, and groping in stormy seas to find the Madagascar route amid "great arguments between the captain, the pilot, and the master, with others who understood navigational matters," the *St. Paul* missed India altogether and was smashed onto the shores of Sumatra in January 1561, despite the final prayerful pleas to God in front of the banners and holy relics unfurled on the upper deck before which all had knelt in prayer.[33] Several survivors of this voyage and the subsequent desperate trek to safety had reached Goa and settled there, reshaping their lives in various ways, when Ricci arrived in India in 1578. Among them were Francisco Paes, who was to be made captain-major of a China-Japan voyage in 1585 (and still lived on as auditor-general of Goa in 1601); Antonio da Fonseca, who married and brought up a family and subsequently entered the Jesuit order after his wife's death; Francisco Fernandes, a young ship's boy at the time of the wreck, who grew up to become crier at the Goa auction market; and the faded gentleman Pero Barbosa, a verger in the Goa church, so destitute that he begged daily for alms from the religious orders and from the wealthy households in the town.[34]

In the absence of any surviving accounts by Ricci of his 1578 voyage to Goa, we cannot be sure of his own views on navigational matters, though we have two sets of indications. On the positive side we know that in his Chinese-language theological writings he used the image of the ship's pilot (along with those of the archer, globemaker, architect, and printer) as an example of a man whose skill lay behind apparently random phenomena, but this may have been simply an echo of his Thomist reading. Ricci argued that the way a ship was guided across difficult seas, by a pilot whose existence was unknown to an observer watching from afar, could be used as an analogy to the way God directed human destinies even though sight of him was denied to mankind.[35] We also know that he profited from the two occasions on which the vessel carrying him to India crossed the equator to do some observational work that later helped him: in a note appended to his Chinese map of the world he wrote, "When I came from the West to China and arrived at the equator, I saw for myself that the North and South poles were equally on the horizon, without the least difference in altitude."[36] On the negative side, we know from others that his ship, the *St. Louis,* ran aground at the very entrance to Mozambique harbor, shipping a good deal of water and perhaps risking more deadly damage; this must have been a considerable shock, one compounded by the very extent of the dangers already surmounted.[37] And there is certainly a heartfelt literalism in another passage from his Chinese theological works, in which Ricci wrote that the men of the sixteenth century were like "those who have seen their ship break up after a wreck; they find themselves in the wide sea among the crashing waves. Now sunk under the water, now bobbing up, they are tossed here and there at the will of the wind. Each thinks of his own plight, and no one thinks of saving his fellows. They grab onto whatever comes to hand—planks, sails, ropes, debris—they seize it, they clutch it to them, they will only leave go when their life ends."[38]

Ricci's contemporaries were attuned to the ups and downs of a seafarer's life, and poked fun at pilots even as they were realistically aware of the technical difficulty of their work and of the dangers to which they were exposed. Cervantes and Shakespeare serve to make the point. Cervantes gave to Don Quixote—as he sailed down a small river in a skiff, convinced that he was crossing mighty oceans—the chance to chide Sancho Panza for his ignorance of "the colures, lines, parallels, zodiacs, ecliptics, poles, solstices, equinoxes, planets, signs of the zodiac and points, which are the measures of which the celestial and terrestrial spheres are composed."[39] Unable to assess the exact distance they have traveled, since he has not brought his instruments with him, Don Quixote contents himself with the guess that they have traveled around two thousand miles (Sancho's guess is that they have moved five yards). Don Quixote continues:

"If I had only an astrolabe here with which I could take the height of the pole, I would tell you how far we have gone; though if I know anything we have passed, or soon shall pass, the equinoctial line which divides and cuts the opposing poles at equal distance."

"And when we get to this noxious line your worship speaks of," asked Sancho, "how far shall we have gone?"

"A long way," replied Don Quixote, "for we shall have covered the half of the three hundred and sixty degrees of earth and water the globe contains according to the computation of Ptolemy, who was the best cosmographer known, when we come to the line I mentioned."

"By God," said Sancho, "but your worship has got me a pretty fellow for a witness of what you say, this same Tolmy or whatever you call him, with his amputation."[40]

Shakespeare's depiction is at once more specific and more allegorical. In the opening act of *Macbeth* one of the witches makes reference to a woman whose "husband's to Aleppo gone, master of the *Tiger*," an allusion that many among an early-seventeenth-century audience would know to apply to the fate of the English merchant Ralph Fitch, who had sailed to the eastern Mediterranean market town of Aleppo on the ship *Tiger* before being arrested in Hormuz as a spy in 1583 and transshipped to Goa's notorious and effective jail, a story recorded in graphic detail in the second volume of Hakluyt's *Voyages,* which appeared in 1599.[41] The continuation of the witch's speech, in which she talks of the disorientation of the navigators as they tried to gain their bearings in wildly veering winds, would certainly have won weary acknowledgment from any who had sailed with the India fleets, as would the same speech's stark epilogue:

> Sleep shall neither night nor day
> Hang upon his pent-house lid:
> He shall live a man forbid.
> Weary se'nnights nine times nine
> Shall he dwindle, peak and pine;
> Though his bark cannot be lost,
> Yet it shall be tempest-tost.
> Look what I have.
> SECOND WITCH. Show me, show me.
> FIRST WITCH. Here I have a pilot's thumb,
> Wrack'd as homeward he did come.[42]

It is a curious but not impossible thought that travel literature of the day gave Shakespeare the idea of introducing Macbeth to the audience in the same breath as a brave yet harassed pilot: such pilots, like Macbeth, being men forced by life to make decisions of great moment under an opaque heaven that gave them little help, driven by stubborn pride to desperate acts that destroyed both them and those in their charge. Europe of the Counter-Reformation was avid for such tales, and life provided them abundantly. We find the historian Gian Pietro Maffei—whose historical work electrified Ricci when he first read it in 1581—not only devouring the same Portuguese disaster tales but also incorporating experiences from the group of Jesuits who sailed with Ricci into the growing drafts of his comprehensive history of the Indies.[43]

Ricci sailed from Lisbon to Goa in early 1578, with a little fleet that consisted of three ships, the *St. Gregory,* the *Good Jesus,* and the *St.*

Louis. The fourteen Jesuits were divided among the three vessels in groups of four or five: Ricci, along with Michele Ruggieri and three others, was assigned to the *St. Louis.* This was the flagship, commanded by the captain-major of the fleet, but the choice was otherwise not encouraging. Two years before, the *St. Louis,* despite good weather, had had a nightmare voyage in which, of the eleven hundred and forty people packed aboard, around five hundred had died of fever and other diseases caused by filth and overcrowding, not counting those who succumbed later after landing at Goa.[44] But Ricci and his friends were fortunate to be sailing in a period when King Sebastian of Portugal had ordered that carracks not be so huge as to be unmanageable, nor so crowded as to guarantee the spread of disease, and to these wise commands—forgotten by Sebastian's successors—they may have owed their lives.[45] Yet space, as always, was costly, and when the Jesuits came aboard on the night of March 23 many sailors and soldiers on the three ships had already sold their cabin space to traders to store their goods, or to wealthy passengers seeking extra room.[46]

Though Ricci's account of this journey has not survived, by good fortune the narratives of three of his fellow voyagers on the *Good Jesus* and the *St. Gregory* have been preserved; thus we know that the priests on the *Good Jesus* endured grim conditions, a tiny cabin jerry-built of rough planks on the upper deck, in which the four of them could only just find room to stretch out at the same time, along with a tiny storage cupboard for water and other supplies such as their stocks of oil and vinegar, wine, cheese, and ship biscuit. Those on the *St. Gregory* were better off, in a cabin in the stern jutting over the rudder that had three windows and an opening directly over the water to serve as a makeshift latrine, through which they could hear the pounding of the waves.[47]

All three accounts agree it was dawn on March 24 when the three ships moved out to sea before a favorable wind, leaving behind the din of the docks where the slow building of an armada—ultimately to total more than eight hundred ships—was under way in preparation for King Sebastian's planned assault on the North African coast.[48] A

75

crowd of pleasure craft scudded around them to speed them on their way, while from above the harbor came the sound of the bells tolling in the Church of the Wounds of Christ, the patron church for the pilots and master mariners of the India fleet.[49]

It was on this sea voyage, six months long, crossing the equator twice, that Ricci first lived in the world as a practicing man of the church, though he had not yet received holy orders and was therefore noted in the Jesuit documents of the trip as "Brother Ricci," a "student of theology."[50] The ship was a microcosm of the life ahead, with its mixture of dangers, hitherto unexperienced social relations, physical discomforts, and opportunities for austere or public devotion. Ricci's own training in the Jesuit college in Rome had prepared his body for physical rigors, but as his fellow Jesuit missionary Nicholas Spinola wrote on board the *Good Jesus,* all one's patterns shifted in the equatorial heat and cramped conditions. The very act of sleeping was denied one, since all one could do was "to sweat all the night through, stretched out on a plank with a tiny mattress, in a terrible stench and a host of lice and bedbugs." Everything rotted or stank in the incessant heat and damp: the ink faded out of the books, metal knives and spoons rusted, robes smelled of rotting wool, the drinking water grew putrid and the foods insipid, as gums swelled, teeth and jaws ached intolerably, and heads thumped with pain.[51]

The sailors were rough company, and the Jesuit fathers tried to restrain their worst behavior: intervening as mediators in the fights that swirled among bored groups, especially on hot summer nights, or to abate their ceaseless swearing by an ingenious system of fines, accumulating a fund that could be used later, by common agreement, for some devotional purpose of benefit to all. When the sailors chose to go to confession a new problem arose, for the priests often sought in vain a solitary spot in which to hear their lurid tales—it seemed that on such small and crowded vessels every cabin and bulkhead had ears.[52] Yet the boredom among the ship's crew was presumably increased by other activities of the fathers, who were diligent in rounding up and throwing overboard playing cards and dice and confiscating the many books, in a babel of languages and often illustrated, that they considered obscene and that seem to have been a constant feature of shipboard life.[53]

The favorite pastime that remained seems to have been shark hunting: some sailors showed great ingenuity in fashioning cloth models of the omnipresent flying fish, decorating the models with two long chicken feathers, embedding heavy metal hooks inside them, and then skimming them up and over the waves until a shark leaped and took the bait.[54] Other sailors would catch one shark with a crudely baited hook on a tough rope and, after spiking out its eyes, would slit its throat and throw it back into the sea; then all on board with time on their hands would line the ship's rails, watching with shouts of excitement as the other sharks converged to gorge upon the victim, until, unable to eat further, the feasters swam in lazing circles round the boat and could be killed in turn. Carried away by their sport, four sailors once fell into the sea when a massive fish smashed the plank hung over the side on which they were standing, but they were rescued before they themselves were eaten.[55]

In groups, each on their own ship, the Jesuits managed to conduct their own rituals of devotion: one hour of prayer after dawn, confessions every eight days, reading the *Spiritual Exercises* and Jacopone da Todi's devotional poems, or practicing acts of penance in their tiny cabins, performing the twice-daily "examinations of conscience"[56] that Ignatius of Loyola had seen as so important to the growth of spiritual life, reciting the litany at least once each day and singing the office at night in two-part harmonies, as crewmen knelt in the darkness.[57] On saints' days there would be full processions around the ships, with fathers in vestments and boy acolytes holding candles, carrying relics and the host.[58] On the feast of Corpus Domini (May 29, 1578) seventeen crew members dressed in varied costumes and acted out a two-hour drama of the battle between the devout and the devils in the temptations of Anthony of Padua, a saint of Portuguese origin to whose invocation the crew responded with fervor.[59] The saints' days gave such a particular rhythm to life at sea that when contrary winds stuck Ricci's ship inside Mozambique's harbor, causing the travelers to fear they might miss the favorable sailing dates for Goa, and when even a new solemn procession with the head of St. Gerasina lovingly displayed on August 12 nevertheless failed to change the wind's direction, many among the ship's complement reasoned that God saw no reason to have them celebrate the Assumption of the Virgin (August 15) at sea, since they had already given her watery offerings on the day of her Annunciation (March 25), on her Visitation (July 2), and doubtless would be still at sea, approaching Goa, on the feast of her Nativity (September 14).[60]

On quiet days of fair weather, there were other tasks for the Jesuits to perform: King Sebastian, as they left Lisbon, had given them a present of herbs and vegetables, and these they stewed in pots for those who were sick on board.[61] Some sailors fell strangely ill, as if possessed, and then ritual prayers could be followed by more thorough-going exorcisms.[62] But if the ship were becalmed, especially in dangerous equatorial waters, then solemn were the new processions around the decks, as treasured relics like the heads of virgin martyrs or that of Boniface (who once led an army of eleven thousand virgins) were paraded past the kneeling sailors, candles flickering in devout hands and the chanted liturgy rising above the altars erected on deck where devotional pictures of the Virgin and her Son were displayed. The fathers interceded directly for wind to get the ships moving once again, adding to their own prayers the effective device of persuading each sailor to promise a share of his pay or his allowance of oil to burn in lamps upon the altar of Our Lady of Beluarte in the little church maintained by the Dominicans on the island of Mozambique.[63] And in stormy seas, like those near the Cape that washed over the ships, smashing against them hour after hour in the heaving dark, the priests heard confessions constantly (all shame of fellow shipmates hearing one's sins now cast aside), and they tossed the little wax Agnus Dei into the sea to calm the waves—battling their own fatigue and sickness. Francis Pasio, one of the Jesuits traveling with Ricci, listed as a criterion for their survival on these long voyages that there be at least four priests on any one ship, able to serve turn and turn about when things were desperate.[64]

In a letter written during October 1578 after arriving in Goa, Pasio added quite casually that his ship, the *St. Gregory*, had loaded aboard "three or four hundred blacks" while in Mozambique,[65] and quite probably Ricci's *St. Louis* took on as many more. There were "an infinity of slaves for sale, both Muslims and gentiles, captured by one side or the other in their wars," shipped from mainland Africa to Mozambique and bought by the Portuguese there for use in India, making an East African equivalent for the West African traffic that fed the mines and plantations of the Caribbean, Peru, and Brazil. Persuading these slaves to embrace Christianity even as the ship crossed the Indian Ocean was a joyful task for the priests, and most slaves chose the faith after they had seen their first comrades die; in many cases Muslim slaves were baptized if they agreed to spit at the prophet Muhammad's name. Some could receive a swift absolution at death, for even on the month-long journey from Mozambique to Goa, in what seem to have been ideal conditions for those days, with fresh water and provisions on board in plenty, eighteen slaves died on the *St. Gregory*, while on the entire voyage, out of five hundred white passengers, only three had died—one ship's boy and one sailor who fell overboard and drowned, and one sailor who came on board at Lisbon with a fever that could not be cured.[66]

Mozambique was Ricci's first experience of that chain of bases that made up Portugal's overseas empire and were to mark the steps of his journey—on to Goa, to Malacca, and finally to Macao. Though barren and uninviting, the island was the first land that passengers, priests, and crew had seen since the Canary Islands four months before, and many were in despair at being delayed from landing. The island had no fresh water and grew virtually no food, everything having to be brought over from the mainland; but there were stockpiles of wine and dried biscuit, as well as fruit preserves, rice, millet, and fowl, and the finest wild pig the travelers had ever tasted. These must have been joys enough, plus the chance to stretch legs that had lost the facility for walking, all this while refreshed by worship in the church that lay under the protection of the fortress's guns, with a chance for quiet prayer or for service in the enormous hospital, one of the island's landmarks.[67] But these pleasures faded into the background once the ships reached Goa. Just as one priest on the *St. Gregory* had written that the joy of sighting even a misty spit of dangerous shore after months at sea had brought all the passengers onto deck in paroxysms of excitement, shouting "Terra, terra!," and could only be compared in terms of human joy to "the joy we will feel when our souls reach heaven,"[68] so did another write that the hills of Goa, washed deep green by winter rains, and the palm trees and elegant homes at the hills' feet, were "like nothing so much as a tapestry in which artifice depicted every aspect of freshness that one could imagine."[69] And who could describe the joys, after five and a half months of rationed and brackish water, of washing one's whole body and all one's clothes, splashing, splashing, splashing in the cold water that gushed from the springs and the fountains in the Jesuit college at Goa?[70]

The remaining long sea voyages of Ricci's life, those during 1582 from Goa to Malacca, and from Malacca to Macao the same year, had none of the drama of this first one, though he was ill enough on the last stage of the journey to Macao to feel the fact worth mentioning in his letters home.[71] (Just after he landed the few survivors of the terrible wreck of that year's Portuguese carrack trading with Nagasaki returned to Macao, with harrowing tales of their weeks as castaways on the hitherto unexplored island of Formosa.[72]) The closest Ricci came to repeating the ecstasy of his first moments at Goa was on two occasions in China, around two decades later. The first came in 1595, after he was at last given permission by the Chinese to travel north from Shaozhou to Nanchang and felt waves of nostalgia at the sight of ice and snow, the first he had seen for many years, as he told his brother in a rare letter home to Macerata.[73] The second was in the summer of 1598. Ricci had been given permission to travel to China's subsidiary capital, the great Yangzi River city of Nanjing, something he had long desired, but when he arrived there by boat in early July the war with Japan in Korea had just flared into its second phase. Since China's imperial court had issued edicts for the arrest of all suspicious-looking foreigners, no one dared to invite Ricci home or even to rent him lodgings, nor did he himself dare to travel on land except for brief journeys in a covered sedan chair. Instead, he was compelled to spend the summer months under the broiling sun of central China in a cramped and stifling boat out on the water, "with the greatest discomfort," as he wrote in the *Historia*, "since the boat not only was small but had few facilities."[74] But as soon as the military tensions eased, a wealthy Chinese official, Zhao Kehuai, invited him to spend eight to ten days as a guest in his country residence at Juyong, a day's ride from Nanjing. Here Ricci was housed in a setting that he described later with a lyricism that recaptures some of the joys of the moment: his lodgings were on high ground within the palace complex, a chamber "beautifully made, ornamented and painted, with three doors, one facing south, the two side ones east and west; these led to a covered walkway with exquisite balustrades, and beyond that lay a garden with many trees giving shade." In this lovely setting, on an altar designed for pagan gods but made his own for the space of a few precious days, Ricci was able to place the painted triptych of Christ which he carried with him in a covered case, to light incense beside it, and "to stay there all through the day, reciting his office and recommending himself to God."[75]

The intensity of these experiences may have something to do with the fact that the most significant dream of Ricci's life—or at least the only one that he felt was worth recording both in his letters and in his *Historia*—occurred as he was traveling by water between Nanjing and Nanchang, the cities that represented the poles of heat and ice to him. Ricci's boat was nearing Nanchang but making little headway against a strong contrary wind blowing off the Boyang Lake, and he was brooding about the difficulties of his mission when he dozed off. He described the ensuing experience in a letter to his childhood friend from Macerata, Girolamo Costa:

I must not forget to tell you one dream, which I had a few days after arriving in this place. I was standing, made melancholy by the sad outcome of my attempt, and by the travails of the journey, when it seemed to me that I met a man I did not recognize, who said to me:

"So is it you who have just been traveling through this land, seeking to destroy its ancient laws and replace them with the law of God?" And I, astonished that this person could penetrate so deep into my heart, asked in return: "Be you devil or God?" And he replied, "Not the devil but God." So I threw myself at his feet, weeping, and said, "If you, my Lord, know this, why up to now have you given me no help?" And he answered me, "Go forward to that city"—and here it seemed to me that he was showing me Peking—"and there I will help you." I entered the city filled with faith, passing through it without any difficulty. And this was my dream.[76]

The instruction to "go forward to that city" carried echoes of the mystical experience of Paul on the road to Damascus, and the vision of Christ the Saviour experienced by Ignatius of Loyola in the chapel at La Storta, during 1537, as Ricci was surely well aware.[77] He records that he awoke, his eyes still full of tears, and recounted the dream to his only companion on the boat, his language teacher and friend, Zhong Mingren, a Chinese convert and candidate for entry into the Society of Jesus, baptized as Sebastian, who had made the unpropitious journey to Nanjing and back with him.[78]

Much of Ricci's knowledge of China came from his journeys over her rivers, lakes, and canals. He had early learned that most Chinese would not venture far by sea, for sea travel and even life near the coast had become too dangerous. As Ricci phrased it, "Two or three boatloads of Japanese would land on China's coast and advance inland and seize towns and large cities, put them all to the sack and burn them, without there being anyone to resist them."[79] Certainly this had been true enough of the 1550s, but Ricci found it hard to accept the prevalence of these fears half a century later: "It is a matter of amazement to us," he observed, "that even though the journey by sea is shorter and more convenient, so great is the fear that the Chinese have of the sea and of pirates that they are unwilling to transport their goods by sea— though several have suggested it to their king, and in the old days they always used to do it." Instead they had focused their energies on their inland waterways, which were like nothing Ricci had experienced in

Europe. He quoted the common belief among Westerners that in China as many people lived on water as on land; and "even if this is not true," he added carefully, "nevertheless it is something that appears to be true to those who have only traveled by way of their rivers."[80]

Ricci was always enough of a European strategist to keep his eyes open for technical details that might later prove of use, and so even in the *Historia* written at the end of his life we find him observing of the Yangzi River, near its junction with the Boyang Lake, that despite the rapid currents there and the danger of drowning, "it appears to me that galleys and ships with mizzen sails could get as far as this area from the sea."[81] At times he and other Jesuits gave such careful details of their river and canal travel that their accounts could serve—as Chinese averse to foreigners had always warned—as bases for military planning by a hostile army contemplating invasion.[82] But more often Ricci's eye was drawn to the majesty of the boats themselves or to the splendid bustle of river life. Writing to his Roman school friend Giulio Fuligatti, Ricci put things into a familiar Italian perspective: these rivers were larger than the Po, he said, and some of the boats were so huge that their central cabins—with their high ceilings, ten or more windows, paintings and other decorations, dozens of tables and chairs—were the size of the chapel in the Roman college. Such boats had other rooms for retiring and sleeping, even kitchens and dispensaries: they "could be taken for fine houses were they on land." The boat specially built to sail on the Grand Canal linking Peking and Suzhou for the celebrated eunuch Ma Tang was even more splendid, with lacquered woodwork overlaid in gold and trellised window shades.[83]

The crowds of boats on East China's major inland waterway, the Grand Canal, could barely be comprehended. They covered the surface from shore to shore, piling up for days before the massive locks that controlled flow levels on the waterway; sometimes parting hurriedly as the boat of a grandee or court eunuch with special priority came racing through, sometimes capsizing if unprepared for the sudden rush of water released from one of the locks. On the banks thousands of coolies toiled to tow the loaded boats, while thousands more stood available, waiting for work.[84] Misery and plenty predictably intertwined: along the canal Ricci saw great storehouses of ice to keep the fruit and fish from the south fresh on their long journey to Peking; he also saw more than a thousand corvée workers in a single groaning team pulling log rafts composed of precious wood, some of the rarest trees being worth three thousand ducats each, he was told; the rafts, so huge and heavy they could be moved only five or six miles in a day, were destined to be used in rebuilding several imperial palaces that had recently burned down and for the emperor Wanli's giant tomb.[85] Chinese contemporaries would have agreed with this view of the barge-worker's suffering: as one of them wrote at this time, after the coolies had been working day after day on the canal under the blazing sun with no adequate clothing to protect them, "their backs are chapped like the scales on a fish."[86]

During the long reign of Emperor Wanli, from 1573 to 1620, which included the entire period that Ricci lived and worked in China, because of the emperor's refusal to get involved in the mundane matters of administration and politics, the eunuchs who acted as his intermediaries with the bureaucrats achieved quite extraordinary power.[87] Ricci rapidly learned that eunuchs controlled the lucrative transport on the Grand Canal, and so he traveled with them when he could—an influential eunuch could speed one's passage past lock after lock where normally one might pay massive fees and still be kept waiting four or five days. Ricci recounted how he and a fellow Jesuit once rented cabin space from a eunuch on a cargo boat carrying a load of fruit up the canal to the capital. The Jesuits negotiated a rate with the pilot of sixteen ducats for the trip from Nanjing, half payable in advance and half on arrival. The eunuch then threatened to throw them off the ship bag and baggage unless they paid him an extra eight ducats as well; by careful negotiation the Jesuits managed to satisfy him by simply paying the balance in advance of arrival in Peking.[88] Chastened by the experience, and short of cash for the return journey, Ricci tried to save money by taking space on a small boat returning empty from the capital. The price was cheap enough, but the boat was so decrepit and the pilot so poor that he could afford no coolie labor to speed their progress. So they made only a few miles a day, and ended up getting iced in at the northern river port of Linqing. After several weeks of enforced inaction, Ricci, ever restless, left his companions with the baggage on the boat and traveled south alone, bowling swiftly down to Suzhou along the side of the canal in a passenger wheelbarrow—a form of transport he had never tried before and which he found fast and convenient.[89]

China's huge rivers were dangerous, as Ricci also well knew. He had experienced disastrous floods when he was a student in Rome, during years when heavy rains had brought the Tiber high over its banks, ruining houses and farmland and causing a doubling of grain prices, and riots in the streets.[90] But he had been in China only three years when he witnessed a much more terrible flood: the waters of the West River engulfed the areas of Zhaoqing prefecture where he was living, causing damage made even worse by an earthquake that struck at the same time. Local Chinese records report that ninety different communities suffered some loss, that 21,759 homes were destroyed or damaged, while the crops on more than one hundred thousand acres of land were lost and thirty-one people drowned.[91]

Of the Yellow River Ricci later wrote: "This river brings much harm to the parts of China through which it passes, both because of its floods and its frequent changes of course. For these reasons the mandarins sacrifice to it, as if to a living spirit, with many superstitious rites."[92] Ricci is silent concerning the knowledge he had of these "superstitious rites," but as he read more deeply in Buddhism during the later years of his life he might have gained an inkling of the many religious tales the Chinese told of men and water.

The last great age of Ming naval exploration (under the eunuch admiral Cheng He, early in the fifteenth century) furnished the story of a sailor who fell into the sea and was miraculously rescued because he believed devoutly in Guanyin, the goddess of mercy.[93] Other Chinese stories described events closer to home, like the case of the devout Buddhist fruit-merchant Shen Jihuan. Shen was traveling across Lake Tai in the winter of 1593 with a cargo of oranges, the story ran, when his boat was caught in a sudden storm that darkened the waters and whipped up waves big as houses. Oars and sweeps were lost, and the boat started to sink. Shen cried aloud for help, and to the amazement of watchers on the shore two golden figures raised his boat out of the waves and brought crew, Shen, and cargo safely to its haven. The two golden figures were guardian spirits, touched by Shen's known devotion in reciting the Diamond Sutra every morning before going to work and carrying a copy of the same sutra always with him. Thereafter in the Lake Tai area, where Ricci had many friends—indeed, it was past those very shores that he traveled in his wheelbarrow five years later—Shen was known as "Fruit-seller Shen the Buddhist."[94]

More touching still, perhaps, though from an earlier time and place, was the case of the Buddhist monk Dongji: unable to swim, Dongji was prevented, by a swiftly flowing river in spring spate, from reaching a sick friend to whom he sought to bring solace. But greatly daring, and putting his faith in the Buddha, he wrapped the sutra in his robe, placed the bundle on his head, and stepped out into the stream. Easily he walked across as if the water had been only a few inches deep and safely reached the other shore. But as he reached dry land again he found that the sutra and wrappings had vanished. Lamenting the loss at his sick friend's house, to which he hastened, he saw the bundle there, resting on a table. Seizing it joyfully, he found that the wrappings were soaked as if they had been in a rainstorm; but the text of the sutra within was bright and clear.[95]

Ricci knew the pains of such loss of sacred texts and the joys of recovery. For many years of his mission to China, he had yearned to have a set of the magnificent Plantin Bible, that Bible he had first seen when it was brought to India in 1580 as a present—and hoped-for tool of conversion—for the Muslim emperor Akbar.[96] It was not just the meticulous scholarship in various languages that made the book so precious, and not just its religious content. It was, rather, its appearance, the very weight of the volumes, the fineness of the paper, the delicacy of the leather bindings, the fact that there were eight volumes, each filled with type from cover to cover. The converts in China had complained repeatedly of the frail bulk of Christian works available to them, and had asked the Jesuits how they could counter those Chinese scholars who mocked them by stating that all of their Christian wisdom could be contained in little treatises a few pages long. In desperation some of the Jesuit fathers had printed devotional books, still in Latin but with Chinese characters added to the text, so as at least to transliterate books that they were not yet skilled enough to translate. These texts remained incomprehensible to their readers, and yet were gratefully received as a step in the right direction, since they brought some added weight to Christianity's claims.[97]

The Plantin Bible therefore provided everything they yearned for. The eight immense folio volumes of this Bible, printed in Greek, Latin, Hebrew, and Chaldean, and illustrated with superb copper engravings made by the leading masters in the Low Countries, represented a pinnacle of Counter-Reformation expenditure, determination, and devotion. The Bible had been made between 1568 and 1572 by Christopher Plantin in Antwerp under contract to King Philip II of Spain; it had cost the king in excess of 20,000 florins to get the project under way, and had occupied up to ten of Plantin's presses and more than thirty of his skilled workers for much of the period. It had entailed the painstaking accumulation of different type fonts, clearance of the text with the doctrinal experts of Rome and the Inquisition, and the hiring of multilingual proofreaders, along with batteries of skilled binders, colorers, line-rulers. The skins of eight thousand sheep had been needed to provide the parchment for the thirteen most luxurious sets destined for royal hands, and 1,900,000 sheets of fine paper were required to print the rest of the edition of 1,200 copies.[98]

At last in late 1603 a copy of the precious volumes, donated to the China mission by Cardinal Santa Severina, reached Macao, and in February 1604 Father Gaspar Ferreira was assigned to take the Bible to Peking, with other supplies and presents. He reached Nanjing in April and was on the outskirts of Peking in early August.[99] But here, as Ricci wrote in a letter to General Acquaviva's assistant, Alvarez, the Peking fathers suffered a "shipwreck" of their own: Ferreira arrived just as catastrophic rains had swollen all of China's northern rivers, and in the raging flood waters of the Beihe, which had already washed away hundreds of houses on the edges of the city and brought destitution to thousands of families, Ferreira's transport boat broke apart, spilling its contents into the torrent. Seventy ducats' worth of wine for the Mass sank immediately and could not be recovered. Pictures, reliquaries, and other religious articles drifted away. Most agonizing of all, the polyglot Bible, just at the end of its voyage halfway round the world, tumbled into the flooded river.[100]

But the Plantin Bible did not sink. The eight volumes floated off in their wooden storage box and were fished from the water by some Chinese in a nearby boat. Brother Sebastian Fernandez, a Chinese Jesuit from Macao who had been with Ricci in many an emergency before, saw the boatmen open the box and look with incomprehension at the mixture of types; he bargained with them while their disappointment was fresh and bought the volumes back from them for a handful of copper coins worth three-tenths of a ducat, or three *giulii,* in the Italian equivalent of the Chinese currency at the current exchange rate. The Bible was worth at least three hundred ducats at current prices, Ricci told Alvarez, and "it was God's will that we were able to ransom back our book for no more than three *giulii,*" about one-thousandth of its true value. The volumes were not ruined—they were just "a little damp," as Ricci put it—and their gilding was in place and the bindings holding.[101] With an eye for the dramatic, Ricci displayed the eight volumes for the first time to his Peking congregation after Mass on the morning of the Feast of the Assumption of the Virgin Mary, and they had the desired effect: "The beautiful printing and the majesty of the book filled [the congregation] with admiration, and they could form a conception of the beautiful doctrine that was inside even though they could not read the words."[102]

Flood and death were parts of river life, and the Jesuits were always aware of the dangers. The very first house Ricci built in China, in Zhaoqing, had itself been badly flooded, and one of the first serious attacks launched against mission property was led by angry villagers who wanted the Jesuits to donate materials to shore up their levees against encroaching waters.[103] Ricci often commented in his letters on the horrors of such floods and of the paradox that "these rivers which make all of China so beautiful and fertile also bring such great damage." He had also seen, as he told General Acquaviva, the effect of the floods that followed after savage rainstorms: "a vast number of houses collapsed, or completely flattened, possessions lost, crowds of people suffocated either in their houses or in the river which flooded over."[104] One cannot help wondering if, for just a moment, as Ricci prayed with his congregation beside the rescued Plantin Bible, he remembered that the three *giulii* he paid to ransom the book was also the cost of a ten-year-old boy during times of natural catastrophe. He would have known the exact price from the fact that a friendly eunuch he met once on the Grand Canal gave him a present of a child who had cost exactly that.[105]

Sometimes the beauty of the natural setting, the convenience of water travel, its turbulence and its deadly power, all flowed together. "Contrasts are never lacking and never will be lacking," Ricci wrote to Girolamo Costa from Peking in 1605, "but with these winds the ship of St. Peter sails on its way."[106] And so it was in the spring of 1595. Ricci was working in Shaozhou at the time, when he received an invitation to visit a senior military official who was passing through the city en route to a military assignment in Peking concerned with logistical planning for the Korean campaign. This official—we know his name only in Ricci's transcription as "Scielou"—had a twenty-year-old son who had fallen ill. Scielou, having heard much praise of Ricci's scientific skills, sought his services as a doctor to cure the youth; Ricci in turn played for time, bartering his healing knowledge for a transit pass to Peking. Scielou agreed to the deal and granted the necessary permits. We can be almost certain that the cause of the young man's illness—described as "grief and shame" because of his failure in the state examinations—gave Ricci the idea of training him in Western memory methods, so he would recover his morale and be able to take the exams again, this time with success. For Ricci had almost no medical knowledge, and undertaking such an assignment with no hope of success would have been perilous indeed.[107]

Scielou, in his suite of vessels full of costly possessions, family and consorts, servants and guards, headed for the north, telling Ricci to join him as soon as possible. Ricci seized with elan this splendid chance to get out of the unhealthy and hostile environment of Shaozhou, wrapping up the affairs of his five-year Shaozhou residence in a day and a half. He left the mission in the hands of his younger associate Cattaneo—new to China, and with almost no knowledge of the language as yet—and of two senior Chinese brothers of the Society of Jesus. Ricci himself took two younger Chinese novices and two of his most trusted servants and hired a boat to carry them northward. But swiftly though they moved, they could not catch the official entourage, which by virtue of Scielou's rank could call on unlimited supplies of free boat-pulling labor to haul his huge boats upstream.[108]

Ricci had still not managed a rendezvous when he reached the northern town of Nanxiong, which he had visited three years before and where he had made some converts among wealthy Chinese merchants. This was the terminus point for the navigable section of the southward-flowing Bei River. Crew and passengers had to alight here and carry their possessions up the steep flights of steps carved into the upper reaches of Meilin Mountain, over the crest, to the loading docks of a second river, the Gan, which would take them north to the center of China. Dense crowds of travelers and merchants tramped and jostled on the fine stone track, but several Christian converts came to help Ricci make the portage, and he himself rode in a carrying-chair through the crowds, past inns and shops and squads of guards that remained vivid in his memory a decade later. Once at the peak, Ricci savored the immense view across the province of Guangdong behind him to the south and the still-unexplored Jiangxi to the north. At the river town of Nanan, he made yet another transfer, for Scielou had a boat waiting for him and the two of them started the long downstream trip to Ganzhou. On quiet days Ricci was invited to join Scielou in his official vessel and they talked together of science and religion, leaving Scielou's son's problems aside for a later date. They entered Ganzhou to the exuberant roar of full military salutes from arquebuses and muskets fired by honor guards of soldiers Ricci guessed to be three thousand in number, spread along three miles of riverbank; here Ricci rented his own boat and crew, to be more independent for the dangerous descent of the rapids that lay ahead, where two larger rivers met in a rocky defile of sudden winds, fast currents, and whirlpools. The "Place of Eighteen Currents," the locals called it.[109]

The first boat to have a minor accident was the one carrying Scielou's consorts and children, which struck a rock and began to sink, but since this was an area of shoals and the boat was built high, it settled on the river bottom the family scrambled to the superstructure and were rescued with some ease by Ricci and his crew, who were following close behind. Ricci forfeited his boat by this generosity, for Scielou forbade his consorts to transship again, in the searching light of day, ordering them to remain where they were until nightfall decorously shrouded their movements; in its place, Ricci was given a berth by Scielou on one of his baggage vessels and thus continued his journey.[110]

He was now alone with Scielou's hired crew, except for the company of one of the young Chinese novices, who as a boy from a converted Chinese family had studied in Jesuit schools in Macao before being sent to join Ricci in the Shaozhou mission in 1592. This young man was called always by his Portuguese name of João Barradas, and was loved and trusted by Ricci, who felt personally responsible for his welfare.[111] The anguish of the next few minutes pierces the hurried words of a letter that Ricci wrote later that year to his superior Edoardo de Sande in Macao:

We reached the place called Tien Chutan, where the current runs swiftly and the water is very deep, at the foot of a tall mountain, and the thundering of the water was so great that when I saw it I began to pray fervently that it subside. For the ships in [Jiangxi] rivers have high masts and no keels, and I realized how easily they might turn over in the thundering water; but no matter how much I beseeched them, the pilot and the sailors were so careless that they took the ships into the rapids under full sail, and in a moment our ship was turned over and spun around, along with two others in which were the mandarin's possessions. Thus did I and João Barradas, as we were traveling together, get sent to the bottom. But God aided me because in turning I caught hold of some ropes dangling from our ship, which by divine providence I found between my hands, and was able to pull myself up onto a support of the same ship. And seeing my writing case and bed floating there on top of the water, I was able to stretch out my hand and pull them to where I was, after which some sailors, swimming back to the boat and climbing aboard, helped me to clamber back up. But João Barradas went to the bottom in such a way that the current carried him away and he never appeared again.[112]

Scielou, distraught at the loss of his possessions, and Ricci, in despair at the loss of his friend, sent boatmen to search the river. The divers produced a good many sodden objects for Scielou's perusal but could find no trace of Barradas's body. Scielou give Ricci the money necessary "for the funeral rites," but since there was little that could be done in the absence of the corpse, the cash really amounted to compensation money for the Jesuits.[113] When yet another squall battered the few boats of Scielou's that had reached the lower river, he resolved to continue his journey by land, since the fates were clearly against him on the water. Ricci also thought seriously of abandoning the whole journey, but at the last moment decided to continue on to Nanjing with some of Scielou's staff who were going to attend to their master's business there. Along with the shock, his main sense was one of surprise: he had never expected, as he wrote to General Acquaviva, "that God would choose to have me shipwrecked in a river, when I had never been shipwrecked on the seas although I had passed across so many."[114]

FOUR

THE SECOND IMAGE: THE HUIHUI

F or his second example of how to construct a memory image, Ricci chooses the Chinese ideograph yao.[1] It is an easy ideograph to write but hard to translate: it can mean, variously, to want something or to need something, or that something is important, or that something must be done. The reader must always be swayed by the context. Thus in the very first translation of the Ten Commandments, made by Ruggieri and Ricci in 1584, yao is the first word in the first commandment, bearing the force of "shall" in "You shall have no other gods but me."[2] In a collection of basic prayers and dogmas of the Catholic faith, which Ricci published (with the permission of the Goanese Inquisition) around 1605 under the title Fundamental Christian Teachings, yao is used to translate the word "fundamental."[3]

To present these multifaceted ideas in the form of a memory image that the reader will remember, Ricci first cuts the ideograph in two horizontally. This yields two separate ideographs, the upper one meaning "west" and the lower one "a woman." Ricci does not simply create the memory image of a woman from the West, however, since that

would not have the resonances he seeks. He does something more complicated, creating an image the description of which can be understood in two quite different ways.

By the first of these, the interpretation that most Chinese would initially be drawn to, Ricci describes the image that will stand for *yao* as being "a woman from the Xixia territories, who is a Muslim." He arrives at this formulation by associating sounds and ideas and playing with the words along lines taught him by his own memory masters: the top half of the ideograph *yao* has the meaning "west" and is pronounced *xi; xi* forms the first half of the name Xixia (which designates an ancient kingdom that once flourished in China's western regions); the bottom half of the ideograph has the meaning "woman"; the area once occupied by the Xixia kingdom is now the home of most of China's Muslims (the *huihui*), who drifted there over the long caravan routes that stretched across central Asia. That, at least, is one interpretation, and we can guess that in Ricci's eyes this woman would have an exotic look, evoking the world of the nomads from the very edges of the settled Chinese borders; she would wear the vivid dress, the felt boots, the braided hair common to those of that harsh terrain.

But there are other and more complex resonances to this image of *yao,* and Ricci leaves open the possibility that his definition of the image could be translated thus: "a woman from the northwest, who is a *huihui.*" By this interpretation *Xixia* simply gives a rough geographical location, and the word *huihui* is not restricted to Muslims. Ricci knows well, from conversations with Chinese scholars and from his own studies and observations, that the term *huihui* is also supplied to the scattered communities of Jews in China and to the descendants of the Nestorian Christians who can still be found there. The Jews of Ming China were distinguished by the term *"huihui* who reject the sinews" (in reference to Jacob's wrestling with the angel), while Nestorians were called *"huihui* of the cross."[4] Thus for Ricci the tribeswoman who is a *huihui* suggests a tighter link to those ideas of fundamental belief or obligation that inhere to the word *yao.* She reminds him that if the triple systems of Confucianism, Taoism, and Buddhism have been internalized in China, the triple systems of Islam, Christianity, and Judaism are tolerated but not allowed to have separate identities. And in this might there not lie a fundamental truth, since the latter three share an underlying acceptance of the one true God?

In the southeast corner of the reception hall the two warriors are still locked in combat. Ricci takes the tribeswoman who means necessity and places her in the northeast corner, close enough to the two men so that she will not be lost sight of but not so close that she might be visually confused with them. She will stay there, in the quiet light that suffuses the memory palace, calm and unmoving, for as long as he chooses to leave her.

While Ricci was living in Zhaoqing in 1584, he drew a map of the world, with the names of the countries written out in Chinese phonetic equivalents, and displayed it in his mission house. Zhaoqing was a large and prosperous town—three times the size of Seville, according to one Western visitor—and the many wealthy locals who came to visit Ricci were surprised and interested to see their own country in a global context. One of them, without Ricci's permission, copied the map and had wood-block prints made of it; these circulated so widely, and proved so popular, that Ricci decided to create a fuller and more accurate version, since the first draft had been done in haste.[5] He worked off and on at these improvements between 1584 and 1602, when he printed his own version of the map, filling it with the latest information on new discoveries, elaborating various sections, and adding flattering essays written in praise of his knowledge by local scholars who had seen and admired his cartographic work. Ricci's short explanatory notes on various countries, written in small but clear Chinese characters, served to introduce his civilization to the curious even when he himself was not present. In the 1602 edition of the map, tucked into the space off the west coast of

Italy, between the peninsula and the island of Sicily, he appended the information that the territory belonged to "The Holy Father, who is celibate, and concerns himself only with the Catholic religion, residing in Rome. All the Europeans who are in the Roman Empire revere him."[6] And in the Atlantic Ocean off the west coast of Europe, Ricci wrote:

> Here are more than thirty kingdoms which all follow the administration of the ancient kings. No superstitions are allowed here but everyone holds to the religion of the Lord of Heaven, the supreme ruler. There are three classes of those in authority: the highest occupy themselves with religion, then come those who judge temporal affairs, and lastly those who devote themselves to arms. These countries have all the cereal grains, metals, fruits, and wine made from grapes. They study astronomy and philosophy and believe in the five relationships. Kings and people alike are powerful and rich: in all seasons they have relations with other lands, and their travelers and merchants voyage to all the countries of the world.[7]

In a notation placed at the eastern end of the Mediterranean, he identified Palestine as the "Holy Land" where "the Lord of Heaven was born." Constantinople, Medina, and Mecca were named, though without comment; a small area in northeast Persia just south of the Caspian Sea was designated as being *huihui* territory, but again there was no comment.[8]

Ricci's reticence was of course deliberate: the Chinese would be unlikely to be drawn to the religion he was preaching if they knew that deep fissures of belief existed in the Western world from which that religion came. Ricci himself knew well enough that the Catholic faith was under assault in Europe, for he had grown up in surroundings of constant religious contention. Especially in the Rome of the 1570s when he was a novice, the church's battles were kept to the fore through ceaseless preaching. The preachers were found not just in the great churches—though here the pope's private preacher, Father Toledo, the Jesuit Father Benedict, the Franciscan Panicharella, the Capu-

97

chin Lupus, all spoke with especial eloquence and had their own public followings—but also out in the streets and marketplaces, in the piazzas, in the crowded public gardens of summertime, and among the swirling crowds of out-of-town laborers who came to be hired in the vineyards and elsewhere. Some Jesuits wandered in the streets and through the countryside accompanied by choristers, and used "pleasant song" to inspire the workers and "eased their labor with this singing." Preachers worked, too, among the prostitutes in the brothel areas and in front of the houses of known usurers. The Jesuits were particularly active in these street ministries: one observer mentioned seeing them standing on convenient market stalls or window ledges to view their audiences, moving the crowd with their words and handing out free gifts of knotted whipcord so the devout could mortify themselves later in private.[9]

In St. Peter's itself the Jesuits were appointed to hear the confessions of not only the citizens of Rome and other Italians but all pilgrims visiting the holy city. They set up a system for the rotation of bilingual confessors, each fluent in Italian and one other language—English, Polish, French, Spanish, Flemish—the name of this second language being displayed on a placard above the confessional where the priest sat holding a white rod of office. If a pilgrim could not find a confessor who understood him, one would be summoned from the nearby house of the Penitentiaria, where twelve Jesuits were always on call; and if the need was for an expert in Greek or Syriac or Arabic they called upon Father Baptista Romanus, a recent convert from Judaism, whose newfound Christian faith was matched by his phenomenal language skills. By the 1590s the Jesuits could produce priests to speak in any of twenty-seven different languages.[10]

The excitement of this polyglot atmosphere was supported by the presence of foreign books. The libraries in all the Jesuit colleges in Rome were already excellent in the late 1570s, "ful of the best bookes for every facultie," as the exiled English Catholic Gregory Martin noted, adding in surprise that the Jesuits even had fonts of foreign type.[11] These resources were supplemented by the remarkable Vatican library, which was kept open three days a week for general readers (on Mondays, Wednesdays, and Fridays), with fires always lighted on winter days to keep the rooms comfortable. Montaigne, visiting there in March 1581, was delighted at the generous access he was given to the books and astonished to see—among the papyri and Greek manuscripts, rare editions of Virgil, Seneca, and Plutarch, handwritten works of Thomas Aquinas and an autographed copy of Henry VIII's attack on Luther—"one book from China, unusual in nature [*le caractère sauvage*], the sheets made of some material much more delicate and translucent than our paper; and because this cannot absorb the ink very well the writing is only on one side of each sheet, the sheets then being doubled over and folded."[12]

Mission fervor was omnipresent, constantly renewing old ideas of spiritual crusade. By express decision of Ignatius of Loyola, in his *Constitutions* for the Jesuit order, which were amplified by Pope Julius III in his bull of 1550, all Jesuits pledged as follows: "We are to be obliged by a special vow to carry out whatever the present and future Roman pontiffs may order which pertains to the progress of souls and the propagation of the faith; and to go without subterfuge or excuse, as far as in us lies, to whatsoever provinces they may choose to send us—whether they are pleased to send us among the Turks or any other infidels, even those who live in the region called the Indies, or among any heretics whatever or schismatics, or any of the faithful." This vision was held with equal force by General Acquaviva.[13] Gregory Martin, fully aware of the effects of these vows on the minds of the Jesuits, described the mood among them in Rome during the years 1577 and 1578, the very period when Ricci was preparing to receive his own assignment:

> Some of them God suffereth to die, the more to declare their charitie, when the thing is so daungerous: the rest he preserveth, to shew his merciful power, and that he accepteth their good wil, and spareth his servants bicause he wil use their service longer. No lesse charitie and zeale is it, or greater perhaps, (the fruite undoubtedly incomparablie more) that so many of them with the like franke spirit and fervent affection desire to be sent as it were into an other world, to the barba-

rous Infidels of both Indiaes, to convert them to the faith, which thing for the great daunger many waies, and the smal probabilitie (as a man would thinke) to doe great good, might justly make very good men to stagger.[14]

Ricci gave only one clue, late in his life, of how he had himself felt at this time—apart, of course, from the example of his life itself. In a letter from Nanchang on October 12, 1596, to his school friend Giulio Fuligatti, who had stayed in Italy, Ricci reminisced on how the two of them had dreamed of joining the missions in the Indies, of becoming a part of the "mighty armies" that were traveling to "untended forests": but he reassured Fuligatti that the life of faith in Italy was as dramatic as in China, since "one needs no thrust of steel to be a martyr, nor need one embark on a long journey in order to be a pilgrim."[15]

The Jesuits were probably trained as well as anyone in the world at the time for mission service overseas. To a rigorous curriculum in theology, classics, mathematics, and science was added the methodological training of the "disputations." These events, usually held on Sundays after dinner, were conducted in one of two ways: in one, a student presented a given point of theology and then defended it against a forceful range of counterarguments by his fellows—who had been given twenty-four hours to sharpen their arguments; in the other, a teacher presented a heretical position, leaving it to the students to undermine this "devil's advocate" by the force of their own skills. Though there was danger that these sessions might become merely formulaic, when rigorously conducted they gave extraordinary training to the young in structuring argument, analyzing their own faith, and sharpening their techniques of memory. This last was accomplished by adapting the methodologies taught by Quintilian and Cicero—originally used in legal and rhetorical contexts—to the domain of theology.[16]

These disputations were backed by impressive displays designed to emphasize the symbolic importance of the struggle being enacted. At special services in the pope's chapel the gospel and epistle for the day were recited both in Latin and in Greek to remind all listeners that the two were parts of the same Catholic church and that the pope was lord of both; but to show the faded state of the Greek church, lights were dimmed and ritual dispensed with as the Greek was read, the lights returning to full glory only when the Latin text was returned to once again. And in the twice-daily readings of the Bible at mealtimes in the Jesuit seminaries, the Greek variants (along with the Hebrew) were always discussed along with the Latin if they were needed in exegesis to dispel a heretical argument.[17]

Yet these various procedures, for all their ingenuity and symbolic weight, did not amount to a formal training in the doctrine of the enemy. Long before, in the late thirteenth century, a courtier and scholar named Ramon Lull had used his experiences in the religiously mixed community life of the island of Majorca—where recently victorious Catholics controlled a population containing many Jews and Muslims—to suggest that the church take seriously the task of learning foreign languages and holding public debates with distinguished representatives of rival faiths, the better to combat them. Lull suggested that his own works be translated into the heretics' languages; that "men should go to the Tartars and preach to them and show it to them; and that there should be Tartars at Paris who should learn our writing and language before returning with this knowledge to their own country."[18] In his earliest important work, *The Book of the Gentile and the Three Sages,* Lull presented a protracted "conversation" in which a gentile questioned first a Jew, then a Christian, and finally a Muslim on such matters as God the creator, Moses as prophet, the Messiah, the Resurrection, the meaning of heaven and hell, and Muhammad and the Koran. Lull left it open which of the three options the gentile finally chose, closing the book on a scene of elaborate courtesy as the Jew, the Christian, and the Muslim apologized to each other for any remarks that might have caused unintentional offense.[19] But in later years, in fact, Lull moved to a position of extreme and public antagonism to Islam, so that any ideas of true tolerance swiftly faded. Coincidentally, it was in the same period of the thirteenth century that Franciscan preachers, who had been well received by the Mongol regimes of central Aisa, brought back their initial reports on Buddhism. These included preliminary accounts of Buddhist prayer, meditation, texts, and saints, quite accurate in various aspects, but this information aroused little interest in Europe and was not followed up in any consistent way in European schools.[20]

The idea of the parallelism between Judaism, Catholicism, and Islam nevertheless received a further underlining in the midfourteenth century from Giovanni Boccaccio, who used this idea for one of the first stories in the *Decameron*. The story concerns a subtle Jew being quizzed by the sultan Saladin, who is after the Jew's money. Seeking to trick the Jew into an indiscretion which he can exploit, Saladin asks the Jew which of the three religions is "truly authentic." The Jew ducks the question with an allegorical tale of three rings: A rich man, dying, wishes to follow the family tradition of leaving an exquisite ring to the son who most pleases the father and would head the family in his turn. But this particular dynast loves three of his sons equally, and sees them as being of equal talent. So he secretly has two perfect copies of the ring made, and gives one to each of the sons. Only after his death do the three sons find they all have a ring, and are therefore forced to share management of the family and the whole inheritance between them. "The question of which of the sons was the true and rightful heir remained in abeyance, and has never been settled," wrote Boccaccio. "The same applies to the three laws which God the Father granted to His three peoples, and which formed the subject of your inquiry. Each of them considers itself the legitimate heir to His estate, each believes it possesses His one true law and observes His commandments. But as with the rings, the question as to which of them is right remains in abeyance."[21]

This kind of acceptance of Islam seems still to have been widespread in Italy in the midsixteenth century, despite the rigors of the Counter-Reformation. The miller Menocchio, first investigated by the Inquisition in 1584, the year after Ricci entered China, believed the Holy Spirit had been given "to heretics, to Turks, and to Jews: and he considers them all dear, and they are all saved in the same manner."[22] It is possible from Menocchio's descriptions of paradise and some of his other beliefs that he had seen a copy of the Koran, or at least discussed it, since an Italian translation had begun circulating in 1547.[23]

Some of Ramon Lull's ideas—especially the complex "art" he developed, combining mnemonic, magical, and organizational techniques for mastering and organizing the forces of the world—had a considerable vogue in the sixteenth century in France and Italy, but there was still no consistent development of training in Arabic, let alone in the languages of India, China, or Japan, and Ricci would have had no chance to learn these languages in school.[24] Apart from the Ottoman alarms of his Macerata childhood in the late 1550s, Ricci's first experience of the power of Islam undoubtedly came when he reached Goa in late 1578. Goa had been a Portuguese possession ever since it was seized from the Muslim sultan of Bijapur by Afonso de Albuquerque in 1510, so it was not surprising that it had become such a thriving center for religion, war, and trade. The city was the base for the viceroy, appointed by the crown, who oversaw Portugal's Indian possessions, and was administered by a municipal council of Portuguese noblemen, magistrates, and leaders of merchant guilds. These men saw to the defenses of the city, supervised its economic life, managed the public works, and fixed the food prices for the local population of some three or four thousand Portuguese, scores of Catholic clerics of different nations, and perhaps ten thousand Indian city residents, as well as the Indians in the more than thirty communities that lay outside the city walls but on Goa island.[25] Yet if Goa was Portugal's greatest bastion in the East, it was also vulnerable, hard to arm and supply, and often in only tenuous connection with its key outposts at Mozambique and Hormuz.

Muslim power seemed all the greater in comparison to the condition of the Hindu residents on Goa island and the neighboring territory of Salsette, for the Hindus had been forced into subjection by the dominant Christians, their temples totally obliterated, many of their rites and feasts forbidden, with recalcitrant Brahmans sentenced to confiscation of property and life in the galleys. Other regulations forbade non-

Christians to head the commercial guilds and forced many to work without remuneration on Portuguese ships in the docks.[26] Complicated laws gave almost all Hindu orphans over to the Jesuit fathers of St. Paul in Goa for education and fostering "until they were old enough to decide their religion for themselves," a process that led to predictable pressures for their conversion.[27] Accounts from the period of Ricci's residence in Goa speak with pleasure of the sight provided by the schoolchildren of the Goa college, some as young as five and none over sixteen, as they danced before the altar in the church with bells on their legs, then formed up into the ranks of a little "children's army" and passed and repassed in review across the broad square in front of the church, firing off real muskets into the air in joyful salutes to the Lord. Groups of boys, some of them orphaned choristers shipped out from Lisbon, ran through the streets singing the religious songs the Jesuits had taught them. In the nearby mission school Ricci and the other newly arrived Jesuits watched more than four hundred local children assemble, boys in one line, girls in another, listened to them chanting aloud, first in local dialect and then in Portuguese, the Lord's Prayer, the Ave Maria, and the Ten Commandments, and then saw them, at a signal from their priest, spit in unison upon the ground at the mention of their former gods.[28]

By contrast to this subjection of the Hindus, Muslim power was on the increase. Throughout the midsixteenth century, a group of Muslim Indian rulers had been steadily whittling away at the power of the last great Hindu kingdom of Vijayanagar in the Deccan, and the sultan of Bijapur, the state bordering on Goa, was a constant threat to the Portuguese community. Some records show how Muslim vessels forced Christian priests to land and hide on shore, while others describe Muslim customs officials demanding large dues from traveling priests and attacking them and their acolytes if they refused.[29] On occasion Portuguese who had themselves converted to Islam led attacks on Goa's environs, and during the siege of Goa by the sultan of Bijapur during 1570–71 so many people died that their corpses polluted permanently what had once been a healthy and beautiful spot: "From that time it has not been so healthy here," wrote Ricci's traveling companion, Pasio, "apparently because of the great number of Moors who were killed then and must have corrupted the air."[30]

The immense empire being forged in northern India by the Mogul ruler Akbar dwarfed all these other dangers. Ricci shared the common presumptions of his time about Akbar's might, writing that the ruler had "seventy kingdoms, and could put 300,000 cavalry in the field and 20,000 elephants," and his first surviving letter—to a friend in Coimbra in 1580—discusses his excitement at the prospect of Akbar's rejection of Islam and probable conversion to Christianity.[31] Ricci was led into this baseless optimism by Akbar's favorable reception of certain Portuguese priests and advisers, and his dispatch of the courtier Said Abdullah Khan on a diplomatic embassy to Goa in 1579. The ambassador brought a letter requesting that two Catholic missionaries be sent to the capital of Fatehpur Sikri with "the chief books of the Law and the Gospel," so that they could discuss their religion with Akbar; a promising development, "seeing how it was a common saying of the Moors that the Christians were like brute animals in what concerns the understanding," as one Jesuit put it.[32] To show his sincerity Akbar even sent two mules so the missionaries could travel in comfort. Ricci described the glittering scene as Goa's viceroy and leading civil, military, and religious figures welcomed the ambassador with music. He could not restrain his excitement at the visit the ambassador made to the Jesuit college, library, pharmacy, church, and refectory, at the ambassador's profound veneration for the painting of the Virgin Mary, at his attentive listening to the church choir, and at his participation in a debate on theology held in his honor by sixteen or more Jesuit fathers. "We hope for nothing less than the conversion of all India," wrote Ricci, describing the departure of three priests bearing the newly arrived eight-volume Plantin polyglot Bible as a gift for Akbar; though, with some prescience, Ricci added, "In saying that these are Muslims I am also saying what difficulties we can expect the devil to put in our way, as he has in the past."[33]

In the event, though Akbar scrutinized the polygot Bible with some care (kissing each volume reverently, according to Jesuit accounts), invited the Catholic priests to protracted debates on religion with senior Muslim clerics, promised to teach his son Portuguese, and watched a celebration of the Mass, he showed little further interest in Christianity.[34] Akbar often seemed too dazed at their meetings to take in the finer points of what they were saying, the missionaries at Fatehpur Sikri observed, since he was "full of opium and a certain drink made from opium peel, musk nuts and nutmeg, *bhang* and other things of that kind, which so stupefy a man as to make us think he sleeps the sleep of Endymion."[35] Summarizing these various reports, Ricci eventually concluded that Akbar had never been sincere in his desire for conversion, but had been motivated to invite the Jesuits to his capital either by "a certain natural curiosity to know some new things about other religions" or because he had certain political goals for whose attainment Portuguese help might prove useful.[36]

While the Jesuits proved wrong in their hope that "the said Mogul king is disillusioned and has realized well that Muhammad is wrong and that the law he gave is false and very false," some of them continued to draw solace from the fact that at least "this king is a very great enemy of the Jews."[37] Certainly in this aspect of his thought Akbar was in line with the policy of the Goanese Inquisition. Ricci was distressed by the activities of the Inquisition against the Jews known as the "New Christians," or *Conversos*—members of families of Jewish origin who in the years after the expulsion of the Jews from Portugal in 1497 had been forcibly converted to Christianity—and he had the courage to tell General Acquaviva so in the first letter that he wrote to him in 1581.[38]

Curiously enough, the jumpiness of the Inquisition about the dangers from Jews or former Jews probably had more validity during the years 1578–82, when Ricci happened to be in Goa, than at any other time before or since. For after the defeat of King Sebastian at Alcazarquivir in 1578, when nervousness in Portugal and her dominions reached a fever pitch because the monarch's death without issue left the whole future of the country in doubt, fear of the Jews resurfaced dramatically. As if in response to the Jews of Morocco, who had feared that a victorious King Sebastian would force them to convert to Christianity, and had exulted openly at his death, celebrating it annually thereafter as a second deliverance, almost as soon as the battle was over, rumors began to spread in Portugal that King Sebastian was not dead—no one had seen him die—and that he had escaped to Europe. Pretenders to his name appeared, and the cult of *Sebastianismo* was born, the belief that one day he would return and lead his people back to freedom. *Sebastianismo* blended imperceptibly with a different and equally dangerous underground current that flowed from the writings of one Gonçalo Anes, known as "The Prophet," a Portuguese shoe-maker who earlier in the century had written visionary tracts on the coming of a new messiah. His works spoke in bold but vague terms of a "Hidden One," an *Encoberto,* a prince who would form a Utopian universal monarchy under Portuguese rule. These writings enjoyed such wide popularity among the Jewish New Christians that the Inquisition had banned them in 1541, and Anes himself had been made to stand trial and recant.[39]

When the Spaniards, as of 1580, took over Portugal, Anes's writings served to fan the excitement of patriotic Portuguese who believed in *Sebastianismo,* whether Old or New Christians. In 1581 the Inquisition once again issued an order banning the reading of his works. Furthermore, King Philip's other great rival to the throne of Portugal—besides the shade of King Sebastian—was the popular Don Antonio, the son of a Portuguese prince of royal blood and a converted Jewess named Violante Gomes. Though Spanish troops forced Don Antonio to flee Portugal in 1581, he received moral support and some military backing from various enemies of Spain, and in 1582 he was still holding out in the Azores, despite the defeat of a small French fleet sent to help him. (The French supported Don Antonio because of his promise to yield Brazil to France if he should regain his kingdom.) Only in the summer of 1583 were the Azores taken by Spain and this potentially dangerous threat to Philip's maritime empire was removed.[40]

Ricci would have known a good deal about Jewish suffering in Europe, having seen some of it at first hand. When he was a child of eight there had been a spirited assault on the Jewish practice of usury in Macerata, and in 1564, when he was twelve, much local publicity was given to an attempt to prohibit a Jew who ran the Macerata slaughterhouse from selling meat during Lent, save under special dispensation.[41] Ancona had been, at least for a time, a haven for Jews expelled from Spain and Portugal, and Ricci may also have had some knowledge of their activities there, especially since persecutions of the Ancona Jews by the Inquisition led to a trade boycott of the city by the Jews in the Middle East, and worried Ancona Catholics tried to have the Inquisition proceedings transferred to Macerata.[42] But it was above all in Rome that Jews were conspicuous, either as representatives of a policy of conversion or else as its enemies. When Ricci was a novice in Rome, the Jews there were living under the stringent laws of 1555, which forced them to live in a constricted ghetto and to be locked at night (and during Passion Week) in their own crowded streets. Each Saturday, at two o'clock in the afternoon, they had to attend a service in the church of the Company of the Blessed Trinity—the men gathered on benches in front of the pulpit, the women out of sight in one of the upper balconies—where they were surrounded by crowds of curious Romans and visitors to the city. With those willing to undergo conversion (known as catechumens) in white robes and the newly baptized (called neophytes) in black sitting among the Christians, the Jews heard the Jesuit Father Passevino (or sometimes Lupus the Capuchine, or Father Francisco Maria) and a converted Jew (most commonly one named Andreas) preach to them of the Messiah, of the captivity, and of the true meaning of Solomon's glory, using the very texts they had heard, interpreted so differently, in their own synagogues that morning. After 1578 baptized Jews were admitted to the new Hebrew Seminary, endowed by Pope Gregory XIII with 100 crowns a month, to learn Latin and Hebrew in addition to their native Italian. Their numbers swelled even more a year later with the coming of the youths whom the newly converted former rabbi Baptista Romanus himself brought back to Rome from the Middle East.[43] Those Jews willing to be baptized, often "removed from their brethren which now cannot abide them," as Gregory Martin phrased it, were trained by special teachers in the house of the catechumens; when they were considered ready, they joined in one of the mass baptisms of the newly converted held twice a year, at Easter eve and Whitsun eve, at Constantine's font in St. John Lateran's under the direction, in Ricci's time, of Thomas Goldwell, bishop of St. Asaph, himself in exile from his native Wales.[44]

The Jews of Rome also played an important part in the economic life of the city. Because the church continued to forbid Christians to lend money at high interest, Jews dominated the business of usury as they had in the past. They were prominent, too, in the garment trade, and even after the ghetto laws had been passed, they were allowed to come once a week to the Piazza Navona, where their colorful displays of clothing, wall hangings, and draperies were one of the sights of the city. Jewish entrepreneurs were active in trying to bring new industrial ventures to Rome: they experimented with cloth production—the ruins of the Colosseum were briefly the base for this operation—and with the manufacture of silk. Roman interest in the silk trade soared briefly upon news that a Venetian Jew had developed a means of hatching silk worms twice a year. One inventor in the furniture business developed a collapsible bed and desk set (it failed to sell), while another anticipated the machine gun with an assemblage that mounted fifty arquebuses in a row.[45] Whether they flourished in business or not, the Jews had to submit to random economic exploitation by both lay and ecclesiastical forces. And especially those who had converted needed to be constantly on guard in case they were accused of backsliding, a charge that would bring the Inquisition to investigate them, with all its fearsome rigors. Gregory Martin described the Inquisition of the 1570s as operating "against Heretikes, Apostataes, Inchanters, Conjurers: where al meanes are used to save their soules, and al courteous release and dimmision geven to them that wil be reformed." To give force to these words there were the ashes of a dozen Jews who had been burned at the stake in Ancona alone.[46]

Throughout the sixteenth century the Portuguese were quite aware of the flights of Jews from the country, whether to Ancona (where the Papacy initially promised them a refuge) or to Goa and Cochin. In Goa, the Inquisition was formally inaugurated under its own grand inquisitor in 1560, but well before this (in 1543, to be exact) it had claimed its first victim, a New Christian physician named Jeronimo Dias, burned at the stake presumably for practicing Jewish ceremonies in secret.[47] By the 1560s the number of Jews established south of Goa, in the realm of Cochin, was so high that the Catholic clergy mockingly referred to the local Indian ruler, whom the New Christians sometimes served, as "The King of the Jews."[48] After priests had been expressly sent south to root out this *"perfidia judaica,"* some of these Jews were arrested and sent to Goa for trial.[49] Agents of the Inquisition were especially on watch for "white Jews"—Portuguese who had heard of Cochin as a Jewish haven and managed to reach Goa via Turkey and Hormuz; they seem to have been considered more dangerous than the "black Jews," those who had intermarried with the indigenous southern Indian population or natives who had been converted to Judaism at some earlier date.[50]

Life for the Jews grew even harder after Bartholemew de Fonseca, a favorite of King Sebastian, was appointed inquisitor at Goa in 1571. Not yet thirty at the time of his appointment, Fonseca took fanatical delight in his assignment. He saw India as being "undermined" (*sola-pada*) by New Christians—or "God-killers" (*mata-Deus*), as he preferred to call them—and boasted often of the number of trials he had held, of jails he had filled, of those "whose fathers and grandfathers I have burned, and whose bones I have disinterred."[51] Two months after Ricci landed at Goa in September 1578 one finds Fonseca writing triumphantly that he had "filled the land with fire and the ashes from the dead bodies of heretics and apostates."[52] From one of his early letters we know that Ricci felt uneasy at the prevalence of these deadly autos-da-fé in India. This uneasiness must have been exacerbated by the two great autos-da-fé of 1575 and 1578 in Goa—in the first, nineteen people were burned, two for Lutheranism and seventeen for Judaism; in the second, seventeen more were killed, this time all for "Jewish heresy."[53]

The Jesuit position on all this was delicate. Autos-da-fé were not only exercises in terror but also elaborate social gatherings, occasions for splendid rituals both in the churches, where investigations were carried out, and in the streets, through which long, decorated processions of victims and judges passed (many who recanted or confessed and were forgiven joined the march, along with the smaller number of people who faced death). Autos-da-fé were also—through the confiscation of the property of those found guilty—major sources of money for the church and the inquisitorial staff.[54] The Jesuits generally served as the confessors for those found guilty and facing death at the stake, and they played an official role as assessors at the trials and as cosigners of the sentences of the guilty.[55] On the other hand, the Jesuit order itself, thanks in part to the intensive hunt for the most intelligent possible new recruits carried out by General Mercurian in the 1570s, had numerous New Christians of Jewish origin in its own ranks, several of whom (including one priest who sailed out with Ricci on the *St. Louis*) had ended up in India in responsible positions.[56]

The Jesuits in India directed a good deal of their energies not to Muslims or Jews but to the slightly more receptive communities of indigenous Christians that were numerous to the south of Goa. Here again, as we can see from his letters, the young Matteo Ricci was an absorbed observer. These "St. Thomas Christians," as they were commonly known, presented the Catholic fathers with both problems and opportunities. According to traditional church accounts, the apostle Thomas had followed the trade routes across Asia Minor and down the west coast of India, making numerous converts in Cochin before traveling on to present-day Madras, where he was martyred.[57] Europeans had long had a generalized knowledge of these Malabar Christians, as they were also called, and after some initial confusion (in which the

111

first Portuguese navigators to reach South India had worshiped before images of the Hindu goddess Kali, believing them to be images of the Virgin Mary), they established contacts with the true South Indian Christians. These Christians gratified their "discoverers" by requesting Portuguese protection against the local Muslim rajas; swift to make the most profit from such an opportunity, the Portuguese promised protection in return for a virtual trade monopoly over the entire output of the highly prized Cochin pepper crop.[58]

More careful examination of the Malabar Christians' doctrines showed that they believed Mary to be the mother of Christ rather than the mother of God—a distinction that branded them as Nestorians, a splinter group within the early church that had been declared heretical—and that they still clearly drew their spiritual inspiration and their pastoral leadership from the Syrian church.

Sixteenth-century Catholics divided over how to proceed with these new charges, and their divisions led to extraordinary muddles. Thus one of the bishops of the Cochin church was condemned for being a heretic by the churchmen assembled in the Council of Goa, while at the same time he convinced the rulers of Portugal and the pope of his doctrinal orthodoxy, and apparently was even considered for a cardinal's hat.[59] By the time Ricci arrived in India the popes had decided to assign jurisdiction over the Cochin Christians to two rival bishops, both of whom had connections with the Nestorian Syrian patriarchs and yet claimed total orthodoxy within the Roman church. The Portuguese were suspicious of both, for they wanted candidates loyal to their interests. One of these bishops, Simon, had more support from Franciscans, and the other, Abraham, more from the Jesuits. The Jesuit-supported Abraham gained the upper hand, and further strengthened his position by establishing a major seminary at Vaipikkotta with Jesuit help; here some fifty students studied Latin and Chaldean liturgy and theology while celebrating their services in Syriac. But the situation remained so fluid that when in November 1579 Ricci was sent to Cochin to recuperate from a dangerous illness—it was some kind of fever that proved almost fatal to him, and led to the deaths of several of his fellow Jesuits in Goa that same month—he still found it hard to sort out the relative claims of the two bishops.[60]

What was clear to Ricci, despite the jurisdictional tangles, was that certain liturgical irregularities had been corrected. Early observers of the Malabar priests had noted:

> They wear their tonsures reversed, hair in the place of the tonsure, and the head around it shaven. They wear white shirts, and turbans on their heads, they go barefoot and wear long beards. They are extremely devout and say Mass at the altar as we do here, with a cross facing them. He who says it walks between two men, who help him, one on each side. They communicate with salted bread instead of the host, and consecrate thereof sufficient for all who are present in the church; they distribute the whole of this as if it were blessed bread, and every man comes to the foot of the altar to receive it from the priest's hand.[61]

Ricci was able to see, however, that a gratifying change had taken place and that now there were "no differences between our two churches save that of language." Even that could be swiftly remedied if Rome would send a printing press to Cochin so that the exact wording of the Roman breviary and missal could be transposed in a new bilingual text.[62]

We know from other writings that Ricci was upset that the more talented Indian students were denied training in advanced theology by jealous or nervous Western priests within the Goa community, and that the local Indians, "however much they know, are rarely given much credit in comparison with other white men."[63] From this we can guess that he was sympathetic to Jesuits who had tried to prevent the application of the Inquisition's rigors to native Christians, at least until they had had a grace period of twenty years in which to try and adjust their differences with Rome. But this tolerant stance had not prevailed, for in the decade or so before Ricci's arrival some three hundred and twenty local Indian Christians had been submitted to "examination" by the Goa Inquisition.[64] Ricci obviously felt that the Indian Christians' changes in ritual and dress were thorough and satisfactory. He wrote on January 18, 1580, to his Coimbra theology teacher, Emanuele de Goes, a man who could be expected to have a keen interest in such details:

> They dress now after the fashion of the Portuguese clergy (and have shaved off their beards), say Mass wearing vestments made in the same way as ours, and present the wafer at Mass, not loaves as they were wont to do; they give communion to the people "under the appearance of one substance" [*sub una tantum specie*], are using the whole range of sacraments more often, and have now added those of confirmation and of extreme unction which previously they never practiced. They build their churches in our style.[65]

Less than four years after writing these lines Ricci was himself sitting, with shaved head and beard, shrouded in the robes of a Buddhist monk, in the southern Chinese town of Zhaoqing. Believing that this was how religious men in China should dress in order to be esteemed as holy, he had forfeited the luxury of being an outside observer and had himself entered the ambiguous world of cultural adaptation. His decision was calculated: with the Chinese intrigued enough by his foreign prisms and clocks and books to come in droves to his little house, he could then engage them in conversation on religious matters. The painting of the Virgin and Child displayed on an altar in his little chapel would given further visual stimulus to his words.[66]

Ricci could persuade himself that he had made the right leap. He wrote to his school friend Fuligatti in November 1585 about the little group of Westerners gathered in Zhaoqing: "Would that you could see me as I am now: I have become a Chinaman. In our clothing, in our looks, in our manners and in everything external we have made ourselves Chinese."[67] He had—like many Europeans before him—seen an apparent parallelism between many of the outer manifestations of Buddhism and Christianity: the priestly robes, the chanting of plainsong (*canto fermo*) in their services, the espousal of celibacy and poverty, the temples, statues, towers, bells and even some of the carved or painted images. Thus he could joke that merely by being partly Italian (cropping his hair very short) and partly Portuguese (shaving off his beard) and by following the basic Christian rituals, one would be viewed by the Chinese as a Buddhist monk.[68]

It took Ricci several years to learn that he had developed the wrong external image. Similarity did not bring prestige, and as Ricci began to understand the low social status of most Buddhist clergy he drifted away from his preliminary position. In 1592 he was writing apologetically to General Acquaviva, "To gain greater status we do not walk along the streets on foot, but have ourselves carried in sedan chairs, on men's shoulders, as men of rank are accustomed to do. For we have great need of this type of prestige in this region, and without it would make no progress among these gentiles: for the name of foreigners and priests is considered so vile in China that we need this and other similar devices to show them that we are not priests as vile as their own."[69] Supported in his conviction that he had to abandon Chinese priestly dress and appearance both by influential Chinese scholars and by his own superior, Valignano, Ricci made the final break in the summer of 1595. He wrote to his friend Edoardo de Sande in Macao:

> We have let our beards grow and our hair down to our ears; at the same time we have adopted the special dress that the literati wear on their social visits (as opposed to that of the bonzes that we used to have). I sallied out for the first time in my beard, and in this dress that mandarins use for paying their visits, which is of purple silk, and the hem of the robe and the collar and the edges are bordered with a band of blue silk a little less than a palm wide; the same decoration is on the edges of the sleeves which hang open, rather in the style common in Venice. There is a wide sash of the purple silk trimmed in blue which is fastened round the same robe and lets the robe hang comfortably open.[70]

In this garment, with his silk shoes decorated with embroidery, Ricci must have cut a finer figure than at any time since he walked as a schoolboy in Rome: Italian students in the Roman college (who were under special papal protection and stipend) wore full-length robes of blue or violet; the other students, who paid their own way, came from foreign countries, or received some lesser stipends, had to be content with simple black gowns, like the majority of students elsewhere in less prestigious schools.[71]

This major shift in Ricci's perceptions of relative social status in China was rather slow in coming. In his first assessment, made after he had been in China just about one year, he concluded that there were three religions of major significance in China, those of the Confucian literati, the Buddhists, and the Taoists. That of the literati was the most important, he felt, although they believed neither in paradise nor in the immortality of the soul and thought that what the others said about demons and the afterlife was "a joke" (*una burla*).[72] A year later, in October 1585, as he wrote General Acquaviva, he had realized that the question was more complex: in essence, the Chinese literati could be considered as holding a cluster of beliefs similar to those of the Epicureans in the ancient Greek world; by contrast, the lower classes in general could be likened to "Pythagoreans," since their belief in the immortality of the soul was coupled with a broader belief in the transmigration of souls into both the human world and the animal kingdom.[73]

This analysis in turn slowly yielded to another, in which Ricci saw that within each of the general bodies of doctrine that one could call Buddhism and Taoism there were near parodies of the Christian trinity, in which three separate deities were fused into one. The belief that a type of false trinity was embedded in the religion of Islam had long been a tradition among the Christians of medieval Europe; the discovery of similar false trinities in China prompted Ricci to observe that here was a perfect example of the devil's work, "showing clearly how the father of all lies, who is the author of all this, has not yet lost his incredible pretensions of seeking to be similar to his own Creator."[74] Ricci also acquired a more subtle appreciation of the ethical values toward state and family that lay at the heart of Confucianism, and of the meaning of their ceremonies to ancestors and to Confucius, the Confucian school serving in a sense as "the true temple of the literati"; but he now saw that just because Confucianism maintained a strictly neutral stance toward the existence or nonexistence of an afterlife, so it was that many Confucians "belonged to one of the other two sects along with their own."[75] Thus did Ricci arrive at a quite accurate assessment of the new synthesis of China's three major religious schools, a synthesis that led in turn to the growth of late Ming syncretism: "The commonest opinion held here among those who consider themselves the most wise is to say that all three of these sects come together as one, and that you can hold them all at once; in this they deceive themselves and others and lead to great disorder by its appearing to them that as far as religion is concerned the more ways of talking about religion there are, all the more benefit will that bring to the kingdom."[76]

As Ricci got a sharper picture of these three basic schools of religious and ethical thought in China, so did he also discover a distorted yet mirrored image of the three groupings he had known in Europe: Islam, Catholicism, and Judaism. Before he even reached China he had probably read something about the prevalence of Islam there, since both Galeota Pereira and Gaspar da Cruz had mentioned this fact in their published reports, and had speculated—rather wildly—on the ways that the Muslims had arrived in the Far East and how they propagated their religion.[77] After one year in China he had learned little more, and though noting the presence of "Moors" added that he "had no idea" how they had got there.[78] Then, as he found out more about the patterns of trade that led Muslim merchants by overland routes from Persia through central Asia to western China in search of such items as jade, musk, and rhubarb, Ricci began to get a sharper picture of the strength of these hundreds of thousands of "Saracens," "Moors," or "followers of the Turkish sect," as he called them on different occasions.[79] The first time he visited Peking, in 1598, he was intrigued to hear that two Muslims from Arabia who had brought a gift of lions to the Ming court had stayed on in the capital, loaded with honors, and he sent one of the Chinese Christians to meet with them and learn more about their background.[80]

Because of the nature of the trade routes, most Muslims in China were settled in the northwest, in the areas of Shaanxi and Gansu province that had once constituted the domain of the old Xixia kingdom destroyed by the Mongols in 1227. Ricci could not have known the details of the collapse of the Timurid Empire, of the waves of emigration among Muslims that followed in central Asia, and of the fact that as the Iranian state converted to Shiite beliefs most of those coming to China were Sunnis, who thus had severed many of their old political and economic ties with western Islamic lands. But he had not been long in China before he became aware of how much the religion of Islam had spread. He recorded that the scholar-official Zhu Shilu (who had originally been the source of Ricci's introduction to the inkcake maker and publisher Cheng Dayue) tried to persuade him to settle in Nanjing in 1599 on the grounds that it was an area tolerant of outsiders, "there being such an enormous number of Saracens who followed the religion of Muhammad living there already."[81] Ricci also recorded that numerous Muslims were in the port city of Canton, where he believed they deliberately spread rumors concerning the wickedness of the Portuguese so that they might disrupt the growing Western trade there.[82] Yet Ricci also professed to see that despite their numbers the Chinese Muslims were comparatively weak in their own faith:

> Since in the far western regions China borders on Persia, at various times many followers of the Muhammadan religion entered this country, and their children and descendants multiplied so much that they have spread over all China with thousands of families. They are residing in nearly all provinces, where they have sumptuous mosques, recite their prayers, are circumcised, and conduct their ceremonies. But as far as we have learned, they don't act as missionaries, nor try to spread their religion, and live subject to Chinese laws and in great ignorance of their own sect, and are held in low opinion by the Chinese.
>
> For these reasons, they are treated as native Chinese, and not being suspected of plotting rebellion they are allowed to study and enter the ranks of bureaucracy. Many of them, having received offical rank, abandon their old beliefs, retaining only their prohibitions against eating pork, to which they have never become accustomed.[83]

Ming Chinese Muslims did make some important modifications to their past practices, by building mosques in pagoda shape, for example, abandoning the minarets and having the muezzin call the faithful to prayer from a post just inside the door of his mosque.[84] But the tenacious survival of Islam in China in this period, shown by such evidence as the spread into central Asia of Chinese texts in Arabic transcriptions, the slow but impressive growth of a Chinese-language Muslim literature, and the development of regional power bases in the west that were eventually to threaten the stability of the Chinese state itself—all point to a level of wishful thinking in Ricci's analysis.[85]

The same was by no means true for the other two religions in this group, Nestorian Christianity and Judaism. Ricci had been surprised to find pockets of Christians in Nanjing and elsewhere in central China, but they amounted to only "five or six families" and seemed to have lost almost all their earlier beliefs, making their churches into temples and in many cases even converting to Islam. The only traces of Christianity among most of them were that they seemed to have some knowledge of the psalter and they ate pork, over which they made the sign of the cross.[86] Local Chinese scholars also knew—by firsthand observation or from popular tales—that the Nestorian Christians grew their hair long, and they used this information to persuade Ricci to abandon the shaved head of a Buddhist priest.[87] From linguistic evidence Ricci speculated that the first Nestorians in China originally came from Armenia; that they were migrants from some branch of the Eastern church was further suggested to him by an old bell he saw in Peking on which were incised a church, a cross, and some letters in Greek. Different informants told Ricci of persecutions earlier in the century—or of lies deliberately fabricated by Chinese Muslims about forthcoming persecutions—that had scared the Christians out of their own faith.[88] When during 1608 Ricci finally sent a Chinese Jesuit lay brother and a recently converted Kaifeng resident to Kaifeng in Henan to try to unravel the mystery, they were able to locate several Christians but found them totally unresponsive: "They would not admit to the brother that they were descended [from the Christians], either out of fear that he was questioning them with the intention of harming them, or because these sons [of the church] wished to be taken for Chinese and were ashamed of the fact that they came from foreign origins—which brings little honor in any nation and is particularly humiliating among the Chinese."[89]

Even more tantalizing was the news given to Ricci in 1602 by a certain "Moor" that in those same far northwest regions of the former Xixia kingdom, where Muslims were now so numerous, there were also "certain white men with flowing beards who had churches with bell towers, ate pork, worshiped Mary and Isa (as they called Christ our Lord) and adored the Cross."[90] Ricci naturally wanted to ascertain the accuracy of this tale, since it suggested that these Christians had held stoutly to their faith and pointed to a major link with the earlier church; but the distances were huge and, as he wrote sadly to General Acquaviva in July 1605, "for lack of the few *scudi* we need for the journey we have not been able to send anyone to find how many there are and whence they came." It was to be left to Ricci's successor Jesuits to make the discovery that these Christians were also Nestorians, as those in India had been.[91]

Much of Ricci's early information on these Christians came from Chinese Jews, and Ricci himself pointed to the irony that these same Chinese Jews were much more forthcoming about their faith than the Christians were.[92] Discovery of Jews in China startled Ricci more than the evidence about the Muslims (who were after all strong in Southeast Asia and in India, as he knew well) or the Christians, about whose existence in the East rumors had long abounded. Both in his letters and his *Historia* Ricci lingered on the fascinating moment when a sixty-year-old man named Ai Tian came to see him in his Peking residence on a summer day in 1605. After some initial confusion—Ai mistook a painting of the Virgin, Christ Child and John the Baptist for one of Rebecca with Jacob and Esau and concluded that Ricci was therefore Jewish—he told Ricci of the seven or eight Jewish families in Kaifeng, of their synagogue, which had cost ten thousand *scudi*, of his two brothers who knew Hebrew, and of the even larger Jewish community in Hangzhou. Ricci showed Ai the Hebrew parts of his Plantin polyglot Bible, which Ai recognized but could not read.[93] In an attempt to unravel the history of the Jews in China—conflicting accounts placed their arrival anywhere from the first to the seventh century A.D.—Ricci sent a Jesuit to the Kaifeng synagogue. He was courteously received and was able to observe that the synagogue's Hebrew Pentateuch was indeed similar to the same books in the Old Testament and that the antiquity of this community was attested by the fact that their Hebrew texts were "without points as in the old fashion." Though few in the Jewish community could now read Hebrew, most continued to practice circumcision and refrained from eating pork; those who lived in Peking neglected the dietary rules on the grounds that they would have died of hunger if they had adhered to the letter of the law.[94] Ricci found several Jews disgruntled with their own religion and their ignorant rabbi, and he was fairly confident that there was a good chance of converting them to Christianity; only lack of time, he wrote, prevented him from putting this theory to the test. He also claimed in the *Historia* that because of his fame as a scholar and religious man a group from Kaifeng invited him to refrain from pork and come live with them as their rabbi.[95]

Ai once told Ricci that since the Jews did not eat pork the Chinese simply referred to them as *huihui,* linking them to the Muslims although the followers of the two religions held each other in abhorrence. Ai added that, having read about Ricci in a Chinese book circulating in Kaifeng which spoke of Ricci's monotheism, and knowing that Ricci was not a Muslim, he had immediately assumed he must be a Jew.[96] In a similar vein Chinese friends urged Ricci to take up official bureaucratic office just as the Muslims had done, and Ricci was intrigued enough to ask Valignano his opinion, since the presence of mosques and the open circulation of the Koran gave Islam an advantage that Christianity lacked.[97] Ricci himself realized (as Ramon Lull and Boccaccio had centuries before) that the common bonds of monotheism and acceptance of the same early prophets gave a certain affinity to Christianity, Islam, and Judaism. When he published his first detailed book on Christian doctrine in Chinese, which spoke of Christ as prophet and teacher but did not present details on the Crucifixion, he discovered that "many copies were bought by Saracens who think it like their doctrine."[98] He told Acquaviva in August 1608 that his books were being bought "by followers of the Moorish religion" because "they thought it spoke of God in better fashion than any of the other books in China." So did Confucian literati in the Nanchang area charge that the Jesuits "distribute certain pictures of a Tartar or a Saracen which they say is that of their God, come to this earth, who can give men riches and prosperity."[99]

Although Ricci threw off the robes of a Buddhist monk, he failed to gain the new identity as a Confucian which he sought. When in 1602 he was at last allowed to prostrate himself before the empty dragon throne in a dawn audience—empty because Emperor Wanli no longer received ceremonial visitors—he was trained in the court etiquette by three Chinese Muslims who also accompanied him to the ceremonies, since the Chinese courtiers simply assumed that Ricci and the Muslims were "fellow countrymen." In the Board of Rites hostel he lodged with "Saracani" who could talk with ease to him about the worlds of Venice and Spain, Portugal, Hormuz, and India.[100] The emperor, pleased by Ricci's presents to the court, and intrigued enough by what he had heard about the Jesuits to want to see them, though not to meet face to face, commissioned court painters to make a full-length portrait of the Jesuits in Peking. According to Ricci's eunuch informants who witnessed the scene, the emperor looked at the finished portrait for a moment and said, "They are *huihui*."[101] This was not just a question of beards and robes but of China's serene indifference to foreigners. The huge and cosmic battle that lay at the heart of European history as Ricci knew it was reduced in China to a semideprecating phrase.

This is not to say that Ricci ever lost the sense of his fundamental missionary vocation, and when his spirits were at a low ebb there were always others to cheer him on. During his most dejected period in India, for instance, he had received from the Jesuit historian Gian Pietro Maffei a copy of the preface to Maffei's massive history of the Portuguese expansion in Asia. Initially Ricci had not been particularly responsive to Maffei's questions about Indian geography and politics, and had rather tartly observed that Maffei might do better to get his information from "an honorable Moor or an extremely intelligent Brahman."[102] But when he read Maffei's new introduction his mood completely changed. What Maffei did, in those few pages, was to present the explorations of the world conducted by the Spaniards and the Portuguese over the previous century as equivalent, in force and importance, to the role of Abraham and his descendants in preserving God's word, or to that of Rome in the development of the Papacy. Global exploration, international trade, and evangelization had now flowed together in one mighty enterprise. Knowledge of this process, wrote Maffei, had value: It could bring joy at the sight of Christianity spreading, sorrow at the strength of the evils it encountered, or bittersweet fear at the thought that God might bring the world to an end because his purpose was accomplished. He himself, wrote Maffei, had no fears save that of raising doubts and disbelief because of the amazing nature of the story he had to tell.[103]

Maffei made a bold claim for the interlocking of specific human destinies with God's long-range plans for mankind, and (after polite disclaimers) stated with equal boldness his determination to explore God's purpose:

Wise men are right to say that we should do better to adore the Eternal Being, who at all times rules all things, in quiet simplicity and respectful silence, rather than try rashly or vainly to penetrate his secrets and his designs. For while there is nothing more wondrous in itself than the celestial order, so constant and so regulated in all its aspects, there is at the same time nothing harder for human weakness to fathom. Nevertheless, to the extent that the mind of man is capable of reason, and the burden of his mortality lets him raise himself up and judge events as they are, it seems that divine providence lays the foundations of all that it plans to do far in advance, and that it leads toward the perfection of its goals by secret ways and unnoticed movement.[104]

Ricci was clearly astonished by the methodology and language used by Maffei in his short introductory essay: "I was completely overjoyed by the introduction to your history," he wrote back to Maffei, "and others who read it will rejoice as well. Though I cannot be a good judge of all your material—partly out of ignorance of it, no less than because of the love I bear you, which makes me unable to be unhappy at anything you do—I must not fail to say that if 'one can know a lion by his claws' so have I come to have a great concept of history just from reading this introduction, as others will after me."[105]

The general of the Jesuit order, Claudio Acquaviva, skillfully fostered this sense of excitement—compounded of service to God and a sense of participation in history—through the letters that he sent to his missionaries in the field. The Far East missions, he told them, offered "precious opportunities" in the current "troubled state of the church," and were a triumphant vindication of the Lord's great prophecy recorded in Isaiah 41:18:

> I will open rivers on the bare heights,
> And fountains in the midst of the valleys:
> I will make the wilderness a pool of water,
> And the dry land springs of water.[106]

The news of thousands of Christian conversions in Japan had been inspiring enough, he wrote to Ricci and his co-workers in May 1586, but "now, however, it is from China that the good tidings are brought to us; for here God's blessing has also crowned our efforts and we hail the bright dawn of faith upon this vast empire." In response to the possibilities of the China mission, he added, Pope Sixtus V had authorized a special jubilee.[107] At times he too weakened, wrote Acquaviva in 1590, grew worried that so many able men had to be withdrawn from equally crucial problem areas of Europe, felt overwhelmed at having to "organize these distant ventures, to choose leaders for them, to direct their labors"; but at such moments it sufficed to recall the words of St. Ambrose that "the body of Jesus Christ is the church, and we are the sweet

odor that issues from his body" or else the words of St. Paul in
1 Corinthians (1:23) that the "Jews demand signs and Greeks seek
wisdom, but we preach Christ crucified, a stumbling block to Jews and
folly to Gentiles."[108]

No one, for Ricci, exemplified this spirit of adventurousness and
faith in a hostile world better than the Jesuit brother Benedetto de
Goís, and though the two never met, Ricci questioned Goís's companions avidly for information about his remarkable journey and was later
to write about him in more detail than he did about anyone else, Chinese or Western. In a four-year journey spanning the period 1602–1605,
Goís walked and rode from Akbar's city of Agra via Afghanistan and
Turkestan to the northwestern frontier of China, just inside the Great
Wall. A former soldier, born in the Azores, a fluent speaker of Persian,
he traveled disguised as an Armenian merchant, accompanied by an Armenian Christian convert named Isaac, in the train of four hundred or
more Muslim merchants and pilgrims grouped together for protection.
His journey was partly designed to open up a shorter route between Europe and China than that by the current long and dangerous seaways,
where Protestant raiders now harried Catholic shipping. But more im-
portantly the goal was to discover, once and for all, whether there was a
"Cathay" distinct from China, an isolated community of Christians
somewhere in the reaches of central Asia where the Great Khans of
Kambaluc had once ruled; for traveling merchants continued to bring
back stories of people there who worshiped the cross and the Virgin
Mary in churches, touched their heads with holy water, partook of
bread and wine in their services, and were led in prayer by celibate
priests robed in black.[109]

In Kabul, wrote Ricci, Goís befriended a noblewoman from Kashgar, a devout Muslim who was returning from the pilgrimage to
Mecca. Since she had run out of money for the expenses of the last
stage of her journey, Goís sold six hundred *scudi*'s worth of fine indigo
dye that he was carrying with him to trade in China and lent the
money to her. She amply repaid his trust by giving him, when at last
they reached Kashgar, a quantity of finest jade worth four times that

amount.[110] Yet by one of those twists of fate that had marked his whole journey, his very prosperity now aroused the greed and hostility of the other merchants. While Goís lingered almost a year and a half in Xuzhou on the Gansu border, ignorant of the Chinese language and trying either to reach the fathers in Peking by letter or else to get permission from the authorities to travel there with a merchant caravan, he was systematically defrauded of all he possessed and abandoned by all save his companion Isaac. Eleven days after one of the Peking Jesuits at last reached him, in March 1607, with money to escort him back to the capital, Goís died.[111]

Now the faithful Isaac was on his way back to India, Ricci wrote to his close friend Girolamo Costa in March 1608, and so "the whole exhausting journey had not been made in vain." Some questions of faith and geography had been cleared up for all time:

> It will now be clear to the viceroy of India, and to all the Jesuits, that there is no other Cathay, nor ever was one, but just this China. And this city of Peking is Kambaluc, and the King of China is the Great Khan. As for those Christians who people have said were in Cathay, they are no other than those who arrived here in the past, and who retained for themselves the term "adorers of the cross" without themselves knowing what that cross really represents. These people are, in everything, gentiles: but since their temples look like those of Christians and have candles and altars, and since their priests wear capes and pray in plainsong, therefore the Moors thought that they must be truly Christians, and brought the news to the Jesuits that there was a large Christian community there.[112]

So at least Ricci wrote back to his friends in Europe, though we don't know how much he talked about these dramatic events, or their ambiguities, with his Chinese acquaintances. The news of Goís's death, of course, came not long before Ricci's own, and it must have dramatized certain baffling and conflicting ideas about comparative religious beliefs that Ricci was not free to articulate directly. As if to underline the ambiguities, Ricci had titled the book in which he talked most

126

clearly of the tragedies of life *Ten Discourses by a Paradoxical Man* (*Jiren Shipian*). In Italian, Ricci referred to this book as *The Paradoxes,* but the Chinese title would have said far more to his Chinese readers than that. For the phrase "paradoxical man," the *Jiren* of the title, was taken by Ricci from the ancient Taoist classic known as the *Zhuangzi,* written in the third century B.C. It appears in the sixth chapter, where the Taoist philosopher explains to his readers how the ceremonies of the world differ, and how the True Man of old behaved.

> The True Man of ancient times knew nothing of loving life, knew nothing of hating death. He emerged without delight; he went back in without a fuss. He came briskly, he went briskly, and that was all. He didn't forget where he began; he didn't try to find out where he would end. He received something and took pleasure in it; he forgot about it and handed it back again. This is what I call not using the mind to repel the Way, not using man to help out Heaven. This is what I call the True Man.[113]

These true men had no need of conventional human ceremonial customs, wrote the Taoist, and the laws of this earth had little relevance to them, for "they have joined with the Creator as men to wander in the single breath of heaven and earth." In the passage which follows, the first phrase of which Ricci chose as the title of his own book, a disciple asks Confucius who or what the "paradoxical man" is, and how we can define him. Confucius replies: "The paradoxical man appears paradoxical in comparison to other men, but he is a companion to Heaven."[114] It was as a paradoxical man in this sense that Ricci the Christian could accept his label as Ricci the *huihui,* and place the Xixia tribeswoman with the same label in his memory palace. For he knew that his God would see through the apparent ambiguities of his situation and claim him, when he came to die, as a companion in his heavenly kingdom, just as he had claimed those true men of old.

FIVE

THE SECOND PICTURE: THE ROAD TO EMMAUS

For the second of the pictures for Cheng Dayue's "Ink Garden" Ricci chooses one that illustrates the story of how Christ, after the Resurrection, encounters two disciples on the road to Emmaus. Ricci carries the text from the Gospel according to Luke, chapter 24, in his head:

That very day two of them were going to a village named Emmaus, about seven miles from Jerusalem, and talking with each other about all these things that had happened. While they were talking and discussing together, Jesus himself drew near and went with them. But their eyes were kept from recognizing him. And he said to them, "What is this conversation which you are holding with each other as you walk?" And they stood still, looking sad.

Then one of them, named Cleopas, answered him, "Are you the only visitor to Jerusalem who does not know the things that have happened there in these days?" And he said to them, "What things?" And they said to him, "Concerning Jesus of Nazareth, who was a prophet mighty in deed and word before God and all the people, and how our chief priests and rulers delivered him up to be condemned to

Murmulj ot uos inieu for.   Edun. aus ob hoesjwuieleci excnait.

death, and crucified him. But we had hoped that he was the one to redeem Israel. . . ."

And he said to them, "O foolish men, and slow of heart to believe all that the prophets have spoken! Was it not necessary that the Christ should suffer these things and enter into his glory?" And beginning with Moses and all the prophets, he interpreted to them in all the scriptures the things concerning himself.

So they drew near to the village to which they were going. He appeared to be going further, but they constrained him, saying, "Stay with us, for it is toward evening and the day is now far spent." So he went in to stay with them. When he was at table with them, he took the bread and blessed and broke it, and gave it to them. And their eyes were opened and they recognized him; and he vanished out of their sight. They said to each other, "Did not our hearts burn within us while he talked to us on the road, while he opened to us the scriptures?"

It is a passage full of ambiguity and hidden meanings, and the fathers of the church discussed every detail of it over the centuries with rapt attention: Why "seven" miles? Because the disciples were still trapped in the cycle of Christ's Passion and were on *their* way to the seventh day, which would bring understanding of his Resurrection, but had not yet reached it. Was "village" the right word for Emmaus, or was it not rather a fort or a castle? Why did only *one* disciple give his name? Perhaps because the other was the evangelist Luke himself, who hid his presence out of innate modesty. Had Christ changed his form, so they did not recognize him, or was it merely that their eyes could not yet clearly see his true nature? Why did the disciples say they "had hoped" Christ was their savior? Had they lost their faith so totally and so soon? Why did Christ "appear to be going further" when they reached the village? Had he misled the disciples deliberately? If so, how could such an act of deception be compatible with his divine nature? And into how many pieces did he break the bread as they sat down to eat, and what was the significance of each?[1]

Ricci cannot cram all these thoughts, details, and exegesis into the space allotted to him by Cheng Dayue. As with the story of Peter in the waves, he creates his own version of scripture, to which he gives this title: "Two disciples, after hearing the truth, reject all vanity." He does not attempt to give a Chinese rendering of the word "Emmaus." The point of this story is in the journey, not the destination:

At the time the Lord of Heaven, to save the world, endured his pain here on earth, two of his disciples were fleeing along the road together. As they talked over what had happened, they were sad. The Lord of Heaven changed his form and, without warning, joined them. He asked the reason for their sorrow. Then he explained the words of the Holy Scriptures, which had foretold how the Lord of Heaven must endure pain and suffering so as to save the world, after which he would return to his heavenly kingdom.

This shows that we should not cleave to the joys of this world, or shun its sufferings. When the Lord of Heaven came down to earth, had he wanted happiness he could have had happiness, had he wanted suffering he could have had suffering—and it was no mistake that suffering was what he chose. In the sufferings of this world there is stored great joy, in the joys of this world there is stored up great suffering. Can one deny that this is the highest wisdom? Awakened to understanding, those two disciples gave themselves over to a life of bitter pain as ordinary people quest for jewels and cash. Their bitter pains were over long ago, and the reward for their love of suffering is an eternity in the land of heaven.[2]

So Ricci makes the journey to Emmaus a story about reason and explanation on the one hand, and about stoic acceptance of suffering on the other. The prolonged acceptance of that suffering will lead, at last, to bliss.

Had he had his copy of Nadal's *Images* with him, Ricci would probably have chosen illustration number 141 to give to Cheng Dayue: it shows Christ seated at table in Emmaus with the two disciples, handing the bread to the disciple on his left with his right hand, while servants bustle in with extra plates of food and the host and hostess look on reverently. But since he does not have Nadal, he chooses another of the Wierix engravings from the cycle on the Passion, the cycle from which he had drawn the wrong picture of Peter. These two engravings are fine foils for each other. The picture of the disciples in the boat shows poor people hard at work on the water, straining at their nets; the Emmaus picture shows gentlemen of leisure—booted as if for a long march, it is true, and carrying stout staves, but clearly elegantly attired—deep in conversation before a grand palace or castle.

The Chinese artist who works for Cheng Dayue cannot quite catch the subtlety of shading and gesture by which Wierix shows Christ pointing in one direction while his disciples urge him in another, nor can he clearly replicate the background vignette in which, transposed in time within the same painting, Wierix lets us see, in a room in the mansion to which Christ at last agrees to go, Christ breaking the bread for the two disciples who sit beside him.[3]

But that does not matter. The dinner is gone from the story altogether, and any Chinese who comes across Cheng's book will be able to see the intensity of the conversation in which the three figures are engaged, and catch the way in which three men, though dressed for movement, seem frozen for an instant in their stillness. If the Chinese viewer can also read the accompanying text, he will realize that the two figures flanking the Lord of Heaven are fleeing no more from whatever it is that has happened but are learning to accept it. And he will understand that Christ in the center, one hand half raised in gentle admonition, his hardships now over, is preparing to return once again to his heavenly kingdom.

Ricci was a child of seven in Macerata, just beginning the study of Latin, when in 1559 the Jesuits in Rome published their first major book, an expurgated edition of the *Epigrams* of Martial. The establishment of a printing press owned and operated by the Jesuit order had been a project dear to the heart of Ignatius of Loyola in the years before his death in 1556, and he had personally taken an active part in trying to find an appropriate font of type—first pursuing the possibility of receiving one as a gift from Duke Cosimo de' Medici of Florence and then, when the duke refused to be drawn, trying to purchase one through intermediaries in Venice for what seemed the very fair price of forty ducats. Ignatius found the Venetian type face too small as well as antique in style, and he rejected the Venetian deal; he had died by the time a satisfactory font was found for sale in Rome itself, 30,000 letters for only twenty ducats, in both large and small sizes, roman and italic.[4]

This quest for the ideal type face, along with the publication of the Latin classics, marked the last stages of the Jesuits' formal entry into the world of late Renaissance humanism. The choice of Martial's *Epigrams* for their first major publication was expressive of their goals: many of Martial's epigrams were sexually explicit in amusing, even savage ways, yet this offensive material could not obscure—may indeed have contributed to—the fact that Martial was regarded as one of the supreme Latin stylists of the classical age. As the Jesuits competed in a world in which the purity of Ciceronian expression had become the new norm, ousting the rough and ready colloquial Latin of the late Middle Ages, they found they could not afford not to study Martial just because he was obscene.[5]

The Ignatian answer was therefore to encourage Jesuit scholars to produce editions of great works that would remove all traces of offensive material, but still keep the grandeur of such moral lessons as they might contain and teach the style adequately. This task Ignatius entrusted to the scholar and musician Andreus Frusius, and though Frusius also died in 1556, he had by then already completed his expurgated edition of Martial, so that the Jesuit press in Rome could go ahead and publish it. Frusius had performed the same service for the poet Horace, and an edition of that work was published at the Jesuit press in Vienna.[6] The Ignatian vision of "removing from the classics everything that might offend the innocence of youth" did not die with Frusius.

The Jesuit press continued to expand under the direction of a German master typesetter, who used Jesuit students as his proofreaders, and began to meet Ignatius's goal of providing not only purged texts but also cheap editions of classical and devotional texts that even the poorest students could afford, including his own *Spiritual Exercises* and the *Constitutions* of the Society. An Arabic font was added in 1564, under the direction of the converted Jew Baptista Romanus, and the press produced as its first Arabic works a translation of key Council of Trent documents, an Arabic grammar, and an Arabic translation of the New Testament. A font of Hebrew type was acquired in 1577 and was used to develop grammars and teaching materials in that language also.[7]

The thorough but inevitably rather broad strokes with which Ignatius had outlined his plans for Jesuit colleges had been much refined by the time Ricci attended the Roman college in the 1570s. Though the Macerata schools had prepared him to a level at which he could and did initially think of proceeding directly to the study of law, his decision to enter the Jesuit order brought him back into a stricter curriculum that had evolved over the previous decade and been precisely formulated in guidelines of 1566.[8] Formal training in "humane letters," the junior level of training within the Jesuit university, was carried out in the faculty of languages. Ricci was twenty-one at this point, but some of the pupils there might have been as young as ten. Here the youths learned the detailed grammar of the Latin they had already begun to speak—instruction was in Latin, and the boys were expected to speak Latin to each other during school hours; they began Greek, and took intensive courses in rhetoric, poetry, and history. These courses finished—they took from two to four years, depending on the school and the caliber of the pupil—the boys moved to the higher faculty of arts, "arts" being defined as those natural sciences that could be learned from reason—logic, physics, metaphysics, moral philosophy, and mathematics. These courses in turn could be followed by training in law, medicine, or theology. If theology was chosen, one of three courses could be followed: Scholastic theology, the application of reason to the data of

God's revelation as taught by Thomas Aquinas; historical theology, a careful examination of the church's decrees and canon laws; and the detailed study of Sacred Scripture itself.[9]

Ignatius's terse instruction that the students "should commit to memory what their masters have assigned" was taken literally and was echoed by other Jesuit directors of instruction during the years of Ricci's schooling. Ignatius also introduced an air of challenge into the atmosphere of the school by suggesting that study be linked to the innately competitive instinct of the young: "For the greater progress of the students, it would be wise to place together some of equal ability who are likely to spur one another on with holy rivalry."[10] Possibly it was some such "holy rivalry" that motivated Ricci and his friend from Urbino, Lelio Passionei, to develop their own private system of "memory places" while they were studying together in Rome, an enterprise that Ricci recollected with nostalgia twenty years later when he was living in China.[11]

While Ricci was a student in Rome a number of books were available that could have enabled him to extend his formidable memory even beyond the limits suggested by the *Ad Herennium* and the writings of Quintilian and Soarez, though we do not know which he actually read. His ability later in life to memorize rapidly lists of four or five hundred Chinese ideographs might have been due in part to the techniques developed by theorists like Host von Romberch, whose book first appeared in Venice in 1533. Romberch worked out elaborate schemes for identifying storage spaces in memory cities according to occupational categories—shops, libraries, slaughter yards, schools, etc.—and developed complex "memory alphabets" based on human, plant, and animal figures or on logically interconnected sequences of objects.[12] At the same time, the actual choosing of memory images to be fixed in the memory places had grown more subtle and sophisticated. The levels to which these memory experts would go in devising vivid memory images that one would never forget was well shown in the work of Guglielmo Grataroli, an alchemist and physician also interested in designing dietary regimens that would strengthen the human memory. Grataroli's book on memory-place systems, first published in Zurich in 1553, was available in a Roman edition by 1555. Acknowledging the prevalent theory that memory images should "move one to laughter, compassion, or admiration," Grataroli developed a tripartite system of place, object, and figure. After designing a memory location on conventional lines, he then positioned in each an object—a chamber pot, a box of salve, a bowl of plaster were his first three examples—and then had separate figures, each based on individuals he knew well and each carefully named, jolt the scenes into mnemonic action. Thus in rapid sequence Grataroli presented his friend Peter as picking up the chamber pot full of urine and pouring it over James, Martin putting his finger in the ointment box and wiping it over Henry's anus, and Andrew taking some plaster from the bowl and smearing it over Francis's face. If one could link these vignettes by pun, analogy, or association of ideas to given concepts, one could be guaranteed never to forget them.[13]

It was Ricci's masterly ability to combine these two different types of mnemonic technique—vivid imagery and lengthy sequence—that led him into his earliest enthusiasm for China and on to some of his most dramatic public successes there. The nature of his mnemonic skills ensured that when he had to start learning Chinese, on his arrival at Macao in late 1582, far from being dismayed by the difficulty of the language he was excited, almost triumphant at what he called the "leap" he had made, as he wrote to his former rhetoric teacher Martino de Fornari in February of the following year:

I have recently given myself to the study of the Chinese language and I can promise you that it's something quite different from either Greek or German. In speaking it, there is so much ambiguity that there are many words that can signify more than a thousand things, and at many times the only difference between one word and another is the way you pitch them high or low in four different tones. Thus when [the Chinese] are speaking to each other they write out the words they wish to say so that they can be sure to understand—for all the written letters are different from each other. As for these written letters you would not be able to believe them had you not both seen and used them, as I have done. They have as many letters as there are words and things, so that there are more than 70,000 of them, every one quite different and complex. If you would like to see examples I can send you one of their books with an explanation appended.[14]

Ricci went on to describe what he considered to be the monosyllabic structure of Chinese, and he noted the universalistic attributes of an ideographic script in which "lies the advantage that all the countries which use this kind of writing can understand each other's correspondence and books even though the languages are different, something which is not at all the case with our letters." Ricci carefully studied the formation of the individual ideographs so that, after only five months in Macao, he felt he could write out correctly any ideograph he was shown. He added (in language his former rhetoric teacher surely appreciated), "I have already placed in my head a goodly number of them."[15]

One can sense a reason for the excitement lying behind Ricci's emotional language: if Chinese had "as many letters [i.e., ideographs] as there are words or things" and if one could learn quite swiftly to subdivide each ideograph into component parts, each of which also had a separate meaning, then it would be easy for someone well trained in mnemonic art to make each ideograph into a memory image. This process was speeded by the fact that Chinese made an encouraging contrast with Greek grammar, which Ricci had been unhappily trying to teach for some years in India. Unlike Greek sentences, which had to be remembered in all their detailed complexity, a Chinese sentence could be presented in sharp detail as a series of images: as Ricci observed, "What is of help in all this is that their words have no articles, no cases, no number, no gender, no tense, no mood; they just solve their problems with certain adverbial forms which can be explained very easily."[16]

It took Ricci another twelve years to reach the point at which he had learned so much Chinese by his methods that he was ready to explain those methods *in* Chinese. From his surviving letters we can chart some of the steps of his arduous progress. In mid-1584, having been given permission by the Chinese to settle at the town of Zhaoqing in late 1583, Ricci was doing some preaching and hearing occasional confessions. By October of that year he was beginning to speak without an interpreter and felt he could read and write quite well (*mediocremente*); in November 1585 he had advanced to fluency in speech and could read almost everything if he got some help from a Chinese assistant. There he stuck for a while, weighed down with work and aggravations. In 1592 we find him still unable to read many books because "of the lack of a teacher, whom we never seem able to keep for more than a year or two, for various reasons," until, urged on by his superiors, he made a final and successful effort. In December 1593 he announced a crash course on the "Four Books"—the introductory collection of Confucian classics known as *The Analects, The Mencius, The Doctrine of the Mean,* and the *Great Learning,* which the Chinese used in their schools—and was experimenting with translating them into Latin. He had taken an experienced and learned tutor so that "in my old age [he was forty-one!] I make myself a schoolboy again." By October 1594, after taking two long lessons a day for ten months, the breakthrough came: "I have plucked up enough courage so that I will be able, from now on, to compose on my own."[17]

How he managed to draw the strands of these studies together in Nanchang in 1595, putting his new-found confidence in his knowledge of Chinese alongside his own rigorous memory training, and cleverly playing on the desire for book memorization on the part of his Chinese acquaintants, Ricci described in a detailed letter to his superior in Macao, Edoardo de Sande, which bubbles with the joy of achievement:

One day, when I was invited to a party by some holders of the first-level literary degree, something happened that gave me a great reputation among them and among all the other literati in the city. The thing was that I had constructed a Memory Place System for many of the Chinese ideographs, and being in good relations with these literati and desiring to gain among them some credit, and give some evidence of what I knew of Chinese letters, understanding how much this mattered to the service and glory of Our Lord and to that which we were intending, I told them that they should write down a large number of Chinese letters in any manner they chose on a sheet of paper, without there being any order among them, because after reading them only once, I would be able to say them all by heart in the same way and order in which they had been written. They did so, writing many letters without any order, all of which I, after reading them once, was able to repeat by memory in the manner in which they were written: such that they were all astonished, it seeming to them a great matter. And I, in order to increase their wonder, began to recite them all by memory backward in the same manner, beginning with the very last until reaching the first. By which they all became utterly astounded and as if beside themselves. And at once they began to beg me to consent to teach them this divine rule by which such a memory was made. And immediately my fame began to spread so swiftly among the literati that I couldn't even keep a counting of all the degree holders and other important people who came to ask me if I would be willing to teach this science and took me as their master, and paid me courtesies as they would to a master, and also offered me money as they would their masters.

I replied to them that I do not take money for teaching my doctrine, and that now, not yet being fully settled, and not having a friend with me, nor a house prepared, and being so terribly busy with these social visits—I just could not agree to it. But when I had eventually settled in and set up a house I would try to satisfy them. For in truth this Memory Place System seems as if it had been invented for Chinese letters, for which it has particular effectiveness and use, in that each letter is a figure that means a thing.[18]

Despite Ricci's disclaimers to de Sande that he was not teaching the memory method, we know from a letter to General Acquaviva that he *was* doing so by November 1595.[19] And though he claimed to be vigorously denying Chinese rumors that he could remember any book that he came across after only one reading, a letter to his friend Lelio Passionei (now living in Modena) shows that he was, in fact, quite deliberately fanning the flames of Chinese enthusiasm: "They claim that I have no need to read a book more than once for it to remain from then on forever in my memory. And though I swore to the contrary they were not willing to believe me—particularly because, when arguing with them over some of their [philosophical] books, on some occasions for fun [*per ricreazone*] I would take from my memory one of their compositions and then at once recite it, word for word, and backward."[20] The memorization of such classical works was of course crucial to ambitious Chinese youths entering the examination ladder for bureaucratic office; as Ricci shrewdly observed: "Great is the rejoicing that is made in the city by the magistrates and by the parents of all those who obtain a passing grade, for as they are heathens they think that this is both their glory and their paradise."[21] Ricci had already met one senior official (the military mandarin Scielou, who nearly led him to a watery grave) whose son had had a physical and mental collapse after failing the state examinations, and as he came to write down his thoughts in his book on mnemonic method, he played on this desire, asserting that "if a student were trying to recall what he had read of the *Classics*, then such-and-such a chapter, such-and-such a page, such-and-such a line would be as vivid as if before his eyes."[22]

By impressing the Chinese with his memory skills, Ricci hoped to interest them in his culture; through interesting them in his culture he hoped to draw them to an interest in his God. The culture that he brought to China and slowly learned to translate and reinterpret was essentially that body of knowledge he learned during a year at the Jesuit college in Florence—from late 1572 to October 1573—and subsequently in the faculty of arts in the Roman college, where he studied between late 1573 and 1577.[23] In broadest terms, this consisted of moral philosophy on the one hand and the mathematical sciences on the other; both these were, in the 1570s, expanding ferociously, and the huge body of material had to be marshaled with the utmost care. In the world of moral philosophy the decision by Ignatius and his successors to try to train young Jesuits to be at the intellectual forefront of the cultural life of their time added immeasurably to the work that each student had to undertake and to the amount of literary work that he had to try and absorb. A heightened appreciation of Latin style led to the need to memorize key classics like Cicero's orations, Quintilian's rhetoric, Martial's epigrams, and long selections of Horace, Ovid, and Virgil, in addition to famous "set pieces" like Livy's version of Hannibal's oration to his troops; while the growing interest in Greek meant that one had to progress through Aesop to Pindar's odes, Hesiod and Xenophon and on to Plato's dialogues, Aristophanes' *The Frogs* and long sections of Homer. From all these examples one had to cull not just the style and the content but modes of delivery and types of argumentation, so that one developed one's own declamations in accepted fashion.[24]

At the same time one had to be deeply versed in the complex interconnections that existed between Christian and pagan antiquity and in the texts from both traditions, since the period of the Counter-Reformation saw a resurgence of the eclectic doctrine known as neo-Stoicism, in which elements of later Greek and early Roman thought were blended with Christian currents of thinking to create a variant of Christian humanism. Here again, memory of a wide range of texts was essential, more for their moral content than for their stylistic power. Thus Seneca, with his calm, strong views on old age and death, and the former slave Epictetus, with his prescriptions for protecting one's personal integrity in a harsh and unpredictable society, both became parts of Ricci's mental world.[25]

When Ricci wrote from Peking to his friend Girolamo Costa in the spring of 1608, near the end of his life, that "I find myself so totally lacking in books that most of the things that I am now printing are things that I have been holding in my memory," he was possibly thinking most clearly of these Stoic or humanist works: the book he published in Chinese that year under the title *Ten Discourses by a Paradoxical Man* contained an almost word-for-word transcription of Planudes' life of Aesop, along with extensive paraphrases of Epictetus. Since extended quotations from such exotic Western works were rapidly picked up by contemporary Chinese scholars and circulated in their own essay collections, the need to be both clear and accurate was paramount.[26] A similar use of memory had doubtless been present in earlier work: in *On Friendship,* which he published in 1595, Ricci drew freely on quotations from dozens of classical authors anthologized in Andrea de Resende's work of the same title. Though we can't be sure that Ricci didn't carry Resende's work with him as he traveled, it is not likely. It is more probable that he had learned numerous passages from Resende while in school and carried them in his memory, a supposition made more likely by the fact that Ricci slowly expanded his observations on friendship from seventy-six to one hundred, as if he were slowly remembering new ones and adding them to his store.[27] A somewhat similar process might have taken place with the selections from Epictetus which Ricci published in Chinese in 1605 under the title of *Twenty-five Sayings* (*Ershiwu yan*); though rearranged and emended, all these passages came from the *Encheiridion,* or so-called *Manual,* distilled from Epictetus's larger philosophical works. Ricci might also have carried this book with him; again, it is more probable that he had memorized selections of Epictetus in his classes and called them up out of his memory when he found a use for them in the Chinese context thirty years later.[28] In the collection of songs that Ricci was ordered to compose by Emperor Wanli in 1601, so the eunuchs could have something to sing as they played on the harpsichord that Ricci had presented to the court, Ricci certainly drew on youthful memories of poems by Horace and essays by Seneca and Petrarch that he then cleverly wove together.[29]

It is somewhat harder to see how conventional memory techniques were applied to that other major subdivision of learning which Ricci absorbed, namely, the mathematical sciences. Here Ricci's teacher at the Roman college had been Christopher Clavius, whose influential reworking and analysis of Euclid's *Elements of Geometry* appeared in Latin in 1574, just as Ricci moved on to a higher level of studies in the faculty of arts. Clavius was a brilliant teacher as well as a man who believed passionately in the value of scientific knowledge at a time when many senior Jesuit teachers did not and were actively dissuading their students from mathematical studies.[30] Clavius emphasized how the careful exploration of natural phenomena aided one's reflections on the spiritual world. Himself an outstanding mathematician and astronomer, who was to become a friend of Galileo, he used to tell the young Jesuits in the Roman college that "it was essential that students understand the sciences to be both useful and necessary for the correct understanding of the rest of philosophy," and he reminded them of the bleak example of those professors who made absurd mistakes in interpreting Aristotle and Plato because they lacked a basic understanding of mathematics.[31]

Clavius had a clear sense of what his students should learn in the college: "The number and motion of the celestial spheres, the multiplicity of observations, the effects of the stars—which vary according to their various conjunctions, oppositions, and relative distances one from the other—the division of connected matter without end, the ebb and flow of the sea, the winds, the comets, the rainbows, exhalations and other meteorological matters, as well as those proportions between motion, quality, action, distance, reaction, etc., about which mathematicians have written so much."[32] The teachers would have to be above average, wrote Clavius, to get the discipline of mathematics across effectively; while the students would have to work with rare intensity to get through the material he thought was essential for them. First-year students (*los lógicos*) could do the first four books of Euclid in four months, practical arithmetic in a month and a half, the planetary spheres in two and a half months, geography in two months, and—if time remained in the school year—they could end up with the fifth and sixth books of Euclid. Second-year students (*los philósophos*) could study the astrolabe (for calculating planetary and stellar motion) for two months, planetary theory for four, perspective for three, and theories of clockmaking and ecclesiastical computation for whatever time remained. A few outstanding students would be allowed a third-year reading course on their own, in which to investigate more advanced theories of the spheres and to study the making of perpetual calendars, planetary tables, use of quadrants, and the like.[33]

Ricci, who had Clavius as his mathematics teacher for four years at the Roman college, was probably in this group who were given advance help. His training in theology may even have been slowed by the demands of his mathematical work, since he finished his theological courses only in 1580, while living in India.[34] Like most other literate Westerners, he would have had first-hand experience of the effects of Clavius's fascination with the "ecclesiastical computation" that was listed for second-year students, since Clavius's famous reformed calendar—named in honor of the current pope, Gregory XIII—went into effect in Europe in October 1582 and in the Far East the following year, just after Ricci had entered China with Ruggieri and was settling down in Zhaoqing.[35]

All his life Ricci maintained an affectionate relationship with Clavius. They exchanged books and correspondence, and Ricci introduced his teacher to Chinese readers as the greatest mathematician since Euclid and Euclid's true successor. While Ricci, in his Chinese writing on mathematics, simply romanized Euclid's name with the rough approximation "Oujili"—not neglecting to say that Euclid had been born "around a thousand years ago," which would lead any Chinese interested in the matter to think that Euclid had been a Christian mathematician rather than (as was the fact) a pagan Greek who lived in 500 B.C.—he gave Clavius the Chinese name Ding. This was an amusing pun, akin to those used in memory-palace building, by which the name Clavius was transformed to the Latin word *clavus* or "nail," and the word "nail" then translated into Chinese quite correctly as *ding*. *Ding* was one of the simplest Chinese ideographs to write, almost identical to the European capital *T;* the Chinese, of course, were aware how much easier it was to write than most other ideographs and used to say of a stupid man, "He can't even recognize the ideograph *ding.*" This saying must have seemed wryly apposite to Ricci as he began his attempt to introduce Western mathematics to the Chinese literati.[36]

The central role of mathematics in the thinking of the Catholic church had been spelled out by Thomas Aquinas in the thirteenth century. He had seen it as an admirable early topic of study for the young because of its methodology of proceeding in a straightforward manner from a thing to its properties, so that it was "the easiest and most certain of human sciences." At the same time, mathematical knowledge fitted in well with the basic premises of mnemonic theory, since the mind, holding onto what was well arranged, found in the harmonious order of mathematics something particularly easy to remember—the arrangement of Euclid's geometrical propositions being a good example.[37] Imagination and intellect combined to make geometry possible; this science showed both man's power and his limitations in the natural order of being; it was a triumph of man to attain to mathematical knowledge, but proof of his weakness that he even needed to. God and the angels, as Aquinas argued, had no need for mathematical tables and graphs, since they would see all things in a single, unified vision.[38] Mathematics therefore seemed to offer a special kind of precision: "Intermediate between natural and divine science, it is more certain than either of them." At the same time it was emotionally untrammeled: "Provided a geometer makes a true demonstration, it is of no importance how he stands in regard to his appetitive part, whether he be joyful or angry."[39]

In their network of schools that spread across Europe in the sixteenth century, the Jesuits emphasized the sciences, not only to compete with Protestant schools which were doing the same but also to please the elite and the nobility who had come to value such studies above all others. By placing emphasis on mathematical skills the Jesuits proved that they stood at the frontiers of modern knowledge and had inherited the dominant thrust of late Renaissance Italian humanism. If they rejected Copernicus's heliocentric theory and continued to teach an astronomy based on an unmoving earth surrounded by seven crystalline spheres, that was because they valued the antiquity and religious correctness of this system and found the evidence for rejecting it inadequate.[40] The discovery of a new star in 1572 and the sighting of a major comet in 1577, both of which events occurred while Ricci was in school at Rome, caused widespread debate among Western scholars and astronomers and pushed Clavius to reexamine some of his assumptions, but ultimately his views remained unchanged.[41]

Once Ricci had become familiar with Chinese language and scholarship, he could hardly dismiss their scientific knowledge in the way that he had their religious practices. Observational astronomy in China, for instance, was excellent, and both the 1572 supernova and the 1577 comet had been recorded in careful detail by the Chinese, with regard to exact date of appearance, apparent size and brightness, and course of motion.[42] But he could try to convince the Chinese that the theoretical background to their methodology was still unsound; as he put it in his preface to his Chinese version of Euclid's *Elements of Geometry,* "From the time I first arrived in China it was my humble opinion that although those studying geometry had full confidence in their textbooks, yet there was no discussion of the fundamental principles. But without good roots or foundation it is hard for something to be firmly constructed, and hence even the most refined scholars could not explain the reasons for their conclusions."[43] Ricci claimed special abilities to cure this lack. Not only did he firmly present himself as the pupil of Clavius, and Clavius as the intellectual heir of Euclid, but he also presented himself rather confidently as representative of a specific Italian intellectual tradition:

My remote Western country, though small in size, is unique among all other nations in the analytical rigor with which its schools examine natural phenomena. For this reason we have many books that investigate such phenomena in the fullest detail. Our scholars take the basic premise of their discussions to be the search for proof according to reason, and they don't accept other people's unsubstantiated opinions. They say that investigation using reason can lead to scientific knowledge, while someone else's opinions lead only to my own new opinions. A scientific knowledge is absence of doubt; opinion is always accompanied by doubt.[44]

Ricci went on to summarize for his Chinese readers very much what Clavius had taught him. The great river of mathematics had four main branches: arithmetic, geometry, music, and astronomy-plus-chronology. Ricci elaborated this general idea in a hymn to the manifold subcomponents of mathematics:

146

These four main branches subdivide into a hundred streams. One measures the magnitude of the universe; as with the thickness of the successive superposed heavenly spheres, the distance from the earth of the sun, moon, and stars, and their comparative magnitudes, the diameter of the earth and distances on its surface; also the heights of mountains and hills, lofty buildings of all kinds, the depth of pits and valleys, the mutual distance of two places, the area and boundaries of fields, of city walls, and palaces, the volume of storehouses, or of large containers. Another subdivision computes the sun's rays, so as to explain the sequence of the seasons, the varying length of day and night, and the hours of sunrise and sunset, and thus deduce latitude and longitude; the exact moment that years, months, and days commence; the equinoxes and solstices, the years to add an extra month, or the month to which one adds an extra day.

Another subdivision constructs instruments such as spheres for observing the heavens and earth, and the movements of the sun, moon, and the five planets; for regulating the eight classes of musical instruments, and marking the passage of time by clock so as to help the daily life of the people, and to regulate the sacrifices to the Supreme Lord. Again another subdivision regulates the arts which work in water, earth, wood, and stone; builds cities, erects towers, terraces and palaces, from the roof to the foundation; opens canals, forms reservoirs and builds bridges. And all these not merely to make them ornamental and beautiful, but to make them so strong that they will not fall into ruins even after thousands of years.

This was only a beginning, continued Ricci. Mathematics also subsumed the whole world of mechanical devices for lifting weights or moving goods; it covered irrigation and drainage mechanisms for deserts and marshes, locks for waterways, the science of optics, the knowledge of curvature of planes, the techniques of perspective and chiaroscuro. Last in his list came geography, the science of representing the earth—mountains, seas, kingdoms, continents, islands, and districts, "all laid down in miniature," each detail "answering to the points of the compass," and all fitting together in scale "so as to avoid mistake and confusion."[45]

While he was in China, Ricci did some work in virtually all of these subbranches of learning: horology, optics, observational astronomy, surveying, music, geography, geometry. For most of these areas his memory of what he had learned in school could be supplemented by information drawn from the few books he brought with him. Calculating eclipses, estimating latitudes, constructing integrated and adjustable sundials that would be accurate at any location, even making the large-scale map of the world that brought him such fame in China, were not so immensely difficult when he had with him copies of Mercator's map of 1569, Ortelius's map of 1570, the immensely detailed tables for estimating latitude that he had in Clavius's *Sfera* and Alessandro Piccolomini's *Sfera del Mundo* and always carried with him on his travels.[46] Clavius's books, especially, were not merely theoretical; they came with the most meticulous working drawings and notes that showed the student not only how to use the equipment but how to make it, down to the last joint in the wood and bolt in the frame.[47]

Especially after 1596, when Ricci received a gift copy of Clavius's new book on the astrolabe (which had been published in Rome in 1593), with its scores of pages of meticulous tables and charts, he had a powerful new tool for astronomical calculation; once again Clavius's precision and complete practicality combined to put into Ricci's hands a means of computation that had led European scholars to dub the astrolabe "the king of instruments" and to write affectionately flattering dialogues in its honor.[48]

How much Ricci saw other types of power flowing into him because of his mastery of mathematics and astronomy we cannot tell; though certainly in parts of Europe at this time the books of Euclid that were now made available to new generations through Clavius's skillful translation and annotations were as much a candidate for magical use as for what now might be called "scientific." Prefacing the English version of Clavius's Euclid that appeared in London in 1570, the magus John Dee threw a challenge in the face of his "Brainsicke, Rashe, Spitefull, and Disdainfull countreymen" and tried to make them understand how the newly proven laws of mathematics supported astrology, that "Arte mathematicall, which reasonably demonstrateth the operations and effectes, of the naturall beames, of lighte, and secrete influence: of the Sterres and Planets";[49] Dee tried to prove, further, that Euclid's precision reinforced his own valued science of "Anthropographie," which used man as the sacred mathematical measure of all things, and even led to that great and final science which would be "Archemastrie," the "performance of complet Experiences" and the only means to "bryng to actuall experience sensible, all worthy conclusions by all the Artes Mathematicall."[50] Ricci might not have used this language, but its nature and content would not have surprised him.

Geography may have been last on Ricci's list of the subfields of mathematics, but his achievements here were very great. He performed the major feat of constructing an accurate world map with all the place names transcribed into Chinese—a map that went through scores of unauthorized printings, and ended up in a giant version of six separate panels each over six feet wide in the inner chambers of the Peking palace of Emperor Wanli. This is not to say that Ricci did not have help in its composition: the work of patient scholars has shown that Ricci translated many of his brief descriptive essays on the Americas and northern Europe direct from Plancius's map of 1592, which was sent to him in China, while the passages on central Asia were not even translated but merely transcribed from the twelfth-century Chinese scholar Ma Duanlin's encyclopedia, the *Wenxian tongkao*. In the case of both Plancius and Ma Duanlin, Ricci took over wholesale much totally fanciful material that belied the apparent scientific rigor of his work.[51]

In any case, the important aim for Ricci in all this was to involve the Chinese in his scientific achievements so they would prove more receptive to the Christian faith. It was in this spirit, as he told Clavius, that he carved messages in Chinese into the bases of his adjustable sundials, pointing out the frailty of human endeavor if it was not backed by some understanding of God's grace, and warning those who were watching time pass on the sundial's face that they could neither recapture the past nor foresee the future but must do good in the present, when they had the chance.[52]

In the field of personal relations Ricci reinforced such messages through his analysis of friendship. The small book on that subject which he published in 1595 for a Ming nobleman in Nanchang (and then republished in expanded form in 1601 with several flattering prefaces by his Chinese friends) brought him, according to his own report, more prestige and admiration among the Chinese elite than anything else he wrote, a view that is reinforced by comments made about the book by leading Ming scholars.[53] Ricci presented friendship as something beyond financial gain and other material considerations, a bond that united two discrete bodies in one heart. Friends were to be truly recognized when times were bad—when things were going well friendships were so easy to sustain that they lacked deep significance.[54] From Seneca, Ricci quoted the thought that he had no regrets for his dead friends, since he had anticipated their loss while they lived and remembered them as still living after they had died; from Cicero he took the idea that one who does not seek to help his friend at all times is not a true friend but a merchant; from Martial he quoted the sardonic epigram that if one's friends were few one would have less joy but, at the same time, less sorrow; from Plutarch came the conceit that a man who chose his friends from among the worthless would be like a man entering a dyer's shop, who would inevitably be splattered.[55] All these sentiments would have sat well enough with Ricci's Chinese readers, and there would have been nothing surprising to them either about sentence 24 in the *Friendship*, "The damage caused by my friends' excessive praise is even greater than the damage caused by the censure of my enemies." All that startles us now is that this phrase comes from Erasmus, who had been severely criticized by Ignatius of Loyola, and who in the late sixteenth century was not normally considered proper fare for Jesuit readers.[56] That Ricci was happy to use Erasmus suggests that he was seeking the fullest range of significant quotation, not just the narrowly orthodox.

Ricci used his Chinese friends to circulate the *Friendship* and other works, confident that the moral message would shine through. Since he did not push the more intransigent side of the Christian teaching, it was easy for senior Chinese scholars to accept him as a near equal. To take a simple example, once Ricci had become friends with the famous Confucian scholar Guo Zhengyu, he used Guo to transmit his writings to the equally eminent Zou Yuanbiao. Zou read the works out of courtesy, and found little to argue with in Ricci's presentation. Since Zou's letter to Ricci has fortunately survived, we can trace the nature of this Ming intellectual's response to the Jesuits in some detail:

> I received a letter from my respected friend Guo, which exceeded all my expectations; and with it came your own handwritten note. I truly felt as if I was one of those who had traveled to islands far away and been able to meet with an extraordinary person, my joy showed on my face. You and two or three of your colleagues are eager to spread your teachings concerning the Lord of Heaven to China—this intention seems to be a worthy one, and as I examined its message there seemed no difference from what our own sages have taught.
>
> The works of our sages, and of the Confucian scholars who came after them, have all been recorded completely and in the greatest detail; can you agree with me that there is no major difference? If there are places where things are not identical, then it is because aspects of the practice are not the same. If you examine a copy of the *Book of Changes,* you will see that the hexagram *qian* is concerned with "the government of heaven." The people of our humble land have always understood heaven; can you agree with me as to that?[57]

Ricci might not have agreed totally, but he could certainly use the hexagram *qian* to bolster his arguments that the Chinese, in their earliest classical texts, had a concept of the divine power that was not far from the Christian one. This hexagram, composed of six unbroken lines, was defined by the Chinese as having the power of "the creative," and as leading to "sublime success, furthering through perseverance." An early commentary on the same hexagram noted that "Great indeed is the sublimity of the creative, to which all beings owe their beginning, and which permeates all heaven," and the commentator added that the "holy man" who understood this process "is clear as to the end and the beginning" and realized how "each thing receives its true nature and destiny and comes into permanent accord with the Great Harmony."[58]

Personal relations and training in science came together in the methodology of conversion that Ricci developed by the late 1590s; and one can certainly say his hope that some important Chinese scholars might be brought into the Christian faith through serious discussion of scientific matters proved to be justified. One of Ricci's first friends in China, Qu Rukuei, although he first came to Ricci because he believed him to have alchemical powers, stayed on to study Clavius's *Sfera* and to do a preliminary translation of the first book of Euclid, and he was converted in 1605. This translation, even if tentative and uneven, attracted the attention of several talented mathematicians in southern China.[59] If we cannot be sure it was Euclid that first drew the Shanghai scholar Xu Guangqi into Ricci's orbit in 1600, Euclid certainly became the cement of their friendship after Xu converted to Christianity, passed the highest levels of the civil service exams, known as the *jinshi,* in 1604, and received a post in the elite Hanlin Academy in Peking. He and Ricci worked every morning for a year, going through Clavius's interpretative edition of Euclid line by line, until they had finished a polished joint translation of the entire first six books, which they published in 1607.[60] This translation in turn deeply impressed the senior bureaucrat Li Zhizao, who had been drawn to Ricci out of admiration for his cartography; after lengthy conversations on the meaning of this geometry and joint collaboration on several mathematical works, Li was finally converted in 1610, just before Ricci died.[61]

The receptivity of these Chinese scholars to the Western science that Ricci presented is worth remembering. These were not society's sweepings who sought to acquire prestige by adopting Western thought. Qu Rukuei was from a distinguished family: his father, Qu Jingchun, had been one of the highest ranked scholars in the national *jinshi* examinations of 1544, had served as senior editor of one of the great Ming encyclopedia projects, and had ended a distinguished bureaucratic career as president of the Board of Rites.[62] Li Zhizao was from a military family in the Hangzhou area and had passed the *jinshi* examinations in 1598; he was already launched on a career in the Board of Public Works when he met Ricci.[63] Xu Guangqi came from a commercial family and had spent a period in the 1580s as a peripatetic tutor—sometimes a mark of a floundering career in Ming China—but in 1597 he had managed to pass the intermediate level of examinations with distinction and, as we have seen, after passing his *jinshi* exams in 1604 he was named to the Hanlin Academy, the most coveted of all intellectual posts in the entire country.[64]

But a thorough indoctrination in traditional norms of Confucian doctrine did not disqualify any of these men from understanding Western science: it is worth emphasizing that in each of the fields that interested these men the most—chemistry for Qu, cartography for Li, and geometry for Xu—there was a long and sophisticated history of indigenous Chinese experimentation and achievement, even though the Jesuits rarely mentioned this.[65] What Ricci could offer them was partly new data, of course, but also new perspectives in which to judge their existing knowledge, and a sense of purpose that came from the belief that with his help they were recapturing a lost Chinese past. This feeling was well articulated by Xu Guangqi in his introduction to the version of Euclid that he wrote down and polished from Ricci's dictation. China's ancient rulers and scholars had once had total mastery in computation, music, and mechanical invention, wrote Xu. Only in the time of Emperor Qinshi Huangdi (during the late third century B.C.) had the skills been vitiated by that emperor's destruction of scholarly books, as a result of which China's scholars became "like blind men shooting at random at the target and never hitting, or like those who had only a blurred sense of form, scanning an elephant by a firefly's light, losing sight of the tail if they focused on the head."[66] Li Zhizao was even clearer about China's past attainments in a preface he wrote for Ricci's world map that was printed along with it; he pointed out that China's geographical knowledge had made important breakthroughs during the Yuan dynasty, and that even Ricci's map was not detailed enough to show all the countries that had paid tribute to

China in the past. Ricci himself noted that Li had devoted "a whole year" to a careful analysis of the mathematical principles behind his own calculations of the size of a terrestrial degree of latitude. Only after being satisfied that they represented "immutable law" did Li recommend that Ricci produce a new, enlarged version of the map to which he would give his own imprimatur.[67]

Ricci shared with all these men a love of books and printing. He had an exaggerated view of the extent of Chinese literacy—"few are there here among them who don't know something of books"—but he noted correctly that all religious groupings tended to spread their message through books rather than through preaching or public discourses.[68] With his customary interest in such details he studied the making of the Chinese ink sticks that were used by all scholars and their mode of paper-making and bookbinding. He noted that Chinese books tore easily and didn't last long because their paper was too thin; and he handed out good quality Western paper, a few sheets at a time, so that scholars could see the difference, just as he emphasized the binding and gilding on the small library of books he had with him.[69] He was also interested in the scholar-calligraphers who seemed to flourish in all Chinese cities, where they either got money by writing out important memorials for less skilled mandarins or sold their own work; he was amazed that the elegant transcription of one memorial could cost eight ducats, while even a few lines of calligraphy could sell for a tenth of a ducat;[70] he was less impressed by the professional scholars, often skilled in mathematical subjects, who were ready to write books for other people and literally give up their rights to their own names.[71]

Always alert for aspects of Chinese society that would help the missions, Ricci seized on printing and operated on quite a massive scale. The very first version of a Christian devotional work in Chinese, which he prepared with Ruggieri in 1584 (from an earlier Latin version probably drafted in India), after winning approval from the Zhaoqing prefect, Wang Pan, was then run off in an edition of 1,200 copies in the Jesuits' own residence.[72] One wonders if Ricci had been one of those students in Rome assigned to help the German master typesetter with the making of books in the Roman college, for he was clearly at home with the technical details of printing. He carefully noted how the Chinese artisans could carve an entire reversed page of calligraphy onto their blocks of apple or pear wood as fast as European typesetters could set a folio page of metal type, and he pointed out that the big advantage of the Chinese system was that one could run off a small edition and keep the blocks for later reprinting, and that minor changes could be made swiftly and cheaply.[73] Though he felt that the number and complexity of Chinese ideographs were something of an "impediment to science" and that the Chinese printed much harmful or useless material in this way—he could hardly say less, given the huge volume of Buddhist and Taoist materials that was printed each year—he nevertheless felt that this outpouring of scholarly energy prevented many Chinese youths and adults "from falling into those vices to which the natures of men are inclined."[74]

At one point Ricci also noted that the Chinese remembered what they read and repeated it to others, and that the missionaries could benefit from this trait of theirs, but unfortunately he didn't follow up this remark with any analysis of Chinese memory training. In presenting the case for his own mnemonic system Ricci obviously tried to impress the Chinese with the fact that the system had been used successfully by royalty in the distant past: he wrote of "the king of Bando," who learned the languages of the twenty-two countries he ruled (in reference to Mithradates of Pontus); of "the king of Balaxi," who knew the names of all the soldiers in his army of hundreds of thousands of men (in reference to Cyrus of Persia); and of "the king of Liweiya," who sent an envoy to Rome, the envoy remembering the names of the thousands of officials he met there (referring to Pyrrhus's envoy Cineas).[75] None of these names would have had any specific significance to the Chinese readers—they served merely as imposing incantations.

What is striking about this list of exemplars is their almost total inapplicability to the concerns of the Chinese literate elite, a fact that graphically highlights the shortcomings of such a literalness of approach in translating a European text to Ming China. All three examples are wide of the target in the Chinese context. Going on embassies to foreign courts was not a mark of respect—indeed, it was almost never done by Chinese—and if one *did* go one would have no reason to want to remember the names of the foreigners; foreign languages were of no concern to a Confucian literatus, who expected that foreigners desiring to communicate with him would, like Ricci, learn Chinese; and few officials sought a military career of any kind—indeed, military service even at the senior level was widely regarded as an inferior occupation, as Ricci knew.[76]

One wonders if, in leisurely conversation with some of his scholarly Chinese friends, Ricci roamed beyond these three examples, which he probably drew from the brief section of Pliny's *Natural History* that dealt with memory, where all three Western examples that he used are listed.[77] The Latin humanist and Stoic writers he had been raised on, such as Cicero, Quintilian, and Seneca, all provided fine examples that the Chinese might have warmed to more readily, for they had attributes that the Chinese themselves valued. For example, Seneca, remembering two thousand names in sequence or two hundred random lines of verse, would have struck a Chinese chord, as would Theodectes with his ability to recall any number of poems after a single reading, and Charmadas, who could remember the entire contents of the books in the libraries he visited.[78] Such figures from the Western past could have claimed a kind of equality with Chinese scholars of the past famous for parallel feats: doubtless any of Ricci's educated Chinese friends could have told him of Ni Heng of the Eastern Han, who remembered all the stone tomb inscriptions after he returned from a long journey; or Xing Shao, who remembered the whole Han dynastic history after five days and could always recall all the poems written at a party; or Lu Jiangdao of the Tang, who after one reading could recite books both forward and backward; and the formidable Zhang Andao who, having grown up in seclusion, had always thought that *everyone* remembered books after reading them once through, until he was politely corrected.[79]

It is interesting at least to speculate how the two traditions, the

Confucian and the classical Roman, could have been drawn into discourse through Ricci's Christian mediation, with the varying acts of memory providing the common ground. Conversation concerning these examples would have been an ideal way to raise questions of human as opposed to divine power, and to analyze the place of reason in human affairs. The parallels that one can find, all of which would have been in the conscious minds either of Ricci or of his Chinese friends, are indeed remarkable. If Julius Caesar could, in Pliny's words, "dictate or listen simultaneously, dictating to his secretaries four letters at once on his important affairs—or, if otherwise unoccupied, seven letters at once," could not Liu Xuan in the Sui dynasty listen to, and retain, five items of information being delivered to him at the same time?[80] If Lucius Scipio could name the citizens of Rome and Themistocles list all the citizens of Athens, had not Su Song, serving in the Nanjing area, been able to retain all the area population registers in his own head? As well as which he had developed a kind of chronological "placement" system of his own, based on the traditional dynastic *Histories*.[81] The matched examples could be found also in varied commercial or recreational spheres. Hortensius recalled every price of every item sold at auction, while Chen Jian recalled each detail of his accounting books and the produce of his looms;[82] Scaevola, riding back to his home in the country, could replay in his head every move of the pieces in the board game he had lost, while Wang Can could do the same with a game of Chinese checkers (*weiqi*) where he had been only a spectator.[83]

As with arguments about memory, or with analyses of geometry, so with the humanism of the Stoics—one could use it when necessary to edge a discussion touching on religion to a higher stage. The convert Xu Guangqi once told Ricci that his greatest fear was that his son might die, and it is hard not to imagine Ricci's mind racing to the memory chamber in which Epictetus was stored, for this fear had obsessed Epictetus also. "When you are fond of something," Epictetus had written in Greek and Ricci translated into Chinese, "remember to ask yourself, 'What is its nature?' If you are fond of a jug, say, 'I am fond of a jug,' and when it is broken you will not be upset. If you kiss your wife or child, say to yourself, 'I am kissing a human being'; then when they die you will not be upset."[84] Or again, as Epictetus wrote in another passage that Ricci translated, "Never say about anything, 'I have lost it' but only 'I have given it back.' Is your child dead? It has been given back. Is your wife dead? She has been given back."[85] In all such cases, ran the Stoic argument paraphrased by Epictetus, "If you make it your will that your children and your wife and your friends should live forever, you are silly; for you are making it your will that things not under your control should be under your control, and that what is not your own, should be your own."[86]

After such messages and teaching had been absorbed by Xu or Li, Ricci could lead them on to the deeper arguments buried within Christian faith itself; arguments that he himself had written out and printed in his *True Meaning of the Lord of Heaven* (*Tianzhu shiyi*), a summary of Christian doctrine presented in the form of a dialogue between a Chinese and a Christian scholar. Yet even in such a book Ricci led the Chinese scholar into his crucial argument via the classical tradition, as in a central passage in chapter 3. Here Ricci began by describing "two famous philosophers from the West, one called Democritus, who was always laughing, and the other Heraclitus, who wept without ceasing. Their utterly different conduct in fact sprang from the same cause, for both of them saw how the men of their day ran after the false goods of this earth. Democritus, by his laughter, mocked their folly; Heraclitus, with his tears, showed his compassion for them."[87] From this Greek bastion Ricci then advanced, hoping to draw his Chinese readers with him:

> God only has us born into this world in order to test us and to have us practice virtue. So this life is for us but a journey, we are not here forever, nor does our final goal lie here below. It is only after our death that we will reach it. Our true homeland is not on this earth, but in heaven, and it is in that direction that we should turn our eyes. Present time is all that the animals have for happiness, and that is why they are built to look at the ground. Man is created for heaven, and his

head and eyes are raised high so he can always see whither he is bound. To put one's happiness in earthly things is to descend to the level of the beasts.[88]

Even as Ricci struggled to present his reasons concerning God and the soul to the Chinese, and to sustain four overlapping roles as missionary, teacher, friend, and guide, he remained always pupil and schoolboy to himself, struggling to explain the unexplainable, escaping from Epictetus only to fall back toward Plato. In one of his strongest passages in the *True Meaning of the Lord of Heaven* he reached out to all Chinese literati known and unknown with these words:

> The Christian religion instructs us perfectly on these rules, but men do not understand what is in front of their eyes. Everything they cannot see seems opaque to them. If a pregnant woman is thrown into prison, and gives birth in a dungeon, her son will grow up knowing neither sun nor moon, ignorant that there are such things as mountains and rivers, a human race, a universe. A large candle serves as his sun, and a small one as his moon. The few people he sees in the prison are the human race to him. He can think of nothing better than this. He is not aware there is hardship in his prison, he stays there peacefully, he does not think of leaving. But if his mother should speak to him of the splendor of the stars, of the fine objects owned by the wealthy, of the wide expanse and wonder of the world, of the loveliness and the loftiness of the sky, he will come to understand that he has only seen some pale echoes of the sun, that his prison indeed is narrow, dirty, stinking. From that time on will he not cease wanting to make his home there? Will he not think, day and night, of freeing himself and going to live in joy amid his parents and friends?[89]

Not only did this weave echoes of Clavius most artfully into the argument, along with Plato's *Republic* (Book 7), but the final image was beautifully chosen, for the joys of company and society were a focal part of Ming upper-class life, as Ricci knew all too well. Indeed, one can chart the stages of his physical and spiritual journey by the tables at which he sat, for as he once said, everything in China, including religion, was discussed at table, over meals or with a cup of tea in one's hand.[90] In South China, in the 1580s, Ricci made cautious journeys out to the houses of the rural poor, where families gathered around a make-shift altar, careful blessings were offered in stumbling Chinese, and the meal, as Ricci put it, "pleased us more for the goodwill it showed than for the variety of the dishes, though there were plenty of them and, in their way, very good."[91] In central China in the early 1590s we find him in the home of a newly converted Christian merchant, enjoying lei-surely banquets, now that the convert had given up his Buddhist di-etary practices, while they pursued their discussions of the Lord's design.[92]

In Nanjing at the end of the century, protracted dinners at the houses of great officials began to be commonplace, Confucian scholars inviting the fashionable Buddhist clergy of the area to come and dis-pute with Ricci. He left a careful record of how he spoke between the courses of human nature and the goodness of God, and of how he struggled to retain every detail of argument and counterargument for eventual publication in his anti-Buddhist writings.[93] And then came the world of Peking after 1601, an endless succession of dinner parties, often three or more a day. For Ricci the search for acceptance was now over, but exhaustion mounted under the press of social commitment and constant intellectual exegesis.[94] One Chinese contemporary noted that the Jesuit "ate and drank exuberantly" on these occasions, and there is little doubt that the ceaseless social rounds took their toll.[95]

In Peking, the pressures on Ricci were worst every third year, when the candidates from all over China poured into the city for the triennial *jinshi* exams, many bringing introductions to Ricci or letters and greet-ings from friends that he could not ignore. Not surprisingly it was in a *jinshi* year, 1610, that Ricci's life ended; he came back one early day in May from a round of visits and lay down on his bed in the Jesuit mis-sion, exhausted, with a headache. When told he would probably be better soon, Ricci replied, "Far from it. This illness is caused by having too many things to do, and will prove fatal."[96] The concern felt for him by both his Jesuit fellows and his Chinese friends led to his being examined by seven different doctors who prescribed, between them, three different courses of treatment.

On May 8, in the evening, he made his general confession to Father de Ursis. The following afternoon he slid into a delirium that lasted through the night and well into May 10. During this time he babbled ceaselessly of his desire to convert the Chinese and their emperor. The evening of the tenth he received extreme unction. There was no question of his writing any more; he had already burned his personal letters, put his other manuscripts in order, and sealed up a final note to General Acquaviva. Suddenly, however, he turned to his companions and in a weak but audible voice said: "I have the very greatest love for Father Coton, who is living at the court of the king of France; although I do not know him personally, I had decided to write to him this year and to offer him my congratulations for the glory he has rendered to God, and to let him know personally how things stand in this mission. Make my excuses to him, for now such a task is quite impossible for me." In the context of Ricci's delirium his conversation has a clear enough logic, for after King Henry IV had abjured Protestantism the Jesuit Pierre Coton had become his confessor, a role he carried out with great skill in difficult circumstances. It is probable that in his last hours Ricci dreamed of being confessor to China's long-lived emperor Wanli. Coton's seems to have been the last name Ricci uttered. On May 11, in the evening, he sat up straight in bed, closed his eyes, and died.[97]

SIX

THE THIRD IMAGE:
PROFIT AND HARVEST

T he memory palace stands on its elevation, suffused in an even light. The reception hall is still silent, yet inside there is more for the mind to dwell on. In the southeast corner are two warriors, locked in combat; in the northeast corner waits the Xixia woman, who is a *huihui*.

For his third memory image Ricci chooses the Chinese character *li,* meaning profit. To compose an image that the Chinese will remember, he divides the ideograph for *li* vertically down the middle, thus yielding two new ideographs, one of which means "grain" and one "blade" or "knife." From these two components Ricci composes his memory picture, "a farmer holding a sickle, ready to cut the crops in the field."[1]

As usual, there is rather more to the memory image than is at once apparent. In this case, the resonance is given by the fact that this ideograph, *li,* is the same one that Ricci has chosen for his own Chinese name, though he uses the form *ly,* which he has adopted as the pronunciation in his own personal system of romanization. At one level this *ly* is no more than a phonetic approximation of the first syllable, *"ri,"* of his name, and given the absence of the rolling *r* in Chinese, *ly* is a good

enough equivalent. But there are scores of words pronounced *ly* in Chinese, and many of them would be suitable. It is as if Ricci senses the word's ambiguities in the context of his own mission work ("What will it profit if we gain the whole world and lose our own souls": Mark 8:36) and in the contexts of local survival and barter ("What will it profit us if we slay our brother and conceal his blood?" as Judah asked his brothers, before they, agreeing, drew Joseph from the pit where they had left him and sold him to the Ishmaelites for twenty pieces of silver: Gen. 37:26–28). A decade later, Ricci leaves one tiny hint to later generations of his awareness of these cross-cultural implications. In using Western letters to transcribe the Chinese version of his name that he appends to the colophons on the paintings he gives to Cheng Dayue, Ricci twice identifies himself as "A man from Europe" and then spells his name "Ri": twice he identifies himself by his Jesuit mission affiliation, and on these occasions he romanizes his name "Ly."[2]

Ricci takes this new composite figure representing profit, in the form of a harvester who bears his own name, and places him in the northwest corner of the reception hall, to the left of the Xixia woman who is a *huihui* and diagonally across from the two grappling warriors. He will stay there, ready to gather in his crops, for as long as Ricci so instructs him.

In Ricci's time, search for financial profit overlapped and cut across differences of religious creed. The trade-offs could be bleak.

For instance, the converted Jews of Portugal, having been fined so mercilessly by the Inquisition that they faced total ruin and began shipping their holdings out to Flanders and Italy, at last in 1577 agreed to a deal with King Sebastian by which he would give them a ten-year exemption from all fines for heresy if they provided him with 250,000 ducats for his African campaign. They provided the money, King Sebastian was killed, and his successors revoked the deal, seeing in Sebastian's death divine retribution for such a tainted bargain.[3]

When the prince of Parma advanced with his Catholic Spanish troops to attack Protestant-held Antwerp, the Protestant leader, William of Orange, warned the citizens that they must breach the great ocean dike of Blauwgarendijk and flood the plains around Antwerp, thus ensuring that the city could be supplied by sea if Parma managed to block the River Scheldt. The Antwerp butchers' guild prevented William's advice being followed, on the grounds that the flood waters would ruin the business they made in grazing 12,000 head of cattle on the reclaimed land between Antwerp and the dike. Since Parma did block the Scheldt, and no supplies could be obtained, in August 1585 the city fell to the Spanish army, the Protestant pastors were expelled, and Antwerp returned to the Catholic fold.[4]

While Ricci lived in China, though mail was always slow and uncertain, couriers usually got through successfully to Shaozhou or Peking from Macao, and the life of the missions could be coordinated with developments in the outside world. But in 1609 the young Chinese Christian courier assigned to bring the mail from Macao decided that the time had come to save the money that had customarily been given to the guards on the Macao-China border at Xiangshan. Deprived of their cash, the guards arrested the courier as a spy and took him to the local magistrate. The magistrate interrogated him and sent him to the prefect. The prefect interrogated him again and sent him to the intendant, who beat him savagely and ordered him imprisoned for life. With fine attention to detail, the intendant also ordered the twenty-five letters the courier carried translated into Chinese line by line (with the forced assistance of those Portuguese who happened to be in Canton for the trade fair), and then placed them on permanent deposit in the Canton archives. Since the letters contained material that the Chinese found suspicious—such as details on the running of Jesuit schools in Macao and on defense problems connected to a feared Dutch attack—the Chinese authorities ordered the Jesuits in Shaozhou to whom the letters were addressed to leave the country.[5]

The Catholic church's attitude toward money and property accumulation had never been settled; its responses ranged from vows of perpetual poverty to soaring cathedral spires. Ignatius of Loyola gave his views on the need for Jesuit poverty in the reflections on "Christ the King" that he appended at the end of the first week of the *Spiritual Exercises*. Those making the exercises were to hear in their minds these words of Christ: "It is my will to conquer all the lands of the infidel. Therefore, whoever wishes to join with me in this enterprise must be content with the same food, drink, clothing, etc. as mine. So, too, he must work with me by day, and watch with me by night."[6] But as if aware how inapplicable these instructions were for ordinary men in the world, Ignatius asked those making the exercises to take a broader view of human choices in their meditations on the fourth day of the second week; he placed this meditation on the same day—but coming just after—the powerful meditation on the "Two Standards," in which men had to reflect on the choice between Lucifer and Christ, between riches, honor, and pride on the one hand and poverty, a willingness to be held in contempt, and humility on the other. In Ignatius's words:

This is the history of the Three Classes of Men. Each of them has acquired ten thousand ducats, but not entirely as they should have, for the love of God. They all wish to save their souls and find peace in God our Lord by ridding themselves of the burden arising from the attachment to the sum acquired, which impedes the attainment of this end. . . .

The First Class. They would like to rid themselves of the attachment they have to the sum acquired in order to find peace in God our Lord and assure their salvation, but the hour of death comes, and they have not made use of any means.

The Second Class. They want to rid themselves of the attachment, but they wish to do so in such a way that they retain what they have acquired, so that God is to come to what they desire, and they do not decide to give us the sum of money in order to go to God, though this would be the better way for them.

The Third Class. These want to rid themselves of the attachment, but they wish to do so in such a way that they desire neither to retain nor to relinquish the sum acquired. They seek only to will and not will as God our Lord inspires them, and as seems better for the service and praise of the Divine Majesty. Meanwhile, they will strive to conduct themselves as if every attachment to it had been broken. They will make efforts neither to want that, nor anything else, unless the service of God our Lord alone moves them to do so. As a result, the desire to be better able to serve God our Lord will be the cause of their accepting anything or relinquishing it.[7]

These meditations would have had a literal resonance for someone like Ricci, since he had been raised in a world that relished money and its uses. Even if his hometown of Macerata was no great place (according to Montaigne, who visited it in the spring of 1581 en route from Rome to Ancona), and had few really beautiful buildings, it was still pretty enough, perched atop a conical hill in fertile country, with a new and imposing entrance gate bearing the gilded inscription *"Porta Buoncompagno,"* which marked it as the terminus of the road from Rome through the papal Marches, and as the legates' headquarters for the regions.[8] The big central square, with its bell tower and cathedral church, the palace for the papal legate, the merchant hall, the narrow stone street that led gradually down to the secondary square where the Jesuits' school stood, the other streets that curled around the contours of the hill, following the lines of the walls, or that swooped at intervals downhill, breaking into jagged flights of steps, all must have been known to him, almost foot by foot, and might well have provided the ground plan for the memory places he fixed in his mind. And the local wine was good, evaporated half away by heat to make it stronger, sold alongside the roads in which the constant movement of human travelers, on foot, in pilgrims' robes, carrying banners and crucifixes, showed one was approaching the shrine of Loreto.[9]

Ricci also knew Florence well, for he had spent almost a year there in 1572–73, as a twenty-year-old, after taking his first vows.[10] It was Florence that Ricci used as a yardstick for measuring Chinese cities when he visited them for the first time: Nanxiong, the busy river entrepôt in northern Guangdong province, where he converted the merchant "Giuseppe," was "the size of Florence"; the administrative center of Ganzhou, which he visited with the mandarin Scielou, was "larger" than Florence; and Nanchang, described by Ricci as "jammed with alchemists, curiosity seekers, scholars, and those interested in studying memory-place systems," was "twice the size"—even though in this latter case familiarity reduced it to "the same size" in a later letter.[11] It was about friends in Florence, too, that Ricci reminisced to his former rhetoric teacher when he first described his attempts to learn Chinese.[12]

Rome, even if Ricci did not mention it much in his letters or his *Historia,* was also very much in his thoughts. One of the few books he had brought to the Jesuit residence next to the church of St. Andrew's Quirinale when he enrolled as a novice there in 1571 was the *Mirabilia Urbis Romae,* with its tales of the imperial city's past glories and illustrations of its former splendors.[13] When he was in China he asked for the latest and most expensive illustrated books on the city to be sent to him there, so he could give the Chinese some sense of what Rome was like. As he told his former schoolmate Fuligatti in a letter of 1596, if he could get the general of the order or some of the teachers at the college to send some such books, "it would be worth many *scudi* to us here, and gain us much credit among these people; and if the expenses are too much for you let's arrange it in such a way that you can write to me what the cost will be and I'll send [the cash] to you from here, or something that is of equivalent value."[14] Thirteen years later he wrote to General Acquaviva's assistant, Alvarez, rather petulantly: "I've requested that a *Roman Antiquities* be sent from Europe many times, one with copper engravings, so that I can show it to these people. I don't know if nobody has sent one because my letters never arrived, or because they couldn't find one for sale. At this point I'd like to remind Your Reverence that this is something that would have excellent results here, and I beg you to apply yourself to this matter with some diligence, and send it to me here at the court in Peking."[15]

Ricci had left Rome before the immense spate of rebuilding under Pope Sixtus V in the late 1580s transformed the face of the city and at last completed the dome on St. Peter's as conceived by Michelangelo thirty years before. Nor had he seen the new Roman college built by Pope Gregory at an estimated cost of 400,000 ducats between 1581 and 1585. But he had already been able to form an idea of the splendid new church of the Jesuits, the Gésu, begun in 1575 by Cardinal Farnese, uncle to the prince of Parma, which when Ricci was a student was already being used for Mass, for preaching, and for hearing confessions, although it was only half-completed.[16] And Ricci had naturally witnessed the pomp with which Rome celebrated festive occasions. Perhaps the finest was Corpus Christi day, when massed dignitaries of the church walked in procession down the long avenue shaded with canvas that stretched from the papal palace to the gates of St. Peter's. The sides of the tented arcade were hung with the finest tapestries and the armorial bearings of all the cardinals, the posts supporting it held garlands of green leaves and flowers, while from the windows along the route bright cloths were displayed by the citizens. Swiss Guards and mounted cavalry in red-velvet uniforms marched beside the singing choirs and the crowds of worshipers, each of whom held two white candles, while borne in his litter came the pope himself as trumpets blew clarions and cannons roared from the castle of St. Angelo.[17]

Ricci had been a student in Rome during the 1575 jubilee, when tens of thousands of pilgrims flocked to Rome from all over Italy, in groups up to a thousand strong, providing a spectacle that dazed Angelo Pientini when he came to record it, as it dazed Gregory Martin when he transcribed Pientini's account for English readers:

What shal I speake of other Companies from other Cities, (some onely of gentlemen and nobles) whose several varieties in notable points of devotion and charitie, their furniture for golden and silver Crosses and Crucifixes, for banners and streamers of most costly silke and velvet with al kind of holy pictures thereupon, their provision of vestments, Altar clothes, sacred vessel, Instruments and quiers for the solemnitie of Masse al their journey and in the holy Citie; and especially their holy devises, for goodly and godly shewes in every Companie, some representing death and damnation, some heavenly joyes, other some the Church Militant, other the Church Triumphant, the

Orders of Angels, the varietie of Martyrs and Martyrdoms with the instruments thereof; the diversitie of Saincts, the puritie of Virgins, the
stories of the Old Testament, the state of Penitents; these and a number of the like able to move a Christian hart.[18]

Ricci found lesser but still impressive proofs of the church's splendors when he reached Goa in 1578. The three-naved church of St. Paul
in Goa, with its magnificent high altar, was enriched with a huge
painting of the conversion of St. Paul, made in the 1560s by Father
Emmanuel Alvares, and with a tabernacle built by Brother John
Gonçalves and gilded by Father Marcos Rodriguez. There he attended
evensong services, led by five priests accompanied by a choir of close to
one hundred orphans and native Indian catechumens being prepared
for baptism, who sang to the music of a host of instruments, including
tamborines, trumpets, flutes, violas, and a clavichord. There he revered
the cross given to the church by the former general of the Jesuit order,
Francis Borgia, a cross made from the wood of the true cross itself, so it
was said, and celebrated Mass among crowds so large that more than
thirty priests were needed to serve them all.[19] Goa was a cosmopolitan
place, and in the Jesuit residence Ricci found he was joining a group
that included the English novice Stephen Cudner, who served as librarian; the Portuguese fathers Martin da Silva, the superior, who preached
each Sunday, and George Carvalhal, who taught theology; Brother
Roger Berwouts, a Fleming, who ran the dispensary and the refectory;
to whom were added the new Italian arrivals, fathers Rodolfo Acquaviva and Francis Pasio, who were put to work in the hospital.[20]

Ricci's letters also show that he loved the structure of the Jesuit residence, which was being expanded under his eyes, with its outbuildings
and chapels and dormitories; the whole struck him as being a totally
integrated "machine," even though work was still under way on the
bakery, laundry rooms, and stables.[21] Indeed, the compound was like "a
garden of many and lovely flowers," wrote a long-term resident in the
month Ricci arrived. "It is a paradise of delights, if I might use the
phrase, because in its material fabric, in its size, style, and appearance it

is the best of all those in the Company, as all agree who have come here from the other main provinces of the Order."[22] One father felt that in size and beauty it could be compared only to the residence in Milan, and the Jesuits could indeed believe themselves back in Europe as they listened to the singing of the choir, accompanied by organ and trumpets, and the sweet sounds that rose above the gardens and fruit trees.[23] Francis Pasio, who had traveled to Goa at the same time as Ricci, was amazed to find a world of startling cleanliness where even the poorest—black slaves being everywhere, cheap to buy and cheap to feed—wore shorts and trousers of freshly washed cotton, and silk was in abundance for the wealthier. He found glazed chinaware in such profusion that it was used not only for eating and food storage but even for chamber pots to be kept under the bed for nightly use.[24]

But it was far harder to develop such magnificence in Goa than in Rome. Just to find talented artists and craftsmen was difficult enough. The Jesuits did not permit Hindus to paint Christian themes, nor would any devout Muslim paint such images.[25] Even Jesuit artists were restricted in their work. There is the documented but unexplained fact that Marcos Rodriguez, a native of Bruges in Flanders, who lived in Goa from 1563 to 1601 and wished to devote his life to art, was confined to the production of small-scale works; his superiors confiscated many of his tools and equipment, forbade him to sculpt the crucifixes he loved to make, and deflected a request from the fathers in Japan that he be allowed to travel there. As the dispirited artist wrote to the general of the order in 1591, "My inspiration goes for nothing."[26]

This shortage of talent may lend some credence to the curious accounts of the virtual kidnapping in 1583 of the English painter James Storie (or Story) after he had been imprisoned along with three English travelers in the jail at Goa. It was Father Marcos Rodriguez who initially acted as interpreter for the group, since the four prisoners knew no Portuguese but two of them had fair Dutch; the father was referred to affectionately by one of the imprisoned men, Ralph Fitch, as "a Fleming named Marco . . . who befriended us." John Linschoten, a shrewd Dutch trader and navigator who had lived long in Goa, took a less sanguine view, claiming that Marcos had been secretly informed that the prisoners "had great sums of money, and sought to get that for the Order." Linschoten continued with an interesting analysis of Storie's fate:

> And although the fathers knew that he was not one of those who had the treasure, yet, because he was a painter, of whom there are few in India, and that they had great need of one to paint their church, which would cost them great charges to bring from Portugal, they were very glad of him, and hoped in time to get all the rest, with all their money, into their fellowship.
>
> To conclude, they made this painter a Jesuit, and he continued some time in their college, where they gave him plenty of work to perform, and entertained him with all the favor and friendship they could devise, all to win the rest to become their prey. But the other three remained in prison in great fear, because they did not understand any who came to them, neither did any one understand what they said.[27]

Fitch and another friend finally fled secretly from Goa, forfeiting the sureties that they and some bondsmen had put up for the viceroy. But Storie stayed on in his comparatively gilded cage until, according again to Linschoten, he finally got his freedom:

> When the English painter, who had become a Jesuit, heard that his countrymen were gone, and found that the Jesuits did not use him with so great favour as at first, he repented himself; and not having made any solemn vow, and being counselled to leave their house, he told them that he made no doubt of gaining a living in the city, and that they had no right to keep him against his inclination, and as they could not accuse him of any crime, he was determined not to remain with them. They used all the means they could devise to keep him in the college, but he would not stay; and hiring a house in the city, he opened shop as a painter, where he got plenty of employment, and in the end married the daughter of a mestee [Indian-Portuguese half-caste], so that he laid his account to remain there as long as he lived. By this Englishman I was instructed in all the way, trades, and voyages

of the country between Aleppo, and Ormus, and of all the rules and customs observed in the overland passage, as also of all the towns and places on the route.[28]

Goa had been a Portuguese possession ever since it was seized from the Muslim sultan of Bijapur by Afonso de Albuquerque in 1510, so it was not surprising that it had become such a thriving center for religion, war, and trade. But the Macao peninsula had also become a thriving community by the time Ricci arrived there in late 1582, even though the Portuguese had resided there less than thirty years. Macao was in a curious state, since it remained technically an annex of Xiangshan county and subject to the jurisdiction of the Chinese county magistrate. Macao residents were liable to property searches and seizures, and were cut off from China by a well-guarded wall through which the Chinese were allowed to pass only twice a week and then only with official passes.[29] The population of Macao totaled around ten thousand by 1582, of whom perhaps four or five hundred were Portuguese men, the others being their Indian or Chinese consorts, the mixed-race children of these unions, black slaves, members of the various religious orders, and three or four hundred resident Chinese families who served as interpreters as well as shopkeepers and artisans. There were three churches, a large hospital, and a charitable foundation.[30] The Jesuit church was especially handsome due to the fact that its original plain wooden roof had been replaced by a tiled one in 1571—the roof being the gift of a captain-general of the Macao-Japan trade, Antonio de Vilhena. Ricci even had a little house in the grounds of the Jesuit compound, built in anticipation of his coming by his friend Michele Ruggieri—who had been sent from Goa to Macao in 1579 and at whose insistence Ricci had been transferred also—at a cost of thirty ducats donated by local residents; here Ricci was able to plunge into his Chinese studies in peace and quiet, assisted by a group of baptized Chinese Christians who helped him as teachers and interpreters.[31]

Any sense of isolation from the wider world that Ricci might have experienced, however, was an illusion, for every detail of the trading success or failure of the Macao merchants affected the Jesuits' hope for expansion. Macao's fortunes, in turn, depended primarily on the Portuguese carracks, or "black ships," that sailed once each year from Goa, via Macao, to Japan. The right to command this flotilla, granted to members of the nobility, important financial figures, and military leaders by the Portuguese crown, virtually guaranteed enormous profits (barring shipwreck) because of two phenomena of late-sixteenth-century economic life in the Far East. One was the different ratios of gold to silver in China and Japan, for in China silver was the dominant metal of exchange, was scarce, and was in constant demand, whereas in Japan silver was less popular as currency and was also mined in bulk. Therefore by buying silk in China with silver obtained in Japan, and then shipping that silk to Japan for resale, skillful traders could make as much as a 30 or 40 percent return on their investments; if they could include shipments of Chinese gold and exchange that for silver in Japan, their profits could rise as high as 60 percent.[32] The second was the Ming emperors' prohibition of direct trade with Japan as a result of the incessant raids on Chinese shipping and coastal towns by Japanese pirates. Though some Japanese traders began to search for new markets in the Philippines and Southeast Asia, and experimented with buying silk made in Vietnam and as far afield as Bengal or Persia, most were content to deal with the Portuguese. And it was the Portuguese traders in Macao who were perfectly situated to act as middlemen, without fear of competition from China's own aggressive and skillful merchant community.[33]

With an eye to maintaining their profits at the maximum level, the traders in Macao worked out a system by which the purchase of silk from the Chinese was supervised by three elected "procurators"; these three men (one was often a Jesuit) ensured that silk purchases made at the biennial trade fairs held in Canton were shared among all eligible citizens, with the intent of giving to each man such a share that "the profits therefrom are enough to support his family for a year in keeping with his station."[34] The procurators fixed the total annual silk quota at a maximum of 1,600 piculs for the entire Macao community (each picul being approximately 133 pounds in Western weight). This silk was subsequently sent to Japan on the vessels commanded by the king's captain-major and sold as one unit at a fixed price to a consortium of Japanese merchant buyers—thus preventing the Japanese from forcing down the price by holding off on purchases. All traders were under strict instructions not to sell any silk outside this fixed quota, and never surreptitiously to transship Japanese investors' silver back to Macao for investment in silk, as many Japanese not surprisingly requested. Church and state collaborated in enforcing these bans: excommunication was the penalty for shipping Japanese silver illegally, as well as confiscation of the precious metal, while heavy fines were levied on those who sold silk in Japan outside the monopoly agreement—fines as high as 400 ounces of silver in the documented case of one greedy ship captain.[35]

Since the demand for silk was so great, profits were high for the Japanese as well, and during the civil-war years of the late sixteenth century different Japanese nobles bargained hard for the benefit of having the black ships come to harbors they controlled; the great Japanese general Hideyoshi was particularly active in the trade, ordering his agents to buy up close to one hundred thousand pounds of raw silk in Nagasaki during 1581, and as much again at Satsuma the following year. In the 1560s the Jesuits tried to push trade in the direction of Japanese nobles who might seek conversion to the Christian faith: after 1571 the ships went regularly to the swiftly growing port of Nagasaki, where the ruling families were Christian. For some years at the end of the century the whole city of Nagasaki was even technically owned by the Jesuits, after a newly converted Japanese nobleman deeded it to them.[36]

One of the most successful early traders with Japan in the 1550s was the surgeon Luis de Almeida, a generous endower of charities in Japan, where he founded a shelter for orphans and a hospital for those suffering from leprosy and syphilis. In 1556 Almeida formally joined the Jesuit order, donating some 4,000 ducats, which the Jesuits promptly invested in the silk trade. Profits were high, but also erratic; in the disastrous wreck of the "black ship" in 1573 during a typhoon off the Japanese coast 500 people were drowned and nearly 800,000 ducats' worth of goods were lost.[37] It was the visitor to the Indies, Ricci's former teacher Alessandro Valignano, who worked out during 1578 the details of a new commercial agreement under which (barring such catastrophes) the Jesuits' Japan mission could be guaranteed some of the income it needed. Valignano obtained permission from the Macao council for the Jesuits to be granted fifty bales of Chinese silk in each annual lading of 1,600 bales; he estimated that the Jesuits would be able to buy the silk from Chinese dealers for 90 ducats per bale at a total cost of 4,500 ducats and sell it to Japan for 140 ducats a bale, or 7,000 ducats in all. The gross profit of 2,500 ducats would of course be reduced by freight charges and other taxes of 13 percent on the total shipment, but could be expected to yield a net annual profit of about 1,600 ducats. By a clever codicil to this agreement, Valignano got the Macao council to agree that in cases where all the silk was not sold in Japan, the Jesuits would not share in any loss that might be incurred by other traders; rather, the Jesuits' fifty bales would always be counted as having been sold among the first parts of any deal, so that their income would be constant. From other documents we know that the Macao-based Jesuits could also leave unsold silk with the Japanese fathers for sale at a later date, thereby saving the cost of shipping it back to Macao, as well as holding bulk silk on consignment in Japan for other traders after the ships had departed, a procedure that could net them a further 2,000 ducats in certain years.[38]

The morality of Jesuit involvement in this trade was certainly open to question. At the Council of Trent, which had ended not long before Valignano came out to the East, senior churchmen had urged penalties of suspension or even excommunication for those indulging in such trading.[39] Yet deprived of the great landholdings that brought rich revenues in Latin America, or of a major mercantile base backed by ship-building and regular dues as provided in Goa, the Jesuits in China and Japan felt they had no choice but to invest in such trade if they were to continue their charitable and mission works. They continued to put money into Portuguese carracks on the Nagasaki run, as they did into the great Spanish galleons that traveled each year between Acapulco and Manila. Often the arguments they used verged on the specious: that it could not be called trading if one did not literally *touch* the silk being shipped, or that one was not engaged in a business deal if one did not set foot in a Chinese market.[40] At the very beginning of his mission to the Far East in the 1570s, Valignano thought it necessary to check with the Jesuit general Mercurian, pointing out that the trade was indeed technically handled entirely by middlemen and was justified by the mission's poverty. Before answering, Mercurian checked in turn with Pope Gregory XIII. Only when the pope gave his consent did the general formally agree to Valignano's procedure, though of course by the time this permission reached Macao three years or more had passed since the original decision had been made. Despite this papal permission, Jesuits in Macao and Japan continued to have qualms of conscience about the whole business, and some of them petitioned that Jesuit involvement in the trade be banned; only in the later 1580s did General Acquaviva reaffirm Mercurian's position and instruct the Jesuits to continue their financial investments.[41]

When Ricci arrived at Macao in late 1582, he found that his superior Valignano, always seeking new ways of obtaining financial backing for the Eastern missions, had with him in the town four Japanese Christian converts from noble families whom he was escorting back to Europe for a series of royal audiences. The four young men were hard at work in Macao learning Latin, Portuguese, and Spanish and developing an appreciation for European music. Yet the events of that year only underlined the fragility of the whole financial structure based on sea-borne trade, for of the two carracks that went to Japan that July with cargoes of silk, one was wrecked off the coast of Formosa and sank, although passengers and crew were rescued; while of the little fleet of three ships on which the four Japanese nobles finally embarked in December, one ship was soon wrecked off Singapore and the ambassadors' own vessel was swamped and had to be lightened by throwing overboard hundreds of thousands of ducats' worth of cargo, despite which she still ran aground near Malacca.[42]

The loss of ships and cargo on the homeward run to Goa and Europe had important long-range effects on Jesuit finances, especially if the ships went down before reaching Portuguese-controlled Malacca, where they would have to pay massive transit dues, some of which would later reach the Jesuit missions in the form of payments remitted back to them by the crown.[43] But a shipwreck like that of the 1582 carrack heading for Japan, in which 200,000 ducats' worth of goods were lost, the Jesuit share of which was a full 8,000, brought an immediate crisis to the fledgling China mission, as Ricci noted. It was not just that the Jesuits lost their own money; the money from the silk ships "supported the whole city" of Macao, and when the city lost so much few would be disposed to help the Jesuits with any further alms; the Jesuits suffered twice, as it were. This was all the more serious because, though Ruggieri and other Jesuits had been able to accompany the Portuguese traders on their biennial visits to the Canton trade fairs and had even been loaned space in the hostels used by tribute emissaries passing through Canton, they had been unable to get permission from local Chinese officials to set up a permanent residence, and always had to return to Macao after the trading season was over.[44]

It was in this politically hectic and economically difficult period that the Macao-based Jesuits managed, in 1582, to get their first permission to reside in China, thus bringing to reality the great dream of Francis Xavier, who had died off China's coast in 1552 (the year of Ricci's birth). Their mission remained economically precarious through the following years, torn by the feuds that set off Spaniards against Portuguese, and left them constantly at the mercy of shifting winds of Chinese favor. Nevertheless, in this inhospitable context the Jesuits managed to make small yet steady gains. Throughout the 1580s there were only two or three Jesuit priests in China, accompanied by no more than one or two Chinese novices and six or seven domestic servants, all of whom were restricted for most of the decade to the Zhaoqing mission. The number of Chinese who converted to Christianity in a given year averaged around fifteen, of whom many were elderly and sick; the number of those baptized seemed more impressive, but the fathers acknowledged that most of these were infant children on the edge of death.[45] By the 1590s, though the Zhaoqing mission was closed by the Chinese, there were greater successes in the three new mission centers of Shaozhou, Nanchang, and Nanjing; now six to ten priests, with numerous novices, began to count their converts in the dozens, some of these converts being men of successful scholarly or commercial background.[46] After 1601 and the opening of a fourth mission, in Peking, the number of Jesuit priests rose to seventeen, and conversions rose to a hundred and fifty a year or more, many of these being from rich and influential families.[47] A pinnacle of a kind seems to have been reached in 1605, when three members of a cadet branch of the Ming imperial house were converted together. Translating these men's princely titles—with some poetic license—as "king," the Jesuits aptly gave the three the baptismal names of Caspar, Melchior, and Balthasar.[48] Ricci, around this time, boasted that Jesuit successes in China not only promised to be as great as those in Japan had been, but indeed might rival anything "that had been done from the beginning of the Apostles' preaching down to our own time."[49]

Surviving letters by Ricci and Ruggieri show how obsessed they were, from the start of the mission, with the strategy of seeking success by providing correct gifts for the Chinese, for they saw that this might be the key to their whole enterprise. In a preliminary shopping list sent to the general of the Jesuit order in 1580, Ruggieri had requested illustrated books showing stories from the Old Testament and depicting the mysteries of Christ's Passion, an illustrated guide to Christian lands (so the Chinese could begin to understand that Europe was a civilization rather than a collection of unruly merchants), and a richly decorated Bible.[50] A year later Ruggieri was asking if the pope might be able to give them "alms" of one thousand ducats, which could be brought out to Macao by Portuguese merchants. He was in these early, optimistic days planning for a possible conversion of Emperor Wanli himself, since he requested religious reliquaries, a "magnificent Bible in four languages, decorated and rich" (in obvious reference to the eight-volume Plantin polyglot Bible just given to the Indian emperor

Akbar), tapestries containing scenes from the Old Testament and the New which could be used "to decorate the Chinese emperor's rooms," and all the furnishings for a luxurious chapel in which the Chinese emperor could assist at Mass. Ruggieri added that his "Chinese friends" had also specifically recommended that he give the Chinese monarch two clocks—one large one for the palace that would chime the hours and be heard from a great distance, one small or domestic in size, like "that which Cardinal Orsino gave to the pope in the year that I left Rome" (i.e., in 1577).[51]

For the next several years, before they had really learned enough Chinese to explain complex scientific ideas in that language, the Jesuits used the clock as one of their key elements in winning Chinese favors. This decision was made all the more practical by the comparative impoverishment of China in clockmaking technology, for the glories of the complex escapement mechanism of the old Song dynasty clocks driven by water and sand, and the ingenious decorative and mechanical devices that went with them, had never been recovered after China's clockmaking artisans had been forcibly relocated after the fall of the Northern Song in 1127. In the Europe of the 1570s and 1580s, however, a revolution was taking place in the science of clockmaking, especially with the development of small, powerful, coiled-steel springs as the drive mechanism, which enabled miniaturization of clocks to proceed at a startling rate in European manufactures. This in turn led to expansion of sales to the middle classes, instead of just to rich people or public institutions that had hitherto been the main customers. With this expansion came specialization of labor in the technological world of clock production and further refinement in design, decoration, and manufacture.[52] Ruggieri had a general sense of these technological developments, and in 1583, when repeating his request for clocks to the new general of the order, Claudio Acquaviva, he asked for "a clock of metal, a palm high, which has the counterweights inside, since those that have [the weights] outside are not so pleasing to these gentlemen here."[53] Ruggieri had already given away the best of his clocks to the ranking military official in Canton in order to win his support for the mission, but this present, as might have been predicted, merely increased the pressure from other officials for identical gifts. It must have seemed providential to Ruggieri when Ricci arrived in Macao in August 1582 bearing another such clock, which had been presented to the China mission by the Goa father provincial, Vincentino Rodrigo; for the governor-general of the two southeast provinces of Guangdong and Guangxi had been asking for a clock with some insistence, despite the fact that he had already been given more than one thousand ducats' worth of the finest velvets, camelots, and crystal mirrors, as well as a pair of eyeglasses. (These last were a special gift from Father Ruggieri, who was laid up in bed with a particularly painful abscess, brought on by a local doctor's inability to find a vein properly when trying to bleed him, and felt nervous that his enforced absence might irritate the mandarin.)[54]

Ruggieri, now recovered, and Francis Pasio (who had come to Macao on the same ship as Ricci) traveled to Zhaoqing in late 1582, carrying their clock for the governor-general; he received both it and them on December 30, 1582—according to the old-style calendar, not the new Gregorian calendar, which only took effect in the Far East later the following year—gave them lodging in a Buddhist temple, and seemed disposed to let them stay permanently.[55] But as the Jesuits in China learned, and were to keep relearning, the Chinese bureaucratic system did not offer much in the way of long-term guarantees in return for such gifts. The governor-general was recalled from office in the spring of 1583, and the Jesuits had no choice but to leave their residence and return to Macao. Despairing of any permanence in China, Valignano ordered Pasio to leave for Japan; Pasio had already sailed when the new governor-general allowed the Jesuits to settle in Zhaoqing once more. This time it was Ricci who accompanied Ruggieri, and they reached the city on September 10, 1583.

This first residence in China inaugurated a new kind of financial struggle, which Ricci was to wage until he died in Peking in the spring of 1610. Indeed, so absorbed was Ricci in problems of landownership, lodging, and real-estate prices that his writings give detailed information on this aspect of the late Ming economy not easily obtainable else-where. In their first base at Zhaoqing, west of Canton, the local prefect "assigned" them a plot of land on the edge of a temple complex. The site was outside the city walls, on the banks of a river, in an area of market gardens and small cottages, pretty though very small.[56] Here the Jesuits decided to build a house of brick, two rooms on each side of a central hallway, with windows spaced in the Western manner, and a veranda at the back with a view of the river, rather than building around a central courtyard in Chinese style. By the end of the first phase of construction the Jesuits had spent well over 250 ducats.[57] Some of this money they had brought in with them, some they got by selling a glass prism, some as a gift from the wealthy Macao resident Gaspar Viegas, and a hundred ducats came in loans from Chinese in Macao. But since the site had no room for a decent church, Ricci and Ruggieri began buying up small adjacent parcels of land—including some "petty houses"—so they could have a church and "a slice of gar-den." At least twenty ducats went on these investments, which may have led to a good deal of local resentment. When they were forced to leave Zhaoqing in 1589 by newly appointed officials unsympathetic to their mission, the viceroy offered them sixty ducats for the structures, and though they protested with some vigor, knowing that the viceroy intended to use the house for himself and that the sum was far below the market price, they had no choice but to accept.[58]

In Shaozhou, north of Canton, which was their next base, Ricci was willing to put up eight to ten ducats for a site about 130 feet by 80 feet on the edge of the city by the river, but hearing of his interest the owner raised the price to eighty ducats. In this case, because of the owner's greed, Ricci seems to have been given permission to build by local officials without ever coming up with the purchase price, which presumably also led to considerable hostility from the original owner. Once again, desire for expansion led the Jesuits to eye a neighboring site, a parcel of fields with two ponds which were going for fifty ducats.[59] These investments were made with remittances from Macao, but by the time Ricci moved yet again, to Nanchang in Jiangxi province, the funds were so unreliable that they initially decided to rent, with fifty ducats which the church had made available to them; in the event, few Chinese were willing to rent to them, and local officials refused to give them formal permission to purchase. So Ricci ultimately bought a small house for sixty ducats, inside the city walls this time, contenting himself with oral permission from the mandarins, using the fifty ducats' rental money plus the extra he made by selling his elaborate adjustable sundials.[60] This house never proved suitable, since it was small and subject to constant flooding, yet when, after Ricci had left, his successor Jesuits decided to pay 1,200 ducats for a splendid house that could be converted into a novitiate, they were prevented by public outcry and ended up getting a poor price on the small house and having to buy a new one, not much larger, for 500 ducats; this new purchase turned out to be in disputed ownership and led to complex legal negotiations.[61]

By the time Ricci started to hunt for housing in Nanjing and Peking, on the national stage, as it were, he had become an experienced and skilled negotiator. Needing large houses for his fellow Jesuits, their numerous staff, and various novices, converts, and visitors, but also knowing that purchase of large houses by foreigners was bound to cause anger and resentment, he adopted the device of looking for houses which the Chinese claimed were haunted. By this means he got a house in Nanjing with room "for eight to ten missionaries" for four hundred ducats and a few years later one in Peking with "about forty rooms, large and small," for seven hundred ducats.[62] In both Nanjing and Peking, Ricci rented for at least a year before buying, to allay local suspicions and to get a better sense of what local brokers had to offer. In both cities, too, he tried to arrange for large sums of money to be remitted direct from Macao by letter of credit, though in both cases he was swindled, leading him to conclude "that in credit matters we see clearly we can trust nothing from the Chinese."[63] And in both cities Ricci fought successfully to evade the basic responsibilities of service and taxes that came from owning such holdings: in Nanjing by persuading the magistrate to let them off night patrol and watchmen's duties in their area, and in Peking by winning a permanent exemption from urban taxes—a considerable savings, since these were estimated at five ducats a year.[64]

The contrast of this final economic expertise with their stumbling earlier attempts could not have been greater. In the spring of 1584, after only a few months' residence in China, Ricci and Ruggieri, struggling to build a house and church, to feed themselves and the servants who lived with them, and to meet all the expenses of their interpreters and their interpreters' families, had run out of all the money they'd brought into China. There is almost a sense of inevitability in reading that at this point the Zhaoqing prefect Wang Pan told them he'd help them if they got him a clock from Macao, and of course the Jesuits hurried to do his bidding.[65] Much of their work in China was to depend on these shifting whims or sudden lurches of mandarin taste. With Wang Pan behind him, Ruggieri, who might otherwise have had to slip humiliatingly back through the gate into Macao, broke and discredited, arrived instead in the city by water, riding the prefect's splendid barge propelled by more than thirty oarsmen. And when he found that the residents of Macao, short of ready cash themselves and full of anxiety at the delayed return of that year's trading vessels from Japan, were unwilling to give the Jesuits any further alms with which to buy new clocks, Ruggieri simply sent the best of the Macao clockmakers to work with Ricci in Zhaoqing. Where or how this man had been trained in metallurgy and clockmaking is unknown; Ricci called him "a Canary Islander who had come from India, black-skinned," but added no other details except that he was a master craftsman. Wang Pan assigned two Chinese metalworkers to work alongside the black craftsman, and the polyglot team proceeded, apparently successfully, with some participation by Ricci himself, to construct a working clock. Ironically enough, after all the labor, no one in Wang Pan's residence could regulate the clock properly. Perhaps it was out of balance or wound incorrectly. For whatever reason, Wang gave it back to Ricci, without rancor, and Ricci hung it in his own residence.[66]

During this time, while Ruggieri continued his fund-raising in

Macao, Ricci was leading a hand-to-mouth existence, even selling one of his prisms of Venetian glass to get money for current expenses— selling it in fact for twenty ducats, which he knew full well was far more than it was worth.[67] Ruggieri, on the other hand, who had only managed to raise a loan of 100 ducats initially, had a change of fortune in the early spring of 1584 when the 1583 ships finally returned, having merely been held up in Japan longer than they expected after a disastrous fire had destroyed much of Nagasaki. He was now able to rejoin Ricci at Zhaoqing, bringing with him more than 400 ducats, some of which had been given as another gift by Gaspar Viegas, the rest probably coming from the Jesuit share of the trading vessels' voyage, which was reported to have been unusually profitable.[68] And as if that was not a fine enough turn of the wheel, a year later General Acquaviva sent four more clocks, all spring-driven (*horiuoli di molla*); one "for the table" was conventional enough, chiming the hours and the quarters on a series of different notes, but the three others—reflecting the rapid improvements in European horology—were all so small that they could be worn on a cord around the neck. To this trove King Philip's agent in Manila added yet another, also spring-driven and of the "very finest workmanship."[69]

In the light of these swings between near bankruptcy and sudden affluence with the arrival of rare objects or large quantities of silver bullion, one can understand why so many Chinese thought that Ricci must be some kind of alchemist. Not surprisingly, he repeatedly denied that he had any special alchemical skills, but he was never able to quash the stories altogether. In late Ming China there were two major areas of alchemical experimentation, both connected with Taoist religious beliefs: one was dedicated to the making of elixirs of immortality, the other was based on the transmutation of base metals into silver. In both areas, mercury—commonly termed quicksilver in the West and cinnabar in China—was a prime ingredient because of its color, its weight, its consistency, and its remarkable ability to be amalgamated with other metals.[70] Ricci guessed that the Chinese found it plausible to believe that he was an alchemist specializing in the transformation of metals because Portuguese traders did indeed buy up large amounts of mercury in Canton, which they shipped to India and Japan in boats that later returned laden with silver. Since the Jesuits did not admit to any outside sources of income, it was logical for the Chinese to think they were literally creating this silver, or else had contacts with Portuguese alchemists who were doing so.[71] But there is little doubt that Ricci's attitudes reinforced the Chinese conviction that he was an alchemist: not only was he active in laboratory experiments and the making of scientific apparatus, but he was reticent on financial matters. He might even have hinted that he did possess special powers, since we know that he once told a fellow Jesuit that he "thought it the lesser evil to confess to being an alchemist than to confess that he depended financially on Macao."[72]

Intriguingly enough, the Chinese who put two and two together in associating mercury and silver production were on the right track. The Spaniards' massive silver-mining operations at Zacatecas in Mexico and at Potosí in Peru—the latter mentioned by Ricci in a notation on his world map as a major world silver source—had begun to decline in the late sixteenth century after the richer ores that could be cheaply smelted had been exploited. This decline was halted, and a new boom begun that had major effects on the global economy, by the application of the mercury-amalgamation process for treating lower-yield silver ore. This technique, first developed at mines in Germany, was applied to the Potosí mines in 1572, and from then on the production of Latin American silver—hence the financial power of the Spanish empire—was based on a precise correlation with available mercury supplies.[73] Until the mercury mines at Huancavelica in Peru were exploited early in the seventeenth century, the Spaniards depended mainly on massive shipments of mercury across the Atlantic from their own deposits in Almadén, supplemented by the deposits of Idria. English privateers knew the importance of this trade well enough, and they worked as hard to intercept Spain's outward-bound mercury transport ships as they did the returning galleons loaded with silver. As Captain Thomas White noted in 1592, after his ship the *Amity* had captured two Spanish cargo vessels carrying 1,400 chests of mercury between them, "by this capture of quicksilver, the King of Spain lost for every quintal a quintal of silver, that should have been delivered to him by the mine-masters in Peru, amounting in value to £600,000."[74] Ricci had a close Jesuit friend in Peru, his fellow Maceratan Battista Ferro, and we know not only that they kept in touch but that Ricci hoped to have Ferro transferred to the China mission, a plan he dropped only in 1599 when tensions between Spaniards and Portuguese had grown so great that interchanges between the missions came to a virtual halt.[75]

Ricci also studied such details as the transportation of ambergris from Southeast Asia to Canton by the Portuguese, and the passionate desire of the Ming imperial court to obtain this product, since it was believed to become a life-giving drug when added to mercury in elixirs.[76] It is logical to suppose he had some knowledge of the shuttle trade that flourished briefly after the 1580 union of Spain and Portugal until national differences resurfaced: this trade saw much Chinese mercury shipped to Japan, and the promise of direct shipments from China to Manila was taken seriously enough to lead to correspondence between the Manila governor and the archbishop of Mexico. In an unusual passage of economic analysis Ricci wrote very lucidly about these trade possibilities, saying that Spain's desire to trade directly with China had been deliberately sabotaged by the Macao Portuguese, who feared that the Spanish would dump too much Latin American silver in the Canton market, driving down prices and wrecking their profitable financial deals there. Since the Portuguese had been generous with their alms to the Jesuits, the Jesuits must support them in their desire to remain independent.[77]

Throughout his life in China Ricci never threw off this association with alchemy. In the early days of the mission in Zhaoqing, the missionaries underwent a serious crisis when a dishonest convert claimed to have proof that the Jesuits had alchemical powers; on the basis of his contacts with Ricci, he procured cash and women before he was finally exposed.[78] To complicate matters, there were abandoned silver mines in the hills outside Zhaoqing; in these mines lived gangs of homeless people who often preyed on the local villagers and thus further spread the view that silver production and illegality somehow went together.[79] A rumor that the Jesuits were expelled from Zhaoqing in 1589 because they had refused to yield up their alchemical secrets for making silver out of mercury not only gained local currency but was later published in a Chinese book and had wide circulation in Ricci's own lifetime.[80]

Ricci's fame as an alchemist preceded him to Nanchang, itself famous for practitioners of alchemical arts, and there was no way he could disprove the stories. As he wryly wrote to one of his closest friends, Girolamo Costa, in October 1595, this "fame" could never be deflected, because "the more I assure them that I know nothing about these matters, the less they believe me."[81] On Ricci's first brief visit to Peking in 1598, a senior eunuch in the court sent his staff to welcome Ricci and sound him out on his alchemical skills; when he learned that Ricci could not turn mercury into silver, the eunuch ordered him to leave the city.[82] At the very end of his life, Ricci was still dogged by this reputation, as he showed in a rather exasperated letter to Pasio of 1609. That same year, his close friend Qu Rukuei, who had once sought Ricci out to study alchemy with him and had then become a Christian, had so fallen back into his alchemical studies that he had to be urged to undertake a general confession and follow the *Spiritual Exercises* of Ignatius to be steered back onto the right path.[83] The Chinese scholar Shen Defu, who had lived near Ricci during the last years in Peking and got to know him well, wrote in his reminiscences of Emperor Wanli's reign: "Because Ricci did not practice usury, and yet seemed to have everything that he needed in abundance and never ran short, people suspected that he must have mastered the arts of the forge and the fire," in other words, that he could create his own money supply by magical means. Shen added that he personally did not believe Ricci was an alchemist.[84]

The same kind of ambiguity ran over into Jesuit relations with the Chinese generally, especially in the areas of service, where the line between independence and sycophancy was often a thin one. Almost from the first, both Matteo Ricci and Michele Ruggieri found themselves running errands for the Chinese. Thus in the summer of 1585 Ruggieri went to Macao on commission from the governor of Guangdong province to buy plumes that were demanded by the court in Peking. These feathers, especially the more luxurious ones, were in great demand among the Chinese, who had asked Ruggieri for them before, either because they wanted to use them as gifts to the court or because they had been amazed and delighted by the pictures and designs made from different colored feathers—"rendered so well that they appeared to be painted by hand"—that a certain Franciscan friar had brought from Manila to the Canton area in the late 1570s.[85] In one of his more lyrical moments Ruggieri thought of trying to obtain a live ostrich for Emperor Wanli: "A living ostrich would be a wonderful present for the King of China," he wrote to General Acquaviva, "because he so much values their feathers, and any living animal or bird that is not native here is highly prized."[86] Though the Jesuits never got entangled in the logistical niceties of shipping live ostriches to Peking, they nevertheless took their feathers seriously: feather goods were featured in a catalog of presents for a projected Spanish embassy to Wanli in the 1580s, and, presumably in reference to the Aztec custom of using feathered costumes for ritual and even for war, Ricci identified various Latin American countries in terms of their feather production in the first world map he created for Chinese eyes in 1584.[87]

Ricci himself received a request from Peking, relayed to him by Zhaoqing officials in 1589, for several bolts of fine European scarlet woolen cloth, and he made the trip down to Macao in a boat provided by the mandarins. In Macao he used his contacts with local Portuguese merchants to buy everything the Chinese wanted, and "at a very good price," to boot.[88] An even tighter meshing of bilateral trade and mission policy occurred in 1585, when the brother of the former Zhaoqing prefect came from his home district far to the north, in Zhejiang province, with a load of fine silk that he hoped to sell at the Canton trade fair. Unable to dispose of the goods as he had hoped, he turned to the Jesuits, and in return for his undertaking to let them accompany him when he returned to Zhejiang so they could open a new mission there, the Jesuits arranged for Portuguese traders to buy up this particular batch of silk on the spot, and for a decent price.[89]

In each of these cases there was a clear mission purpose along with the financial manipulation: in the first, after making his feather purchases, Ruggieri was able to bring the missionary Edoardo de Sande back with him into China; in the second, after buying his scarlet cloth, Ricci had a chance to confer lengthily with Valignano; in the third, Ruggieri's silk trading gained him the opportunity to explore the mission possibilities in a new province.

In similar fashion, though the Jesuits were not a mendicant order, they showed from their earliest days in China a willingness to accept whatever alms were available. Ruggieri accepted free lodging and even a little food and fresh fish from officials in Canton at the dawn of the mission; Ricci accepted incense for the burners in their first chapel, and oil for the altar lamps there, from devout Chinese donors; he and Ruggieri together accepted loans from the Chinese in Macao to help them complete the building of their first house in Zhaoqing.[90] At other times there were cash gifts from the Chinese, left genteelly along with calling cards when they came to visit Ricci out of courtesy or curiosity, sometimes as much as ten ducats, sometimes five, at others just a handful of copper coins.[91] Some officials left sizable presents after seeing religious pictures like the small triptych of Christ, which Ricci carried in a protective glass case, or when they were given Christian religious tracts: the local army commander in Zhaoqing left three ducats after being given a version of the earliest commentary on Christianity that Ricci and Ruggieri had put into their still-tentative Chinese, and the ambassadors from Cochin China, passing through Zhaoqing en route to Peking, left silver and incense in exchange for several copies of the same little book. Other Chinese scholars gave chairs and tables, or decorative items for the various rented residences that the Jesuits had at different times.[92]

How much to accept was always a delicate problem, though most gifts could be justified one way or another. Ricci nearly always accepted means of travel, since this was so very expensive, and senior officials who were in a position to offer it normally got their conveyances free from the state. Thus even when short of ready cash he could travel in style, on luxury junks pulled upstream by toiling coolies, on boats escorted by troops and watchmen, on horseback to a picnic, or in sedan chairs with groups of up to eight bearers and pack animals for his baggage.[93] Even when he went out to dinner, wealthy Chinese hosts would pay his sedan-chair carriers and tip his accompanying servants. At other times generous Chinese friends simply gave large sums of silver to ease the pains of the journey, especially once Ricci was well known, or paid his expenses for a given journey in advance without telling him, so that a delighted Ricci, preparing to argue the bill for two cabins and the storage space for all the accoutrements of a chapel on a long-distance boat trip, would be told there was no charge since a friend had already given the boatman double what the trip could possibly cost.[94]

Such random Chinese generosity eased individual moments of Ricci's life, but could not support the work of the mission in any serious way, and would tail off to nothing whenever the political climate swung against the missionaries. In 1585 Valignano worked out an agreement with the viceroy of India, confirmed by King Philip II "in perpetuity," that each of the China missionaries should receive 100 ducats a year and some jugs of wine for the Mass. This sum would be derived from the transit dues collected from merchant ships at Malacca and transferred to the Jesuits by Portuguese traveling to the trade fairs each March and October.[95] In addition to income from the Japanese silk trade and from these royal allowances, the China Jesuits received numerous massive gifts from the Macao Portuguese, especially in the 1590s—one gift of 500 ducats for support of a native Chinese clergy, another of two silver chalices for use on the altars in China, others of hundreds more in cash or deeds to homes.[96]

There is no doubt that many donors were truly devout and wished the Jesuits well in their mission work in China, having no ulterior motive beyond the good of their own souls and the saving of Chinese ones. But others may have been prompted by gratitude to the Jesuits for help with a difficult financial-legal problem, the return of runaway

THE MEMORY PALACE OF MATTEO RICCI

slaves. Ricci himself was involved in these transactions and wrote quite openly about them; he had little reason to hide such matters in a world in which each Portuguese family in Macao had an average of five or six black male slaves (without counting those slaves' wives and children) and the Jesuits themselves in China had several black "Kaffir" and "Indian" servants and doorkeepers who were surely not free wage-laborers.[97] Many slaves fled from their masters in Macao and came into China, wrote Ricci, indenturing themselves there to local Chinese military commanders. The Chinese welcomed these slaves as "brave and spirited men," especially those whom the Portuguese had trained in bearing arms; some of the slaves were Japanese, "whom all the Chinese fear in war," while others were black Kaffirs and Javanese who still, even if less feared, "brought terror to the enemy."[98]

The Jesuit tactic was to try to identify those fugitive slaves who had been baptized as Christians, and to persuade them that it would be better in the long run to return to their masters and resume their lives in the Christian environment of Macao rather than to live out their lives among the heathen Chinese, especially since the Chinese in any case also "treated them just like slaves." When slaves expressed willingness to return, the Jesuits would negotiate with their owners and the bishop of Macao for full pardons; they then helped the slaves to get back across the border. "This not only helped the souls of many who might have been lost among the gentiles," as Ricci put it, "but also made a profit of many thousands of ducats for their owners who thus recovered slaves often of great value."[99]

If the Chinese were aware of these deals, the knowledge can only have increased the suspicion they had generally of Jesuit activities. Dislike of Macao among the Ming Chinese was widespread, as Ricci observed in one of his letters to General Acquaviva, and extended to any Chinese who made the decision to live there:

> Since Macao is at the outermost border of China, all those from there are held to be foreigners and people who can bring harm to China, and they are regarded with suspicion. And anyone who has

dealings with the place is seen as a mean person, suspected everywhere. So much so that in charges they might be bringing against each other, wishing to speak ill of their adversary, the Chinese will say, "He's a man who makes a habit of going to Macao." And this I've seen for myself.[100]

This passage suggests that the Ming Chinese had begun to realize that Macao had become an independent foreign enclave, and they thus extended the same hostility to Chinese Macaoans as they did to any Chinese settling overseas and hence abandoning their traditional values—that being the Confucian view. Ricci might have been even more determined to distance himself from the Portuguese if he had seen the description of them in the Ming scholar Zhang Xie's guide to foreigners and foreign travel: "The Portuguese are seven feet tall, have eyes like cats, and mouths like orioles: their faces are like white ash. Their beards are tightly curled, like black gauze, while the hair in their heads is almost red." Zhang added to his analysis some thoughts on the power of the Catholic priests who accompanied the Portuguese: they seemed to be numerous and powerful, had major influence on national policy, and chanted from their sacred books as criminals were being led to execution.[101]

Such patterns of fear and dislike had dogged the mission since its inception in 1583 when Ricci, settling in Zhaoqing, had to promise the Chinese officials—who were being violently pressured by their own townspeople—that he would not bring anyone else from Macao into the area. Ricci tried to disarm criticism by telling the Zhaoqing authorities that he sought to settle in their peaceful city *just because* it was "so far from the din of trade and other worldly things of Macao," but local Confucian degree-holders found this unconvincing. They warned that Ruggieri and Ricci were to Zhaoqing what the earliest Portuguese had been to Macao—an innocent-looking handful who would grow in numbers until it proved impossible to eject them.[102] When popular pressures at last forced the Jesuits' eviction from Zhaoqing in 1589, one of the reasons given was that the Jesuits' newly built house was on a river, and that down this river, traveling in swift illegal boats, they would speed at intervals to Macao to tell the Portuguese there all of China's secrets.[103]

To see the final pattern of Ricci's solution to the problem of trade and profit in China, one must backtrack to his use of presents. Ruggieri's ostrich had been but one unusually imaginative example in an endless drama—part dream, part reality—of what should or should not be given to the Chinese so as to achieve maximum success for the work of the church. At the most grandiose level Philip II's factor in the Philippines, Juan Battista Roman, seeking to open a port in China for Spanish commerce in the early 1580s, had suggested that Spain should send a royal embassy to Emperor Wanli's court, offering the emperor gifts worth from 60,000 to 70,000 ducats: these should include a dozen or more horses from New Spain; velvet, brocades, and cloth of gold; Flemish carpets, Venetian prisms and mirrors; large clocks, oil paintings, and glassware; red and white wine; swords and other gilded arms.[104] The Jesuits had backed the idea of such an embassy, and after the idea for the original one had foundered for lack of Spanish support, Valignano kept alive hopes for a formal papal embassy from Rome to Peking, suggesting that gifts costing from 4,000 to 6,000 ducats should be sent from the pope to the emperor, conveyed by four Jesuit fathers.[105] In the final event, the gifts that were to make possible Peking residence for the Jesuits for more than a century were procured for a little less than the 900 ducats that the rector of the Macao Jesuit establishment was able to scrape together after the loss of the 1599 carrack, plus whatever objects Ricci had with him at the time in China.[106] Nevertheless, it took eight packhorses and more than thirty porters, as Ricci proudly noted, to carry these gifts into Peking on a January day in 1601: there were three religious paintings, one of them the triptych of Christ in its glass case, one of the Virgin Mary and Child with John the Baptist in attendance, and one of the Virgin and Child together. (This last split into the three boards it was painted on when it was dropped by clumsy porters, and would thus have been worthless to European connoisseurs, as Ricci rather sardonically noted; but the breakage made it look all the older to the Chinese and thus enhanced its value.) There was one large clock, with hanging weights, and one smaller desk clock, spring-driven; a gilded breviary, and a handsome edition of Abraham Ortelius's cartographic masterwork, *Theatrum Orbis Terrarum.* There were prisms and hourglasses, colored belts and bolts of cloth, European silver coins, a rhinoceros horn (a valued commodity in traditional Chinese medicines), and a small harpsichord designed to be played not by means of a keyboard but by plucking the strings with a plectrum. (There would also have been a small hand organ with bellows, made to order for Ricci in Macao, but it arrived in Nanjing after he had already left for the north.)[107]

The Jesuits' loving itemization of these gifts shows how much store they set by them even as they knew how little they had cost by comparison with earlier, more grandiose plans. Believing that this was how European powers should show their wealth and skills to China's withdrawn but mighty emperor, Ricci was shocked to see how casually some other foreign tributary embassies treated this ritual gift-giving: in Peking's hostel for foreign visitors, where he was initially lodged, he found both how little store the Chinese set by their visitors, whom they put in tiny cubicles without furniture "like sheep stalls," and how the foreigners in return showed their contempt by presenting cheap metal swords with tacked-on wooden handles, "breastplates" that were no more than thin iron plates held together with oakum, or scraggly horses that looked ready to keel over—all things "sure to make you laugh," said Ricci.[108]

But the gift-giving and the lodging in the foreign hostel brought the Jesuits a government allowance from the Board of Rites consisting of rice and meat, salt, vegetables, wine, and firewood, enough for five people to live on, and a full-time servant to wait on them. Once out of the hostel, after ceaseless petitioning, the Jesuits got oral permission from the court, relayed through eunuchs, to rent a house in Peking; the state allowance of food for five was continued, and with it came eight ducats in silver each month. A few weeks later a senior official sympathetic to Ricci guaranteed the cash equivalent of the food allowance in case of nondelivery (which had happened too often for the Jesuits' comfort), another six ducats a month.[109] These were not lordly sums, but they were comforting, and they kept pace with still more gifts, such as the casually delivered present of silver worth forty ducats, along with bolts of cloth and furs, from the grand secretary Shen Yiguan in 1602. Reciprocating as convention required, Ricci gave Shen's son a prism of Venetian glass. As Ricci noted elsewhere, because of the purity of the light filtered through them, some Chinese believed these prisms to be worth anywhere from 200 to 500 ducats and called them "precious stones beyond price," whereas in fact any one of them could be replaced in Europe for eight *baiocchi* (a *baiocco* being a copper coin worth less than one-hundredth of a ducat in Italy).[110] With such varied sources of income now available, the Jesuits could ride out the temporary crises caused by the loss of the silk ships to storms or to privateers; above all, the open Chinese financial support offered to Ricci and his colleagues in Peking—plus the great distance that separated Peking from the cities of the south—laid to rest, for a time, that vexing problem of trying to prove the Jesuits were not bound hand and foot to the Portuguese in Macao.

Most of Ricci's successes were the result of careful calculation, not accident, though he could salute the occasional splendid windfalls brought to the Jesuits by others in their personal search for profit. It particularly pleased him, for instance, that Chinese non-Christians were trying to make a bit of extra cash by printing copies of his *True Meaning of the Lord of Heaven* and other religious books and selling them in the provinces, thus circulating the Christian message more widely than the Jesuits alone could ever have done.[111] But generally he took a hard look at the tasks confronting the mission and planned for a wide range of contingencies. The many New Testament exhortations concerning workers in the fields bringing in the sheaves and gathering a golden harvest were in his mind, but he was cautious not to claim—or expect—too much. "The time at which we now find ourselves in China," he told Girolamo Costa in 1599, "is not yet that of the harvest, nor even that of sowing, but rather of opening up the wild woods and fighting with the wild beasts and poisonous snakes that lurk within."[112] And nine years later he wrote to the same friend that though now in China, with four separate Jesuit bases established and the number of Jesuit fathers and brothers at work risen to twenty, he could claim they truly had a grand "machine"—a word with great resonance for Ricci, which he had used in praising the residence at Goa almost thirty years before—nevertheless he still felt "the fruit here is at the stage of sowing rather than that of harvest."[113]

How he used music to prepare for that possible harvest is illuminating. Though Ignatius of Loyola had expressly forbidden choral music in Jesuit services, fearing that it would distract the priests from their sacred duties and lead to the perception among laymen that the Jesuits were similar to the monks of other religious orders, this was one area in which his will had not prevailed, and the use of music—both sung and played—was widespread and popular in the order in Ricci's day.[114] Somewhat surprisingly, in view of his many other skills, Ricci was not a musician and had little ear for music despite the extensive knowledge of music he had doubtless obtained in Rome and Macerata. He did not have much sympathy for Chinese music. He noticed its effectiveness in public martial display and in religious services, but he found it hard to trace its harmonies, and he missed the keyboard instruments and four vocal lines to which he had been accustomed in Europe.[115] Nevertheless, one of the presents he had carried across China with him, and had finally been able to present to the court in 1601, was a small harpsichord. This present would have been a mere curiosity, perhaps indeed virtually useless, had not Ricci used some leisure time in Nanjing during 1600 to have the Jesuit father Lazzaro Cattaneo—who was a good musician but couldn't leave Nanjing because of his pastoral responsibilities—teach the newly arrived young priest Diego Pantoja to play several sonatas and also to tune the instrument.[116] Ricci subsequently took Pantoja with him to Peking and when, as Ricci had hoped, the emperor was intrigued enough by the harpsichord to order the Jesuits to teach four of his eunuch musicians to play it, Pantoja was ready and able to instruct them.

Again, Ricci's tact and anticipation were manifest. Since two of the four eunuchs were young and able to learn the Western music rapidly, while one elderly eunuch of seventy found the going very rough, Ricci had each of them taught only one piece, so that the older eunuch, even if slower—he took a month to learn his piece—would not lose face at court. While waiting, Ricci and the younger eunuchs composed eight songs in Chinese that could be sung with harpsichord accompaniment.[117]

Ricci's lyrics dealt, predictably, with moral and religious themes. He wrote of the striving of the human heart toward God, of the folly of our desire for long life, of how the grace of God fills the world more surely than the harmonies of musical instruments fill the hall in which they are played, of how youth glides by before we have time to think of leading a moral life, of how God makes us most glorious yet we debase ourselves, and of how death spares no one, being neither in awe of the king's palace nor compassionate to the poor man's hovel. The language was not particularly elegant but was designed to fit the pattern of short, sung lines while making its moral points in the clearest way possible. This is the second song of the cycle:

> A shepherd boy fell sad one day,
> Hating the hillside on which he stood;
> He thought a distant hill he saw
> More beautiful by far,
> And that going there would wipe away his sorrows.
>
> So he set off to that distant hill,
> But as he drew near to it
> It looked less good than it had from afar.
>
> O shepherd boy, shepherd boy,
> How can you expect to transform yourself
> By changing your dwelling place?
>
> If you move away can you leave yourself behind?
> Sorrow and joy sprout in the heart.

If the heart is peaceful, you'll be happy everywhere,
If the heart is in turmoil, every place brings sorrow.
A grain of dust in your eye
Brings discomfort speedily;
How can you then ignore this sharp awl
That pierces your heart?

If you yearn for things outside yourself
You will never obtain what you are seeking.
Why not put your own heart in order
And find peace on your own hillside?

Old and new writers alike give this advice:
There's no advantage to roaming outside,
Keep the heart inside, for
That brings the profit.[118]

Ricci's little cyle of eight songs became immediately popular in China among the intellectual elite, according to his own account, and copies were rapidly printed and circulated. Chinese bureaucrats who heard the songs, or read the words of the text, remarked to him how glad they were that such sentiments were now being made available within the court, where there was some room for moral improvement.[119] Because of the stern laws restricting access to the inner court to all save the imperial family, the eunuchs, and the concubines, Ricci of course would never hear the words he had written sung by the court musicians to Pantoja's music, but he had devised a number of plays on words within the songs themselves that must have given him quiet satisfaction when he imagined the eunuchs—or perhaps the concubines taught by them—chanting his words within the walls of the Forbidden City. For instance, in the final couplet of the second song in the cycle, quoted above, he contrasted the shortcomings of the life "outside" with the "inside" world. The words he used for "outside" and "inside" (the Chinese *wai* and *nei*) represented one of the great polarities in traditional Chinese political and moral thought, and could be applied not only to the differences in mental states, or in location, but also to the differences between barbarian foreigners and residents of the Middle Kingdom, or to the difference between the world outside the walls of the inner palace and the sheltered and secretive world within. Since the word for profit, *li* or *ly,* which ended the song, was also the word Ricci had taken for his own name, each time someone in the court sang the words "Keep the heart inside, for that brings the profit," he would also in fact be singing "Living inside the court, there's Ricci." It was not yet quite true, of course, but he hoped to get there eventually; and in the meantime those unheard voices would be carrying his dreams up into the quiet evening air.

SEVEN

THE THIRD PICTURE: THE MEN OF SODOM

For the third picture that will be placed in Cheng Dayue's book, Ricci chooses one of a series of prints telling the story of Lot's life, made by Crispin de Pas the Elder in Antwerp. De Pas illustrated Lot's life through four pictures. In the first, the Lord, having heard of the sin of Sodom, announces he will destroy the city. In the second, he blinds the men of Sodom as they strive to break into Lot's house to abuse the men (in fact they are angels) who have been sheltered there. In the third, Lot, his wife, and his two daughters flee the city under the angels' protection, just before the city is destroyed and Lot's wife, who has turned back to look, is transformed into a pillar of salt. In the fourth, the two daughters get their father to drink himself to dizziness and then sleep with him, so as to perpetuate their family line.[1]

Ricci wants the Chinese to be aware of the sin of Sodom and of the city's fate in the words of Genesis 19:24–25: "Then the Lord rained on Sodom and Gomorrah brimstone and fire from the Lord out of heaven; and he overthrew those cities, and all the valley, and all the inhabitants of the cities, and what grew on the ground." Unfortunately, as with St.

201

inspirande Possicit   et Got tri

Peter on the water, there is the slight problem that none of the four pictures available quite fits what Ricci wants to say. In the event he chooses the second picture from the de Pas cycle, because it shows the turmoil of the moment best: the angel stretching out his hand to blind the men of Sodom; Lot, hands clasped, pleading with them to desist; the men themselves tumbling to the ground or still reaching to seize the stranger, under the distant towers of their proud city. To make his point Ricci gives the story a clarity the Bible version does not contain, and though he had not spelled out the names of the Sea of Galilee or of Emmaus in his first two pictures, in this one he includes the closest transcription he can manage of the word "Sodom" so that the Chinese will have a focus for future discussion with the Jesuit fathers. He is careful, of course, that the syllable "ma" he uses to render the *m* sound at the end of Sodom is quite different from the "ma" of his own Chinese name. He titles his essay "Depraved sensuality and vileness bring on themselves the heavenly fire":

In ancient times the people of So-do-ma gave themselves up to depraved sensuality, and the Lord of Heaven turned away from them. Among them lived one pure man named Lo, so the Lord of Heaven sent his angels to get [Lo] to leave the city and go to the mountains. Then down from heaven rained a great fire of consuming flame, men and animals and insects were all burned up and nothing was left, even the trees and rocks were turned to ash and sank into the ground. From the mire was formed a lake that brought forth stinking waters and still today serves as testimony to how greatly the emperor of heaven hates unnatural sensuality and perverse lusts.

Lo was able to keep himself pure amidst the perversity, so heaven blessed him. Most people can behave well in the presence of goodness; but to stay pure and upright in the midst of unnatural customs, that truly calls for a courage that is rarely encountered. The wise man is happy when amongst good customs, and uses them to strengthen himself; he is also happy among evil practices, and uses them as a sharpening-stone for his own character. He can trust his own guidance in any circumstances.[2]

When one places this text of Ricci's next to the picture, one gets an even stronger effect than de Pas had intended. For it is these people whose faces we can study, these lofty domes and towers etched so sharply against the stormy sky that are going to be destroyed in the fire. It is across this piazza that will spread the noisome, eternal lake. And since the picture has only Lo and the angel, without the daughters and the wife, much cumbersome exegesis can be saved. Why the wife became a pillar of salt, or why the daughters slept with their father in these texts of long ago—the explanation of such problems can be left to another time and place.

When Pope Paul IV died in August 1559 at the age of eighty-three, the city of Rome dissolved in rioting and celebration. A crowd stormed into the elegant headquarters of the Inquisition and ransacked it, destroying records, releasing all the prisoners they found there, and finally setting fire to the building. The imposing statue of the pope recently erected on the Capitol was knocked to the ground. Somebody derisively placed a yellow hat—of the kind Paul IV had ordered the Jews of Rome to wear—on the statue's head as it lay in the street. Others dragged the main bulk of the statue away and threw it into the River Tiber. The pope was buried at night, almost furtively, "as deep as possible" in a vault in St. Peter's, and the tomb was kept under guard; outside, the streets filled with vendors hawking lampoons and satires on the dead pontiff and his three notorious nephews, the Carafa brothers.[3]

The irony of this reaction was that Paul IV had passionately wanted reform of the church and had lived a spartan, dedicated, deeply devotional life. But in pursuing his reformist policies he had roused hostility in all quarters. It was his intransigent hatred of Spain, his determination to curb Philip II's pretensions and recapture the Kingdom of Naples from the Spaniards, that had brought the duke of Alva's troops to the gates of Rome and the troops of the duke of Guise, in France's ill-fated counterintervention, into the streets of Macerata. Pope Paul had followed a ruthless policy of suppressing all public entertainments in the name of morality, arresting men found with their mistresses in the confines of the Vatican and sentencing them to life in the galleys, banning all hunting and even all dancing so that throughout the year in Rome, as a contemporary wrote, it was "as if we were in the midst of Lent."[4] He had launched a merciless campaign against the Jews in Rome and in Ancona, arresting Christians who had Jewish mistresses, forcing the Jews themselves to live in enclosed ghettos, and forbidding them to trade in any foodstuffs with Christians or to act as physicians for them; by forcing the Jews to sell most of their property in the papal domain, he acquired vast estates for the church at around half a million ducats—about one-fifth their true value. He attended the key policy meetings of the Inquisition punctiliously every Thursday, and gave the inquisitors totally new powers, such as the right to pursue those guilty of sexual misconduct as well as those guilty of heresy or errant doctrine: those who sexually abused women or procured prostitutes were arrested; those convicted of sodomy were executed, some by public burning.[5] In this last context, it was especially ironic to the Roman citizens that one of the pope's three powerful nephews, Cardinal Carlo Carafa—besides living in a style of almost unimagined splendor and having a passion for hunting and gambling—was a notorious philanderer whose amours with lovers of both sexes seem to have been common knowledge to all but the pope. The mocking poems to the cardinal's young male lover, with their echoes of Ovid's love poems and Textor's description of Ganymede, written by the great French poet Joachim du Bellay who was then living in Rome, were merely the most elegant of the many insulting writings that circulated at the time. Carlo Carafa was executed by his uncle's successor, Pius IV, in 1560— dying in particularly horrible pain because the ropes with which the executioner was trying to garrot him broke twice just as he was losing consciousness.[6]

Ricci was only a child in Macerata while these events were unfolding and can have known little of them, save from travelers and perhaps from sermons. But the moral of the tale was a universal one: it spoke to the interconnections of power and weakness, to the overlap between moralistic censoriousness and public contempt of conventional norms. It fitted perfectly with the biblical vision, as one might find it in the book of the prophet Isaiah, where the fate of Sodom was an allegory for the fate of the earth, constantly reiterated by an angry God. To Isaiah, the beggars in their misery, the gorgeous women with bells tinkling on their feet, the concubines, the drunken men in their vomit, the eunuchs, all spoke for a world of Babylon that could destroy others as swiftly as it would be itself destroyed. Here sodomy was the punishment for idolatry, as fire and brimstone were the punishments for sodomy; here Isaiah cried out to the good king Hezekiah, "Of thy sons that shall issue from thee, which thou shalt beget, shall they take away; and they shall be eunuchs in the palace of the king of Babylon."[7]

It was not just from rumors and from the biblical prophets that Ricci derived some knowledge of the potent presence of luxury, poverty, and vice in the cities of his time. Macerata had rung with scandals during his childhood, and was filled with stories of the murders that sprang from sexual passion, or of the social problems caused by those born out of wedlock.[8] During the 1570s, also, Macerata was agitated by debates as to where to locate the prostitutes' dwellings, whether to concentrate them all in one place and, if so, where; each choice by the city fathers aroused predictable opposition from local residents.[9]

The streets of Rome, by the same token, had as broad a spectrum of human nobility and degradation as one could find in any city of the time. The more religious one was, indeed, the more one might see, for beggars tended to cluster around each church according to whether special services were scheduled there. There were "so manie and so miserable persons," wrote Gregory Martin, who "hedge in the way on both sides, that I never saw the like." Among the crippled, the mad, the blind, the mute or deaf, Martin was told, were many who had refused the shelter of the city's charity hospitals, preferring to lie out in the streets and take their chances from the city's church-bound passersby; for they hoped to get more from casual charity than the seven daily coppers ordained for their support by Pope Pius IV.[10] He probably did not know, any more than Ricci did, that many of these beggars were carefully organized by their own secret leaders into some nineteen subgroups or "specialties," and were carefully coached in such roles as appearing diseased, maimed, veterans of Turkish wars, or possessed by the devil, so as to get maximum public sympathy.[11] Yet both would have been fully aware of another side of the city's constant social misery, since the unwanted children of the desperately poor or of prostitutes were kept in the city's consciousness—and conscience—by the great processions in which they paraded, sometimes over four hundred strong, to selected churches on saints' days, to manifest the charity they had received. Ignatius of Loyola had particularly concerned himself with the fate of these children, and had helped set up charitable foundations to nurture them.[12]

In the late sixteenth century there were between six hundred and nine hundred registered prostitutes in Rome, charging anywhere from one to twelve ducats, and many more who were reduced to this means of making a living for smaller sums in times of dearth. Those who were associated in some ways with prostitution—providing lodging, procuring, serving—numbered perhaps ten times more, and this out of a population that totaled only around one hundred thousand. Papal attempts to limit prostitution to certain narrow corners of the city failed repeatedly, and major banks were driven to insolvency if the women chose to act in concert and withdraw their money all together.[13]

How one viewed the pattern of social exploitation and misery naturally depended on one's angle of vision. Gregory Martin was impressed by the sternness with which prostitution was controlled in Rome during the 1570s, even though he recognized that a papal attempt of 1567 to ban them from the city altogether had failed. He described the way the prostitutes were restricted to certain quarters of the city, and so "plagued by lawes and Ordinances" that one could see "how small comforts they have toward their beastly living." Forced to wear short veils over their faces and a special style of dress, denied the right to make wills, to have Christian burial, or to ride in coaches, they were kept in perpetual humiliation.[14] But Montaigne, as he sojourned in Rome in 1581, was more impressed by the prostitutes' omnipresence; he described how taking coach rides or strolling to view the prostitutes was a major Roman pastime, the prostitutes displaying themselves at their windows or on their balconies "with such deceptive art that I am often amazed how much they attracted our gaze. And often, having on impulse dismounted from my horse and had the door opened for me, I was filled with admiration to see how much prettier they had appeared to be than they really were." Other Romans would eye the women through specially designed holes cut in the roofs of their carriages, a kind of "stargazing"that a Roman preacher described, in an amusing wordplay which Montaigne appreciated, as "the making of astrolabes out of our coaches."[15]

However Ricci opened or closed his eyes to the situation in Rome, beggary and prostitution, with the addition of slavery, would have been even more obvious to him during his residence in Lisbon, between 1577 and 1578. An international trading city, headquarters of the overseas Portuguese empire, Lisbon was filled at once with local merchants, workers bound for the Indies or Brazil, the widows of sailors dead at sea, and impoverished farmers or their children who had fled the arid countryside.[16] Slaves were everywhere in Lisbon, according to the Florentine merchant Filippo Sassetti, who was also living in the city during 1578. Black slaves were the most numerous, but there were also a scattering of Chinese and Japanese among them. One could watch potential buyers putting these slaves through their paces in the streets before deciding to purchase, making them run and jump and opening their mouths to check their teeth; they cost anywhere from thirty to sixty ducats a head.[17] In Goa, one found the same social derelicts, and a new element, the mixed population of half-caste Chinese and Indians, born often from the melancholy trade in kidnapped children that the Portuguese—with the willing assistance of Chinese petty criminals—had built up in Macao.[18]

The Jesuits had slaves working for them in Goa—it was not a society in which white men did any kind of physical labor—and slavery was commonplace in Macao, where slaves outnumbered freemen five to one.[19] Ricci discussed quite openly in his *Historia* his activist role in returning runaway slaves in China to the Portuguese authorities in Macao, and he himself had black slaves—*"gente negra dell'India"* and a *"cafro assai negro"*—with him in China, at least during the early years of his mission, to work in the Jesuit residence as household staff and watchmen.[20] Other blacks served him as interpreters in the years before he learned Chinese well—they may have been the offspring of marriages between Chinese residents of Macao and black slaves, whose children were raised as Christians and spoke both Chinese and Portuguese, making them ideal for the job. Ricci acknowledged on one occasion that these blacks frightened the Chinese, and references to them do not occur later in his mission; he probably switched gradually to Chinese servants as his language improved.[21]

There was also a steady sale of Chinese as slaves overseas, as Ricci knew. He had no moral judgment to offer on this practice, only the observation that this might be one of God's ways to get the Chinese converted to Christianity, since sometimes these slaves were bought by Spaniards and Portuguese and were later converted by their masters or local priests.[22] Many of those sold overseas had not been slaves in China but were kidnapped in southeastern China and sold to foreign buyers at a surprisingly consistent rate of fifteen to twenty ducats each for girls or boys; some were from educated families, and ended up as secretaries or assistants to Portuguese historians and military men. The traffic continued, despite a decree stipulating an incredible fine of one thousand ducats for any Portuguese found guilty of buying or selling Chinese slaves which was put on the books by the Goa viceroy in 1595.[23]

Ricci placed much of the blame for Chinese slavery on the Chinese themselves, and linked its extension throughout Chinese society to defects in the Chinese character, such as their combination of lust and timorousness.[24] In taking this stance, he was giving a sort of analogy to his view of Chinese society in general. In no sense was he an uncritical admirer of China, as he is sometimes taken to be; he was in fact profoundly torn about how to assess the country and its government, and he never reached a synthesis. He merely presented two sets of irreconcilable views which, between them, doubtless he felt approximated reality.

On the positive side there was much that he could admire in its own right, and even compare favorably to Europe. China's geographical size and diversity, the enormous range of crops grown there (almost the only things he found lacking were olives and almonds), the small, beautifully tended market gardens, the love of flowers, the porcelain from Jiangxi—"the finest and loveliest thing in the world"—their ingenious use of coal for cooking and heating, the connoisseurship concerning antique bronzes, ink paintings, and calligraphy, the sophistication and cheapness of Chinese printing, all roused his admiration.[25] Of the Confucian moral system he took a favorable, even an idealized view, since he wished to prove to the rulers of his own church that the Chinese would be natural converts. Their funeral rites and ancestral ceremonies were not superstitious, he concluded, and the Confucian ceremonies conducted by the magistrates were divorced from religious significance, even though they did burn incense and offer animal sacrifice; being a follower of Confucianism itself was like having membership in an academy rather than being a believer in a specific theological creed. Certainly the Chinese had a pantheistic view of the universe, and the rich were given to polygamy, but apart from that—and if they would eschew Buddhism and/or Taoism—they "could certainly become Christians, since the essence of their doctrine contains nothing contrary to the essence of the Catholic faith, nor would the Catholic faith hinder them in any way, but would indeed aid in that attainment of the quiet and peace of the republic which their books claim as their goal."[26]

To aid in the attainment of this morality, the Chinese had an integrated bureaucracy, supervised by a staff of censors whom Ricci likened to the five magistrates who had imposed order in ancient Sparta. Thus despite the emperor's power China had "many elements of a republic," for the emperor responded always to his ministers' initiatives, and those same ministers had the final say over the disposition of the huge annual income of one hundred and fifty million ounces of silver that came in from taxes and dues.[27] Even in their religious practices the Chinese showed little of the kind of "indecent behavior" toward their own gods that had been so common among Romans, Greeks, and Egyptians. Indeed, one could say that "none of the gentiles known to us in Europe fell into fewer errors in regard to matters of religion."[28]

But serpents lurked in these ideal gardens. At one point in the middle of his *Historia* Ricci set up an elaborate rhetorical structure to make the point, as he described the Buddhist temple complex outside Shaozhou to which he was invited when he first visited the city:

> We found there a level valley, sheltered at the end and on both sides by mountains of medium height, covered with fruit trees and other decorative trees that stay green all the year round. The land was all sown with rice and other vegetables, irrigated by a stream that never ran dry, but coursed through the middle of the valley to the green mountains beyond, a copious flow of pure water that bathed everything there.[29]

Yet this lovely site, this veritable Chinese Eden, was the home of the shrine to a monk who, eight hundred years before, had made a mockery of asceticism, in Ricci's eyes, by letting maggots feed on his own torn flesh. Those Chinese monks who now lived there had lost even this sense of distorted piety, and made a fitting contrast to the lyrical landscape: "They live in a truly dissolute way, and not only do many of them have wives and children, which is forbidden by their monastic rule, they are also robbers, and killers of those who pass along the road."[30] So had the people of China and their rulers slid downward from a state of nobler and partially forgotten purity into a cycle of dishonesty and greed in which terrible beatings were commonplace and watchmen were needed to watch the watchmen in a land that crawled with thieves. The exquisite external courtesy of the Chinese hid a situation in which no one could trust anyone else—not one's fellow provincials, not one's friends, not one's relatives, not even one's own children. The economic life of the country, too, was fractured, for there were always two prices for every object in the markets—"one for the local people and one, which is much less, for the officials who are numerous everywhere" and could buy at these fake prices whatever they wanted from artisans and merchants, so that many honest workers were forced to flee.[31]

In a letter to his former schoolmate at the Roman college, Giulio Fuligatti, only shortly after he entered China, in November 1585, Ricci had described the terror of their ruler in which the ordinary people lived: the magistrates held their public audiences with more pomp and show than did the pope in Rome, he wrote, while the emperor was locked up in a miserable magnificence amid his palaces, his women, his eunuchs, his songbirds, and his flowering trees, like the Assyrian despot Sardanapalus.[32] Ricci later elaborated on this idea, observing that the emperor had grown so frightened that he held no more audiences for his courtiers and did not dare go out unless privately in one of a procession of identical carriages; the ruler seemed "as if in the land of his greatest enemy who wishes to kill him" rather than in his own domain, and his life became "like a reflection of hell."[33]

This reflection of hell, for Ricci, was composed of many elements. One was the grandeur that he dwelt on at length. The great courtyards in the Forbidden City palace, where Ricci went in 1602 to prostrate himself in gratitude before the empty throne, could have held 30,000 people, he wrote, and the emperor's elephants, the three thousand royal guards, and the huge walls all increased the sense of majesty and power.[34] Both in his *Historia* and his letters he marveled at the size of the trees brought from southern China by water to reconstruct the imperial palaces, of the huge cedar beams that were priced anywhere from one thousand to three thousand ducats by the time they reached the capital. He had stood at the door of the Jesuit residence and watched the foundation stones for the palace buildings come rumbling by on gigantic carts hauled by one hundred mules—each stone also costing one thousand ducats, he was told, although they came from quarries quite nearby, while the palaces themselves were costing an estimated three million gold pieces, perhaps thirty million ducats or more at contemporary levels of exchange.[35]

The construction of Emperor Wanli's tomb at the Ming imperial burial grounds, ringed by mountains, to the northwest of the capital, was on an even vaster scale, and with a corresponding rise in the cost of stone, lumber, bricks, and transportation. The emperor attended with passionate interest to every phase of this tomb construction, which had begun before he was twenty.[36] Ricci and his young musician friend Diego Pantoja both cleverly played on the emperor Wanli's interest in the splendor of his tomb; when he sent them a list of questions about European customs—relayed by court eunuchs—which included a question on royal funerals, the Jesuits prepared a careful response in which they dwelt on all the details of Philip II of Spain's death and burial, which had occurred in September 1598. They told Wanli (again, via the eunuch messengers) how King Philip's inner coffin of lead had been placed inside another of wood, and then both placed within a sepulcher of stone in a specially constructed church.[37] They also gave him a religious print of the genre known as "The Name of Jesus," which showed the Holy Roman emperor, the pope, and various kings and queens kneeling between the angels and the inferno at their day of judgment; this so captured Wanli's imagination that he had his court painter copy it on a large scale in color. The success of this venture led them to offer Wanli a large picture of the piazza and church of St. Mark's in Venice, and a book containing a whole series of detailed prints of the church of San Lorenzo in King Philip's palace at the Escorial, though this latter, they learned to their chagrin, was kept for himself by a senior eunuch and never reached the emperor.[38] The emperor Wanli apparently roared with laughter when told that European rulers sometimes lived on the upper floors of their high buildings, so absurd did such an idea seem to him. This prompted in Ricci the reflection that "thus are all people kept content to remain in the modes in which they were brought up."[39] Yet ultimately this enigmatic figure of Wanli, so apparently autocratic at one level, so hedged in with restrictions at another, had a powerful effect on Ricci. If we may judge from his intense admiration for his younger Jesuit contemporary, Pierre Coton, which he expressed on his deathbed, Ricci may have dreamed at some level of one day becoming confessor to Wanli, as Coton had for that reconverted Catholic Henry IV, king of Navarre and France.[40]

But Ricci was never to speak to the emperor, let alone convert him, and in a world in which the emperor restricted his conversation to his palace women and eunuchs, the power of the latter was bound to rise, for they became the only intermediaries with the bureaucrats outside the palace walls. All of Ricci's dealings with the emperor were conducted via the eunuchs, and here again he had a split view of the situation, as one might expect from someone who read the Bible with care. For in the book of Daniel (1:3–4) had not Nebuchadnezzar called on his chief eunuch to select from the captured Israelites those who were "skillful in all wisdom, and cunning in knowledge, and understanding science," so that they might be trained in the Chaldean language and fitted "to stand in the king's palace"? As Ricci labored at his scientific works with the eunuchs of Peking, it is clear from numerous examples that many of them impressed him favorably. In addition to the four eunuchs from the palace music department to whom he taught his songs while Pantoja taught the harpsichord, there were four other eunuchs whom he taught to wind and service the palace clocks in 1601, and those with whom he assembled the clocks' exquisitely carved and decorated outer casings; and besides these were the eunuchs from the department of mathematics who helped him assemble the twelve sets of the giant map of the world that the emperor—on a sudden whim that could not be refused—ordered to be delivered for himself and his family in the early months of 1608. These men became "our friends" to Ricci, and when they visited the Jesuits' Peking house they behaved in the "most affectionate way" (*con molto amore*).[41]

Other examples show that he also got on well with several eunuchs who had real power in the political world. Ricci knew that, though often "from the lowest classes of society," under Wanli they were also "the servants, councilors and, moreover, friends of the king, so we can say they govern the kingdom."[42] The old eunuch Feng Bao—megalomaniac, deaf, and eager for one of Ricci's Venetian glass prisms though he might be—received Ricci with extreme pomp and graciousness at his palace in Nanjing in 1599. And the eunuch Ma Tang, who had emerged by the 1590s as one of the most powerful figures in the country—prominent officials warned Ricci that they could never try to boss Ma Tang—overwhelmed Ricci with the acrobatic shows he invited him to in Tianjin during 1600: jugglers tossed three large knives at once, acrobats swiveled huge porcelain pots on their feet and then proceeded to do the same with porcelain drums and large wooden tables, a boy dancer produced a model figure and then frolicked and tumbled with it on the floor in a startlingly realistic way—all of this was "charming," as Ricci had to admit.[43]

Eunuchs were at the forefront of at least three major crises during Ricci's residence in China, to all of which he referred in his historical writings. In one crisis during 1598–99, after the war with Hideyoshi, the accidental burning of part of the Peking palaces brought eunuchs to central and southern China in search of funds, in pursuit of which they recklessly thrust into people's houses, tyrannized and blackmailed to get their quotas, and caused massive risings of townsmen and manual laborers in such cities as Linqing and Suzhou.[44] It may have been in connection with the unrest and terror of the time that a courier traveling for Ricci between Nanchang and Nanjing was robbed and murdered, and his corpse then thrown into the river.[45]

The second case involved the wave of terror launched by Emperor Wanli and his eunuchs in 1603, following the appearance of an anonymous pamphlet, circulated in Peking, which attacked the emperor's favorite consort, and those who were conspiring to make her son heir apparent in place of the emperor's unloved elder child. Ricci wrote vividly of the unlicensed arrests at this time, the omnipresent spies, the torturing of literati, and the death of the influential Buddhist monk Zhenke. Zhenke did not survive the beating of thirty blows with a bamboo pole that Emperor Wanli ordered him given because of his alleged complicity in the writing of the pamphlet. Zhenke, a deeply religious and ascetic man, and a fine scholar and essayist who was friendly with many of China's leading intellectuals of the time, including the great dramatist Tang Xianzu, was sixty when he died. In a harsh aside that showed how deeply his hostility to Buddhism had become rooted, Ricci noted that people despised Zhenke because, though "he was wont to boast of caring nothing for the things pertaining to his body, afterward, while being beaten, he cried out like any other profane mortal."[46]

The last instance concerned the eunuch Gao Cai, who recklessly persuaded the emperor to send officials to Manila in pursuit of the rumor that there were, in Luzon, mountains of solid silver and gold. The presence of this Chinese expedition, and the ever-growing number of Chinese traders and artisans settling in the Philippines, persuaded the Spaniards that an invasion was imminent and led to the terrrible massacre of 1603 in which close to twenty thousand Chinese lost their lives. Ricci's main worry was that the Peking Jesuits might be associated with the Spaniards' acts, and he described his anxieties at the time in a letter of early 1605 to his friend Maselli in Rome: "There was much talk at court here about the matter and we were afraid some harm might come from it, because we had always been careful not to let ourselves be known as friends of [the Spaniards] up to the time of this event." This deception was almost ruined when a letter written by a Spaniard in Manila was brought back to Fujian province by one of the Chinese officials who had gone to the Philippines. As Ricci continued,

It was translated into Chinese and sent on to Peking, with the description that it had been written "in the year 1603 of the Lord of Heaven" which is just the same form I had used in my catechism. But God chose to have no one notice this, except for Dr. Paul, whom I warned not to say anything to anyone else. And another thing that helped us in not being known as people of the same religion was that they translated the name of God into Spanish as Díos while we use the Portuguese form, which is Deus.[47]

This care the Peking fathers took to separate themselves in the Chinese view from the Spaniards and the Philippines was probably made easier by the eunuchs' intense preoccupation with their own affairs, and the disintegrating influence or involvement of the upper bureaucracy with government. The "Dr. Paul" that Ricci referred to in his letter was the Shanghai scholar Xu Guangqi, the convert who was helping Ricci translate Euclid, and Xu clearly felt it quite correct to keep this damaging evidence away from his colleagues in the Hanlin Academy, some of whom, especially the Buddhists, might have been happy to use it against Ricci.

Ricci could, by 1605, be fairly confident that when there was a payoff in the air for someone, little action would be taken to harm him. Corruption could be protective, in a way:

> This king is extremely cruel to the eunuchs of his own palace and often has them beaten to death on the smallest pretext. Thus none of them concentrate their attention on business from outside the palace, unless it is the kind of matter that promises to provide a good sum of money. And the court mandarins have learned to do the same thing, which is to demand money from those who come from the provinces on court business, making these provincial mandarins pay them a part of the money they have flayed from the people in the countryside and the cities. So has this city become a true Babylon of confusion, full of every sort of sin, with no trace of justice or piety in anyone, or any desire on the part of anyone to cleanse himself.[48]

The rhetoric of this piece is astonishingly like the kind of charges that Reformation priests had launched against Rome and its corrupted popes as the "whore of Babylon," an echo reinforced by Ricci's charge that the Buddhist church itself represented "a Babylon of doctrines so intricate that no one can understand it properly, or describe it." In this corrupted city of Peking, wrote Ricci in his moralistic mood, lived "an effeminate people, given to pleasure" (*gente effeminata, deliziosa*).[49]

As a friend of the rich, Ricci was at least familiar with some of the social background of these excesses, because he had written that before a departure from an office or a city one often attended "seven or eight such parties, given by one's friends, so as to both receive and give favor." He showed that this was not a casual observation by the precision of his remark that Chinese "wine is rather like beer and not very strong, and though you get drunk, if you drink too much you feel fine the next morning." Yet he belied this jocularity in the picture he gave of the prevalence of massive drunkenness in Peking—of city streets down which staggered "men full of wine, tumbling to the ground, speaking and doing countless insulting things." The only difference here between the poor and the mandarins was that the latter, shaming their office by their debauches, could be carried home in the curtained seclusion of their sedan chairs.[50]

Ricci had a clear view of the misery and poverty in Peking. We cannot tell if he knew of the roving street gangs there, often composed of that most desperate of social flotsam, youngsters who after being castrated by their parents' orders had failed to get palace jobs and now drifted around, tyrannizing poor tradesmen.[51] Nor do we know if he understood all the complex patterns in the shifting Peking exchange rates between the silver of the well-to-do and the copper coins used by the poorer classes that led thousands of the poor to die in the 1590s even while the system of charitable relief was collapsing because of inept management and bureaucratic neglect.[52] His friend and convert Xu Guangqi was an expert on the miseries of the poor; he could have described for Ricci the old warehouses full of straw or animal fur where in winter, for the price of a copper coin, beggars could burrow in at night to avoid freezing to death.[53]

We do know that in the course of his visits to talk on scientific and religious topics with the Confucian elite of the city Ricci crisscrossed Peking, for he has left an unforgettable picture of himself riding in the streets, wearing a black veil over his face as all the wealthier locals did to shield themselves from the biting dust storms that made Peking such a nightmare in the dry months. As Ricci traveled thus, on a rented horse or mule, carrying with him his printed street directory of the houses of the notables, he could take advantage of the anonymity his veil afforded to gaze around with extra care.[54]

Ricci remarked of China that "this country is full of slaves." He ascribed this state of affairs partly to the natural lust of the men: "Unable to live without women, and not having the money to buy them, they sell themselves into slavery to some rich man, so that he will give them as wife one of his woman slaves; thus they and their children remain slaves forever more." Others, who had enough money to marry free women, found themselves unable to support their children and subsequently sold them for two or three ducats, "less than one would pay for a pig or a worn-out horse," wrote Ricci sadly, and this low price was the going rate even when there was no famine in the land; when there was, prices dropped to a tenth of that level.[55] Ricci went much further than this in certain passages of his original draft of the *Historia* which were cut from the published version of the book by his cautious Jesuit editors in the seventeenth century. Ricci saw, embedded in the Chinese character, a sensuality that made the males unwilling to wait until maturity—which he saw as twenty years of age—before choosing sexual partners. Many young men had their first women when they were fifteen or even fourteen, with the result "that many became so weakened that they could never thereafter have children." Besides this, he wrote, "the entire kingdom is full of public prostitutes, quite apart from the cases of domestic adultery, which are well enough known. Just here in Peking alone they say that there are forty thousand on public display; these women do this either because they chose to or, which is a much graver injustice, because they were bought by impure men, who by force made them earn their living in this filthy way."[56] Ming contemporaries would have endorsed at least Ricci's observation on the numbers and the visibility of prostitutes, noting that they could be found even in small villages, and could be counted in the thousands in the larger cities. In Peking (as in Rome), they were registered by the state and had to pay a tax; and though they did not lounge literally in the doorways, as they did in Florence, the brothels had special doors, hinged in the middle, so that when the upper half was hanging ajar passersby could gaze at leisure at those for sale within.[57]

The Jesuits themselves in China had to face disquieting charges of sexual misconduct. They had not been long in Zhaoqing when a Chinese convert accused Father Ruggieri of committing adultery with a married woman of the town, a charge in which the woman's husband concurred, claiming that he had beaten the truth out of her. This was a classic case of a shakedown, and Ruggieri was able to clear his name.[58] Father Longobardi was similarly charged in the city of Shaozhou and was cleared only when the woman he was alleged to have slept with was put to the torture by the local magistrate and exonerated Longobardi while, at the same time, confessing to adultery with several other local men.[59] Such rumors were constantly fanned by the Chinese, who staged plays on market days in the little towns, mocking the Christians and the Portuguese, who kept their swords and their rosaries in action at the same time, and let their priests mix indiscriminately with local women. These plays were reinforced by comic prints attacking the Jesuits and their converts, which enjoyed a brisk sale, as well as by lengthy written affidavits posted by the literati themselves.[60]

Ricci may have been thinking of these unfortunate plays when he wrote that the young actors of China were "the vilest and most vicious people in this whole country," and described the way many of them were bought by their masters as children and then taught to dance and sing.[61] But it is more likely that these heavily made-up young male singers enforced the agitation that he felt at the presence of male prostitutes in Peking, and at the obvious extent of male homosexuality there:

That which most shows the misery of these people is that no less than the natural lusts they practice unnatural ones that reverse the order of things: and this is neither forbidden by law, nor thought to be illicit, nor even a cause for shame. It is spoken of in public, and practiced everywhere, without there being anyone to prevent it. And in some towns where this abomination is most common—as in this capital city of the country—there are public streets full of boys got up like prostitutes. And there are people who buy these boys and teach them to play music, sing, and dance. And then, gallantly dressed and made up with rouge like women these miserable men are initiated into this terrible vice.[62]

These lines were written in 1609 or 1610, near the end of Ricci's life, but he had expressed similar sentiments in 1583, when he had been in China only a few weeks, writing to Valignano about "the horrible sin to which everyone here is much given, and about which there seems to be no shame or impediment."[63] In taking this position before he can have had much evidence one way or the other, and in reinforcing it a quarter of a century later after detailed observation, Ricci was expressing a moral outrage totally in line with his times. Indeed, the two men who had published accounts of China before Ricci traveled there had both written in similar terms. Galeote Pereira wrote of the Chinese that "the greatest fault we do find in them is sodomy, a vice very common in the meaner sort, and nothing strange among the best."[64] Friar Gaspar da Cruz said much the same, adding that this "unnatural vice" was "in no wise reproved among them," and that the Chinese expressed surprise when he spoke against it, claiming "that they had never had any who told them that it was a sin, nor an evil thing done."[65] Da Cruz ascribed the vengeance that God took on certain Chinese cities in the late 1550s, in the form of terrible earthquakes followed by lightning bolts that destroyed whole communities, to the prevalence of this vice. He emphasized the point by noting that the Chinese man who brought the news of these catastrophes "was so frightened that it appeared to him as if the whole province of Sanxi was desolated, just as the daughters of Lot, seeing the destruction of Sodom and Gomorrah, thought that the whole world had perished." And da Cruz concluded that this catastrophe and its causes might indeed portend the coming of the Antichrist.[66]

Both Friar Gaspar de Cruz and Father Matteo Ricci were reacting as loyal members of a church that, while in principle committed to a condemnation of all fleshly lusts, reacted with particular vehemence to any male sexual indulgence that did not lead to the possibility of procreation. This moral stand had been given solemnity by the writings of Thomas Aquinas, who identified natural intercourse as being that union of the sexes practiced universally by the birds and animals, an example that humans were told to emulate. Thus masturbation and— from the logic of Aquinas's argument—both homosexual liaisons and male anal intercourse with women were strictly forbidden. In the stern words of Aquinas's *Summa Against the Gentiles,* "after the sin of murder, whereby a human nature already in actual existence is destroyed, this sort of sin seems to hold the second place, whereby the generation of human nature is precluded."[67] Deeply built into this later Christian condemnation of homosexuality was the association of such practices with Islam. The earliest Western translations of the Koran pointed to the apparent toleration of homosexuality that is mentioned there, and numerous late medieval sources referred to homosexuality freely indulged in, to the existence of catamites and male brothels, or to the sexual abuse of male slaves. Among the earliest laws of the kingdom of Jerusalem, established by Christians after the First Crusade, was one calling for the burning of "sodomites," and extraordinarily dramatic descriptions of the Muslims' violating of captured Christian boys, men, clerics, and bishops were circulated in Europe to give added impetus to support for the Crusades. Ricci himself, in fulminating against the painted youths of Peking, used language almost identical to that used by William of Adam in attacking the catamites of Islam three centuries before.[68]

One can see something of the extension of these ideas in a casual remark made by Martin Luther in an otherwise far from casual—indeed, intense and moving—letter that he wrote to his friend Justin Jonas in 1542 in an attempt to reconcile him to the death of his wife in childbirth. "For who is not weary of the abominations of our world?" wrote Luther, "—if it ought to be called a world and not a very hell of evils with which those Sodomites torment our souls and eyes day and night"; here Luther made clear that by Sodomites he meant "Turks,

Jews, papists, and cardinals."[69] Naturally such a mocking association of groups was unacceptable to Catholics, and we find Jesuits like the celebrated Peter Canisius, so dominant in the intellectual life of the order in the 1570s and 1580s, restating an updated version of Aquinas's doctrine on homosexuality with passionate vigor in his *Catechism*. Canisius drew together the classic biblical texts, which included the fate of Sodom and Gomorrah as described in Genesis (chapters 18 and 19), the Lord's comment on the cities as recorded by the prophet Ezekiel (chapter 16), and the dire warning in Leviticus (18:22) that men shall "not deal together carnally" as they do with women, "because it is abomination." Many church fathers, and indeed Luther as well, had interpreted the sin of Sodom to be primarily composed of a mixture of greed, sloth, and indifference to the plight of the poor, but Canisius made it clear that he rejected such a reading as inadequate. The men of Sodom, he wrote, as well as failing to help "the poor and needy" were "guilty of this most abominable vice which fears not to violate the law of God, yea, and the law of nature."[70]

It was very much this type of interpretation that Ricci heard as a schoolboy in Macerata, when Pius IV's fulminations against homosexuality were presented there in 1566. These, too, were the interpretations that the Jesuits took with them as they traveled to the East in the late sixteenth century, reinforced by the general sense of the time that vices of all kinds flourished more easily in hot climates.[71] A Jesuit landing at Goa could write home almost immediately that "the heat is great here by day and night, and most of those in the college sleep without bed covers, wearing always light drawers and a sleeveless shirt, and by day wear only a very light cotton vest; the heat enervates everyone." And we know that the Jesuits in charge of the dormitories in Goa had speedily abandoned the attempt to enforce their customary rules that all those in their care should sleep properly covered, with the window shutters closed.[72]

Some observers, like the Italian merchant Francesco Carletti, were transfixed with admiration at the resulting sensuality; the men in wide-sleeved, dangling, loose white clothes, the women looking as if they were "formed on a lathe," with their limbs "sculptured and in relief, in such a way that the eye can judge exactly how they are made." Striving for a simile that would explain the dress of the Indian women in greater clarity, Carletti chose to say that they were pleated "in the manner in which surplices and other garments of the religious are pleated, without starch, as the water and burning sun of that region are enough to hold those pleats and keep them stiff."[73] The description may well have been accurate, but the association of ideas was altogether unfortunate, and perhaps suggests one reason for the passion with which local clerics moved to root out all thoughts of male homosexuality in the Goa region. Letters from the Goa inquisitor spoke of the spread of this "infamy" and the need for harsh measures. Men caught committing sodomy were publicly burned in Goa, as they were in Rome.[74]

There was nothing localized about the distaste Jesuits expressed, and they were in fact following a line of reasoning and behavior that had been sanctified for the church in the Far East by Francis Xavier himself. In an open letter to the younger Jesuits of the company in Goa, which he wrote from Japan in 1549, Xavier expressed his shock at the extent to which homosexuality was entrenched among the priests of the Japanese Buddhist church, a shock intensified by the casualness with which the whole business seemed to be taken. The priests used the young boys, sent to them to be educated, for their sexual pleasure, and laughed when questioned about it. "The evil is simply become a habit," he wrote; "the priests are drawn to sins against nature and don't deny it, they acknowledge it openly. This evil, furthermore, is so public, so clear to all, men and women, young and old, and they are so used to seeing it that they are neither depressed nor horrified."[75]

Other monks lived openly with nuns, wrote Xavier, and if the nun became pregnant she was aborted with drugs, or else the child was killed as soon as it was born. One Jesuit described Xavier a year later shouting aloud at a startled group of Japanese monks (who had just served him a free meal in their temple) "for the abominable vice of

224

Sodom which reigned amongst them," a charge their abbot did not deign to answer.[76]

By 1580 the visitor in the Far East, Alessandro Valignano, was honest enough to realize that Catholic priests, because of their harsh attitudes and lack of human warmth toward the Japanese students who had come to study in Jesuit houses, might be contributing to a very similar state of affairs: "Worse still, as they lived such unhappy lives in the Church, that is, in our house, many of them went about taciturn and dissembling, falling into coarse and sinful ways, some in order to seek consolation by very undesirable methods, others in order to force [the Jesuits] to open their eyes to the reality."[77] Valignano tried to find some median position that would check the "corrupt character of the people (beyond that corruption to which we are all naturally prone)," and in his rules for the Jesuits' Japanese seminary, drawn up in 1580, he stipulated with meticulous care that the students should sleep on tatami mats, separated by little wooden benches, and that a light was to be kept burning all night.[78] Father Francis Cabral, who lived in Japan almost twenty years, saw no amelioration of the situation when he had been transferred back to Goa. As he wrote in a letter of 1596 to Rome, Japanese homosexuality was the major obstacle to their religious discipline. Their "abominations of the flesh" and "vicious habits" were "regarded in Japan as quite honorable; men of standing entrust their sons to the bonzes to be instructed in such things, and at the same time to serve their lust."[79]

The weight of such dominant views among missionaries in the Far East was such that other Western travelers tended to feel the need to develop complex explanations for an *absence* of homosexuality in certain areas. Thus the Venetian merchant Cesare Fedrici wrote that the enticing slit skirt worn by the women in Burma (Pegu), which is "so strait that at every step they shew their legs and more," had been specially designed by them to woo their menfolk away from their "unnatural practices."[80] A missionary in the same area concluded in 1544 that the absence of sodomy there was because the lord of the realm, answering the entreaties of his queen, had ordered all men to set a tiny bell "between the skin and the flesh of their members" and that this device had successfully stopped the covert practice of the "abominable sin."[81]

Certainly homosexuality among males was prevalent in the Ming dynasty despite laws against it in the statute books, of which Ricci was apparently unaware. Whether there had been a dramatic increase in the late sixteenth century because of the growth of new relaxed urban life styles and changing moral perceptions is impossible to say. The Ming scholar Xie Zhaozhe, a contemporary of Ricci, quoted the tenth-century author Tao Gu to show that "the honeycomb alleys" of the Song dynasty capital had been filled with male prostitutes willing to sell their bodies, and in that respect the later Ming dynasty was not so different. "In today's Peking," wrote Xie, "there are young boy singers who go to all the gentry's wine parties, and no matter how many official prohibitions there are, everyone uses them. . . . As soon as one man had them, then the custom spread, and now every single gentleman uses all his energies to obtain them, it's as if the whole country had gone crazy. This has really come to be absurd." Xie felt that if it had ever been true that male homosexuality was largely a southeastern Chinese practice, as earlier writers posited, that was certainly no longer the case: in Peking, over half the male prostitutes came from the town of Linqing in Shandong province, ending the old dominance of the males from Zhejiang province (especially the two cities of Shaoxing and Ningbo), who had once been the most notorious.[82] Xie added the thought that in the Ming one now found many cases of men dressing up as women, whereas in previous dynasties it had been the women who dressed as men.[83]

Montaigne, during his 1581 visit to Rome, had been surprised to learn that several marriages between Portuguese males had been celebrated in the church of St. John a few years before, and that the couples "went to bed and lived together" for some time before being arrested and burned at the stake.[84] If Ricci ever heard such stories—and this particular incident allegedly took place in 1578, the year after he left

Rome—the global prevalence of such customs would have been amply confirmed for him by the Ming scholar Shen Defu, who became a friend of his in Peking in the early 1600s. Shen wrote in his book of general studies on social customs, the *Bizhou zhai yutan,* that in Fujian province homosexual males often lived together conventionally in households, the elder partner being treated by the younger one's parents as their son-in-law and supported with the money they had laid aside for his marriage portion. The locals had even created a special ideograph to express the closeness and sexual ambiguity of these unions, substituting the component meaning "female" for the component signifying "physical strength" that was conventionally used in the ideograph for "male." One would not find this new ideograph in standard dictionaries, noted Shen.[85] Various other sources corroborate the findings of Xie and Shen on the prevalence of homosexuality in their time. For instance, erotic prints that were widely circulated in the late Ming, though dominated by scenes of heterosexual love, also contained numerous examples either of male anal intercourse with women or of male couplings. In obvious reference to the prevalence of such customs among the upper levels of the literati, these males were described as practicing "the Hanlin Way."[86]

Just as the Inquisition had become particularly active against homosexuality in the pontificate of Paul IV in the late 1550s, when Ricci was a child, so by the end of the century its stern hand had reached around the world to Manila, as Ricci began his China mission. The Spaniards burned several Chinese men at the stake for homosexuality in Manila during the 1580s, a harsh fate that did not escape the notice of Ming scholars. As the Ming geographer Zhang Xie wrote in a succinct comment on the Philippines: "Luzon has the strongest prohibitions against perverse intercourse with boys. Chinese who violate this are thought to act against heaven. They are at once condemned to death and burned on a pile of firewood."[87]

With the sternness of these punishments becoming public knowledge, it was essential that the Jesuits themselves be kept free of all taint, though this was not always possible. As with the charges of adultery

THE MEMORY PALACE OF MATTEO RICCI

launched at Ruggieri and Longobardi, so did other unpleasant rumors collect around the Jesuit residences. The celibate Jesuits, with their black male retainers (at least in the earlier days of the mission) and their young servants and novices, inevitably sparked stories. Ricci wrote that on one occasion he was charged with having kept a Chinese boy, drugged, in his house for three days, the implication being that he had had his way with him before planning to sell him to the Portuguese in Macao.[88] Such charges hung over Western missionaries in general after one Catholic father secretly brought a twenty-year-old Chinese youth—formerly the disciple of a Buddhist priest—out of China with him to Macao, where he had him baptized. Scandalized Chinese threatened to round up Portuguese ships, confiscate all merchandise, and destroy the city unless the young man was returned. Reluctantly the Portuguese yielded, and one of their senior clerics escorted the youth back to Canton and was then forced to watch as the youth was savagely beaten for his indiscretion.[89]

The Jesuits tried to keep a strong moral stance on these issues, one that would preclude further Chinese speculation. In the first version of the Ten Commandments, which Ricci and Ruggieri translated together in 1584, instead of translating the sixth commandment in its simple form as "Thou shalt not commit adultery," they wrote "Thou shalt not do depraved, unnatural, or filthy things."[90] Ricci emphasized the same point far more strongly in his explanation of Christian doctrine entitled the *True Meaning of the Lord of Heaven,* though before coming to it he explained the church's theory of celibacy on eight grounds, in a lengthy elaboration of the arguments for the celibate life that could be found in Paul's epistles to the Corinthians and to Timothy and in Epictetus's reflections on the need for moral men to see to the needs of the world.[91] Ricci's eight points were these: the large population of men competing for sustenance gives those with families no spare time to think of spiritual matters; continence sharpens spiritual perception; poverty when linked to chastity makes it easier to serve as a moral example to others; the goal of spreading the faith across the world demands total commitment; in Europe, where people are passionate to

spread the faith, priests play among the general population a role similar to that of the tax and seed grain that any farmer sets aside from each
harvest; the highest conceivable calling for mankind is to reach toward
God, and since some saw "the world were better to be without food
than without God, the world were better without inhabitants than
without religion," they devoted their whole lives to religion; missionaries must be free of the binding ties of wife and children, and always
ready to travel where they are called, since "if they can't succeed in the
West they must go to the East, if they fail in the East they will go to
the South or North"; and lastly, with chastity one lives nearer to the
angels, is closer to God, and so can fight the devil more effectively.[92]
False celibacy, or the rejection of marriage but not of lust, was worse
than all things, as Ricci wrote in a stern passage that followed his eight
reasons:

> In China there are those who reject normal sex and indulge in deprav-
> ity, they abandon sex with women and instead they corrupt young
> males. This kind of filthiness is not even discussed by wise men in the
> West, for fear of defiling their own mouths. Even the wild animals
> only make their bonds between female and male, none of them over-
> turn the nature heaven gave them. Men who are like this never blush
> for shame; how sinful these men have become. The members of my
> humble society retain all their seed, and do not plant it out in the
> fields. If you doubt the wisdom of this, how much more should you
> question throwing it away into a ditch or a gutter.[93]

In the first week of the *Spiritual Exercises,* Ignatius of Loyola enjoined
each priest making the exercises to apply his whole being to the contemplation of sin, using all the powers of memory, reason, and will to
approach an understanding of God's grace in its contrast to the sins of
the angels, of Adam, and the mortal sin of men that followed from
them. The second exercise of that week was profound contemplation of
the self, of the "loathsomeness and malice" of the sins each man had
committed, until one could see all one's being in the harsh and terrible
clarity of guilt: "I will consider myself as a source of corruption and

contagion from which have issued countless sins and evils and the most offensive poison." This contemplation should lead, not to sorrow, but to an astonished "cry of wonder accompanied by surging emotion" as the maker of the exercises, conscious of the depth of his sin, grew at the same time conscious of the true meaning of the mercy of that God who would forgive such sins.[94] Ricci and his fellow Jesuits in China would have practiced these contemplations in their own making of the exercises, and indeed their general, Claudio Acquaviva, urged them often not to give up those crucial reflections on the "two standards" of Christ and of Satan as they labored in the missions.[95]

In the new directory on the exercises that he worked on with the advice of members of the order during the 1590s, Acquaviva further developed his thoughts on how and to whom the exercises should be administered. His conclusion was that the limitations which Ignatius imposed on use of the exercises should still be followed, especially with reference to excluding married laymen, however devout, from exploring the entire exercises. Acquaviva followed Ignatius in emphasizing that good results came from allowing at least the first week of the exercises to be read by those "who, after reforming their lives, have remained in the world," and in reminding the missionaries that the exercises need not only be given when in retreat but also in the converts' "own homes if possible." This final decision of 1599 was reconfirmed in 1601, when Acquaviva wrote to the missionaries that local superiors "ought to show themselves ready and willing to entertain any who may wish to make the *Spiritual Exercises*."[96]

There are only scattered hints as to how often Ricci led Chinese converts through the first week of the exercises. The first time seems to have been with a wealthy merchant convert named "Cotunhua" in Shaozhou city during 1591, the second time with Cotunhua's friend, the scholar-alchemist Qu Rukuei.[97] In the first case Ricci noted explicitly that Cotunhua was the more ready to make the exercises because he was already prepared in the practice of meditation by his previous Buddhist beliefs; in the second case Ricci believed that Qu, the passionate alchemist, had his soul purged of the fear of death that had driven him to a ceaseless quest for elixirs of immortality.

The delicate point in the exercises of the first week, which both Ignatius and Acquaviva had emphasized, was that one was not to be too literal in one's reflections on the sins one contemplated, especially not so far as the application of the senses was concerned. In the meditations on Christian life it was proper, as Acquaviva wrote, "to picture to oneself, and as it were to see with the eyes of the imagination, the place where the thing on which we meditate occurred." The contemplation of sin, however, raised very different problems: while being aware of the whole range of human frailty, and expressing the deepest contrition for one's own shortcomings, one had to avoid any mental involvement that could lead one to partake, as it were, in the sinful thoughts or act themselves. Ignatius of Loyola had suggested that the best way to reflect fruitfully on sin was to hold the three powers of memory, will, and reason in the tightest possible balance, so that no one of the three powers should be able to gain the ascendancy. Rather surprisingly, Acquaviva had concluded that those who proved to have "greater facility in this matter than others," far from being those without boldness of mind, were in fact those "in whom imaginative powers are especially keen."[98] One might interpret this as meaning that those with the strongest and most far-ranging intellects were able to see all dimensions of this particular exercise, to understand the need for reining in the passions just because they were so aware of their scope and complexity. Perhaps Ricci managed to share some of this insight with Qu and with Cotunhua. His, after all, was the fierce pen that told the Chinese how "men and animals and insects were all burned up and nothing was left"; it was in the grim sharpness of his imagination that "the trees and rocks were turned to ash and sank into the ground."[99]

231

EIGHT

THE FOURTH IMAGE:
THE FOURTH PICTURE

I n the middle of August 1599, Ricci wrote to his friend Girolamo Costa, from whom he had just received two letters, one dated 1595 and one 1596. Letters from Costa often set Ricci to musing, for Costa was also from Macerata, was only one year older than Ricci, and had entered the Jesuit order in Rome in the early 1570s. In this particular case emotions were especially frank since Costa's letters repeated the sad news that both Ricci's parents had died. The news happened not to be true, but Ricci could not know that, and in his reply he dwelt briefly on their passing; he also mentioned how cheered he was at hearing from other friends, such as Nicolo Bencivegni, who had been his and Costa's childhood teacher in Macerata, the man "who during our most tender and most vulnerable years taught us and put us on the road to the state where now we find ourselves." The news from Costa and Bencivegni was good, both about his home region and about the work of the Jesuits there, and Ricci rejoiced in it. Then he added, as if suddenly struck by the thought, "A good many times in the past I have boasted to these barbarians that I come from a

232

land to which Christ our Lord, from many miles away, moved the house in which he and his mother had spent their time on this earth. And they are astounded when I tell them of this and of other marvels that God has wrought in those Western lands."[1]

Ricci was obviously referring, almost with pride of ownership, to the shrine of the Virgin Mary at Loreto, which stood on a verdant site near the sea, among fruit trees and vineyards only a short ride from Ancona. The shrine itself was in the form of a house nine and a half meters long, four meters wide, and five meters high—which was believed to be the one in which Mary received the Annunciation and in which she raised the child Jesus. According to legend, the house had been miraculously transported by angels from Nazareth in the Holy Land, first to Fiume, then to a forest outside Recanati, and finally to Loreto. Initially the house rested unrecognized and abandoned in the woods, sheltering its most treasured relic, a portrait of the Virgin rendered by St. Luke the evangelist; until at the end of the thirteenth century, alerted in a vision, sixteen young men from Recanati traveled to Nazareth and confirmed that the foundations of the Virgin's house that could still be seen there matched exactly the dimensions of the house at Loreto.

So read the descriptive legend hanging in the church, composed in the late fifteenth century and translated into French, German, and Spanish; and so it was confirmed by overlays of papal bulls and reports of miraculous occurrences. The simple house had become, by Ricci's time, a famous shrine enclosed in a glittering marble carapace designed by Andrea Sansevino and paid for by Julius II and his four successor popes, and the fame had brought changes: the wooden ceiling of painted blue on which stars had glistened was removed because of the danger of fire from the candles of the faithful, an ancient cedar statue of Mary and her child was swathed in precious fabrics to preserve it, while Sansevino's marble carapace in turn was contained within a magnificent church, for which Bramante completed the facade in 1571. For all his time in China this shrine would have been present to Ricci, given new richness and meaning by Ignatius of Loyola's instructions to those making the second week of exercises that, after contemplating the Incarnation of the Virgin, they should make special efforts "to see the house and room of our Lady in the city of Nazareth in the province of Galilee."[2]

The grandeur that was added to the once-simple shrine in the late sixteenth century had not vitiated its poignant solemnity, at least according to Montaigne, who visited it in April 1581 and left there the gift of a composite portrait of himself, his wife, and his daughter worshiping the Virgin Mary, the whole wrought cunningly in silver. Noting that the church was "beautiful and large," and that Bramante's over-building was "the most finely worked and of the loveliest marble that one could ever see," Montaigne reserved his greatest praise for the humble little house: "Here there is no ornament, no bench or hassock, no paintings or tapestries on the wall; for it is the building itself that serves as the reliquary." He added, "One finds there more of the real sense of religion than in any other place that I have ever seen."[3] Long after they had returned home, other travelers of the same period remembered the haunting music to which the litany of the Lady of Loreto was set, while Macerata in the 1570s was already the center for a thriving publishing business on Loreto and on the cures worked there in the Virgin's name.[4]

Macerata was a way station on the pilgrim route from Rome to Loreto, and from his earliest years Ricci would have been aware of the shrine and the special focus of devotion to the Virgin Mary that it gave to the region. Indeed in Macerata itself, as all the town knew, the Virgin had appeared to a townswoman, Bernadina di Bonino, just four years before Ricci was born; all through his schooldays a magnificent church was being raised in honor of this event on the very spot where the miracle had occurred. Though marred somewhat by a number of lawsuits that slowed construction, the church of St. Mary the Virgin was completed in 1573 and became one of Macerata's proudest monuments, a worthy addition to the twenty other churches, with their exquisite collections of frescoes and paintings dating back to the Middle Ages.[5] In the presence of this evidence of the Virgin's power Ricci could feel reassured, for strength and gentleness combined in her and reached out to all men. One can catch a fragment of this emotion in the words used by Ludolfus of Saxony to describe his personal sense of the Virgin's fruitful majesty, words that were to touch Ignatius of Loyola deeply, and reach through him to his followers in the instructions that he left concerning the Virgin's role as mediator between sinful mortals and her Son in heaven:[6]

> For just as in springtime, when the sun begins to rise towards the height of Heaven and to pour the life-giving brightness of its rays upon the earth, all plants fettered in winter's frost begin to come to life again; animals and birds hidden in each and every cave and lair and eyrie begin to breathe because of the renewal of such light, and take up their strength again and make their joy known in songs and happy praises; and old and young men exult in its arrival; and the whole surface of the earth is beautifully adorned, celebrating and rejoicing—so it is with us, when the life-giving Virgin comes, clothed with the sun, the preeminent Queen of Heaven. Like the sun, she enters the borders of our hearts, and the remembrance of her pours upon our minds which glow brightly without cloud; for indeed, all lack of feeling is continually melted in the greatness of such a light; all that is dry is watered by the dew of Heavenly Grace; the darkness is put to flight; a new light appears, and the unending theme of joys is built up for us.[7]

That "all lack of feeling" was "continually melted in the greatness of such a light," in Ludolfus's wonderful phrase, may suggest a further reason for Ricci's finding solace in the Virgin Mary's presence. As the eldest of fourteen children, Ricci can have had little attention from his mother, the noblewoman Giovanna Angelelli, and he refers to her only twice in all his letters, once asking to be remembered in her prayers, and once expressing satisfaction that she was spending much time in church.[8] His relationships with his father, his brothers, and his sisters all seem muted if we can judge from his letters, which are filled with complaints that no one in the family ever writes to him.[9] Only of his grandmother Laria did he write with real affection, and it seems typical of the family distances that it should have again been Girolamo Costa, then living in Siena, rather than a relative, who told him when Laria died. "I cannot stop remembering with the greatest tenderness the love that she showed me when I was a little boy," Ricci wrote in 1592, after getting the news, "and how much I owe to her for having on various occasions raised me like my second mother."[10]

Costa's letter bringing the sad news reached Ricci when he was confined to bed with a badly injured foot, suffered when he jumped from the window of the Shaozhou mission house during the nighttime attack by Chinese youths in the summer of 1592. Ricci's lying there in pain echoes, in a softer way, the long and agonizing weeks that Ignatius of Loyola spent in bed seventy-one years before, after a French ball of shot had broken his right leg in the siege of Pamplona. As doctors probed Ignatius's leg for shards of shattered bone, attached a metal brace in an attempt to stop the right leg from permanently shriveling to a shorter length than the left one, and reopened the wound to replace a splinter of bone that pierced through the right kneecap, he drew courage from a vision of Mary and her child that came to him, a vision, he said, that left his heart serene and his flesh never again troubled by thoughts of lust.[11] When Ignatius could walk again, in late September 1521, he first transcribed selections from Ludolfus of Saxony and then went to visit his sister; when Ricci could stand again, in August 1592, he said three Masses in sequence, all in Laria's memory, and thereafter embarked on an exhausting and apparently endless series of legal proceedings involving those who had attacked the mission. All this activity, coupled with the inability of the Macao doctors to correct the damage, ensured that he too would limp for the rest of his life.[12] Later, when the pain came flooding back after a long day's walking or standing in Peking, one can almost hear Ricci murmur the lines that Dante chose to introduce himself and his own quest in the *Inferno:*

> *Poi ch'èi posato un poco il corpo lasso,*
> *Ripresi via per la piaggia diserta,*
> *Si che'l piè fermo sempre era 'l più basso.*

> So having rested, for a moment, my tired body,
> I resumed my way up the deserted slope
> With my firm foot always staying the lower.

That English version can only be a partial translation; for Dante here used the highly resonant language of Aristotle and the church fathers to show how the exhausted pilgrim dragged his left foot behind him as he limped tenaciously forward, given courage by the thought of his Beatrice.[13]

Limping literally and metaphorically toward the light, Ricci had not just the solace of visions and memory but the real presence of devotional objects to give him courage along the way. We can guess that the idea of Loreto as reliquary, caught by Montaigne, was present also in Ricci's mind after childhood visits to the shrine; certainly when he moved from Macerata to Rome as a schoolboy of sixteen he took up residence literally in a city of relics. In the myriad shrines of the city's 127 churches could be found, it was believed, the bodies of St. Peter and St. Paul, the heads of St. Luke the evangelist and of St. Sebastian, the arm of Joseph of Arimathea, and Christ's face imprinted on the linen cloth once held by Veronica. There too were stored the tip of the spear that pierced Christ's side, a piece of the true cross, the head of an arrow that pierced St. Sebastian, the table on which the Last Supper was served to Christ and his disciples, one of the thirty pieces of silver paid for Christ's betrayal, the chains that bound St. Paul, part of the five barley loaves with which Christ fed the hungry multitude, the towel with which Christ washed his apostles' feet, the stairs that Christ ascended to the house of Pontius Pilate, one of the nails that fastened Christ to his cross, and two of the thorns from his crown.[14]

As important as the relics were the special legends that sanctified certain holy places. The church of the Blessed Virgin, Santa Maria Maggiore, for one, was built on the spot where snow fell one August in the reign of Pope Liberius; Romans still called it Our Lady's Church of the Snow. It was here, during one service long ago, that an angel uttered the response to St. Gregory, so that still in Ricci's time the choir did not reply to the blessing "The Peace of the Lord be with you always" in hope that the angel would speak once more the words "And with thy spirit." And there was lovingly kept a part of the shelter and ox's stall where Mary first placed Christ in Bethlehem, of which St. Jerome wrote, "That stall wherein the little infant cried is rather to be honored with silence than with speech too base for it," a pledge of honor understood by the Roman matron Paula, who lived out her life devoutly in this very spot, "the cabin wherein the virgin Childwife brought forth our Lord a babe." Naturally this was the station chosen by the faithful at Christmastime.[15]

Not surprisingly, Ricci took with him such relics as he could on his voyage half-way around the world. We know that he had with him in China, lovingly preserved, a tiny cross made of remnants of the true cross, as well as fragments of the bones of certain saints and a box of soil from Jerusalem; he kept these in his own personal baggage lest they be defiled at the court. At propitious times he gave these away to his converts, some of whom acknowledged their ownership proudly and in public. For instance, in the painting that Luke Li, the founder of the first Marian sodality in China, commissioned to memorialize the Christian converts within his own family, one could see the tiny reliquary holders that hung around their necks, though of course the viewer could not be sure what they contained.[16]

This same Luke Li was the founder of a group of Chinese Christians in Peking who met together to pay particular homage to the Virgin Mary and to devote their lives to good works. He thus lays claim to be the first to bring "Marian sodalities," as such groups were termed, into China. The ideas that lay behind such sodalities were prevalent throughout much of Europe in the Counter-Reformation. Small groups of religious men and women pledged themselves to lives of heightened spiritual service in order to reinforce the work of the large organizations or institutions to which they might already belong. The groups were united by their pledges to attend regular meetings, usually weekly, to make frequent confession and communion, and to explore the modes of social service, reconciliation, and charity that were most

238

needed in their communities. The members did not have to be in orders, and in the midsixteenth century one could find Marian groups among the women of Padua and Naples, among the artisans of Florence, among all social groups in Venice, Genoa, Siena, which engaged in similar activities in hospitals and among the poor. One group even paid for the upkeep of women separated from their husbands while they sought to arrange reconciliations.[17] The first such Marian sodality in Macerata was established in 1551, the year before Ricci's birth, and held its meetings in the church of St. Anthony of Padua until 1566, when the members moved to the even more apposite shrine of the Madonna of Loreto.[18]

Whether Ricci was a member of this group we don't know, but he certainly was an active member of the sodality in Rome, which had been founded at the Roman college by the Belgian Jesuit and theologian Jan Leunis in 1563. By 1569, just before Ricci joined the sodality, it had grown so rapidly that it had been divided into two sections, one for those between twelve and seventeen, of whom there were around thirty, and one for those eighteen and older, of whom there were seventy. As expansion continued, it was subdivided yet again, this time into groups for those over twenty-one, those fourteen to twenty-one, and those under fourteen.[19] These groups of young Jesuits would have worked side by side with numerous groups of lay believers, who were active at Rome as elsewhere. Among groups of laymen that flourished during Ricci's school years in Rome we find those who visited prisons, giving out bedding and pallets, arranging appeals or physicians' visits, paying off debts, or giving spiritual solace to those condemned to death. If death came, then it was the Compania de Morte that gave decent burials to the poor, while the Compania de la Misericordia buried those executed criminals (who confessed themselves Christians) in consecrated ground rather than leaving them hanging on the gallows for the ravens. Other companies solaced the Vergognosi (those of good family, now impoverished, too proud to beg), while yet others mediated in disputes between citizens or looked after the deranged or dangerously mad.[20]

Leunis's special contribution was to give a powerful internal unity to the students of the Jesuit order, with the goal of integrating their scholarship into a life of Christian service. Naturally service in overseas missions became a central focus for much of this energy, and it was significant that Leunis had himself yearned to serve in the Indies, but was prevented from doing so by the fact that he suffered from blinding headaches that led his superiors to order him to stay at home. It was after his headaches ceased following a pilgrimage to the shrine in Loreto that in gratitude he began to meet with the students and to deepen their devotion to the Virgin.[21] From this marshaling of forces in the Jesuit college the ideas that stimulated the group spread to Spain and France, and then out to Portugal and her overseas possessions. There are frequent references to sodalities in Goa, where they were active in helping minister to the needs of the slaves, in converting the Muslims, in trying to eradicate concubinage, and in reconciling the quarrelsome citizenry—this latter no easy task, as in one six-month period some fifteen hundred disputes were recorded as having taken place.[22] Similar groups were also being established in Macao just as Ricci arrived there, and perhaps because of his experiences with the Marian sodalities in Rome or in Goa, Valignano assigned him in late 1582 to head the new Macao congregation of the name of Jesus. This was designed to help recent Chinese and Japanese converts residing in Macao deepen their spiritual life: Portuguese were not permitted to be members.[23]

The Marian sodality in Rome had been given extra prestige by a papal bull issued by Gregory XIII in 1584, which named it the "first and principal" congregation, and the organizational passion of General Acquaviva followed up this lead by formulating new rules for the groups in 1587.[24] Among other things Acquaviva tightened the rules for the officers of the Marian sodalities, instructing them to make confession every two weeks; he also specified weekly Sunday meetings with no outsiders present (unless special dispensation was obtained), ordered the maintenance of secrecy concerning the sodalities' activities, arranged for admission to each sodality by an electoral process conducted by the local members, and banned the admission of women since he deemed them "not conducive to edification."[25]

Luke Li built on this foundation as interpreted for him by Ricci and established the Peking sodality in 1609, the inauguration coming, suitably enough, on the natal day of the Virgin. Ricci's account of this event, which clearly moved him deeply, comes at the very end of the autograph draft of his *Historia,* and the structure of the draft suggests that these may indeed have been the last lines he wrote before his final illness and death. He noted how Luke Li, a former retainer of Ricci's friend Li Zhizao, drew up rules for his little society which was to meet monthly for a sermon and prayer, how the Chinese members gave flowers, wax for candles, and incense to the Peking church, worked on settling disputes and helping prisoners in the churches, and concentrated their main energies on providing decent Christian burial for converts who could not afford it. By Christmas 1609 the sodality had grown to forty members.[26] Thus at one level we can see that these activities were based on the experiences Ricci had had in Rome, and probably partially followed Acquaviva's guidelines, and yet there were also new twists. The concentration on decent burial was particularly likely to appeal to Chinese raised with Confucian ideas of filial piety toward their elders, for whom a dignified funeral was obligatory—Xu Guangqi spent 120 ducats on a cedar coffin for his father, while Li Zhizao provided fifteen ounces of silver for Ricci's. Moreover, the mere prospect of such fine burials probably encouraged the poorer Chinese to seek baptism and attain a posthumous dignity that would otherwise have been beyond their means.[27]

From the very earliest days of the founding of the Roman college's sodality of the Virgin, there had been rumors and accusations that the members formed an elite within the Jesuit schools, and indeed that the sodalities were used expressly for the purpose of identifying the most promising young men so they could be given more rapid advancement. Such rumors were given substance by the existence of secret subgroupings within the sodalities, for as the sodalities grew in size, smaller groups often coalesced to meet in private and pursue their own goals or—as in the case of a group of young nobles in the Abruzzi—to foster a stronger sense of piety. In this latter case it was General Acquaviva himself who not only gave permission for the subgroup to continue to meet but encouraged the formation of similar groups in Rome.[28] The strength of the bonds that could be forged by those who shared this common experience was carried over into China, reinforcing the ties of shared hopes and dangers. Ricci showed this clearly by the way he wrote about Francesco de Petris, a Jesuit father ten years his junior who served with him in Shaozhou until his death in November 1593. Since Petris had entered the Roman college at an unusually young age, the two may have known each other before Ricci left Rome in 1577; Ricci wrote later that Petris "was unable to hide from anyone the deep devotion he felt for the Madonna" and that the young priest had told the Chinese novices in Shaozhou that he had entered the Society of Jesus because the Virgin Mary, in a vision, had urged him to do so. Petris was a devout member of the Marian sodality in Rome, added Ricci, and even on his deathbed continued to chant aloud songs in her praise. After making his final confession, Petris rose from his bed and flung his arms around Ricci's neck. When Ricci gently disengaged himself and tried to reassure Petris that he would recover, the two missionaries remained side by side, bathed in tears that prevented their speaking further. There is no passage so filled with personal emotion anywhere else in Ricci's writings.[29]

General Acquaviva was himself strongly drawn to the cult of the Virgin, a trait that he shared with the founder of the Jesuit order, Ignatius of Loyola. Ignatius had written that the constitutions of the society had been drawn up in part with the help of the Virgin Mary through visions, an observation that led to the wide circulation of a rumor that the *Spiritual Exercises* themselves had been in part "dictated" by the Virgin.[30] Meditations on the Virgin Mary are "unobtrusive and fundamental" to the exercises, according to a leading Jesuit scholar of spirituality, an interpretation given weight by the fact that Ignatius had waited a full year between his ordination and the saying of his first Mass, both "to prepare himself and to beg our Lady that she might desire to place him with her Son." When Ignatius did at last say his first Mass in 1538, it was in the church of Santa Maria Maggiore in Rome and on Christmas Day.[31] General Acquaviva reinforced this underlying theme of the Virgin's centrality to the order in a letter to the Jesuits of May 19, 1586, which Ricci probably saw several years later just before he was evicted from Zhaoqing. The letter was directly geared to aspects of the China mission, since Acquaviva wrote it to notify the missionaries that Pope Sixtus V had authorized a jubilee to celebrate the "bright dawn of faith upon this vast empire" of China; one can imagine the effect of Acquaviva's ringing rhetoric on Ricci as he knelt before the altar in Zhaoqing on which was displayed a picture of the cowled Madonna holding the Christ Child (the Scriptures clasped in his left hand). The picture was a reproduction of the one in the church of Santa Maria Maggiore, which Ricci had brought into China and displayed first in a little house he rented and then in the larger room he built to serve as a church.[32] In his letter Acquaviva wrote:

Mary is the Mother of Him who created all things, and hence she is very properly honored by St. Damascene with the title of Mistress and Queen of heaven and earth. It is my wish, that at all times and in all things—whether in our individual wants or in those of the whole Society—we seek, with a special veneration and unwavering confidence, the protection and patronage of the Blessed Virgin; for she is the refuge of all those that are heavily laden with the weight of their labors, or troubled in soul. Indeed, when I reflect upon the tender devotion of the saints to our Blessed Lady, and the holiness which they attained through their persevering and fervent love of her, I cannot but desire that we all cherish with devoted hearts a veneration for the Mother of God. I do not forget that our holy Father rested all his hopes for the future of the Society upon Mary's protection, and I consequently beg of you to pray that, through her intercession, her honor and her memory may daily become dearer to us. And truly, the exceptional dignity to which the Virgin Mother of God has been raised is such that it must call forth our love and admiration. If we recall the generosity with which she has bestowed upon us her gifts, our gratitude can never equal her goodness to us; and if we reflect upon our own necessities and helplessness, we must be forced to call in to our aid her all-powerful patronage.

The quid pro quo for this devotion would be clear, he concluded: "If we only prove ourselves her faithful clients, she will take us into her confidence and will herself protect us."[33]

Ricci hardly needed reminding of the role played by the Virgin Mary within the order. He had seen her in Mozambique, in his brief days ashore there, after the long voyage from Lisbon, in the shape of "Our Lady of the Bulwark" guarding the Portuguese fortress of San Sebastian; he had seen Akbar's ambassador remove his shoes and prostrate himself before her image in the Jesuit church in Goa; and he had noted that the finest church in Macao was the one dedicated to the Virgin.[34] In China, indeed, she had been almost too potent a force, displacing in the popular Chinese mind the august parties of the Trinity.

Perhaps in part it was the extraordinary realism with which the beauty of her image had been caught—a realism that led Zhaoqing residents to kowtow before her and the prefect Wang Pan to request a copy of her image to send to his aged father in Shaoxing—but the Chinese slowly came to believe that the Christian God was a woman.[35] Her image fused with other visions of benevolent deities from China's own past, and the very realism with which her long robes were painted made it hard for some Chinese scholars to recognize the humanness of her form. As Ricci's contemporary, the scholar Xie Zhaozhe, wrote in his book of observations and reminiscences, "The image used for the Christian God is the body of a woman, but her appearance is most unusual; she's like those figures we used to describe as 'having a human head and a dragon's body.' "[36] Once it had become clear to Ricci that misunderstandings were arising, he considered replacing the main image of the Virgin and Child with one of the mature Christ. The Chinese could not help being "a bit confused" (*un poco confusi*), he noted, because at the same time they saw Mary's image everywhere the Jesuits were teaching them that there was only one God; indeed, they had just translated the Ten Commandments with their unambiguous opening statement to that effect. Since the Jesuits did not yet feel ready to explain to the Chinese the mystery of how Christ had entered the Virgin's womb in the Incarnation, some confusion was inevitable, and removing the Virgin's picture from its prominent position did not end the rumors. That the Christian God was a woman with a child in her arms was a well-established item of knowledge in Nanjing by the end of the sixteenth century, and later Chinese writers continued to circulate the same information in their printed works.[37]

Perhaps indeed Ricci did not do as much as he might have done to dispel these rumors, since, in the days before the missionaries had begun teaching the full burden of the Christian story, the effect of the Virgin's image was so valuable in their work. In October 1585 we find Ricci writing to Acquaviva, asking him for some more small clocks "that could be worn around the neck" and also for some religious pictures, but "not those which show details of Christ's Passion, which as yet they do not understand."[38] Sometime after 1586 Ricci received a very fine oil painting, made in Spain, as a gift from a priest serving in the Philippines. This picture was of the Virgin, Christ, and John the Baptist, and was displayed to great effect in Nanchang and later in Peking. Near the end of Ricci's life other Jesuits were surprised to find a copy of this painting among a pile of some fifty scrolls in the back room of a country villa outside Shaozhou. The owners did not know what it was, but the Jesuits deduced that it had been copied privately by a local painter who was able to view it while it was being conveyed overland from Macao.[39] This was the kind of informal circulation of religious material that Ricci usually encouraged.

Another copy of the Santa Maria Maggiore Virgin reached Ricci via Macao in late 1599, a full-size color reproduction this time, not a print. This copy and the oil painting had a major effect on the eunuch Ma Tang when he first saw them, and he promised Ricci that the Virgin "will have her place in the palace of the king." This promise was fulfilled, for there were two large paintings of the Madonna—one in "ancient style" and one in "new style"—itemized in the gifts that were finally given to Emperor Wanli in 1601, and they were presumably these same two. According to eunuchs who reported the circumstances to Ricci, the emperor was "stupefied" and believed this must be "a living Buddha," but was upset by the paintings' realism and gave them to his mother. She, a devout Buddhist, was also made uneasy by them, and the paintings ended up in the palace storehouse.[40]

This generally pious reception of the pictures of the Virgin and Child contrasts sharply with attitudes to the crucified Christ, as Ricci had encountered them the previous year. One crucifix, which Ricci was carrying in his private baggage, must have been small yet vividly real in the style of the late sixteenth century, designed to give maximum immediacy to the man contemplating it, in line with Ignatius's injunctions to be present as Christ is crucified. Ricci described it as "beautiful, carved out of wood, with blood painted on it, so it seemed alive." The eunuch who found it, however—that same Ma Tang who had admired the Virgin's picture—suspected black magic and shouted aloud, "This is a wicked thing you have made, to kill our king; they cannot be good people who practice such arts."[41] Soldiers were called up and the baggage of Ricci and his companions was ransacked for further clues to their depraved designs, and they were threatened with savage beatings. The main difficulty was, as Ricci noted with honesty, that the eunuch "truly thought it was something evil" and that in the face of the hostile crowd Ricci found it hard to marshal an adequate explanation of the significance of Christ crucified. "On the one hand," as he wrote later (speaking of himself in the third person as he often did), "he didn't want to say that that was our God, it seeming difficult to him among these ignorant people, and at such a time, to talk of these high mysteries, . . . on the other, because he saw all the people turned against him, full of disgust for the cruelty which, it seemed to them, he had done to that man"—that is, to Christ. The explanation he finally gave did not really satisfy Ricci or his listeners; he told them "that they would not understand what manner of thing this was; that this was a famous saint from our land who had wished to suffer this pain on the cross for our sakes; and for this reason we painted him and sculpted him in this way so as to have him always before our eyes, and to give thanks to him for his great goodness." As one Chinese friend said to Ricci, it was really "not good to have someone looking like that"; another suggested that the Jesuits "crush into powder any other crucifixes they had with them, so there would be no memory of them."[42]

In the face of such incomprehension it was more sensible to continue giving visual primacy to the Virgin and Child, despite the difficulties of describing the Incarnation adequately, although images of Christ crucified were still circulated in the form of the small bronze medallions that were worn around their necks by the faithful, as small prints that could be given to converts who requested them, in a plain cross used to ornament the roof of a church, or even by a simple display of the rosary as proof of devotion. At other times, images of Christ were hidden altogether.[43] So Ricci continued to make copies of the Virgin's image, some on paper, some even carved on stone, and to commission new paintings of her from any Jesuit painters with adequate talent whom he could find, and the number of fine versions slowly grew, along with their effect. Father Cattaneo brought yet another Madonna and Child—set in a beautiful background of gilded cornices and pillars—when he came back from sick leave in Macao in 1602. This picture had such an effect on Xu Guangqi when he saw it that it acted as a catalyst to his conversion. Jesuit priests in the south began to carry small pictures of the Virgin with them when they preached—they would cover a small table with an altar cloth and place the Virgin's picture on it, flanked by candles and incense. Slowly the Chinese converts began to make their own printed images of the Virgin, which they stamped on sheets of colored paper and hung outside their door at the New Year's festival and on other religious or festive occasions. Others began to invoke the Virgin's name in exorcism of evil spirits.[44]

In the presence of these images, and with the circulation of gospel stories about Mary, the Chinese began to dream of the Virgin. At least one sick convert dreamed that Mary, robed in white and carrying the child in her arms, stood by his bedside and recommended that he be sweated of his fever; he did so and recovered.[45] And the wife of an official in charge of grain transportation on the Grand Canal dreamed of a woman with two small children and later realized—hearing about the picture from her husband, who had met Ricci—that she had seen the Virgin, Christ, and John the Baptist. When she sought permission to have a Chinese artist make a copy of the painting, Ricci, fearing that the rendition might not be faithful, had one of the Jesuit brothers who was a good painter do it for her.[46]

In a more complicated incident, a Chinese child, desperately ill, had a dream of a woman who came to him carrying a baby in her arms and calling his name, saying she would protect him. After the child recovered and told the dream to his parents, they in turn went to the priest, João Soero, who had baptized their son seven years before, to thank him. In the Jesuit chapel the child saw a painting of the Virgin of St. Lucca and recognized her as his protectress. But at this point, Father Soero, embarrassed, explained that he had never baptized the child, doubting the sincerity of the parents, but had merely sprinkled holy water on him. Now, assured both of their sincerity and of celestial approval, he proceeded to baptize the boy properly.[47]

As the Jesuits spread abroad their own images of the Virgin Mary so did they slowly try to beat back the images used by their rivals from other faiths, through various types of religious persuasion that sometimes ended up as open iconoclasm. Ricci tried to discourage the cruder forms of idol smashing—the "breaking off of hands or feet or whatever they could" from temple figures which some overzealous converts carried out near Shaozhou, or the stealing of idols from temples in order to burn or bury them—for such acts inevitably stirred up local hostility.[48] But his writings are full of praise for other purges carried out by the fathers in full cooperation with their new Chinese converts: for the merchant who gave Ricci forty ducats' worth of the bronze religious statues he used to sell, so they could be melted down; or for another convert who built a furnace in the grounds of his own Peking home so he could melt down the figures that others didn't dare to harm; or an old man of seventy-eight who, over his sons' protests, got the Jesuits to burn his Buddhist images since the family wouldn't let him do so himself.[49] On occasion, if the statues were impressive enough, Ricci sent them to Macao as "battle prizes," in his words, but destruction was more common and extended also to paintings on wood and paper and to the printed word. One young painter burned his entire collection of paintings of religious figures, at which he had been a specialist. Qu Rukuei brought three crates of his alchemical and religious books, whatever printing blocks he had, and a number of original manuscripts to be burned when he was converted, saving only a few that had "special subtleties" which he and the Jesuits studied in common so that they would better learn how to refute such arguments. The military official Li Yingshi, a veteran of the Korean campaigns against Hideyoshi, burned his collection of manuscripts on divination techniques which he had accumulated over many years at great cost.[50]

Both Qu and Li left carefully written statements of faith at the time of their baptism. Qu's in particular was imbued with devotion to the Virgin Mary. Qu ended his confession, in the bulk of which he particularly regretted having dedicated so much money and energy to the propagation of Buddhism, with the heartfelt words of a new Counter-Reformation Chinese rhetoric of Marian faith:

As to the articles of the Christian faith, though I cannot comprehend the grandeur of every mystery, with all my heart I subject myself to them, and believe all that is contained in them. I pray to the Spirito Sancto [a phrase that Qu sounded out in Chinese as "Sanbilido Sando"] to make them clearer to me. I am starting to believe afresh, and my heart is like a fragile and soft ear of corn. Wherefore I beg the Mother of the Lord of Heaven that she will deign to give me spiritual courage and strength, and that she will pray on my behalf to God, that my resolve remain strong and firm, never vacillating, opening up for me the full potential of my soul, and making my spirit pure and clear. And so, with my heart filled with light, and holding fast to both truth and reason, my mouth will open to speak the holy word, spreading and sowing it across the whole of China, so that all may know the holy law of God and submit themselves to it.[51]

That there was indeed unusually deep feeling of affection between Qu and Ricci is suggested by the fact that Qu took Ignatius as his baptismal name, and gave to his fourteen-year-old son the name of Matteo.[52]

It was inevitable that the Jesuits and their converts would spend much—perhaps most—of their energies attacking Buddhism in China, since Buddhism was their central rival in its claim to ethical good and in performance of acts of charity. Buddhist charitable organizations often involved themselves in projects to improve the lot of the poor through endowing hospitals and homes for the aged, giving food or low-interest loans in times of trouble, establishing bath houses, planting trees, and mending bridges; while Ricci was living in Peking there were institutions to give food and medicine to the poor and to provide coffins for those who died indigent. Luke Li, before founding his Marian sodality, had been a member of several Buddhist charitable organizations and the director of at least one.[53] So Christian converts burned statues of Guanyin, the Buddhist goddess of mercy, along with other images and perhaps with an added urgency, since even Christian missionaries themselves had confused her image at first sight with that of the Virgin Mary.[54]

Ricci himself spent a prodigious amount of time trying to demolish the arguments of those Buddhist believers most dedicated to a rigorous life of fasting, even though he acknowledged—as Francis Xavier had before him—that these were often holy men, that they made the most devout converts, and that many of them were particularly adept at moral argument.[55] Ricci met them halfway, in one sense, by keeping to a Buddhist-style diet of vegetables and bread or rice on the Christian fast days, touching no fish, meat, eggs, or dairy products at such times "to conform to the fasting patterns of the Chinese pagans." But he completely rejected the Buddhist explanations of why abstaining from all animal products was necessary—on the grounds of the oneness of all beings, for instance, or because of the doctrine of transmigration of souls. Ricci tried to argue that fasting made sense only if it was undertaken as a penance, to remind oneself of one's state of sin and to keep one's mind alert at all times to the frailties of the body. There was an inherent absurdity in abstaining from something in order to preserve it: "There are Western barbarians who shun pork; so one finds no pigs in their country." Was that the way to protect a species, Ricci asked?[56] Ricci made a similar point about purpose and technique in a slightly roundabout way, by means of the third of the Chinese ideographs that he chose to represent his own Chinese name, Li Madou. Unlike *Li,* which was the common word for profit or harvest, or *Ma,* the symbol of a king on a horse, *Dou* was taken by Ricci from the *Three Character Classic,* the basic Chinese reading primer that was memorized by any Chinese child beginning to embark on the study of his own language. According to this old Chinese text, probably also the first book in Chinese Ricci ever read, Dou was a reflective and scholarly man who saw to the education of his own children with brilliant success because he "knew the right techniques" and was one of the finest examples of the ethical and conscientious man that the Chinese tradition had to offer.[57]

As early as 1585, as we can tell from his letters, Ricci had decided that the lower orders in China were often "Pythagoreans" who tied their dietary habits to their belief in transmigration, and he never abandoned this way of describing them. Ricci's conviction that the pervasiveness of ideas of reincarnation accounted for the great amount of infanticide in China, since the very poor would kill their infants in the hope that they would be reborn soon into a richer family, gave an additional moral urgency to his criticisms. He elaborated on the origin of transmigration theories with Pythagoras in his *True Meaning of the Lord of Heaven* (even spelling out a Chinese transliteration of the philosopher's name—it came out "Pitawoci"—in an attempt to make him more memorable) and explained that Pythagoras had invented the doctrine of transmigration of souls from humans into various types of animal bodies as a kind of allegorical teaching device during a time of particularly lax European morality. From Europe the mistaken doctrine spread to India, whence the Chinese brought it home in error.[58] The doctrine was absurd on a number of grounds, Ricci argued: it denied the fact that mankind is lord of all other creatures and that God put them there to serve him and to be exemplars of certain traits; if properly followed it would make marriage impossible, because one could never know one was not marrying one's own deceased ancestor, even one's own former parents if they too had died; it would destroy the structure of domestic service, since the valet or maid one ordered around might also have been a relative or parent; there could be no beasts used in agriculture, and no draft animals, for one's own begetters' souls might be in those creatures; and were there such a thing as transmigration some memory traces of former existences would inhere in each of us, and this was patently not the case.[59] In his *Ten Discourses by a Paradoxical Man,* which he published in 1608, Ricci elaborated on these ideas, presenting his thoughts as if they were a dialogue held with the convert Li Zhizao after Ricci had been fasting. Here he designed a stronger defense for the Christian view of penitence that could justify fasting at certain times, while restating his opposition to the Buddhist premises on fasting.[60]

One Chinese scholar, Yu Chunxi, took the time to respond to Ricci by letter, asking him why he defamed Buddhism without having taken the trouble to read Buddhist scriptures carefully, and why he felt he had the right to condemn whole generations of worthy Confucians who had been influenced by Buddhism; he pointed out that in any case Ricci's published work showed there was considerable overlap between Buddhism and Christianity in other areas of morality. Yu sent Ricci a reading list of basic Buddhist works that he believed would give him a clearer view of things. Ricci replied at considerable length, explaining the nature of his mission, his use of Western science in pursuit of his ends, his conviction that Buddhism violated the very first of the Ten Commandments, and his feeling that it had not raised moral standards in China despite the two thousand years during which it had been preached.[61] Ricci was proud of his letter, and wrote to General Acquaviva on August 22, 1608, that he had responded to Yu "in such a way that I don't think he'll reply to me in that fashion again, and we are planning to print both the letters, because by so doing we will be able to explain many aspects of our faith." In the case of other scholars, Ricci added, who had sought to use certain publications circulating at the triennial *jinshi* examinations to propagate their criticisms of Ricci, the senior examiner had stepped in and censored the writings on Ricci's behalf "by changing a few words, so that all the criticisms that had been directed against us were made to fall on the idols of the other religions."[62]

In fact Ricci was mistaken in thinking he had silenced Yu by the force of his arguments and the sharpness of his ripostes, for we know that Yu sent both his original letter and Ricci's reply to Yu's own former teacher, Zhuhong, one of the leading Buddhist intellectuals of the late Ming period. As abbot of Yunqi, near the city of Hangzhou, Zhuhong had been instrumental in bringing morality back into Buddhist monastic life and for building up the lay Buddhist devotional movement at the same time. He was unimpressed by Ricci's letter and told Yu that Ricci was not worth refuting since his arguments were so shallow. As to the style of Ricci's letter, which was far better than that in his published works, that was because it had probably been written for him by a Chinese scholar. A few years later Zhuhong elaborated his criticism: the prohibition against taking life was an absolute, but Ricci's discussion of mistreatment of parents was muddling the actual with the merely possible. There were fundamental differences between the two realms:

Marriages between men and women, the use of carts and horses, as well as the employment of servants are all ordinary things in the world. They can never be compared with the cruelty of taking the lives of animals. That is why the sutra says only that one should not kill any sentient being, but does not say that one should not get married or employ domestic animals. The kind of sophistry [used by Matteo Ricci] is a clever play on words. How can it harm the clear teaching of the Great Truth?[63]

Ricci probably never saw Zhuhong's original letter, and he was dead by the time the fuller criticism was published, but he was very aware of another set of detailed criticisms that were directed against him by Huang Hui, a highly regarded Hanlin scholar, also a devout Buddhist. Huang had somehow obtained a draft of Ricci's *True Meaning of the Lord of Heaven,* which he covered with critical marginal comments and circulated among his friends. Ricci was shown a copy, but chose not to respond to Huang directly, since he had no desire "to rouse any further enmity from one who was such a senior mandarin, and powerful at the court."[64]

Ricci left one quite detailed account of how he attempted to handle such disputations. He described an argument that he had over religion with the well-known Buddhist monk Sanhuai at a dinner party in Nanjing in early 1599. While the other guests listened and occasionally intervened, Ricci and Sanhuai argued over the meaning of creation and the role of the human mind in that process. The debate grew so heated that both men were shouting at each other much of the time. While Sanhuai argued for the full creative powers of the mind, Ricci countered with an analysis of the mind's storage capacity and reflective power when it came to the supernatural. The mirror, after all, he told Sanhuai, does not create the sun it reflects. The dialogue was opened to all the guests, as more food was served, on the topic of the innate goodness of human nature; here, in response to the Buddhist priest's ambiguous attitudes and the muddled arguments of the other guests, after one hour had passed Ricci used his memory powers to summarize all the arguments made so far. He then drew on his conceptions of original sin and divine grace to present his interpretation of the innate goodness of the Creator, a goodness that naturally informed the nature of God just as brightness was innate to the sun; he tried to use reason to show Sanhuai that the author of all things could not be of the same substance as man, though Sanhuai remained tenaciously unconvinced. Ricci had not wanted to get involved in this particular debate, he wrote later, and had begged off several times. But in the event it proved useful, and the content of their argument formed part of the revised version of his *True Meaning of the Lord of Heaven.* Indeed, in that work we can still see traces of the dialogue: on the reasons for God's existence in chapter 1, on innate phenomena in chapter 2, on natural goodness in chapter 7.[65]

Just before this debate with Sanhuai, Ricci had met a far more formidable man, the brilliant but irascible scholar Li Zhi, who by this time was seventy-two. Li flattered Ricci by visiting his house in person before Ricci had called on him, by writing two poems for him, by seeming to express his acceptance of many of Ricci's criticisms of Buddhism (through silence at debates in which they were presented), and by enjoying Ricci's work *On Friendship* so much that he shared copies with friends in other provinces.[66] In a letter to a friend, Li wrote how Ricci had learned about Buddhism in India before coming to China and throwing himself into the study of Confucian classics in Zhaoqing, working steadily through the canonical writings with the aid of local scholars. Li added:

> Now he can speak our language fluently, write our script, and act according to our rules of conduct. He is an extremely impressive man— a person of inner refinement, outwardly most straightforward. In an assembly of many people, all talking in confusion with each holding to his own point of view, Ricci keeps his silence and cannot be provoked to interfere or to become involved. Amongst the people of my acquaintance no one is comparable to him. All those who are either too overbearing or too flattering, or those who parade their cleverness or are narrow-minded and lacking in intelligence are inferior to him.[67]

Since Ricci admitted in his own *Historia* that he was occasionally driven to try to shout down the opposition (as in the case of Sanhuai), Li Zhi may have been overstating Ricci's control somewhat; but in any case Ricci reciprocated by noting that Li Zhi—whom many other contemporaries found eccentric, opinionated, and rude—was "prudent and experienced" at the kind of negotiations needed to obtain permission to establish residence in Peking for the Jesuits. The reunion of the two men in Jining city, Shandong province, in the spring of 1600, must have been an emotional and loving occasion. Ricci wrote that Li Zhi and his friends "treated him with such real tenderness [*amorevolezza*] all through the day, that it seemed to the father that he was not at the ends of the world in the midst of the gentiles, but rather in Europe among the most friendly and devout of Christians."[68]

Li Zhi gave Ricci several introductions to Peking friends, and these, added to the ones that Ricci already had from Nanchang, Nanjing, and elsewhere assured that when he finally settled in the capital he was able to mix with some of the most stimulating and talented intellectuals of the day, some of whom admired him and some of whom were sharply critical.[69] Ricci was still hoping to convert Li Zhi in 1603, or at least to build further on the interest in Christianity that he thought he detected there, when he received the shocking news that Li, defamed and imprisoned by hostile local scholars, had slit his throat in prison. "He cut his own throat with a knife," wrote Ricci in an emotional obituary,

> because a mandarin having written a bitter memorial about Li and his writings was told by the king to seize and burn all Li's books. And Li, seeing himself taken and made a mockery by his enemies, and not wishing to die at the hands of the courts, or else—and this moved him more—wishing to show his disciples, his enemies, and the whole world that he had no fear of death, killed himself in this manner and thus put an end to the plots of his enemies.[70]

Ricci's words here suggest that he had read Li Zhi's own essays on death, or had at least discussed them with him. As Li had written in an essay called "Five Ways to Die," death for a worthy cause was the finest, followed by death in battle, death as a martyr, death as a loyal minister unfairly calumniated, and premature death after finishing some good piece of work:

> An intelligent person should elect to die in any one of these five ways. One may be better than another, but each is a good way to end one's life. As for those who die in a sickbed, surrounded by wives and

256

children—one finds them everywhere in the world. . . . This is hardly a
way for a man to die. . . . As man is born for some good reason, how
can he die but for some good cause? But I am already old. I am denied
the opportunity to die in any one of the five preferable ways. . . . How
then shall I die? For those who fail to understand me will I die—just
to give vent to my resentment.[71]

However fond Ricci may have been of Li Zhi, prudence dictated that
after his death Ricci should align himself with those who criticized Li
for immoral behavior, particularly when those criticisms were couched
in a broadly anti-Buddhist context. Thus in the *Historia*, some sixty
pages after writing so movingly of Li, he also quotes approvingly from
the powerful indictment that the president of the Board of Rites, Feng
Qi, had made of Li and all those who tried to syncretize Buddhism and
Confucianism.[72]

This Board President Feng was well known among Ming Chinese
scholars for his support of state censorship of new books, his attempts
to ban ideas from student essays if they did not follow conventional
schools of Confucian interpretation, and his rule that any student
quoting from a Buddhist sutra have his government stipend suspended
for a month.[73] It is certainly unlikely that such a man, with such views
on orthodoxy, holding such high office in that particular ministry,
would have been seriously interested in Christianity and even contemplated conversion, but such was the claim made by Ricci in the second
book of his *Ten Discourses by a Paradoxical Man*, where he wrote that
Feng "strongly inclined toward the true religion of the Lord of
Heaven" but had died before he could put his intention into effect.
Feng, in fact, had died in 1603, five years before Ricci wrote these lines.
What makes them all the more suspect is the fact that the entire opening section of the dialogue, which in the *Ten Discourses* Ricci ascribes to
Feng Qi, had already appeared in quite another place—the *True Meaning of the Lord of Heaven*, begun in 1593 and published in 1603.[74] In this
central passage, ascribed to "a Chinese scholar" in the *True Meaning*
and to Feng Qi in the *Ten Discourses*, Ricci's interlocutor first talks of
the birds and animals, and of how swiftly they grow up and how per-

fectly equipped they are to feed and defend themselves. He contrasts this with the melancholy fate of mankind:

> At the time of our birth our mothers endure great pain, and as the naked baby comes out into the world he opens his mouth to cry, as if he already knew all the hardships of the life ahead. In infancy he is so weak that he cannot even walk, and it's only at around three that he no longer needs support. When they are grown, all must make their livings by painful toil. The peasant works in all four seasons to turn the soil in his plot of land, the merchant spends his years traveling over mountains and seas. The artisans of all the different trades exhaust their hands and feet day after day, the scholars day and night exhaust their brains by thinking. Thus it is said [by Mencius] that the rulers labor with their minds and the poor with their physical strength.
>
> Our fifty years of life are fifty years of pain, and our bodies subject to hundreds of kinds of misfortune. If we examine the medical texts, we find that there are three hundred diseases of the eye alone—how much more are there for the whole body, how can we even count them all? The medicines we need to heal us are bitter to the taste, and the world is filled with animals and insects, large and small, provided with poisons and weapons to do us harm, as if by some common agreement. A tiny insect no more than one inch long can destroy a grown man.[75]

This cry of despair, already poignant enough in the *True Meaning of the Lord of Heaven* when put in the mouth of an anonymous Chinese scholar, becomes doubly so when ascribed to Feng Qi, the passionate anti-Buddhist. For if all his Confucian wisdom has led him only to this deep well of pessimism, Ricci was saying, then nothing but Christianity can help him, nothing but a clear understanding of the intentionally transitory nature of our life on earth, and the possibility of a life of eternal joy for the faithful in the world to come.

To get this message across, every means that skill, artifice, training, and memory could provide had to be called into play: prisms, clocks, paintings, Euclid, tracts, dinners, the fathers of the church, Roman and

Greek philosophers, all under the divine guidance of the mother of God herself. It is not surprising that Ricci boasted at times to the Chinese that he had been born near Loreto, virtually under the shadow of the house where the Virgin Mary had lived and in which the Incarnation took place that made the word into flesh; it was under the Virgin's guidance that he worked and would rescue them from their despair. For if Mary was the garden and the sun, the fountain and the earth, as Ludolfus had said, she was also herself the tower, the castle into which Christ entered, and the water that flowed past the castle was a fountain of tears from the world.[76]

How could one be present at such mysteries? The cloistered monk, in some interpretations, could see himself as a symbol of Christ within the Virgin's womb, but Ricci was not cloistered; he ran around from day to day and snatched what moments of contemplation he could find.[77] And yet in the constant active service out in the world, to which Ricci was pledged, lay a kind of answer. Ignatius of Loyola seems to have seen and seized on one aspect of service, for the sake of all in his order, with a subtle insight. In the first day of the second week of the *Spiritual Exercises,* after the exercitant had fully reflected on the Incarnation, Ignatius led him into the second contemplation, that of the Nativity. He wrote:

> *First Prelude.* This is the history of the mystery. Here it will be that our Lady, about nine months with child, and, as may be piously believed, seated on an ass, set out from Nazareth. She was accompanied by Joseph and a maid, who was leading an ox. They are going to Bethlehem to pay the tribute that Caesar imposed on those lands.
>
> *Second Prelude.* This is a mental representation of the place. It will consist here in seeing in imagination the way from Nazareth to Bethlehem. Consider its length, its breadth; whether level, or through valleys and over hills. Observe also the place or cave where Christ is born; whether big or little; whether high or low; and how it is arranged. . . .
>
> *First Point.* This will consist in seeing the persons, namely, our Lady, St. Joseph, the maid, and the Child Jesus after His birth. I will make myself a poor little unworthy slave, and as though present, look upon

them, contemplate them, and serve them in their needs with all possible homage and reverence.[78]

This single maidservant, who in Ignatius's version is always in attendance to help the Virgin on her travels, in her labor, and after her son's birth, is not found in the gospels. In various apocryphal gospels there are often several relatives or two retainers, one male and one female, but it seems to have been Ignatius's idea to have just the one maid.[79] In the 1570s several Jesuits objected to the maid's being there, claiming she was not scriptural and that her presence offended against their sense of the Virgin's poverty at the time of Christ's birth. They could gain strength for this position from Chrysostum, who insisted that no servant could have been present, and from Ludolfus, who pointed to the Virgin's loneliness and shame as, attended only by her husband Joseph, she was forced "to wander among the men, seeking someplace to rest and finding none." General Claudio Acquaviva, however, insisted that the maid must stay; she had been put there with Ignatius's own hands to help the fathers meditate with maximum piety, she was central to the passage, and she must not be moved.[80] Through the maid's eyes, intimately but without impropriety, Ricci and his fellows could be present in memory and in person at the most mysterious and beautiful moments in the liturgy of their church.

Just before the New Year festival of 1591, Father Antonio Almeida, who was Ricci's only Western companion in the Shaozhou mission, fell seriously ill and had to be escorted back to Macao for medical treatment. Thus as the Chinese began to celebrate their most important holiday of the year, Ricci was left in the city with only one or two Chinese brothers to keep him company. He was depressed at the "coldness" of the local Chinese toward both himself and his religion, and the depression grew worse as the festivities reached their climax and the city shimmered in the blaze of light from the thousands of lanterns hung in the houses, streets, and temples. When cities all over the world were normally in darkness after nightfall, such ceremonies took on extra significance, literally changing the balance between night and day. Ricci wrote how every household in China took pride in its lanterns at the peak of the festival, and how for days in advance the markets were crammed with lantern-sellers hawking their wares and with eager customers.[81] Montaigne had seen the effect in Rome when it seemed to him "as if twelve thousand torches passed and the wax candles filled the street."[82] Gregory Martin was caught up even more vividly in the splendor of the Roman lights. There was nothing more superb than Maundy Thursday, he wrote, when the assembled sodalities of religious laymen marched in their liveries to St. Peter's, each carrying a great decorated crucifix in place of their usual standard and bearing aloft lanterns of glass or translucent horn and long wax candles so that for the space of three hours as the procession passed the streets were as "full of lightes as it were the firmament besett with great starres." Among them walked the flagellants, heads covered and backs bared to show the bloody weals. In St. Peter's itself the form of a great cross shone out, formed entirely of tiny glittering lamps of glass, gleaming like pearls.[83]

Moved by a sudden impulse that night in 1591, Ricci took the oil painting of the Virgin Mary which he had received from the Philippines not long before and placed it upon the altar in the little Shaozhou church. Then he brought out all the candles he could find and lanterns of all shapes and sizes, and anything of glass that would reflect the light, and he hung them all around the walls and placed them on the altar flanking the picture. As these lights began to shine forth, a large crowd of Chinese gathered, first in curiosity, and then to jeer, and finally to throw stones. The lights shone forth as the crowd ripped the clothes off the backs of Ricci's servants, who tried to chase them away. They shone as Ricci ran out to try to rescue the servants. And as he retreated back to the church in the face of the crowd's unwavering hostility the lights must have continued to shine, all around the Virgin Mary's picture, in their small corner of the nighttime city of Shaozhou, until the lamp oil and the candles were all burned out, or until Ricci had extinguished them, one by one.[84]

For the fourth image to be placed in the reception hall of his memory palace, Ricci chooses the Chinese ideograph for goodness, pronounced *hao.* He divides the ideograph vertically down the center to yield two separate ideographs, one with the meaning "woman" and one with the meaning "child."

To create the image of goodness that he seeks, he combines these two elements into a composite figure of a maidservant holding a child in her arms. He makes it clear that she is a maidservant by emphasizing her youth, and describing her hair as still being in the two tufted top-knots that are the mark of young servants in Chinese households. He notes that she is playing with the child she holds.[85]

He takes the servant girl with the child in her arms and places her in the last vacant corner of the reception hall, the one in the southwest. Opposite her are the two warriors locked in combat; diagonally across from her is the woman who is a *huihui;* to her left, the peasant who is profit waits above his harvest of grain.

For the fourth of his pictures that he will place in Cheng Dayue's ink garden, Ricci again chooses a woman with a child in her arms. This one is a print made by the Jesuit fathers in Japan of the Virgin Mary and the Christ Child. This Japanese print was taken from a rendering origi-nally made by Wierix of a painting hanging in a side chapel of the cathedral of Seville. The Virgin holds the Child with her left hand, and in her right hand she holds a rose. Christ holds a bunch of grapes in his left hand and in his lap a goldfinch, its wings outstretched; these are the symbols of his passion and death. His right hand is raised in bless-ing. Three angels hold a crown above the cowled head of the Virgin, whose halo bears the inscription, in Latin, "Hail Mary, full of grace."[86]

For all the other pictures Ricci has written a text, but he does not do

Domina noſtra S MARIA (cui ab antiquitate cognomen) curaſartago ita ſinibi a
æde dum Eccleſia eiuſdem tertiæ EVſebiuſ q̃ rigorat in pariete depicta Vincida
Noſtra Señora De C Antiqua   Inſceñ⁰ Iapo V31

so for this one. Above the picture he writes just two words, *Tien Chu,* meaning "Lord of Heaven."

The inscription below the picture, which he has the artist copy, records that the image was painted in commemoration of King Ferdinand III of Castile's capture of Seville from the Moors, so it thus represents the culmination of the great series of battles fought against the forces of Islam in thirteenth-century Spain. Since those days, of course, Seville has become the city that stands for the fame and wealth of the Spanish empire overseas, the unloading point for the floods of silver bullion pouring in from the New World.[87] A note at the bottom right of the picture mentions that this particular version was made in Japan in 1597, and for any Catholic in the Far East that will recall the twenty-six Christians who—on the orders of General Hideyoshi in his wrath—were crucified outside Nagasaki in that year.

Cheng Dayue's artisans do a commendable job in cutting a new woodblock from the Japanese original. It must surely be on Ricci's orders that they place the bird on Christ's lap, a bird that cannot be seen in the Japanese version; in conversation, as in memory, when correctly interpreted, the bird and the grapes together can lead to a consideration of deeper mysteries. But it is presumably by a slip of the chisel, rather than on instructions from Ricci, that a misprint appears in the Latin words engraved upon the Virgin's halo. The original "Hail Mary, full of grace," *Ave Maria Gratia Plena,* emerges in Ricci's picture as *Ave Maria Gratia Lena. Plena* is an adjective meaning "full"; *Lena,* on the other hand, is a feminine noun that means a woman who allures or entices. If Ricci does notice the slip, he lets it stand.

NINE

INSIDE THE PALACE

He stands on the threshold of the Memory Palace, in his embroidered shoes. The foot that he injured when jumping from the window, so long ago, pulses with pain.

In front of him, as far as the mind can travel, stretch the gleaming walls and colonnades, the porticoes and great carved doors, behind which are stored the images born of his reading, his experience, and his faith.

He sees the eunuch Ma Tang, suffused with anger, grasp the cross of carved wood to which the bleeding Christ is nailed. He hears the shouts of warning and the howling of the wind as the boat keels over, flinging both him and João Barrados into the water of the River Gan. He smells the incense that curls up around his triptych as he places it reverently upon a pagan altar in the luxurious garden temple of Juyung. He tastes the homely food prepared for him by the poor farmers in their country dwelling near Zhaoqing. He feels the touch of cheek on cheek as the dying Francesco de Petris throws his arms around his neck.

266

He has gone farther than he expected into unknown terrain and is not sure how easy it will be to return, should he choose to. *"Facilis descensus averni,"* he writes to Giulio Fuligatti, his school friend with whom once he learned the lines *"sed revocare gradum superasque evadere ad auras."* The words are Virgil's, from book 6 of the *Aeneid,* and he condenses slightly since he is in a hurry, and quoting from memory the verses he chanted as a child.

> The way downward is easy from Avernus.
> Black Dis's door stands open night and day.
> But to retrace your steps to heaven's air,
> There is the trouble, there is the toil.[1]

It is the warning spoken by the Cumaean Sybil as Aeneas seeks permission to go down to the underworld in search of his dead father.

In his pictures, sharply carved, the apostle Peter flounders in the waves, the two disciples pause at Emmaus, the men of Sodom tumble to the ground. In the reception hall the images hold their places: the grappling warriors, the *huihui* woman, the farmer who is his name.

"It often happens," he writes, "that those who live at a later time are unable to grasp the point at which the great undertakings or actions of this world had their origin. And I, constantly seeking the reason for this phenomenon, could find no other answer than this, namely that all things (including those that come at last to triumph mightily) are at their beginnings so small and faint in outline that one cannot easily convince oneself that from them will grow matters of great moment."[2]

He stands on the threshold, a heavy, bearded man, in his robe of purple silk trimmed with blue. The Memory Palace is silent. Behind him wait two women, each cradling a child in her arms. One woman wears a long embroidered dress of extraordinary beauty. Her hair and shoulders are covered by a flowing shawl. She holds a rose. The other wears the simple garb of a servant girl, and her hair is gathered in two tufts to mark her youth and lowly station.

"Though still a young man," he writes to Gian Pietro Maffei, his friend and chronicler of Christendom's expansion, "I have already taken on the trait of the elderly, who are always praising time past."[3]

The two children watch him. One raises his small right hand in blessing; the other reaches out his arms to play. Through the quiet air, confusedly, comes a murmur of sound from the streets of Peking.

He closes the door.

ABBREVIATIONS

DMB: Dictionary of Ming Biography. L. Carrington Goodrich and Chaoying Fang, eds. 2 vols. Columbia University Press, 1976.

Doc Ind.: Documenta Indica. Joseph Wicki, S.J., ed. *Monumenta Missionum Societatis Jesu, Missiones Orientales,* vol. 10 (1575–1577), Rome, 1968; vol. 11 (1577–1580), Rome, 1970; vol. 12 (1580–1583), Rome, 1972.

FR: Fonti Ricciane. Pasquale M. D'Elia, S.J., ed. *Storia dell'Introduzione del Cristianesimo in Cina.* [The annotated version of Ricci's original manuscript of the *Historia.*] 3 vols. Rome, 1942–1949.

OS: The letters of Matteo Ricci, in *Opere Storiche.* Pietro Tacchi Venturi, S.J., ed. Vol. 2, *Le Lettere dalla China.* Macerata, 1913.

NOTES

ONE
BUILDING THE PALACE

1. Ricci, *Jifa,* pp. 20-21. The only surviving versions of this *Jifa,* Ricci's *Treatise on Mnemonic Arts,* list Ricci as author, Zhu Dinghan as collator, Vagnoni (Gao Yizhi, Pfister no. 26) and Sambiasi (Bi Fangji, Pfister no. 40) as editors. (For locations, see *Fonti Ricciane,* 1/376 n. 6.) Zhu Dinghan, a Christian convert and native of Shanxi province, wrote the only extant preface, in which he says "Mr. Gao" was the main transmitter of Ricci's work on memory. I assume this Gao to be Gao Yizhi, the name Vagnoni adopted after his return to China in 1624 when he settled in the same Shanxi town where Zhu Dinghan was living. Vagnoni had taught rhetoric for five years in Turin after his novitiate and later became a brilliant Chinese-language scholar. He probably obtained a copy of Ricci's text when in Nanjing and then revised it in Macao, carrying it to Shanxi and introducing it to Zhu Dinghan sometime after 1624. (See Pfister, pp. 85 and 89, for the details of Vagnoni's life that support such a contention.) From the condition of the current text one would guess that Vagnoni left Ricci's basic six-chapter form unchanged but added the lengthy series of further exemplars at the end of ch. 6, pp. 28-31 (reprint pp. 63-69). Vagnoni or Zhu may well also have ex-

270

panded the lists of examples running through chs. 4-6, since Zhu notes in his preface that Ricci was often rather unclear in his explanations. As fellow Jinjiang residents, Vagnoni and Zhu were natural collaborators, though it is still hard to fix the dates exactly. Vagnoni died in 1640, but Zhu was still living a year later, as he is noted as an honorary licentiate for 1641 (*Jiangzhou zhi*, 8/29). The role of Sambiasi in editing the book is not clear; he did travel to Shanxi in 1628 (Pfister, p. 138) but was not in Jinjiang long, if at all. The imprimatur was granted by Emmanuel Diaz the younger (Pfister, p. 31), who was made vice-provincial in 1623, dying in Hangzhou in 1659.

2. *Jifa*, pp. 21-22.

3. This text is in *Jifa*, pp. 17-18, with one ideograph illegible in the last phrase. This is clearly Ricci's rendering of the famous passage from Cicero's *De Oratore*, 2/86, also cited in *Lyra Graeca*, 2/307. The Cicero original is discussed by Frances Yates in her *Art of Memory*, pp. 17-18.

4. The main outlines of Ricci's career are given in English by Wolfgang Franke in the *Dictionary of Ming Biography* (hereafter cited as *DMB*), pp. 1137-44. More extended treatments are in George Dunne, *Generation of Giants;* Vincent Cronin, *Wise Man from the West;* and George Harris, "The Mission of Matteo Ricci." The French biography in Pfister, *Notices*, pp. 22-42 (no. 9), is still useful, as is the extended survey by Henri Bernard, *Le Père Matthieu Ricci et la Société Chinoise de son temps*. A recent Italian biographical sketch with good bibliography is Aldo Adversi's "Matteo Ricci" in *Dizionario Bio-Bibliografico dei Maceratesi;* the most extended Italian biography is Fernando Bortone's *P. Matteo Ricci, S.J.*, illustrated with maps, photographs, and drawings. All of these works draw massively on the great central source, Ricci's own *Historia*, as transcribed first by Tacchi Venturi and republished, with corrections, by Pasquale d'Elia as *Fonti Ricciane*, cited here throughout as *FR*. The Trigault version of Ricci's *Historia* (translated by Louis Gallagher) is full of Trigault's distortions, deletions, and additions to the original and is not a reliable reflection of Ricci's own views. A recent Chinese essay by Lin Jinshui, "Li Madou zai Zhongguo," unfortunately relies very heavily on this Trigault-Gallagher version but shows a thorough grasp of the basic issues. A good survey of current Ricci scholarship in Taiwan is provided in the special issue of *Shenxue lunji* (*Collectanea Theologica*), no. 56, Summer 1983, which is entirely given over to a collection of essays on Matteo Ricci's China mission.

5. Details on the composition of the *Friendship* book (the *Jiaoyou lun*) are

given in Ricci's letters, edited by Tacchi Venturi under the title *Opere Storiche*, vol. 2 (hereafter cited as *OS*); see p. 226, letter of Oct. 13, 1596, to General Claudio Acquaviva. In this letter Ricci refers to *"l'anno passato"* as the time of composition, and says he wrote the book "as an exercise" (*per esercitio*). Since the book is not mentioned as finished in Ricci's Nov. 4, 1595, letter to Acquaviva (*OS*, p. 210), it must have been completed later in November or in December. Despite this rather clear evidence from the basic sources, the dates of composition have been argued over with considerable bitterness by Pasquale d'Elia, "Further Notes," especially p. 359, and by Fang Hao, "Li Madou *Jiaoyou lun xinyan*" and "Notes on Matteo Ricci's *De Amicitia*." Fang Hao's charges against d'Elia of linguistic incompetence ("Li Madou *Jiaoyou lun*," p. 1854) are more than matched, if not exactly quashed, by d'Elia's countercharge of Fang's blatant plagiarism, in "Further Notes," pp. 373-77.

6. *OS*, p. 211, Nov. 4, 1595: *"ad alcuni ho cominciato ad insegnare la memoria locale"* ("I have begun to teach various people the memory place [system]").

7. *FR*, 1/376. As Ricci writes in *OS*, p. 224, to Acquaviva, on Oct. 13, 1596: *"Per la memoria locale ... feci in sua lingua e lettera alcuni avisi e precetti in un libretto, che diedi al viceré per il suo figliuolo."* (That there were in fact three sons is stated by Ricci in *FR*, 1/363.)

8. There is a biography of Lu Wangai in his fellow Pinghu townsman Guo Tingxun's *Benchao fensheng renwu kao*, juan 45, pp. 32b-33b. Further details on his career and accomplishments are given in the *Pinghu xianzhi*, 15/37 (reprint pp. 1431-32); ibid., 13/5 (reprint p. 1176) shows him as twenty-first in the second class in the *jinshi* exam of 1568.

9. For the children's exam successes, see the governor's son Lu Jian's *jinshi* degree of 1607 in *Pinghu xianzhi*, 13/7a (reprint p. 1179) and other Lus clearly of the same generation in ibid. and *Jiaxing fuzhi*, lists in 45/75-85; also biographies in juan 58. On mnemonic rhymes for alchemists, mechanics, ship pilots, and astronomers, see Joseph Needham, *Science and Civilisation in China*, vol. 5, pt. 4, p. 261; vol. 4, pt. 2, pp. 48, 528; vol. 4, pt. 3, p. 583. An assemblage of famous Chinese mnemonic masters is given below in ch. 5.

10. *OS*, p. 224, Nanchang, Oct. 13, 1596.

11. *OS*, p. 235, to Lelio Passionei, Sept. 19, 1597.

12. *Monumenta Paedagogica*, p. 350, where *"Cypriani rhetorica"* is recommended *"pro classe inferiori."*

13. Soarez, *De Arte Rhetorica,* pp. 58–59.

14. Compare Pliny, *Natural History,* bk. 7, sect. 24 (Loeb ed., p. 563), with Ricci's *Jifa,* p. 14. The *Monumenta Paedagogica* of 1586, p. 350, show Pliny's *Natural History* as an assigned book in the Jesuit school. (This same passage of Pliny is the springboard for the brilliant story by Jorge Borges, "Funes the Memorious.")

15. *Ad Herennium,* p. 221.

16. Quintilian, *Oratoria,* 4/223. The "impluvium" was the water storage tank in the center of a Roman home.

17. I have here elaborated in the visual terms common to the Renaissance tradition three of the verbal mnemonics that are given as examples in *Dictionary of Mnemonics:* p. 18, bones, no. 1; p. 21, cell division, no. 2; p. 57, nerves. I have made the Zulu and the French lady singular, as would have been favored in Renaissance mnemonics.

18. Stahl and Johnson, *Capella,* 2/7, and n. 18. Yates, *Art of Memory,* pp. 63–65.

19. Stahl and Johnson, *Capella,* 2/156–57 (with minor changes) and p. 156 n. 13.

20. Smalley, *English Friars,* p. 114, citing Ridevall's complete jingle *"Mulier notata, oculis orbata,/ Aure mutilata, cornu ventilata,/ Vultu deformata, et morbo vexata";* Yates, *Art of Memory,* pp. 105–6, has a brilliant gloss on Smalley's use of Ridevall's passage.

21. Ricci describes his memory feats in *OS,* p. 155 and *FR,* 1/360 n. 1. He gives the number of ideographs in *OS,* p. 184. Chinese witnesses include Li Zhizao in his preface to Ricci's *Jiren shipian,* p. 102, and Zhu Dinghan, citing Xu Guangqi in his preface to Ricci's *Jifa.* Though Zhu is not included in the indexes to the Ming histories, mention of him can be found in the *Jiangzhou zhi* (ed. of 1776), 8/29, where he is listed as a senior licentiate, second class *(suigong)* of 1641.

22. *FR,* 1/377n., suggests Panigarola as Ricci's source; see the Panigarola manuscript, Macerata. Frances Yates, *Art of Memory,* p. 241, cites a Florence manuscript of 1595 on Panigarola's powers.

23. Ricci, *Jifa,* p. 22.

24. Yates, *Art of Memory,* pp. 62 and 26.

25. Ricci, *Jifa,* pp. 16–17, 22. I translate the Chinese word *shi* as "reception hall."

26. Ibid., pp. 27–28.

27. Ibid., p. 22; Quintilian, *Oratoria,* 4/223; on Dolce, see Yates, *Art of Memory,* p. 166.

28. *OS*, pp. 260 and 283. For Nadal's work, see the discussion by Guibert, *Jesuits*, pp. 204-7.

29. Ricci, *Li Madou ti baoxiang tu,* sec. 2, p. 4; Cheng Dayue, *Chengshi moyuan,* juan 3, sec. 2; Duyvendak, "Review of Pasquale d'Elia," pp. 396-97.

30. Agrippa, tr. Sanford, p. 25 recto.

31. Yates, *Art of Memory,* p. 133.

32. Rabelais, *Gargantua,* tr. Cohen, ch. 14, pp. 70-72; see also the fruitful discussion in Thomas Greene, *Light in Troy,* p. 31.

33. Bacon, "Of the Advancement of Learning Divine and Human," bk. 2, sec. 15, 2, in *Selected Writings,* p. 299. The positive role ascribed to memory for the study of new science is elaborated by Paolo Rossi in *Francis Bacon,* pp. 210-13.

34. *Monumenta Paedagogica,* edition of 1586, continues to list it, p. 350. The first dismissals of Cicero's attribution as author came in 1491 (Yates, *Art of Memory,* pp. 132-33).

35. Yates, *Art of Memory,* pp. 72-104, especially p. 86 on the misreading of *"solitudo"* for *"sollicitudo,"* and p. 101 on Giotto. Aristotle's original text on memory has been translated and carefully glossed by Richard Sorabji in *Aristotle on Memory.*

36. Guibert, *Jesuits,* pp. 167-68.

37. As translated in Bodenstedt, *Vita Christi,* p. 121.

38. Conway, *Vita,* pp. 38 and 127; Bodenstedt, *Vita Christi,* p. 50.

39. Cited in Conway, *Vita,* p. 125.

40. See the 1454 "Garden of Prayer" cited in Baxandall, *Painting and Experience in Fifteenth-Century Italy,* p. 46.

41. Ignatius of Loyola, *Exercises,* par. 47. In the following pages, I try to heed the injunction given by Guibert, in *Jesuits,* p. 167, that discussing Ignatius in terms of his method is like defining a locomotive by its color; I also note Hugo Rahner's comments in *Ignatius the Theologian,* pp. 181-83.

42. Ignatius, *Exercises,* pars. 192, 201, 220. Rahner, *Ignatius,* p. 189, discusses these locations as symbols.

43. Ignatius, *Exercises,* pars. 107, 108, and 124-25.

44. Ibid., par. 50.

45. Ibid., pars. 56, 140-46. For a counter-commentary on Ignatius and the senses see Barthes, *Sade, Fourier, Loyola,* pp. 58-59.

46. Augustine, *Confessions,* p. 266.

47. Rahner, *Ignatius,* p. 158; Wright, *Counter-Reformation,* p. 16.

48. Rahner, *Ignatius*, p. 159.

49. Ibid., pp. 161-62.

50. Ibid., p. 191.

51. Walker, *Spiritual and Demonic Magic*, p. 36 and pp. 70-71 on Ficinan magic; Thomas, *Decline of Magic*, p. 33.

52. *OS*, p. 223.

53. Thomas, *Decline of Magic*, pp. 178-80.

54. Ginzburg, *Cheese and the Worms*, p. 56.

55. Ibid., pp. 13 and 29.

56. Thomas, *Decline of Magic*, pp. 75-77; examples cited from p. 14; ch. 8; and p. 536.

57. Ginzburg, *Cheese and the Worms*, p. 105.

58. Ibid., pp. 83-84.

59. See ch. 3, below, on the sea and the talismans; *FR*, 2/121 on the relics and the cross composed of *"molti pezzi della Croce di Cristo benedetto."* Thomas, *Decline of Magic*, p. 31, notes the ongoing faith in the power of the wax "Agnus Dei."

60. Thomas, *Decline of Magic*, p. 247.

61. Ibid., pp. 333 and 578.

62. Montaigne, *Journal de Voyage*, p. 349.

63. Davis, *Return of Martin Guerre*, p. 37; see her other comments on magic and memory, pp. 60, 76, 102, 107.

64. *Hamlet*, act 4, scene 5, lines 173-74; see the recipes in Grataroli, *De Memoria*, p. 58, and in Fulwood's 1573 English translation at p. E5.

65. Paci, "Decadenza," pp. 166, 194, and 204 n. 400.

66. Yates, *Art of Memory*, quotation on p. 147; memory theater, p. 136; Camillo as "Magus," p. 156. See also Walker, *Spiritual and Demonic Magic*, pp. 141-43, on Camillo, and pp. 206 and 236 for Campanella and Pope Urban VIII. Yates, *Art of Memory*, chs. 11, 13, 14, details Giordano Bruno's system. The coincidence of Bruno's heresy trial with that of the miller Menocchio, mentioned above, is noted in Ginzburg, *Cheese and the Worms*, p. 127.

67. Hersey, *Pythagorean Palaces*, p. 84 on "linee occulte," and pp. 96-105 on the human figure.

68. Winn, *Unsuspected Eloquence*, pp. 51, 58-59; Walker, *Studies in Musical Science*, pp. 1 and 2, 53; p. 67 for an analysis of the sexual images in Kepler's *Harmonice Mundi*.

69. Winn, *Unsuspected Eloquence*, p. 167, and quotation on pp. 178-79.

70. *OS*, pp. 27-28, letter to Martin de Fornari, Macao, Feb. 13, 1583. For

Acosta's 1590 view of Chinese ideographs as "ciphers designed to jog the memory," see Lach, *Asia in the Making of Europe,* vol. 1, bk. 2, pp. 806–7.

71. Ricci, *Li Madou ti baoxiang tu,* sec. 2, pp. 1b–2. See also Laufer, "Christian Art in China," pp. 111–12; Duyvendak, "Review," pp. 394–95.

72. Quintilian, *Oratoria,* 4/221 and 229.

73. *Ad Herennium,* p. 211; Yates, *Art of Memory,* p. 23.

74. Ricci, *Jifa,* p. 22.

75. Examples given in *FR,* 1/112 n. 5 and 113 n. 6. Barthes, *Sade, Fourier, Loyola,* p. 28, discusses the satiric obverse of this in the Sadian order of the rosary, where the old nuns are arranged by "decades."

TWO

THE FIRST IMAGE: THE WARRIORS

1. Ricci, *Jifa,* p. 16, for the image. L. S. Yang, "Historical Notes," p. 24, quotes the *Tso-chuan* interpretation on the components of *wu* being "to stay" and "the spear."

2. Ricci, *Jifa,* pp. 52–61.

3. Ibid., pp. 23–28.

4. Paci, "Le Vicende," pp. 234–37.

5. Paci, "Decadenza," pp. 204–7, especially the detailed n. 403 on p. 204. The Riccis killed were Francesco in 1547 and Costanza in 1588. The peacekeeping attempts are listed on p. 205 nn. 404–7.

6. Paci, "Vicende," p. 265 n. 642.

7. Ibid., pp. 264–68.

8. Delumeau, *Vie économique,* 1/40, 44, 94. On p. 105 Delumeau mentions a "G. Battista Ricci of Loretto" being in charge of the Marche transport routes after 1587. This is the same name as Ricci's father, though the Loreto registration makes the identification unsure.

9. Paci, "Vicende," pp. 238–39.

10. Ibid., pp. 249–50.

11. Pastor, *History of the Popes,* 14/152–67; Paci, "Vicende," pp. 250–53.

12. Paci, "Vicende," p. 231.

13. *Cambridge History of Islam,* 1A/328; Paci, "Vicende," p. 253.

14. Paci, "Vicende," pp. 257–61.

15. Robert Barret, *The Theorike and Practike of Moderne Warres* (London,

1598), p. 75. This passage is cited, with one or two small changes in transcription, by J. R. Hale in his chapter on "Armies, Navies and the Art of War" in *New Cambridge Modern History,* 3/194.

16. Paci, "Vicende," pp. 256–57.

17. See the excellent discussion by J. R. Hale in *New Cambridge Modern History,* 3/196–97.

18. Paci, "Vicende," p. 250 n. 500.

19. Ricci and Xu Guangqi, *Jihe yuanben,* p. 3 (reprint pp. 1933–34); also translated in d'Elia, "Presentazione," pp. 183–84, and Moule, "Obligations," pp. 158–59.

20. The passage appears both in Ricci's *Jiren shipian,* p. 5b (reprint p. 126) and his *Tianzhu shiyi,* juan shang, p. 24 (reprint p. 423).

21. *New Cambridge Modern History,* 3/199–200; Essen, *Alexandre Farnèse,* 4/55–62. A picture of the bridge is in plate 3, facing p. 22, and of the explosion in plate 4, facing p. 60. A second ship, similarly prepared, burned out harmlessly on the shore.

22. Paci, "Vicende," pp. 259–61 on Maceratan troops; Gentili and Adversi, "Religione," p. 51, on the wounding of Fra Ruggero.

23. See O'Connell's vivid account in *Counter Reformation,* pp. 195–203; and Paci, "Vicende," pp. 259–61 for Maceratans in the battle.

24. Groto, *Troffeo,* preface on his tour of the fleet, Section A on the sub-fleets and their commanders, followed by a 120-page anthology of poems in Don John's honor. See also the Greek and Roman analogies in Pompeo Arnolphini's *Ioan. Austriaco Victori Dicatum* (Bononiae: Ioannis Rossii, 1572).

25. See the fascinating example of such paintings reproduced in Sakamoto, "Lepanto," plates 3–6; Sakamoto traces the original print back to a Cornelis Cort engraving from a Giulio Romano drawing. Montaigne noticed a Lepanto victory painting hanging near the St. Sixtus chapel in Rome (*Journal de Voyage,* p. 226).

26. L. A. Florus, *Epitome of Roman History,* pp. 113–15 (correcting misprint); Ricci's three schoolboy books are given in *FR,* 2/553n.

27. Pastor, *History of the Popes,* 18/429–32.

28. Ibid., pp. 433–34, 444.

29. Schütte, *Valignano's Mission,* pp. 76–79, citing Valignano's letter of 1574.

30. Ibid., p. 75, and Brooks, *King for Portugal,* pp. 9–10.

31. *FR,* 2/559, n. 4.

32. *Cambridge History of Islam*, 2A/241-45; on heat and armor, see Bovill, *Alcazar*, pp. 106, 126.

33. Bovill, *Alcazar*, pp. 101-2.

34. Quoted in Brooks, *King for Portugal*, p. 150. On the battle see ibid., pp. 8-21, and Bovill, *Alcazar*, pp. 114-40.

35. Couto, *Decada Decima*, bk. 1, ch. 16, p. 148; *Documenta Indica* (cited hereafter as *Doc. Ind.*), 11/698, on the ceremonies.

36. D'Elia, *Mappamondo*, plate 24; Giles, "Chinese World Map," p. 379.

37. *Doc. Ind.*, 11/673 and 698.

38. On Goa's size, see Sassetti, *Lettere*, p. 280; quotation from Francis Pasio, letter of Oct. 28, 1578, *Doc. Ind.*, 11/365.

39. Ricci's comment in d'Elia, *Mappamondo*, plate 20; opium evidence from Cesare Fedrici, *Voyages*, pp. 202-4; Hakluyt, *Second Volume*, p. 241.

40. His letter of Nov. 25, 1580, to Acquaviva, in *OS*, p. 20, shows some sympathy. The other letters are neutral or cool. See also his comments in Chinese, d'Elia, *Mappamondo*, plate 19.

41. Biographical details in Schütte, *Valignano's Mission*, pp. 30-35, especially nn. 106 and 122; p. 39 n. 167 on stature; p. 42 n. 187, and p. 121 on India walk.

42. Ibid., pp. 44 and 52.

43. Ibid., p. 61, citing letter of Nov. 16, 1573.

44. Ibid., pp. 104-8.

45. Ibid., pp. 117, 120, 155.

46. Ibid., p. 131.

47. Quotations ibid., pp. 272-73, 279.

48. Ibid., pp. 296-97, 308.

49. Ibid., pp. 286-87 for Valignano's report; p. 288 and n. 61 for Acquaviva's response.

50. Noted in d'Elia, *Mappamondo*, plate 16.

51. *OS*, p. 48, Zhaoqing, letter of Sept. 13, 1584, to Giambattista Roman.

52. On these works, see Boxer, *South China in the Sixteenth Century*, pp. lvi-lvii and lxiii-lxv; for da Cruz on hair, ibid., pp. 138 and 146. On Pereira and da Cruz in the context of sources on China in the sixteenth century, see Donald Lach, *Asia in the Making of Europe*, vol. 1, bk. 2, pp. 747-50.

53. Bernard, *Les Iles Philippines*, pp. 48-50; Lach, *Asia in the Making of Europe*, vol. 1, bk. 2, p. 746; Elison, *Deus Destroyed*, pp. 114-15; Johannes Beckmann, *China im Blickfeld*, pp. 52-65. The key letters by Alfonso Sanchez and Giuseppe de Acosta are printed in *OS*, pp. 425 and 450.

Other materials are discussed in John Young, *Confucianism and Christianity*, pp. 141–42 n. 122.

54. *FR*, 1/70.

55. *FR*, 1/65 and 68. By now, Ricci has moved beyond the interpretations offered by Pereira and da Cruz, discussed above.

56. *FR*, 1/343.

57. *FR*, 2/21.

58. *FR*, 1/19.

59. *FR*, 1/28.

60. *FR*, 1/74.

61. *FR*, 1/104 and 67.

62. *Zhaoqing fuzhi*, 22/32b and 33b (reprint pp. 3330 and 3332).

63. So Kwan-wai, *Japanese Piracy*, ch. 5.

64. Huang, "Military Expenditure," p. 49; "Hu Tsung-hsien," in *DMB*, p. 633; Fitzpatrick, "Local Interests," p. 24.

65. Huang, "Military Expenditures," pp. 53–55; compare Cipolla, ed., *Fontana Economic History*, pp. 384–88. *DMB*, p. 1114, "P'ang Shang-p'eng."

66. Huang, *1587*, pp. 168–74, and illustration from Qi's handbooks. Millinger, "Ch'i Chi-kuang," pp. 110–11.

67. Quoted in Millinger, "Ch'i Chi-kuang," p. 104.

68. Schütte, *Valignano's Mission*, p. 286.

69. As in *FR*, 1/67 and 104; Ricci's companion Ruggieri used the same parallel, *OS*, p. 402 (appendix 3).

70. *FR*, 1/100. For Pereira's and da Cruz's descriptions, see Boxer, *South China*, pp. 18–19, 178–79.

71. *FR*, 1/101.

72. *FR*, 1/205–6, 243.

73. *FR*, 1/289–93. Ricci mourned the original Francesco Martines in his letter to Maffei of Dec. 1, 1581; see *OS*, p. 24.

74. Ricci's detailed account is in *FR*, 2/374–79.

75. In a lengthy note in *FR*, 1/292 d'Elia discusses a Jesuit catalogue entry of 1593 (or very late 1592) stating Martines was then twenty-five, i.e., born in 1568.

76. Ludolfus, *Vita Christi*, ed. Bolard, p. 638, right top, following the translation by H. J. Coleridge, p. 190. On the entire flagellation, see Coleridge's rich translation, pp. 188–97, and Ludolfus's haunting details of cold and nakedness, pp. 255–56.

77. A particularly good description is in a Ruggieri letter of Feb. 7, 1583, *OS*, p. 415.

78. See *DMB,* pp. 728–33 under Konishi Yukinaga. Jesuit complicity in these Japanese military plans is discussed by Elison, *Deus Destroyed,* pp. 112–13.

79. *FR,* 2/10–11.

80. Ricci reflection in *FR,* 2/373–74; Schurz, *Manila Galleon,* pp. 85–93; *DMB,* "Kao Ts'ai," p. 583.

81. The outlines of these three other religious orders' early days in China are well sketched by Henri Bernard in his *Aux Portes de la Chine,* especially pp. 59–71, 103–14. The China experiences of the Dominican Gaspar da Cruz and the Augustinian Martin de Rada are translated in Charles Boxer, ed., *South China in the Sixteenth Century,* pt. 2. Paul Pelliot gives a good summary of Franciscan experiences in his *Les Franciscains en Chine,* and also points out shortcomings in the work of Bernard and Wijngaert on the same topic. Ricci's praise for St. Francis and his followers is in his *Tianzhu shiyi,* p. 541. For examples of Ricci's concern at Franciscan tactics, see *FR,* 1/179, 232, 2/269. D'Elia cites an even stronger warning by Valignano to Ricci about other orders' *"herror y zelo desordenado"* in *FR,* 1/187, n. 8.

82. *FR,* 2/372–73; Cooper, "Mechanics of the Macao-Nagasaki Silk Trade," p. 431.

83. *FR,* 2/373.

84. *FR,* 2/388.

85. Furber, *Rival Empires of Trade,* pp. 33–35. On Coen's ruthless methods, see pp. 44–45.

86. See Schilling, "Martyrerberichtes," p. 107; for the disputatious background to the martyrdoms see Elison, *Deus Destroyed,* pp. 132–40. Carletti, *My Voyage,* says that upon landing in Nagasaki he "went immediately to see the spectacle." Boxer, "Macao as Religious and Commercial Entrepôt," p. 69, mentions the martyrdom on silks and other textiles.

87. Stele, cited by Cooper, "Mechanics," p. 424.

88. On savage riots between Japanese Christian crewmen and Portuguese in Macao during 1608, see Boxer, *Fidalgos,* pp. 53–54.

89. *FR,* 1/324.

90. *FR,* 2/370.

91. I.e., in 1601; see Boxer, *Fidalgos,* p. 49.

92. *FR,* 2/370, *"un puoco di muro et un modo di fortezza."*

93. *OS,* p. 374, letter of Aug. 23, 1608.

94. Ignatius, *Spiritual Exercises,* tr. Puhl, par. 327.

95. Ibid., par. 325.

96. *FR*, 1/172–73.

97. *FR*, 1/203.

98. *FR*, 1/246–47.

99. Aquinas, ed. Bourke, p. 259.

100. Phrases from *OS*, pp. 67, 70, 90, 234, 279.

101. *OS*, p. 161. On de Sande, see Pfister, *Notices*, p. 44.

102. Quoted in Conway, *Vita Christi*, pp. 61 and 96.

103. Maffei, *L'histoire des Indes*, preface, p. 3. Ricci praises this "proemio" lavishly in *OS*, p. 24, letter of Dec. 1, 1581. On Maffei, see Villoslada, *Storia del Collegio Romano*, p. 335, and Dainville, *L'éducation*, p. 129.

104. 2 Cor. 11:26, echoed in *OS*, p. 107.

105. *Shaozhou fuzhi*, 11/52b (reprint p. 242) on drought, and 24/36b (reprint p. 481) on the magician (*Yao*) named Li.

106. *FR*, 1/320–22. *OS*, p. 108, letter to Acquaviva of Nov. 15, 1592, gives extra details.

107. Foot pain and treatment consultations can be reconstructed from remarks in *FR*, 1/321 and 323.

THREE

THE FIRST PICTURE:
THE APOSTLE IN THE WAVES

1. Matt. 14:23–33.

2. Ricci discusses this Bible translation, and his refusal, in a letter of May 12, 1605, to Acquaviva's assistant, Alvarez, *OS*, p. 283.

3. Ricci, *Li Madou ti baoxiang tu*, pp. 1–3b; Cheng Dayue, *Chengshi moyuan*, juan 6, sec. 2, pp. 36–38b. For other translations, see Laufer, "Christian Art," pp. 107–8 as amended by Duyvendak, "Review," pp. 389–91.

4. *OS*, p. 284.

5. Nadal, *Evangelicae Historiae Imagines*, no. 44. The illustrations had been commissioned by the Jesuits in Europe with the express purpose of enhancing the value of Nadal's famous work *Adnotiones et Meditationes in Evangelia* for missionaries and priests in their work of conversion. Nadal's own theological reflections were orthodox, learned, and clear, but they lacked that sense of excitement or immediacy that would fix them in the memory. So senior members of the Jesuit order worked for

years to have an illustrated version of Nadal's work published by the great printer Plantin, whose presses—though never idle—were less worked in the 1580s than they had been in the days when he was printing the polyglot Bible. The Jesuits endured many humiliations and invested large amounts of cash to get as many of the biblical scenes as possible engraved from their own drawings by the formidable Wierix brothers; besides being regarded as the best engravers in Europe, the three Wierixes were also well known to be drunkards, lechers, and insatiably greedy for money. True to their reputation they steadily pushed the price per page up between 1586 and 1587, though when the work was finished in 1593 it was a triumph. (The protracted and fascinating negotiations between the Jesuits and Plantin can be read in Plantin, *Correspondance,* vol. 8, letters 1160, 1182, 1188, 1193, 1194.) The full edition of Nadal had 150 folio pictures following the whole life of Christ, from Nativity through the Passion to Resurrection, identifying scenes within scenes by means of letters inserted in the pictures, which were then glossed in notes below. Each picture was also keyed to Nadal's lengthy commentaries, which were designed to help in sermons or in exegesis.

6. *OS,* p. 260, on Diaz agreement; *OS,* p. 283, requests new copies of Nadal.
7. For the placement of this in the full sequence of prints, see Mauquoy-Hendrickx, *Estampes,* pp. 17 and 20–21. The prints are taken from originals by Martin de Vos. Two states of the original print, one by Visscher (51.501.1765:20) and one by Eduardus ab Hoeswinc[kel] (53.601.18:43) are in the Metropolitan Museum in New York. The second was the one adapted by Ricci, and the stigmata are boldly visible.
8. See d'Elia, *Mappamondo,* passim, or outline map in *FR,* vol. 2, frontispiece. J. H. Parry, *Age of Reconnaissance,* p. 139, suggests King John II of Portugal was the first to change the cape's name.
9. Gomes de Brito, *Tragic History* (*1589–1622*), tr. Boxer, p. 1 and map.
10. Ibid., pp. 3–5.
11. As well as Gomes de Brito, above, see Parry, *Age of Reconnaissance,* pt. 1, and James Duffy, *Shipwreck and Empire,* pp. 49–51.
12. Carletti, *My Voyage,* pp. 102–4.
13. *FR,* 1/290n.
14. *OS,* p. 125, letter of Nov. 15, 1594, to Fabio de Fabi.
15. *OS,* p. 113, letter of Dec. 10, 1593.
16. *OS,* pp. 218 and 230.
17. *OS,* p. 268, letter of May 10, 1605.

18. Tacchi Venturi in *OS,* p. 218 n. 1, suggests Matteo's father died in 1604.

19. See examples in Gomes de Brito, *Tragic History* (*1589–1622*), pp. 9–10. Duffy, *Shipwreck and Empire,* pp. 62–63, 73–74.

20. Gomes de Brito, *Tragic History* (*1589–1622*), pp. 20–21.

21. Ibid., pp. 15–17; Sassetti, *Lettere,* p. 280; Mocquet, *Voyages,* pp. 220–21 corroborates the worst details on his 1609 journey to Goa.

22. Gomes de Brito, *Tragic History* (*1589–1622*): p. 116 for wood rot; p. 191 for rotten rudder on the *St. John the Baptist; Tragic History* (*1559–1565*), p. 31, for ropes around stern.

23. *FR,* 1/238.

24. *Doc. Ind.,* 11/312.

25. *Doc. Ind.,* 11/306 and 336, accounts by Spinola and Pasio.

26. Kerr, *General History,* 7/456–60, for Captain Downton's account of such resistance; and Boxer, *Fidalgos,* pp. 59–62.

27. Parry, *Age of Reconnaissance,* ch. 11, "Atlantic Trade and Piracy"; Boxer, *Fidalgos,* pp. 50–51; Schurz, *Manila Galleon,* pp. 306–8, gives *St. Ana* original loot as 2 million pesos and on p. 313 the London sale of the loot remaining as 500,000 crowns. Hakluyt, *Third Volume,* p. 816, says the main loot was "an hundreth and 22 thousand pezos of golde." Spate, in *Spanish Lake,* downplays the haul.

28. Gomes de Brito, *Tragic History* (*1589–1622*), pp. 11–13; Duffy, *Shipwreck,* pp. 70–74.

29. Aquinas, ed. Bourke, p. 70.

30. Stevens, "Voyage," p. 467; for a later view of Stevens in Goa, see Pyrard, *Voyage,* 2/269–70.

31. Gomes de Brito, *Tragic History* (*1559–1565*), pp. 4–6, 59–60.

32. Ibid., pp. 61–67.

33. Ibid., pp. 68–72.

34. Ibid., pp. 8–9.

35. Ricci, *Tianzhu shiyi,* p. 383; ibid., tr. Lancashire, p. 4.

36. D'Elia, *Mappamondo,* plates 3–4.

37. *Doc. Ind.,* 11/343. Ricci mentions Mozambique only fleetingly, in *OS,* p. 67.

38. Ricci, *Tianzhu shiyi,* p. 425; French tr., p. 193. These words are in the mouth of the "Chinese scholar."

39. Cervantes, *Don Quixote,* tr. Cohen, pt. 2, ch. 29, p. 659.

40. Ibid., p. 658. I am indebted to Ian Spence for this reference.

41. Fitch, "Journey," p. 472; Hakluyt, *Second Volume,* pp. 250–65. For a vivid account of Goa jails, see Pyrard, *Voyages,* 2/18–22.

42. Shakespeare, *Macbeth*, act 1, scene 3, lines 19–29.
43. See interlocking of the wrecks of the *São João* and the *São Bento* (Duffy, *Shipwreck*, pp. 26–27) with Maffei's narrative (*L'histoire*, bk. 4, ch. 3, pp. 266–68): and on the details of carrack life from Lisbon to Goa, Maffei, bk. 12, ch. 2, pp. 119–20 with Pasio's instructions, *Doc. Ind.*, 11/366. Maffei had the strength for the task, initially doubted by Procurator Sabinus, *Doc. Ind.*, 11/625–26.
44. *Doc. Ind.*, 10/17, 21 and 709–13; and 11/353 for 1576 tragic voyage. Couto, *Decada Decima*, bk. 1, ch. 16, p. 147 for the commanders, though his dates of the sailings between 1577 and 1579 are garbled; *Doc. Ind.*, 11/160–62, for Jesuit ship assignments.
45. Duffy, *Shipwreck*, p. 52.
46. *Doc. Ind.*, 11/310–11.
47. *Good Jesus* in *Doc. Ind.*, 11/305; supplies, 11/342; *St. Gregory*, 11/338, sought out by sailors wishing to hear the lap of the waves in calm seas.
48. Lisbon 1578 dock life in Brooks, *King for Portugal*, pp. 14–15, 160n.
49. *Doc. Ind.*, 11/305; Gomes de Brito, *Tragic History* (*1589–1625*), p. 30 n. 2 on church; Stevens, "Voyage," p. 463, on a similar send-off the following year.
50. *Doc. Ind.*, 11/161, 375; *FR*, 2/560, plate 22.
51. *Doc. Ind.*, 11/307.
52. Ibid., 11/308–10.
53. Ibid., 11/351 on gambling and books. Wicki, "The Spanish Language," p. 16, gives an analysis of sixteenth-century light shipboard reading.
54. *Doc. Ind.*, 11/358.
55. Ibid., 11/308–9; Stevens, "Voyage," p. 466, has parallel tales.
56. *Doc. Ind.*, 11/310, 351–52. The Jesuit use of "examinations of conscience" is discussed in Guibert, *Jesuits*, pp. 94–95, 190–93.
57. *Doc. Ind.*, 11/351.
58. Ibid., 11/311.
59. Ibid., 11/318.
60. Ibid., 11/347.
61. Ibid., 11/351.
62. Ibid., 11/313.
63. Ibid., 11/342.
64. *Doc. Ind.*, 11/354 for Pasio; 11/339 reliquaries; 11/312 on storm conversions and relics; 11/316 storm services, Natal; 11/316 open confessions; 11/337 in calm; 11/338 saints' heads. The details of the voyage of the *Good Jesus* show graphically the kind of real crisis that Ricci was spared.

The ship had begun the journey in fine style, moving ahead of her two sister ships off the Cape Verde Islands, and speeding down to the Cape of Good Hope before a favorable breeze. Off the southern tip of Africa, however, she ran into massive seas and contrary winds and, unbeknownst to the pilot, was blown backward during two successive nights of storm. Trusting totally to the ship's compass, the pilot turned confidently north when the weather cleared, and held that course—out of sight of land—up what he thought was the east coast of Africa for the long run to Mozambique. He was in fact heading back up the west coast of Africa, in the direction of Portugal, and continued to do so for nine days, covering a full eight hundred miles, despite the anxious queries of his passengers, who were sure something was wrong. At last, after angry and protracted debates, with passengers and crew alike exhausted and soaked, and with provisions and water in short supply, the pilot finally changed his course and sailed for the Cape of Good Hope once again (*Doc. Ind.*, 11/313, 345, *"cosa che mai accadate,"* adds Spinola in heartfelt irritation), rounding it this time without incident. But it was not surprising that when told that because of the lateness of the year they would now have to run directly for Goa without pausing to restock food and water in Mozambique, the soldiers and sailors aboard the *Good Jesus* seized their weapons and briefly threatened mutiny. There was by now a feeling, as Father Nicholas Spinola discreetly phrased it for his fellow passengers, "that the pilot was not really very intelligent" (*Doc. Ind.*, 11/317).

65. *Doc. Ind.,* 11/352.
66. Ibid., 11/341, 352-53.
67. See descriptions in Boxer, "Moçambique Island," pp. 10-15, and *Doc. Ind.,* 11/341, 346.
68. *Doc. Ind.,* 11/376.
69. Ibid., 11/350.
70. Ibid., 11/349.
71. *OS,* 27 for his "grave illness." *FR,* 1/163 n. 9 Pasio notices he had a "light sickness." Here and in *FR,* 2/562 n. 1 d'Elia shows he was in Malacca June 14 to July 3.
72. *FR,* 1/178 n. 3.
73. *OS,* p. 219, letter of Oct. 13, 1596, referring to *"l'anno passato."*
74. *FR,* 2/11.
75. *FR,* 2/15-16. Trigault (tr. Gallagher, p. 304) calls the triptych a crucifix, changing the implications of the scene as he so often does.

76. This version is from a letter of Oct. 28, 1595, to Costa, in *OS*, p. 182; see ibid., p. 119 n. 1 for biography on Costa. *FR*, 1/355–56 has a polished version.

77. Acts 9:6. Ignatian echo caught by d'Elia in *FR*, 1/356 n. 1.

78. *FR*, 1/356 n. 3; for Zhong's life, see *FR*, 1/290 n. 1.

79. *OS*, p. 48; see also examples of Chinese involvement in So, *Japanese Piracy*, pp. 71–73.

80. *FR*, 1/19–20. For the Western belief that half of China lived on the water, see Plancius, *Universall Map*, p. 256 recto. Ricci may be partly echoing Gaspar de Cruz again, as tr. in Boxer, *South China*, pp. 111–14.

81. *FR*, 1/348.

82. See the remarkable details in *FR*, 1/228 n. 3, or Ricci in *FR*, 1/280.

83. *OS*, p. 68, letter of Nov. 24, 1585, and ibid., p. 66 n. 1; *FR*, 1/92; *FR*, 2/110 on Ma Tang's boat.

84. *FR*, 2/19, 102.

85. Ibid., 2/20.

86. Hoshi, "Transportation," p. 5.

87. A fine summary of Wanli's reign is given by Ray Huang in *1587*.

88. *FR*, 2/21. Hoshi, "Transportation," p. 6 for more on private trading, p. 27 on eunuch abuses.

89. *FR*, 2/31 on boat, 2/34 on wheelbarrow.

90. Delumeau, *Vie économique et sociale de Rome*, 2/530–35, 605–6.

91. *Zhaoqing fuzhi*, 22/34a (reprint p. 3333).

92. *FR*, 2/18.

93. *Gujin tushu jicheng*, *ce* 498. (bowu section, juan 106, p. 36b).

94. Ibid., p. 35b.

95. Ibid., *ce* 498 (bowu section, juan 103, p. 21).

96. Ricci comments on this Bible in *OS*, p. 6, letter of Jan. 18, 1580.

97. See Trigault's observations inserted in *FR*, 2/229–31.

98. Voet, *Golden Compasses*, vol. 2, esp. pp. 37–46; Roover, "Business Organization," pp. 237–39; Rooses, *Plantin*, pp. 120–33. Montaigne saw one of these luxury copies in Rome: *Journal de Voyage*, p. 223.

99. *FR*, 2/279 and n. 1.

100. *OS*, p. 282.

101. See Ricci's two letters to Alvarez, *OS*, p. 282 (May 12, 1605), and *OS*, p. 388 (Feb. 17, 1609) on the Bible as *"un puoco bagnata."*

102. *FR*, 2/282; and *OS*, p. 298.

103. *FR*, 1/245–46.

104. Quotations in *OS*, pp. 364 and 344.

105. *FR*, 2/111, taking "three mace or sapéque" as equivalent to three *qian* or *giulii,* following price equivalents given in *FR*, 2/46 n. 5 and 2/211 n. 2. Albert Chan, *Glory and Fall,* p. 88 mentions children being sold for one *qian* in 1594 in Shandong province.

106. *OS,* p. 274, letter of May 10, 1605.

107. *FR*, 1/338-39. The identification of this Scielou with Board of War President Shi Xing, suggested by d'Elia in *FR*, 1/339 n. 1 and followed by Gu Baogu in "Li Madou di zhongwen zhushu," p. 241, does not fit with the known facts. But I have been unable definitely to identify this man among known Guangxi officials.

108. *FR*, 1/341.

109. Scene and journey in *FR*, 1/343-44, also *OS,* p. 103 on Nanxiong.

110. *FR*, 1/344.

111. On Barradas, see Ricci's two passages in *OS,* pp. 128 and 194.

112. *OS,* 132, letter of Aug. 29, 1595, to Edoardo de Sande in Macao; also letter of Nov. 4, 1595, to Acquaviva, *OS,* 193-94.

113. *FR*, 1/345.

114. *OS,* p. 193, Nov. 4, 1595.

FOUR

THE SECOND IMAGE: THE *HUIHUI*

1. Ricci, *Jifa,* p. 17.

2. *FR*, vol. 1, plate 9 facing p. 194 gives the Ten Commandments in Ricci's Chinese version: Exod. 20:2.

3. *FR*, 2/289 and nn. 1 and 2 on the book *Tianzhujiao yao.* The long n. 2 (extending to p. 291) by d'Elia is a fine essay on the methodology and composition of Ricci's work.

4. Ricci discusses the term in *FR*, 1/113; Gen. 32:32.

5. On Zhaoqing's size, see Bernard, *Aux portes,* p. 196. On early map, see *FR*, 1/208-9, and notes.

6. D'Elia, *Mappamondo,* plates 19 and 20; Giles, "World Map," p. 378.

7. D'Elia, *Mappamondo,* plates 23 and 24; Giles, "World Map," p. 377, mentions "twenty-four states" only, perhaps reflecting an earlier state of the map.

8. D'Elia, *Mappamondo,* plates 19 and 20. Ricci's map, Chinese reactions to it, and the various editions are meticulously studied by William Hung in "Kao Li Madou." Kenneth Ch'en, "A Possible Source," also gives in-

valuable information on Ricci's Chinese sources for the map's Asian regions.

9. See Gregory Martin's account of the preachers he heard at Rome in 1577 and 1578 in *Roma Sancta*, pp. 71–74. Also Culley and McNaspy, "Music," p. 222. The roots from which this preaching grew have been analyzed in O'Malley, *Praise and Blame in Renaissance Rome*.

10. Martin, *Roma Sancta*, pp. 68–69, 169, on confessors and Baptista Romanus; Delumeau, *Vie économique*, 1/217 on range of languages.

11. Martin, *Roma Sancta*, p. 175.

12. Montaigne, *Journal de Voyage en Italie*, pp. 223–24; Martin, *Roma Sancta*, p. 240, on open days.

13. Ignatius of Loyola, *Constitutions*, ed. George Ganss, p. 68; for an example of Acquaviva's "active" policy in Constantinople, see Pirri, "Sultan Yahya," especially pp. 65–66 on the Mancinelli mission.

14. Martin, *Roma Sancta*, p. 170.

15. *OS*, p. 214.

16. On *Disputations*, see Ignatius, *Constitutions*, pp. 194–95 (par. 378), and Martin, *Roma Sancta*, p. 164. On formation of the genre, Ganss, *St. Ignatius' Idea of a Jesuit University*, pp. 255–60.

17. Martin, *Roma Sancta*, pp. 103, 116. At St. Basil's monastery, only fourteen miles from Rome, all the services were chanted and conducted in Greek. Martin, p. 152.

18. Hillgarth, *Ramon Lull*, pp. 2, 6, 20; quotation p. 49.

19. Lull, *Le livre du Gentil*, pp. 210–11; Hillgarth, *Ramon Lull*, p. 24, suggests Lull "implicitly recognizes here the necessary role of grace."

20. Lubac, *La rencontre du Bouddhisme*, pp. 35–38.

21. Boccaccio, *Decameron*, tr. McWilliam, pp. 86–89, quotation p. 88. The story is discussed by Ginzburg in *Cheese and the Worms*, p. 49.

22. See quotations in Ginzburg, *Cheese and the Worms*, pp. 9–10, 51, 62.

23. Ibid., pp. 30, 77, 101, 107.

24. Hillgarth, *Lull*, pp. 280–87; ibid., p. 294 for Lull and alchemy; Lubac, *Rencontre*, p. 63.

25. Diffie and Winius, *Foundations of the Portuguese Empire*, pp. 323–34, rough estimates of population made by me from ibid., p. 331 n. 37. Boxer, *Portuguese Society*, pp. 12–13.

26. Costa, *Christianisation of the Goa Islands*, pp. 25, 30–32, 59, 96–97; for an exception to the guild rule, see ibid., pp. 162–63.

27. Costa's words, from his erudite but apologist *Christianisation*, p. 59; also pp. 120–22.

28. *Doc. Ind.,* 11/360–61; on the choristers, see Culley and McNaspy, "Music," pp. 241–42.

29. Costa, *Christianisation,* pp. 14 and 15.

30. *Doc. Ind.,* 11/365; Costa, *Christianisation,* p. 85.

31. *OS,* p. 11 (letter of Jan. 30, 1580) and p. 4 (Jan. 18, 1580).

32. Correia-Afonso, "More about Akbar," p. 58; Renick, "Akbar's First Embassy," pp. 35, 43.

33. *OS,* pp. 4–6, letter of Jan. 18, 1580.

34. Correia-Afonso, *Letters from the Mughal Court,* pp. 58, 83, 110, 115 n. 6.

35. Ibid., pp. 77 and 78 n. 13 (with minor changes); see also p. 53 n. 16 for Akbar's alleged addiction to the opium infusion "post."

36. *OS,* p. 25 (Dec. 1, 1581). See also Renick, "Akbar's First Embassy," pp. 40, 43–45, on Akbar's motives, including his scrutiny of Goa's defenses.

37. Quoted in Correia-Afonso, "More about Akbar," pp. 60 and 61.

38. *OS,* pp. 19–20, letter of Nov. 25, 1581.

39. Brooks, *King for Portugal,* pp. 39–40 and 170 n. 14; Yerushalmi, *Zakhor,* p. 47, on the "second Purim" in memory of Sebastian's death.

40. Brooks, *King for Portugal,* pp. 25–31; Estoile, *Paris of Henry of Navarre,* tr. Roelker, for the French ineptness in this war.

41. Paci, "La Decadenza," p. 174 n. 136 and p. 176 n. 153.

42. On Jews in Ancona, see especially Cecil Roth, *House of Nasi,* pp. 135–39, 149. Also Azevedo, *Historia,* pp. 364–65; Martin, *Roma Sancta,* p. 129; Pastor, *History of the Popes,* 14/274–75.

43. Main details in Martin, *Roma Sancta,* pp. 77–82, 126, 205. Montaigne also described these ceremonies in *Journal de Voyage,* p. 234; Pastor, *History of the Popes,* 14/272–74, discusses Jewish responses to the economic pressures imposed on them, and names some other converts.

44. Martin, *Roma Sancta,* pp. 82–83, 96.

45. Delumeau, *Vie économique,* 1/502–7 details these economic experiments. Martin, *Roma Sancta,* p. 76, on the clothing market.

46. Martin, *Roma Sancta,* p. 241; Pastor, *History of the Popes,* 14/274–75.

47. Baião, *A Inquisição de Goa,* 1/263 on Dias. Azevedo, *Historia,* pp. 230–31 on Cochin; p. 364 on Ancona.

48. Azevedo, *Historia,* p. 230.

49. Baião, *Inquisição,* 1/36.

50. Baião, *Inquisição,* 1/41 and 45, on white and black Jews; Azevedo, *Historia,* pp. 230–31 on conversions and lure of Cochin.

51. Baião, *Inquisição,* 1/185–87, 265.

52. Ibid., 2/55, letter of Nov. 25, 1578.

53. *OS*, p. 20, Ricci's letter of Nov. 25, 1580. Azevedo, *Historia*, p. 232. Pyrard de Laval, *Voyage*, 2/94–95, gives examples of Inquisition excesses in Goa around 1608.

54. Hanson, *Economy and Society*, pp. 76–79, is good on procedures and budgets; see also Baião, *Inquisição*, 1/272 on budget; and 1/187–88 on Fonseca's elaborate procedures. An intriguing discussion of the Inquisition as "demonic theater" is given by Stephen Greenblatt in *Renaissance Self-Fashioning*, p. 77; A. D. Wright, *The Counter-Reformation*, p. 43, discusses the "learned obsession with the demonic" in this period.

55. Costa, *Christianisation*, p. 197.

56. Schütte, *Valignano's Mission*, pp. 60 and 67; Dehergne, *Répertoire*, no. 741, p. 239 on Edoardo de Sande's Jewish grandmother.

57. Summary of early texts in Brown, *Indian Christians*, ch. 2, and Mathew and Thomas, *Indian Churches*, pp. 5–21. Ricci's thoughts are in *OS*, p. 8.

58. Brown, *Indian Christians*, pp. 12–13, 15.

59. This was Mar Joseph; see Brown, *Indian Christians*, p. 22.

60. *OS*, p. 8, Ricci to Goes, Jan. 18, 1580. For his illness and the grim list of the deaths of priests and teenage students see *Doc. Ind.*, 11/699. On the Simon-Abraham controversy and the Vaipikkotta seminary, see Brown, *Indian Christians*, pp. 22–26 and Mathew and Thomas, *Indian Churches*, pp. 27–29. Wright, *The Counter-Reformation*, pp. 140–41, discusses the institutional forms that were developed to handle the Malabar Christians.

61. Cited from Duarte Barbosa, *Description of the Coasts of East Africa* (bk. 2, pp. 600–601), in Brown, *Indian Christians*, p. 283.

62. *OS*, p. 9.

63. *OS*, p. 20, letter to Acquaviva of Nov. 25, 1581.

64. Costa, *Christianisation*, p. 198, believes this was done with "no rigour": ibid., pp. 195–97 on Jesuit arguments against the Inquisition.

65. *OS*, pp. 8–9.

66. *FR*, 1/167 n. 3 and 1/192 n. 3 for Buddhist dress of Ricci. On the other topics, see below chs. 6 and 8.

67. *OS*, p. 72, letter of Nov. 24, 1585.

68. *FR*, 1/124–25, 1/336–37.

69. *OS*, p. 104, letter of Nov. 15, 1592. I translate *"inventioni"* as "devices" here.

70. *OS*, pp. 136–37, letter of Aug. 29, 1595; I render *"roxa escura"* as "purple" here, in light of the fact that Ricci always used the Italian word for purple, *"paonazza,"* when he repeated this description (with variations)

later, in *OS*, pp. 173, 183, 199–200; see also Young, *East-West Synthesis,* p. 16, and *FR*, 1/358, where Ricci judiciously cuts the more flamboyant details.

71. As described by Gregory Martin, *Roman Sancta,* p. 128.

72. *OS*, pp. 48–49, letter of Sept. 13, 1584, to Giambattista Roman.

73. Ibid., p. 57, letter of Oct. 20, 1585.

74. *FR*, 1/128. On the earlier traditions concerning Muhammad, Apollo, and Termagant, see Metlitzki, *Matter of Araby,* p. 209.

75. See his comments in *FR*, 1/118 and 120.

76. *FR*, 1/132; the best introduction to late Ming syncretism is Judith Berling, *Syncretic Religion of Lin Chao-en.*

77. Boxer, *South China in the Sixteenth Century,* pp. 36–38, 219–21.

78. *OS*, p. 48, Sept. 13, 1584: *"no sé cómo."*

79. *OS*, p. 380; *FR*, 1/24.

80. *FR*, 2/27.

81. *FR*, 2/47.

82. *FR*, 1/149.

83. *FR*, 1/110–11. On later Ming Muslim rebellions, see Barbara Pillsbury, "Muslim History," pp. 19–20; Morris Rossabi, "Muslim and Central Asian Revolts," passim; Albert Chan, *Glory and Fall,* pp. 118–19.

84. Israeli, *Muslims in China,* p. 29; Thiersant, *Mahométisme,* 1/53, on minaret suppression.

85. On early Arabic-Chinese transcriptions, see Forke, "Islamitisches Traktat," a remarkable piece of scholarly decipherment and reconstruction. On the early Qing Muslim work by the prolific Liu Zhi, see Israeli, *Muslims in China,* pp. 145–47, and Thiersant, *Mahométisme,* 2/364–68. The same volume of Thiersant gives a lengthy translation of Liu Zhi and Yusuf Mazhu. An important statement by Emperor Yongzheng on Islam is in Thiersant, 1/55–56. Liu Zhi's life of Muhammad, showing a basic eighteenth-century Chinese view of Islam, has been translated and annotated by Isaac Mason, *Arabian Prophet* (Shanghai, 1921).

86. *OS*, p. 290, letter of July 26, 1605, to Acquaviva; *OS*, p. 344; *FR*, 2/320.

87. *FR*, 1/336 n. 1.

88. *FR*, 1/112 and 114, 2/320.

89. *FR*, 2/323; Ricci mentions this reticence also in *OS*, p. 344.

90. *FR*, 2/141 n. 4.

91. *OS*, p. 290; ibid., p. 289 refers to an earlier letter on the same topic, now lost. The famous 718 A.D. Nestorian stele was discovered only in 1625, fifteen years after Ricci's death. See the translation and analysis in *Chi-*

nese Repository 14 (May 1845): 201–29. Henri Bernard, *La découverte de Nestoriens Mongols,* pp. 14–31, reviews their early history, up to Ricci's time.

92. *FR,* 2/323.

93. *OS,* p. 290; *FR,* 2/317–24. Dehergne and Leslie, *Juifs de Chine,* pp. 8–12, summarizes the sources on early Jewish history in China; ibid., pp. 216–18 has a succinct bibliography.

94. *FR,* 1/112, 2/324; *OS,* p. 344.

95. *FR,* 2/324–25.

96. *FR,* 2/316–18.

97. Ricci discusses this conversation and his intention to ask the visitor (Valignano) in his letter of May 12, 1605, to Alvarez, *OS,* p. 281. Valignano died in Macao in January 1606.

98. *FR,* 2/179.

99. To Acquaviva in *OS,* p. 360; on Nanchang literati, *FR,* 2/452.

100. *FR,* 2/141–42, 145.

101. *FR,* 2/130.

102. *OS,* p. 24, letter of Dec. 1, 1581.

103. Maffei, *L'Histoire,* "Proemio," p. 3. On Maffei's earlier problems as a historian, see Correia-Afonso, *Jesuit Letters,* p. 113. For his fame, Martin, *Roma Sancta,* p. 245, and Dainville, *Géographie,* pp. 122–26.

104. Maffei, *L'Histoire,* "Proemio," p. 1.

105. *OS,* p. 24, letter of Dec. 1, 1581.

106. Acquaviva, *Letters* (*29 Sept. 1583*), pp. 47–48.

107. Acquaviva, *Letters* (*19 May 1586*), p. 78.

108. Acquaviva, *Letters* (*12 Jan. 1590*), pp. 110–11, 113.

109. *FR,* 2/398–402, 2/393 n. 1. D'Elia gives a detailed map of his route in *FR,* vol. 2, plate 20, facing p. 396. Bernard, *Le Frère Bento de Goes,* pp. 45–47.

110. See *FR,* 2/437, where Goís sells his jade for 1,200 ducats, "only half its value."

111. *FR,* 2/434–38; Bernard, *Le Frère Bento de Goes,* pp. 102–10; Rossabi, "Muslim and Central Asian Revolts," pp. 172–75, on the Kashgar politics of the time.

112. *OS,* p. 338, Mar. 6, 1608. Ricci also dwells on Goís in *OS,* pp. 347–50 and 391. First news of Goís's arrival in China is *OS,* p. 327.

113. Zhuangzi, *Complete Works,* p. 78, and standard Chinese editions, "Da zongshi" section. Gu Baogu, "Li Madou di zhongwen," p. 248.

114. Here I generally follow Zhuangzi, *Complete Works,* as translated by

Watson, but rephrase and use Ricci's "paradoxical" for Watson's "singular man."

FIVE
THE SECOND PICTURE: THE ROAD TO EMMAUS

1. Aquinas, *Catena Aurea,* pp. 772–79. Ludolfus of Saxony had seen in the story three major focuses for contemplation: Christ's kindness and friendship in seeking to grasp the reason for the disciples' sadness; his humility in speaking to these disciples "of lower grade"; his goodness in explaining, so patiently, the meaning of what they had seen (Ludolfus, *Vita Jesu Christi,* p. 716). The story of Emmaus was to be reflected on, also, in the *Spiritual Exercises,* in the fourth week, as the fifth among the thirteen mysteries of Christ's apparition to various persons on earth (Ignatius, *Exercises,* nos. 226 and 303).

2. Ricci, *Li Madou ti baoxiang tu,* pp. 4–5b; Cheng Dayue, *Chengshi moyuan,* juan 6, pt. 2, pp. 38b–41; Duyvendak, "Review," pp. 391–92.

3. Nadal, *Evangelicae Historiae Imagines,* fig. 141, for the unused image. A copy of the original state of Ricci's print can be seen in the Metropoltian Museum of Art in New York (Prints, Netherlands, Martin de Vos file, 53.601.18:44).

4. Castellani, "La Tipografia del Collegio Romano," pp. 12–13, taking *scudi* as equivalent to ducats.

5. Robert Palmer, "Martial," is an excellent summary and analysis, and has some startlingly explicit translations.

6. On the general strategy, see Dainville, *L'éducation des Jésuites,* pp. 181–84. For the cut Martial and Horace in the curriculum, see *Monumenta Paedagogica, 1586,* p. 435. On Frusius's following of Ignatius's instructions, Castellani, "Tipografia," pp. 11 and 15, and Palmer, "Martial," p. 913. On Frusius as musician, and friend of Ignatius, see Culley and McNaspy, "Music and the Early Jesuits," p. 218.

7. Castellani, "Tipografia," pp. 11, 14–16.

8. Ganss, *Saint Ignatius' Idea of a Jesuit University,* pp. 296–301, and 326–27 on Ignatius's initial statement; Pachtler, *Ratio Studiorum,* pp. 192–97 for 1566 details, including p. 195 on *Ad Herennium.*

9. Ganss, *St. Ignatius' Idea of a Jesuit University,* pp. 44–51, 60. Ibid., p. 304 for instructions on Latin conversation.

10. Ibid., pp. 304–5; Ledesma's instructions in *Monumenta Paedagogica, 1586*, p. 361; Schwickerath, *Jesuit Education*, pp. 493–97.

11. *OS*, p. 235, Nanchang, Sept. 9, 1597.

12. Romberch, *Longestorium Artificiose Memorie*, pp. 22–26, 36, 49–51.

13. Grataroli, *De Memoria Reparanda*, pp. 78–82. Thorndike, *History of Magic*, 5/600–16, has a fine brief biography of Grataroli. These images were too much for Grataroli's 1573 English translator, William Fulwood, who toned them down for his *Castel of Memorie* (London: William How, 1573), filling the pot with water and leaving the anatomical parts unspecified. Grataroli's work, albeit in bowdlerized form, was still circulating in England in the late seventeenth century among university students. Cf. Marius d' Assigny, *The Art of Memory* (London, 1699), especially pp. 72–74.

14. *OS*, p. 27.

15. *OS*, p. 28 and *FR*, 1/36–37. Ricci's example of the word for heaven, *tian* in Chinese, had already been mentioned by Gaspar de Cruz in his account: see Boxer, *South China*, p. 162.

16. *OS*, p. 28.

17. For his stages in learning Chinese, see September 1584 in *OS*, p. 49; October 1584, *OS*, p. 60; November 1585, *OS*, p. 65, *"già parlo correntemente la lingua"*; 1592, *OS*, p. 91; December 1593, *OS*, pp. 117–18; October 1594, *OS*, p. 122.

18. *OS*, pp. 155–56. For de Sande, see Pfister, *Notices*, no. 11; Dehergne, *Répertoire*, no. 741 mentions his grandmother having been a "New Christian," i.e., of Jewish origin. He traveled to Goa with Ricci on the *St. Louis*.

19. *OS*, p. 211.

20. *OS*, pp. 235–36.

21. *OS*, pp. 239–40.

22. Ricci, *Jifa*, p. 18.

23. Bortone, *P. Matteo Ricci*, pp. 35–40.

24. Schwickerath, *Jesuit Education*, p. 494; Schimberg, *L'éducation morale*, pp. 132–33, 139; *Monumenta Paedagogica, 1586*, p. 351; Dainville, *L'éducation des Jésuites*, pp. 168–71. See also Dainville, ibid., pp. 187–88 on the Jesuit *"humanisme de culture et de formation,"* and Villoslada, *Collegio Romano*, ch. 5.

25. Zanta, *La renaissance du stoïcisme*, pp. 12–14, 126–27, 203–5.

26. Letter to Costa, *OS*, p. 336, Mar. 6, 1608. Ricci, *Jiren shipian*, pp. 187–88

on Aesop, and p. 131 for Epictetus. The Aesop sections Ricci used can be found in Planudes le Grand, *La vie d'Esope,* preface and chs. 13 and 14. Though I have seen only the Rouen edition of 1765, I assume the order was the same in the editions of Ricci's day. For circulation of the Aesop passage by a Ming scholar, see Zhang Xuan's *Xiyuan wenjian lu,* ch. 15, pp. 39b–40b; Zhang's biography is in *DMB,* p. 79 (Chang Hsüan).

27. Ricci, *Jiaoyou lun,* passim, and d'Elia, "Il trattato sull' Amicizia," esp. pp. 454, 463–65. The Beitang edition of the 1590 Paris version which d'Elia thinks Ricci used would thus be a later importation; this hypothesis seems reinforced by comparing Ricci's paraphrases with the original Resende version as printed in d'Elia's "Trattato."

28. Epictetus, ed. Oldfather, vol. 2, prints the *Encheiridion* on pp. 479–537. In an elegant piece of scholarship the *Encheiridion* has been collated with Ricci's version of *Ershiwu yan* by Christopher Spalatin in his "Matteo Ricci's Use of Epictetus' Encheiridion."

29. D'Elia, "Musica e canti," gives the Chinese version with an Italian translation. I am grateful to Thomas Greene for pointing out borrowings in these songs from Horace (i.e., *Odes,* ii, 4 and 18, iii, 24); from Petrarch, "Ascent of Mt. Ventoux"; and from Seneca, *Epistolae Morales,* 93.

30. For the place and significance of Clavius's 1574 ed. in the context of Euclid bibliography, see Heath, *Thirteen Books,* 1/105; on the negative attacks on science teaching, see Dainville, *L'éducation des Jésuites,* pp. 324–25.

31. *Monumenta Paedagogica, 1586,* p. 476. For beginnings of Galileo friendship, see Phillips, "Correspondence of Father Clavius," p. 195; also Villoslada, *Collegio Romano,* pp. 194–99, 335.

32. *Monumenta Paedagogica, 1586,* p. 472.

33. Ibid., pp. 471, 478. Clavius's colleague Torres outlined a similar curriculum, phased somewhat differently. Ibid., p. 477.

34. *FR,* 1/207–8, and *OS,* p. 13.

35. *FR,* 1/167n.

36. Ricci and Xu Guangqi, *Jihe yuanben,* preface, pp. 4–5 (reprint pp. 1935–37).

37. As paraphrased by Vincent Smith, *St. Thomas on the Object of Geometry,* p. 6.

38. Ibid., pp. 43–44.

39. Thomas Aquinas, ed. Bourke, pp. 40, 278–79.
40. Dainville, *La Géographie,* pp. 37, 39, 42; Thorndike, *History of Magic,* 6/46.
41. Thorndike, *History of Magic,* 6/73–74.
42. See the Chinese discussion of these sightings in Ho and Ang, "Astronomical records," p. 77.
43. Ricci and Xu Guangqi, *Jihe yuanben,* preface, p. 5a (reprint, p. 1937); Moule, "Obligations," p. 162.
44. Ricci and Xu Guangqi, *Jihe yuanben,* preface, p. 1a (reprint, p. 1929); Moule, "Obligations," p. 154; d'Elia, "Presentazione," pp. 177–78.
45. Ricci and Xu Guangqi, *Jihe yuanben,* preface, p. 2 (reprint, pp. 1931–32); Moule, "Obligations," pp. 155–57; d'Elia, "Presentazione," pp. 179–81.
46. Ricci on Clavius and Piccolomini, *OS,* p. 72. For his use of Ortelius, see Ch'en, "A Possible Source," p. 179. See examples of tables in Clavius, *Astrolabium,* pp. 572–79 for sun in zodiac, and the "tabula sinuum," pp. 195–227.
47. Clavius, *Astrolabium,* p. 43 shows the kind of detailed help with tools, carpentry, and construction of instruments offered by Clavius. For other good examples of working drawings, see Clavius's *Fabrica et Usus Instrumenti ad Horologiorum Descriptionem* (Rome, 1586), pp. 7–12.
48. This book, about eight inches by five, two inches thick with metal binding clasps, 683 pp. long, was both portable and practical. Ricci's thanks after the book's arrival are in *OS,* p. 241, letter to Clavius of Dec. 25, 1597, referring to previous year's events. Dainville, *Géographie des humanistes,* p. 40 on praise for the astrolabe.
49. Dee, *Preface,* A ii (recto) and B iii (recto).
50. Ibid., A iii (recto).
51. For Plancius, see Heawood, "Relationships of the Ricci Maps" and Plancius, *Universall Map,* tr. Blundevile; for Ma Duanlin, Kenneth Ch'en, "Possible Source," pp. 182–90. On the map's early reception and circulation, see *OS,* p. 51 and *FR* 1/207–10. Emperor and map, *FR,* 2/472–74.
52. *OS,* pp. 241–42, to Clavius, Nanchang, Dec. 25, 1597.
53. *FR,* 1/368–69; *DMB,* pp. 1139–40; see the specific praise for a passage from the *Friendship* in Jiao Hong, *Dan yuan ji,* 48/9b, dating from 1603 (my thanks to Cheng Pei-kai for this reference). For Jiao Hong (Chiao Hung) see *Eminent Chinese of the Ch'ing Period,* pp. 145–46.
54. See passages in d'Elia, "Il trattato sull' Amicizia," items 1–3, 5 and 9.

55. For the passages, see d'Elia's identification in "Il trattato": Seneca, item 15; Cicero, item 28; Martial, item 47; Plutarch, item 67.

56. Ibid., item 24; for Ignatius and Erasmus see Guibert, *Jesuits*, pp. 163–66 and n. 36. Gu Baogu, "Li Madou," p. 243, suggests that Ricci also quoted Montaigne: Gu's evidence for this fascinating observation is frail.

57. Zou Yuanbiao, "Da Xiguo Li Madou," in *Yuan xue ji*, 3/39. On Zou (Tsou Yuan-piao), see *DMB*, pp. 1312–14; on Guo (Kuo Cheng-yü), *DMB*, pp. 768–70. I identify Guo as the intermediary on the basis of evidence in *FR*, 2/43 n. 1.

58. Richard Wilhelm, *The I Ching*, tr. Cary Baynes, pp. 4, 370–71. The subtle problems of Ricci's "accommodation" of Christian values to the Confucian ones are well described by Bettray, in his *Akkommodationsmethode*, pt. 5, and by Harris, "The Mission of Matteo Ricci." Young, *Confucianism and Christianity*, pp. 59, 73, 94, 126–28 emphasizes the fundamental but often neglected point that Christianity did in fact threaten the most basic Confucian values. The forthcoming volume by Paul Rule on Christian attitudes toward Confucius, based on his 1972 dissertation for the Australian National University, will examine this interrelationship in even greater depth.

59. *FR*, 1/298, 2/342. For the attractive powers of this first draft, at Shaozhou in 1589 and 1590, see *FR*, 2/55.

60. *FR*, 2/357–58; Joseph Ku, "Hsü Kuang-ch'i," pp. 90–93. For the place of this work by Ricci and Xu in the general history of Chinese mathematics, see Joseph Needham, *Science and Civilisation in China*, 3/52, 110, 446–51.

61. *FR*, 2/476–77.

62. *Eminent Chinese of the Ch'ing Period*, p. 199; *FR*, 1/296 n. 1.

63. *Eminent Chinese*, p. 452; *FR*, 2/168 n. 3.

64. *Eminent Chinese*, p. 316; Joseph Ku, "Hsü Kuang-ch'i," pp. 25–27, 35–36; Monika Ubelhör, "Hsü Kuang-ch'i," 15:2/217–30 has full details on Xu's family and upbringing.

65. On this background see the massively detailed accounts in Needham, *Science and Civilisation in China:* chemistry, vol. 5, pts. 2–5, sec. 33; cartography, vol. 3, sec. 22; geometry, vol. 3, sec. 19.

66. Ricci, *Jihe yuanben*, Xu preface, p. 1b (reprint p. 1922), following the translation by Moule, "Obligations," p. 152.

67. D'Elia, *Mappamondo*, plates 11 and 12; Giles, "Chinese World Map," pp. 368, 371.

68. *FR*, 2/283.
69. Examples from *FR:* ink sticks 1/34; Chinese paper 1/25; Western paper 1/25 n. 5; binding 1/283, 1/196.
70. *FR*, 2/11, 46, 112.
71. *FR*, 2/44–46.
72. This was the *Tianzhu shilu*, later discarded by the Jesuits as too primitive in style and content, discussed in *FR*, 1/31 and 197.
73. *FR*, 1/31.
74. *FR*, 1/38, 2/314.
75. Ricci, *Jifa*, p. 3b (reprint p. 14) for examples. He discusses Chinese memory briefly in *FR*, 2/283.
76. There were some exceptions in the case of Chinese military feats—thus we find early Chinese records which show that Wei Renpu in the period of the Five Dynasties remembered the names of the generals and soldiers at every garrison, their expenses and their wages (*Gujin tushu jicheng, ce* [ts'e] 606, p. 35a, and *Songshi*, p. 8802 [ch. 249]), while Zhu Huan in the Three Kingdoms period remembered not only all the soldiers in his area but even the names of their wives and children (*Gujin tushu jicheng*, 606/32b, and *Sanguozhi*, 1314–17 [ch. 56]).
77. Pliny, *Natural History*, pp. 563–65. Soarez, *De Arte Rhetorica*, p. 59, has Mithradates and Cyrus but not Cineas.
78. Seneca, *Controversiae*, pp. 3 and 5; Quintilian, *Institutio Oratoria*, 4/243, on Theodectes; Pliny, *Natural History*, p. 565, on Charmadas.
79. These Chinese examples can be found in the *Gujin tushu jicheng*, in *ce* (ts'e) 606, pp. 32b, 34a, 34b, 35b.
80. Pliny, *Natural History*, p. 565; *Gujin tushu jicheng, ce* 606, p. 34a.
81. Pliny, *Natural History*, p. 563, on Scipio; Cicero, *De Senectute*, pp. 29 and 31, on Themistocles. Su Song is discussed in *Gujin tushu jicheng, ce* 606, p. 36a and Sibucongkan, ed., *Sanchao mingchen yanxiang lu*, ch. 11, pp. 268–69.
82. Quintilian, *Institutio Oratoria*, 4/225; *Gujin tushu jicheng, ce* 606, p. 35a.
83. Quintilian, *Institutio Oratoria*, 4/233; and *Gujin tushu jicheng, ce* 606, p. 32b.
84. Xu's remark is in *FR*, 2/253. Ricci, *Ershiwu yan*, p. 335, no. 6, following Epictetus, *Encheiridion*, no. 3, p. 487. In his Chinese version Ricci substituted the word "love" for the word "kiss."
85. Ricci, *Ershiwu yan*, p. 338, no. 10, reversing order and specifying "son or daughter"; Epictetus, no. 11, p. 491.

86. Ricci, ibid., p. 345, no. 19, reversing order and closing only with the son's death; Epictetus, no. 14, p. 493.
87. Ricci, *Tianzhu shiyi*, p. 426; tr. *Lettres édifiantes*, p. 194.
88. *Tianzhu shiyi*, p. 428; tr. *Lettres édifiantes*, pp. 195–96.
89. *Tianzhu shiyi*, p. 561; tr. *Lettres édifiantes*, pp. 319–20.
90. *FR*, 1/76.
91. *OS*, p. 56, Oct. 20, 1585, to Acquaviva. Also *OS*, p. 63.
92. *FR*, 1/314–16, with "Giuseppe" in Nanxiong.
93. *FR*, 2/76–79.
94. *FR*, 2/161.
95. Shen Defu, in *Wanli yehubian*, p. 785, saying Ricci "yindan shenjian."
96. *FR*, 2/537.
97. Illness and death in *FR*, 2/538–42. Letters burned 2/546. On Coton's Marian training with Leunis, see Villaret, *Congrégations*, pp. 92–93; on his devotional works, Guibert, "Le généralat," p. 90.

SIX

THE THIRD IMAGE: PROFIT AND HARVEST

1. Ricci, *Jifa*, p. 5a (reprint p. 17). For a late Ming analysis of this "profit motive," see Brook, "Merchant Network," p. 186.
2. Ricci, *Li Madou ti baoxiang tu;* on the transmittal letter and the picture of Peter he writes "Ri," whereas on the "Man from Europe" pictures of Emmaus and Sodom he writes "Ly." I hope this is one more step forward to solving the baffling code that seems built into Ricci's signature form on these paintings. The attempt in *DMB*, p. 215, by the editors, is ingenious but not conclusive, since elsewhere in his writings Ricci used a quite different transcription for *Deus*, as in *Tianzhu shiyi*, 1/3 (reprint p. 381)—namely *Dou-si*.
3. Azevedo, *Historia*, pp. 131–32, using cruzados as the currency. Gomes de Brito, *The Tragic History of the Sea, 1589–1622*, tr. Charles Boxer, p. 55, suggests ducats and cruzados and reals can be equated at this time, all being roughly equal to four English shillings.
4. Essen, *Farnèse*, 3/222–24. *New Cambridge Modern History*, 3/198–200. William of Orange was assassinated on July 10, 1584, before he saw the truth of his warning proven.
5. *FR*, 2/518–20, this being an account by Trigault. The expulsion order does not seem to have been carried out with any rigor, if at all.

6. Ignatius of Loyola, *Spiritual Exercises*, tr. Puhl, sec. 93.
7. Ibid., secs. 150, 153–55.
8. Montaigne, *Journal de Voyage*, p. 256.
9. A detailed plan of the town of Macerata showing locations of all main buildings and walls in the late sixteenth century, designed by Libero Paci and Ceresani Giuliano, is in *Storia di Macerata*, vol. 5, plate 5, facing p. 312.
10. Florence data are sparse: see *FR*, 1/ciii; Bortone, *P. Matteo Ricci*, pp. 35–36.
11. *OS:* Nanxiong, p. 103; Ganzhou, p. 192; Nanchang twice size, pp. 175 (see quote) and 202; same size, p. 235.
12. *OS*, p. 28, to Fornari.
13. *FR*, 2/553n. St. Andrew's and the residence are illustrated in Bortone, p. 27.
14. *OS*, p. 217, Oct. 12, 1596.
15. *OS*, pp. 390–91, letter of Feb. 17, 1609, to Giovanni Alvarez.
16. O'Connell, *Counter-Reformation*, pp. 272–74, and Villoslada, *Storia*, pp. 148–54, discuss the building boom. Martin, *Roma Sancta*, p. 58, describes the Gésu.
17. Martin, *Roma Sancta*, pp. 86–88.
18. Angelo Pientini, *Le Pie Narrationi*, cited by Martin, *Roma Sancta*, p. 231.
19. On St. Paul's church and the painting, see *Doc. Ind.*, 11/358 and nn. 112, 113, 114; Schütte, *Valignano's Mission*, p. 113. Services and choir, *Doc. Ind.*, 11/359, and Culley and McNaspy, "Music," p. 243.
20. *Doc. Ind.*, 11/349–51.
21. *OS*, p. 5, Jan. 18, 1580; *Doc. Ind.*, 11/358.
22. *Doc. Ind.*, 11/329, letter of Petrus Parra, Goa, Oct. 28, 1578.
23. *Doc. Ind.*, 11/319–20, Nicholas Spinola, Oct. 26, 1578.
24. Pasio letter of Nov. 30, 1578, *Doc. Ind.*, pp. 364–65.
25. Costa, *Christianisation*, p. 34.
26. Schütte, *Valignano's Mission*, pp. 236–37, n. 196.
27. Linschoten, *Report*, p. 517. The other three travelers with Storie were Fitch, a jeweler named William Leedes (or "William Bets of Leeds"), and John Newbery. See Fitch, *Letters*, p. 514; Newbery, *Letters*, p. 512.
28. Linschoten, *Report*, p. 520.
29. On the Macao community, see Boxer, *Portuguese Society*, pp. 12–13, 43; Pyrard, *Voyage*, 2/172–73; Fok, "Macao Formula," pp. 144–47.
30. Boxer, "Macao as Entrepôt," pp. 65–66; *FR*, 1/152 for Ricci's summary

of the population; Fok, "Macao Formula," pp. 72–94 on Chinese attitudes to the community; Ptak, "The Demography of Old Macao."

31. Church in Boxer, *Fidalgos,* p. 39; Ricci's house, *OS,* p. 402, appendix 3, Ruggieri to Mercurian, Macao, Nov. 12, 1581. Ruggieri's request for Ricci is in *OS,* p. 398, letter of Nov. 8, 1580.

32. On silver ratios see the detailed account in Atwell, "Bullion Flows," and his table on p. 82. The 60 percent figure is suggested by Kobata in "Gold and Silver," p. 254. Detailed survey of the trade is in Boxer, *Fidalgos,* and the same author's *Great Ship.* An early seventeenth-century account of the Goa-China trade is given by Pyrard, *Voyage,* 2/174–77.

33. Iwao, "Japanese Trade," p. 2. For a contemporary Chinese merchant's account of the Southeast China trade and foreign participation therein, see Brook, "Merchant Network," pp. 202, 205–6. A fine survey of the Chinese economy at this time, and the effect of silver, is given by Cheng Pei-kai, "Reason and Imagination," ch. 1.

34. Cooper, "Mechanics," p. 428.

35. Ibid., pp. 425–26, 430, 432.

36. Overview in Spate, *Spanish Lake,* pp. 151–57; Iwao, "Japanese Trade," p. 7, on Hideyoshi; Elison, *Deus Destroyed,* pp. 94–98 on the donation of Nagasaki; Boxer, *Fidalgos,* pp. 30–38 on details of regular trade.

37. Boxer, *Great Ship,* pp. 37–38; Boxer, *Fidalgos,* pp. 30–31; Schütte, *Valignano's Mission,* pp. 212 and 218 n. 130.

38. Schütte, *Valignano's Mission,* pp. 184–85, 314, rendering the 133-pound "piculs" as "bales" here, and converting *scudi* to ducats. Cooper, "Mechanics," p. 428. There is some inconsistency in Valignano's figures. Further details are in Elison, *Deus Destroyed,* pp. 101–5.

39. Cushner, "Merchants," p. 366, discusses the views of Navarro and Molina.

40. Cushner, "Merchants," pp. 360, 364.

41. Schütte, *Valignano's Mission,* p. 185 n. 388; Takase, "Unauthorized Commercial Activities," pp. 20–22; Boxer, "Macao," pp. 71–72, discusses the skilled middlemen who worked with the Jesuits.

42. Frois, *Tratado,* pp. 17–18. The idea of isolating China from any knowledge of Protestant Europe had not yet become entirely fanciful when Ricci first reached Macao in 1582, and this party of young Japanese princes were conducted for all their travels in Europe through areas controlled by the Spaniards or by the Papacy and its Italian allies, and were probably barely aware of the extent of the Protestant territories. (See the detailed accounts given in Lach, *Asia in the Making of Europe,*

vol. 1, bk. 2, pp. 688–706.) But after 1588, when the English defeated the Spanish Armada and Philip II's great general the prince of Parma proved unable to use his stunning victory at Antwerp for a successful assault on Dutch Protestant power in Amsterdam, the idea of a Spanish-Portuguese dominance of the world's seaways in the name of the Catholic faith was doomed.

43. Boxer, *Fidalgos,* p. 40, citing dues figures of 50,000 ducats.

44. *FR,* 1/178 and 178 n. 3; *OS,* p. 396, Ruggieri to Mercurian.

45. *FR,* 1/cx–cxi; *OS,* pp. 55–56; 1589 was a peak, with eighteen converts of whom several were women.

46. *FR,* 1/314–18, 2/94. More precise numbers can be plotted through the analytical index in *FR,* 3/80, under "Battesimi," broken down by area.

47. Peking area figures of converts, *FR,* 2/356; 1605 locations of priests in China, *FR,* 2/268 n. 3, and 2/276 n. 6. On Peking wealthy converts (and lesser success with the poor), see *FR,* 2/160, 310, 354.

48. *FR,* 2/337.

49. *FR,* 2/270. The exact date of this high point of optimism was probably 1603, on Valignano's last visit to Macao.

50. *OS* (appendix 2), p. 398, letter of Nov. 8, 1580.

51. *OS* (appendix 3), pp. 402, 404, 406, letter of Ruggieri to Mercurian, Nov. 12, 1581. On the Jesuit gift strategy as a whole, see Bettray, *Akkomodationsmethode,* pp. 25–32.

52. The Chinese horological background is meticulously spelled out in Needham, *Science and Civilisation,* vol. 4, pt. 2, pp. 435–546. On European background, see Domenico Sella, "European Industries 1500–1700," pp. 382–84, printed in Cipolla, ed., *Fontana Economic History,* and David Landes, *Revolution in Time,* pp. 67–97. For Landes's disagreements with Needham, see Landes, ibid., ch. 1.

53. *OS* (appendix 6), p. 419, postscript to letter of Feb. 7, 1583.

54. *FR,* 1/161–64. *OS* (appendix 6), p. 415, where Ruggieri elaborates on his woes and the spectacles.

55. *FR,* 1/166 n. 4.

56. *FR,* 1/167–68, 176–79.

57. *FR,* 1/184–88, 192; *OS,* p. 432. The 250 "taels" the Jesuits spent would have been rather more than 250 ducats, though precise conversion figures are hard to fix. *FR,* 2/535 n. 4, equates one tael with one cruzado, though *FR,* 2/352 n. 5, suggests that 450 taels were equivalent to 800 *scudi.* Schütte, *Valignano's Mission,* p. 314, suggests that 20,000 taels in

Japan were equivalent to 30,000 *scudi*. The traveler Jean Mocquet found that in Goa early in the seventeenth century, twelve to fifteen taels were about twenty-five *scudi* (see his *Voyages*, p. 342).

58. Details from *OS*, pp. 420, and 431-32 (Cabral letter); *FR*, 1/264, 278-79; Takase, "Unauthorized Trade," p. 20, mentions similar Jesuit real-estate concerns in Japan. See also Elison, *Deus Destroyed*, p. 102, for Valignano's worries over the rocketing expenses in Japan.

59. *FR*, 1/285-86, and 286 n. 4; *OS*, p. 461, where the price is given in pesos.

60. *FR*, 1/374 and 378.

61. *FR*, 2/448, 465-66.

62. Nanjing house, *FR*, 2/83-84, 93; Peking, *FR*, 2/352.

63. *FR*, 2/30 and 93.

64. Nanjing, *FR*, 2/346; Peking, *FR*, 2/355-56. Similar types of tax evasion are discussed in Geiss, "Peking," p. 74.

65. *FR*, 1/178 nn. 4 and 6; 1/201.

66. *FR*, 1/201-5.

67. *FR*, 1/190.

68. Ruggieri to Acquaviva, Macao, Jan. 25, 1584, *OS*, pp. 419-20; also Boxer, *Fidalgos*, pp. 41-42 and *Great Ship*, pp. 45-46. But the Jesuits' "main support" Gaspar Viegas left for India that same year, see *OS*, pp. 431-33, Francis Cabral to Valignano, Macao, Dec. 5, 1584; Cabral uses the spelling "Villegas."

69. *FR*, 1/230-31, and Ricci letter of Oct. 20, 1585 to Acquaviva asking for more of the same, *OS*, p. 60. Landes, *Revolution in Time*, pp. 87-88, has fine detail on sixteenth-century miniaturization; on p. 99 he notes the intriguing use of fine clocks as "tribute" to Islam.

70. Ricci's explanation is in *FR*, 1/104-7. The full background of Chinese alchemical experimentation is in Needham, *Science and Civilisation*, vol. 5.

71. *FR*, 1/240; the great dramatist Tang Xianzu was also one of those who believed Ricci was an alchemist, in 1592. See Xu Shuofang, "Tang Xianzu he Li Madou," pp. 274, 277-78. Carletti, *Voyage*, p. 146, gives his observations on mercury purchases at this time.

72. *FR*, 2/390 n. 6.

73. D'Elia, *Mappamondo*, plates 9 and 10; Brading and Cross, "Colonial Silver Mining," pp. 553-54; Spate, *Spanish Lake*, pp. 186-94.

74. The patterns of mercury trade are outlined in Cipolla, ed., *Fontana Economic History*, p. 395; Brading and Cross, "Colonial Silver Mining," pp.

NOTES TO PAGES 187-189

562–64. Fernand Braudel, in *Wheels of Commerce*, gives many intriguing facets to the trade; e.g., pp. 323 and 386 on the failed Hochstetter attempt to set up an early-sixteenth-century mercury cartel; pp. 326–27 on Huancavelica and the Fugger control over Almadén; p. 174 on the Seville-Idria connections; pp. 169 and 406 have a late-seventeenth-century trader mentioning 300 percent profit obtained by shipping Chinese quicksilver to New Spain; while p. 379 mentions the Greppi family's bulk buying of mercury in the eighteenth century. Captain White's account of his huge mercury seizure is given in Kerr, *General History*, 7/455. Brading and Cross, op. cit., p. 555 give the precise ratios of mercury to silver production; see also Spate, *Spanish Lake*, pp. 189–92.

75. *OS*, pp. 245–46, and 245 n. 5, letter of Aug. 14, 1599 to Costa; *FR*, 1/217–18 has Ricci's view of tensions.

76. *FR*, 1/240 corroborated independently by *DMB*, pp. 318, 905. See also Fok, "Macao Formula," pp. 93–95, though ambergris is there defined as a "spice."

77. *FR*, 1/216–17; Chan, "Chinese-Philippine Relations," pp. 52, 62.

78. *FR*, 1/240–41.

79. *Zhaoqing fuzhi*, 22/78a (reprint p. 3421).

80. *FR*, 1/313.

81. Letter in *OS*, p. 184, dated Oct. 28, 1595. Nanchang stories detailed in *FR*, 1/359n, 375; *OS*, p. 175.

82. *FR*, 2/29.

83. *OS*, p. 382, letter of Feb. 15, 1609, and *FR*, 2/490 n. 4.

84. Shen Defu, *Wanli yehubian*, p. 785.

85. *FR*, 1/225, 163 n. 7 for such Chinese requests. The Franciscan gift is discussed in Bernard, *Aux Portes*, p. 129. Examples of this astonishing workmanship can be seen in great detail and variety in the special issue of *Artes de Mexico*, n. 137, año 17, "Tesoros de Mexico—Arte Plumario y de Mosaico," especially the essay "Comentarios sobre el arte plumario durante la colonia" by Marita Martínez del Rió de Redo. (My thanks to Diana Balmori for this reference.) The traveler Mocquet also escaped from destitution in Goa by a fortunate profitable sale of feathers—*Voyages*, p. 287.

86. For this *"struzzo vivo"* see *OS*, p. 449, letter of Nov. 8, 1586.

87. *FR*, 1/216 n. 1; d'Elia, *Mappamondo*, plates 5 and 6 in Brazil, 7 and 8 in New Spain, and 15 and 16 in Borneo. Chan, "Peking," p. 135 mentions 6,500 taels' worth of feathers given by Peking merchants to the court.

88. *FR*, 1/266–67.
89. *FR*, 1/227. The background to the mission side of the deal is given in *OS*, pp. 59 and 444, letter by Ricci to Almeida; on the Zhejiang silk trade in the late Ming, see Brook, "Merchant Network," p. 199.
90. Ruggieri's alms and food, *OS*, pp. 413 and 416, letter of Feb. 7, 1583; Ricci's incense and oil, *FR*, 1/195; loans from Macao Chinese, *OS*, p. 420, letter of Jan. 25, 1584.
91. *FR*, 1/74 and 259, lit. "*scudi.*"
92. Triptych, *FR*, 2/16; army commander, *OS*, p. 56; Cochin embassy, *OS*, p. 57; furniture, *FR*, 2/48.
93. Junks, *FR*, 1/341; with troops, *FR*, 1/346; picnic, *FR*, 1/302; sedan chairs, *FR*, 1/345, 2/15, 2/426.
94. Dinner tips, *FR*, 1/370; travel gifts, *FR*, 2/100 and 2/104; advance payment for trip, *FR*, 2/101.
95. *FR*, 1/224, 258.
96. *FR*, 1/334, 2/92.
97. Boxer, "Macao," p. 65 on slaves; *FR*, 1/246 on Ricci's "*cafro assai negro*" and his other "*negra dell' India.*" Use of slaves is discussed in Bettray, *Akkomodationsmethode*, pp. 148–50.
98. Ricci's analysis in *FR*, 1/262.
99. *FR*, 1/262; So, *Piracy*, p. 57, mentions blacks as pirates at this time.
100. *OS*, p. 287, Ricci to Acquaviva, Peking, July 26, 1605.
101. Zhang Xie, *Dongxi yangkao*, 5/6 (reprint p. 183). Zhang refers to Portuguese (Fo-lang-ji) here, but is also drawing material from what he's heard of Manila.
102. *FR*, 1/181, 187, 189.
103. *FR*, 1/264.
104. *FR*, 1/216 n. 1.
105. *FR*, 1/248 n. 1, and 2/7 n. 3.
106. *FR*, 2/91 n. 2.
107. Peking arrival, 2/123; details on these gifts are in *FR*, 2/114, 123 n. 5, 124 n. 1. The missing organ is mentioned in *FR*, 2/90. Shen Defu gives a Chinese contemporary's view of the gifts in his *Wanli yehubian*, p. 784.
108. *FR*, 2/139–40.
109. *FR*, 2/151, 153, 156.
110. Presents and prism in 1602, *FR*, 2/154; early prisms, *FR*, 1/346 and 2/37; value merely eight *baiocchi*, *FR*, 1/255, 2/142. For a meticulous study of *baiocchi:*ducat exchange rates—they in fact stood at around

115:1 in 1567–73—see Delumeau, *Vie économique et sociale de Rome*, 2/660–65.

111. *OS*, p. 386.

112. *OS*, p. 246, letter of Aug. 14, 1599.

113. *OS*, p. 338, letter of Mar. 6, 1608.

114. Culley and McNaspy, "Music," pp. 217–26.

115. In display, *FR*, 1/268; in ceremonies, 2/70; hard harmonies, 1/130; four parts and keyboard, 1/32.

116. *FR*, 2/132. Ricci calls the instrument a *"gravicembalo"* in *FR*, 2/29, and a *"manicordio"* in 2/39. Dehergne, *Répertoire*, no. 607 (p. 193) shows Pantoja was born in 1571, and was in Nanjing during March to May of 1600. For Cattaneo, see Dehergne, no. 158 and Pfister, no. 15. Ricci used Cattaneo's great musical skills to help him analyze Chinese tonal patterns in speech, *FR*, 2/32–33.

117. *FR*, 2/134–35.

118. Ricci, *Xiqin quyi bazhang*, pp. 284–85; d'Elia, "Musica e canti," pp. 137–38. Chinese interest in Ricci's musical work is strong at present: see Yin Falu, "Li Madou yu Ouzhou jiaohui yinyue," and the rejoinders in *Yinyue Yanjiu* 1982, 4/70 and 105.

119. Ricci summarizes his Chinese friends' comments in *FR*, 2/134–35.

SEVEN

THE THIRD PICTURE: THE MEN OF SODOM

1. See listings of the cycle in Verbeek and Veldman, *Hollstein's Dutch and Flemish Etchings*, vol. 16, "De Passe (Continued)," pp. 6 and 7; and Franken, *L'oeuvre gravé*, p. 4, nos. 18–21.

2. Ricci, *Li Madou ti baoxiang tu*, pp. 6–8; Cheng Dayue, *Chengshi moyuan*, zhuan 6, pt. 2, pp. 41–43; Duyvendak, "Review," pp. 393–94.

3. Pastor, *History of the Popes*, 14/414–16; Duruy, *Carafa*, pp. 304–5 and lampoon example on p. 408 (appendix 95); O'Connell, *Counter-Reformation*, p. 83.

4. Pastor, *History of the Popes*, 14/152–67 on the war; p. 233 on perpetual Lent.

5. Ibid., 14/265 and 272–75 on Jews and land; pp. 238–39, 266–68 on punishing sensuality.

6. Ibid., 14/214–26; du Bellay, *Les Regrets*, poem no. 103; Ancel, "La dis-

grâce," 24/238–44; other homosexuality charges made by the cardinal of Lorraine are given in Duruy, *Carafa*, pp. 296–97 n. 4. Death account in Ancel, "La disgrâce," 26/216–17.

7. Quotation from Isaiah 39:7. See also Isaiah 1:6, 1:9, 3:9, 3:16, 10:6, 13:19, 19:14. D. P. Walker, *Ancient Theology*, p. 8, builds from Paul's Romans 1:22–27 to develop the chilling arguments for the role of sodomy in the chain of punishments.

8. Paci, "La Decadenza," p. 204 n. 402 and p. 206 n. 410. Ibid., p. 145, has an amusing fifteenth-century popular song on Maceratan immorality.

9. Ibid., p. 174 n. 139.

10. Martin, *Roma Sancta*, pp. 49, 132, 189.

11. Delumeau, *Vie économique et sociale*, 1/404–8.

12. Martin, *Roma Sancta*, pp. 85 and 185; on Ignatius's concern, see Tacchi Venturi, *Storia della Compagnia*, 1/390.

13. Delumeau, *Vie économique et sociale*, 1/416–27.

14. Martin, *Roma Sancta*, pp. 145–46.

15. Montaigne, *Journal de voyage*, pp. 234–35. In ibid., p. 348, Montaigne compares the prostitutes of Florence to those of Venice and Rome.

16. See graphic descriptions in Duarte Gomez, *Discursos*, pp. 130–31, 156, 186; and Boxer, *Fidalgos*, pp. 227–29.

17. Sassetti, *Lettere*, pp. 125–27.

18. Mocquet, *Voyages*, pp. 285, 307, 343, 351, gives cumulative details on the intriguing example of a Chinese former slave woman married to an Indian Christian doctor.

19. Goa details in Pyrard, *Voyage*, 2/102–4 (for a slightly later period), and Costa, *Christianisation*, p. 24; on Macao figures, Boxer, "Macao," pp. 65–67, and Ptak, "Demography of Old Macao," p. 30; *FR*, 2/433, shows Father Goís arriving in Xuzhou with two boy slaves he bought en route.

20. *FR*, 1/246. On runaway slaves, see *FR*, 1/262 and ch. 5, above.

21. *FR*, 1/204, for the help given Ricci by *"un putto Indiano que sapeva parlare meglio que lui un puoco la lingua cinese"*; and *FR*, 1/246, *"i cinese hanno grande paura."*

22. *FR*, 1/99; I assume by *"altri christiani"* he meant the Portuguese.

23. On prices, see Pantoja in *FR*, 1/99 n. 1 and Mocquet, *Voyages*, p. 342—the figures in *taels* were twelve and fifteen. On slaves as secretaries, see "Ioan Pay" in Mocquet, *Voyages*, p. 333, and Boxer, *Fidalgos*, pp. 224–25. Boxer, loc. cit., gives the fine (in cruzados).

24. *FR,* 1/98–99. Maffei, *L'Histoire,* p. 253, echoes these criticisms.
25. Crops, *FR,* 1/17; porcelain, 1/22; connoisseurship, 1/91; printing, 1/31.
26. Quotation, *FR,* 1/120; also ibid., 1/39–40, 118–19.
27. *FR,* 1/56 and 60. On the Ming censorate in general, see the fine study by Charles Hucker, *The Censorial System of Ming China.*
28. *FR,* 1/108–9, the "indecent behavior" being *"sconcie."*
29. Ibid., 1/281.
30. Ibid., 1/282.
31. Ricci's comments in ibid., 1/93, 110, quotation 1/101.
32. *OS,* p. 70.
33. *FR,* 1/59 and 79, 1/101–2.
34. Ibid., 2/144.
35. Letter of Aug. 23, 1608, to Fabio de Fabi, *OS,* p. 372; *FR,* 1/23 and 2/20, transposing *scudi* to ducats. On gold-to-silver exchange rate of one to eleven, see Delumeau, *Vie économique et sociale,* 2/665–66.
36. Construction finely described in Ray Huang, *1587,* pp. 125–28, and 246 nn. The tomb, the Ting (Ding) Ling, is described by Ann Paludan as tomb no. 10 in her work *The Imperial Ming Tombs* (Yale University Press, 1981). This is the first study that lets us see Wanli's construction in the context of the tomb architecture of his ancestors and descendants.
37. *FR,* 2/174 n. 4.
38. Ibid., 2/131.
39. Ibid.
40. Ibid., 2/541, and conclusion of ch. 5, above.
41. *FR,* 2/471–72 on map and visits; 2/126–28 on the clock case, which to Ricci's amazement cost 1,300 ducats.
42. Ibid., 1/100, calling then *"gente plebeia."* A judicious view of the real extent of eunuch political power at this time is given by Charles Hucker in *Censorial System of Ming Ching,* pp. 44–45.
43. Feng Bao, *FR,* 2/65, though Ricci is sarcastic about the visit; warning on Ma Tang, 2/109; acrobatics, 2/112, which Ricci found *"garbata."* Albert Chan, "Peking at the Time of the Wanli Emperor," p. 136, gives further examples of such acrobatics.
44. *DMB,* p. 331 and references under Wang Ying-chiao; Yuan, "Urban Riots," pp. 287–92; *FR,* 2/81–82 on the fake "mines" under houses, and 2/107 on Linqing.
45. *FR,* 2/93.

46. *DMB*, p. 210 on Cheng Kuei-fei, and pp. 142–43 on Chen-k'o (Zhenke) of the Shen family. Ricci's harsh comments are in *FR*, 2/190. Tang Xianzu's possible connections with Ricci are explored by Xu Shuofang in "Tang Xianzu he Li Madou"; clearly in this case Zhenke was not a mutual friend.

47. Letter in *OS*, p. 259, dated February 1605 by Tacchi Venturi, corrected to May 12, 1605 by d'Elia. Background to the massacre in *DMB*, p. 583.

48. *FR*, 2/30.

49. Ibid., 1/125 on Buddhist Babylon; 1/98 on *"gente effeminata."*

50. Ibid., 1/76, 79, drunkenness discussed 1/101.

51. Geiss, "Peking," p. 185.

52. Ibid., pp. 41 and 191.

53. Xu (Hsü Kuang-ch'i) is quoted in Geiss, "Peking," pp. 175 and 177. On the winter retreats of straw for beggars, see Chan, "Peking at the Time of the Wanli Emperor," pp. 141–42, and Geiss, "Peking," p. 172. Galeote Pereira (Boxer, *South China*, p. 31) expressed his surprise at the absence of beggars in South China. Martin de Rada (ibid., p. 294) saw many later, especially among the blind.

54. *FR*, 2/25 on veil and modes of travel; for dust storms and the residents' veils, see Chan, "Peking," p. 124, and Geiss, "Peking," pp. 33–34, 45–48.

55. *FR*, 1/98–99, converting *scudi* to ducats; see *FR*, 2/111 n. 2 for the boy costing three mace.

56. Compare these passages in *FR*, 1/98 with the cuts in Trigault, tr. Gallagher, p. 86. On women sold as children into prostitution, see Gaspar da Cruz in Boxer, *South China*, pp. 150, 152.

57. Accounts summarized in Chan, "Peking," p. 141. Gaspar da Cruz (Boxer, *South China*, p. 122) noted that blind women were often prostitutes in the south, being dressed and made up by companion "nurses" who shared their immoral earnings.

58. *FR*, 1/241; in ibid., 1/242 n. 6, d'Elia adds other rare sources on this case.

59. Ibid., 2/381–82.

60. Prints and plays, ibid., 2/234–35.

61. Ibid., 1/33; Chan, "Peking," p. 128, notes these boys ousting sing-song girls from popularity at this time.

62. *FR*, 1/98.

63. Cited by d'Elia in *FR*, 1/98 n. 3.

64. Boxer, *South China in the Sixteenth Century*, pp. 16–17.

65. Ibid., p. 223.

66. Ibid., pp. 225–27.

67. Aquinas, ed. Bourke, pp. 220–22, quotation at p. 222. The inconsistencies of Aquinas's use of "natural" in this context are pointed out in John Boswell, *Christianity, Social Tolerance, and Homosexuality*, pp. 319–26.

68. Daniel, *Islam and the West*, pp. 132, 144 (for parallel to Ricci in *FR*, 1/98) and appendix E. Boswell, *Christianity, Social Tolerance, and Homosexuality*, p. 281 and pp. 367–69 on the kingdom of Jerusalem's laws and the stories of violations.

69. Luther, *Letters of Spiritual Counsel*, tr. Tappert, p. 76.

70. Canisius, *Ane Cathechisme*, ch. 149, spelling modernized; Luther, *Letters*, p. 236, an interpretation found also in Luther's *Lectures on the Epistle to the Hebrews*, ch. 13, v. 2 or his *Lectures on Romans*, ch. 12, v. 13; Boswell, *Christianity*, pp. 97–101 discusses the dominance in many early commentaries of the idea of hospitality.

71. Paci, "La Decadenza," p. 195, on Macerata; Boswell, *Christianity*, p. 279 n. 32 for an early statement of this view by Jacques de Vitry; see also remarks by Pyrard, in his *Voyage*, 1/195 and 307 on sodomy in the Maldives.

72. Quotation from Spinola, letter of Oct. 26, 1578, *Doc. Ind.*, 11/320; rules abandoned, *Doc. Ind.*, 10/282.

73. Quotations from Carletti, *My Voyage*, pp. 209 and 212. Equally graphic are the descriptions by the French merchant Pyrard, *Voyage*, 2/112–13.

74. Baião, *Inquisição*, 1/43–45. Costa, *Christianisation*, p. 195.

75. Joseph-Marie Cros, *Saint François*, 2/12. See similar passages in Boxer, *Christian Century in Japan*, pp. 35 and 66; and Elison, *Deus Destroyed*, p. 35.

76. Cros, *Saint François*, 2/13 on abortions, 2/100 on public charges.

77. Cited in Schütte, *Valignano's Mission*, p. 257.

78. Ibid., pp. 279 and 284 on median position, p. 350 on sleeping rules. Elison, *Deus Destroyed*, p. 41, gives Valignano's views on sodomy in a context of his moral views.

79. Cited in Schütte, *Valignano's Mission*, p. 245.

80. Fedrici, *Voyages and Travels*, pp. 210–11.

81. Jacobs, *Treatise* (attributed to António Galvão), pp. 119–21. Other examples are given in Lach, *Asia in the Making of Europe*, vol. 1, pt. 2, pp.

553-54, including a statement by Linschoten of the same tenor (n. 301).

82. Xie Zhaozhe, *Wu za zu*, 8/4b-5 (reprint p. 209); for Xie's biography, see *DMB*, pp. 546-50 under Hsieh Chao-che. The remarks by Tao Gu can be found in his *Qing yi lu*, juan 1, p. 11. Chan, "Chinese-Philippine Relations," p. 71, led me to these passages.

83. Xie Zhaozhe, *Wu za zu*, juan 8, p. 2 in the 1795 edition; for some reason this passage on transvestism is cut from the 1959 Peking reprint.

84. Montaigne, *Journal de Voyage*, p. 231, and p. 481 n. 515.

85. Shen Defu, *Bizhou zhai yutan*, pp. 31b-32. Again, I was led to this passage by Albert Chan's "Chinese-Philippine Relations," p. 71.

86. On this "Hanlin feng," see Robert van Gulik, *Erotic Colour Prints of the Ming Period*, 1/211-12, 222, and vol. 3, plates 4 and 19. Lesbian lovers are pictured in ibid., vol. 1, plates 4 and 17, and at p. 147.

87. Zhang Xie, *Dongxi yangkao*, 12/11 (1962 reprint p. 537); Chan, "Chinese-Philippine Relations," p. 71. Spate, *Spanish Lake*, p. 159, puts the sodomy of the "Sangleys" in contemporary context.

88. *FR*, 1/204. Henri Bernard, in his *Aux Portes de la Chine*, p. 101, elaborates on the Chinese view that the Jesuits were *"séducteurs d'enfants."*

89. *FR*, 1/155 and 1/155 n. 6; Bernard, *Aux Portes*, pp. 100-1.

90. *FR*, vol. 1, plate 9, facing p. 194, gives a reproduction of this Chinese text of the Ten Commandments—the sixth runs *"moxing yin, xie, wei dengshi."*

91. I.e., in 1 Cor. 7:32-33; 2 Tim. 2:3; Epictetus, *Discourses*, bk. 3, ch. 22, pp. 155-59.

92. *Tianzhu shiyi*, pp. 608-14 (quotations from pp. 612 and 613); *Lettres édifiantes*, pp. 361-66.

93. *Tianzhu shiyi*, p. 615; the French version, p. 366, is judiciously bowdlerized.

94. Ignatius of Loyola, *Spiritual Exercises*, tr. Puhl, sec. 58, pt. 5; sec. 60.

95. Claudio Acquaviva, *Letters (Sept. 29, 1583)*, p. 69; *Letters (May 19, 1586)*, p. 82; and *Letters (Aug. 1, 1594)*, p. 130.

96. Acquaviva, *Directory*, tr. Longridge, pp. 277-79; Acquaviva, *Letters (Aug. 14, 1601)*, p. 48.

97. See *FR*, 1/315 and 2/490.

98. Acquaviva, *Directory*, pp. 304-5.

99. Ricci's words from the first paragraph on Sodom, *Li Madou ti baoxiang tu*, p. 7.

EIGHT

THE FOURTH IMAGE: THE FOURTH PICTURE

1. *OS*, p. 245 for quoted portions. On Costa's life, see Tacchi Venturi's comments in *OS*, p. 119 n. 1. Ricci here wrote "Nicola Bencivenni" but gave the correct spelling in an earlier letter, *OS*, p. 122.

2. Beissel, *Verehrung Marias*, pp. 424-28, 435-37. A poem by Tasso in homage to the shrine is in ibid., pp. 440-42. Ignatius of Loyola, *Spiritual Exercises*, tr. Puhl, no. 103.

3. Montaigne, *Journal de Voyage*, pp. 258-60.

4. Beissel, *Verehrung Marias*, p. 483, quoting Adam von Einsiedeln's visit of 1574, and ibid., p. 484 n. 2, for some early Macerata works. Montaigne, *Journal de Voyage*, p. 261, discusses the effect on him made by the cure of Michel Marteau, whom he met there on his own visit.

5. Miracle and church of St. Mary discussed in Gentili and Adversi, "La Religione," p. 43 (bibliography in n. 105). On the names and locations of the other twenty churches, see *Storia di Macerata*, vol. 5, plate 5 facing p. 312, "Macerata alla fine del secolo XVI." The background to Marian devotion in Macerata can be seen in the same volume, pp. 247-93, in the two essays by Mons. Elio Gallegati, "Note sulla Devozione Mariana nel Basso Medioevo." A valuable survey of the holdings of early religious art in Macerata is the Maceratan Tourist Board publication *Pittura nel Maceratese dal Duecento al Tardo Gotico* (Macerata; Ente Provinciale per il Turismo, 1971).

6. Ignatius, *Spiritual Exercises*, no. 63, the triple colloquy.

7. Cited from Charles Conway, *Vita Christi*, p. 13 (with minor changes).

8. He mentions her in *OS*, pp. 99 and 115. On the other children, see Adversi, "Ricci," pp. 357-58.

9. *OS*, pp. 96, 113, 122, 218, 278, 374. An exception is the poignant letter to his father of May 10, 1605, after Ricci heard he had *not* died, *OS*, p. 268.

10. *OS*, p. 97, letter to his father of Nov. 12, 1592.

11. Tacchi Venturi, *Storia della Compagnia di Gesù*, 2/15 (siege), 16-17 (medical treatment), 21 (vision).

12. Ignatius writing and visit to sister, ibid., pp. 22-24. Ricci's Masses after being in bed are mentioned in his letter to his father of Nov. 12, 1592, *OS*, p. 97. On the medical treatment in Macao, and the limp, see *FR*,

1/321–23. Michel de Montaigne, *Oeuvres Complètes*, bk. 3, ch. 11, has the extraordinary essay on the lame, "Des Boyteux." This essay is the focus of a remarkable chapter in Natalie Davis, *Return of Martin Guerre*.

13. *Inferno*, I, lines 28–30, quoted in John Freccero, "Dante's Firm Foot," p. 250, and analyzed in ibid., pp. 252–55. *FR*, 1/321 and 323 on causes of recurrent pain.

14. This is but a small selection from the long list in Martin, *Roma Sancta*, pp. 29–38.

15. Ibid., pp. 39–40, spelling modernized; p. 48.

16. Ricci's own relics, *FR*, 2/121 and 116 n. 7; gifts to others and Luke Li's painting, *FR*, 2/481–82 and 1/261.

17. Villaret, "Les premières origines," pp. 28–37, 44–49.

18. Gentili and Adversi, "La Religione," p. 43.

19. Miller, "Marianischen Kongregationen," p. 253; *FR*, 2/552 n. 3; Ganss, "Christian Life Communities," p. 48.

20. Examples from Martin, *Roma Sancta*, pp. 206–9.

21. Miller, "Marianischen Kongregationen," p. 257; Villaret, *Les Congrégations*, pp. 41–45.

22. *Doc. Ind.*, 11/368; Villaret, *Congrégations*, pp. 43 and 478, and Villaret, "Premières origines," p. 35. For other groups in Bengal, see Correia-Afonso, "Akbar and the Jesuits," p. 62. In Boxer, *South China*, p. 53, Gaspar de Cruz lists the achievements of other religious orders in spreading the cult of the Virgin.

23. *FR*, 1/160, 166; Margiotti, "Congregazioni," 18/256.

24. Hicks, "English College," p. 25; Mullan and Beringer, *Sodality*, doc. 5; Ganss, "Christian Life Communities," pp. 46–47.

25. Mullan and Beringer, *Sodality*, p. 26 and doc. 9, passim. It is in doc. 7, a letter of June 16, 1587, that Acquaviva refers to the reason for the ban on women being *"por no ser esto conforme a la edificacion."* This is an illuminating confirmation of Ranke's stern judgment that Acquaviva was "a man who concealed a profound inflexibility under an aspect of great mildness and great suavity of manner" (*History of the Popes*, p. 198).

26. *FR*, 2/482; Margiotti, "Congregazioni," pp. 132–33.

27. Xu in *FR*, 2/361; Li, *FR*, 2/544 nn. 1 and 3.

28. Early rumors, Hicks, "English College," pp. 3–4; subgroups, Villaret, *Les Congrégations*, pp. 417–19.

29. *FR*, 1/328–30; Pfister, p. 45. For the true date of Petris's death as November 1593 (not 1594, as Ricci wrote), see d'Elia in *FR*, 1/328 n. 1. Ibid., p. 328, Ricci says Petris came to the college as a "boy" (*fanciullo*),

which makes it possible he was there before 1577, when he would have been fifteen.

30. Ignatius of Loyola, *Exercitia Spiritualia,* pp. 62–64, especially n. 17. On Acquaviva, Villaret, *Les Congrégations,* pp. 78–79.

31. Guibert, *Jesuits,* pp. 137 and 37.

32. For Ricci and his pictures, see *FR,* 1/188, 189, 193, and plates 14 and 15 facing 2/126 and 128. Notice Ranke's remark on Acquaviva that "the young clung to him with ardour" (*History of the Popes,* p. 198).

33. Acquaviva, *Letters* (*19 May, 1586*), pp. 94–95, with slight punctuation changes.

34. Mozambique, Gomes, *Tragic History of the Sea, 1589–1622,* tr. Boxer, pp. 186, 271; Akbar, *OS,* p. 5; *FR,* 1/153 nn. 1 and 5 on Macao churches.

35. Wang Pan's request, *FR,* 1/188 n. 2 and 1/193.

36. Xie Zhaozhe, *Wu za zu,* p. 120.

37. Ricci on confusion, *FR,* 1/194. See ibid., 1/194 n. 2 on Zhang Geng (Chang Keng, *Eminent Chinese,* p. 99) and *FR,* 2/85n. on Nanjing.

38. *OS,* p. 60, letter of Oct. 20, 1585. To keep perspective on this, see the discussion of the absence of pictures of the Passion or Crucifixion even in the Sistine chapel at this time, O'Malley, *Praise and Blame,* p. 140.

39. Painting in *FR,* 1/232, 2/4, 2/29; recopied, 2/330.

40. *FR,* 2/110 on Ma Tang; *FR,* 2/123 n. 5 on gifts, 2/125 on empress.

41. *FR,* 2/115, reading *"fattaccio"* for Ricci's *"fatticio."*

42. Ibid., 2/116, 118.

43. Medallions, *FR,* 1/302; prints, *FR,* 2/461, 512; church roof, 1/200n.; hidden, 2/455. A good discussion of the role of the cross at this time is in Bettray, *Akkomodationsmethode,* pp. 365–82.

44. Search for painters, *OS,* pp. 159, 254; Cattaneo Madonna, *FR,* 2/247, 254; on altars, *FR,* 2/330; converts' own images, 2/339; exorcism, 2/335.

45. Ibid., 2/349.

46. Ibid., 2/105 n. 6. The painter was Emmanuel Pereira (*FR,* 2/9 n. 7), a Macao Chinese born 1575, then a novice in Nanjing.

47. *FR,* 2/333–34; Dehergne, *Répertoire,* p. 257.

48. *FR,* 1/318 and 319.

49. Forty ducats (lit. *scudi*), *FR,* 2/349–50; furnace in home, 2/480; old man of 78, 2/248.

50. "Battle prizes," *FR,* 2/94; paintings, *OS,* p. 63 and *FR,* 2/330; painter's whole collection, 2/261; Qu, *FR,* 2/342 and *OS,* p. 269, *"tre cassoni"* of books; Li, *FR,* 1/69 n. 2 and 2/261.

51. *FR,* 2/345. Trigault, tr. Gallagher, p. 470, changes the sense of this passage and downplays Qu's invocation of the Virgin.

52. *FR,* 2/341 and 342.

53. On Buddhist works see Yü Chün-fang, *Renewal of Buddhism in China,* and Geiss, "Peking," p. 40. On Luke Li's devotion to Buddha see *FR,* 2/481; the members tried to sue him for graft when he left to become a Christian.

54. Burnings in *FR,* 2/243, muddles with Virgin 2/398 n. 3. Shen Defu, in *Wanli yehu bian,* p. 785, noted Ricci's tenacious anti-Buddhism, though praising his fairness in debate.

55. On Xavier, Cros, *Saint François,* 2/28; on Ricci, *OS,* p. 55, and *FR,* 1/314-15, 357.

56. Ricci's diet, *FR,* 2/535 n. 1; on pigs, Ricci, *Tianzhu shiyi,* pp. 510, 514; *Lettres Edifiantes,* pp. 273-75. His anti-Buddhist arguments are summarized in Bettray, *Akkomodationsmethode,* pp. 256-66.

57. *Sanzijing,* sentences 13 and 14 in the standard editions.

58. Basic argument in Ricci, *Tianzhu shiyi,* pp. 492-93, *Lettres Edifiantes,* pp. 255-56; lower orders as Pythagoreans, *OS,* p. 57, letter of Oct. 20, 1585, to Acquaviva; infanticide argument, *FR,* 1/99. Variant editions of *Tianzhu shiyi* and its prefaces are examined by Fang Hao in his "Tianzhu shiyi zhi gaicuan."

59. Ricci, *Tianzhu shiyi,* pp. 495-507; *Lettres Edifiantes,* pp. 258-70.

60. Ricci, *Jiren shipian,* ch. 6.

61. Lancashire, "Buddhist Reaction," pp. 83-85 (using the spelling Yü Shun-hsi): the original letters are in Ricci, *Bianxue yidu,* pp. 637-50. (Buddhism, though two millennia old by this time, had been widely prevalent in China only since the fifth century A.D.).

62. Quotations in *OS,* p. 360. For Ricci's other, briefer mentions of similar criticisms, see *OS,* pp. 277, 345.

63. As quoted in Yü, *Renewal,* pp. 88-89; on the earlier letter, see Lancashire, "Buddhist Reaction," p. 86.

64. *FR,* 2/180-81.

65. *FR,* 2/75-79, and Sanhuai biography, 2/75 n. 5.

66. *FR,* 2/66-68 for first meetings; Li was staying with Jiao Hong at this time. The pioneer work on the poems and the Li-Ricci relationship was Otto Franke's "Li Tschi und Matteo Ricci": see pp. 14-17 for his analysis and translation of the first poem; the poem appears in Li Zhi's *Fenshu,* p. 247. There is now an immense body of new scholarship on Li Zhi, which I will not attempt to recapitulate here; a good short biogra-

phy is in *DMB*, pp. 807–18. Li's relations to the dominant philosophical schools of the time are discussed by W. T. de Bary in his edited volume *Self and Society in Ming Thought* (Columbia University Press, 1970), pp. 188–225, and his broader place in the economic and political spectrum is explored in Cheng Pei-kai, "Reality and Imagination."

67. Li's letter to an unnamed friend is in Li Zhi's *Xu fenshu*, p. 35. The translated passage is from *DMB*, p. 1140.

68. *FR*, 2/104–5. Li's extreme syncretism may have drawn him to Ricci, as Li wrote, "Those who discuss the Three Teachings cannot discuss them with a narrow mind" (Berling, *Syncretic Religion*, p. 53).

69. Hung Ming-shui, "Yüan Hung-tao," pp. 214–16, gives a fine introduction to this intellectual circle.

70. *FR*, 2/106.

71. As translated in *DMB*, p. 814.

72. *FR*, 2/184–86.

73. *DMB*, p. 444.

74. Ricci makes the claim in *Jiren shipian*, 1/9 (reprint p. 133). On earlier appearance of the same passage, compare *Tianzhu shiyi*, p. 422 with *Jiren shipian*, reprint pp. 125–26.

75. Compare Ricci, *Jiren shipian*, pp. 125–26 with *Tianzhu shiyi*, pp. 422–23. The only change is that the "nine foot" man of the latter is changed to the "seven foot" man in the former. *Lettres*, pp. 189–90 is quite faithful. The place of this passage in the content of the *True Meaning* as a body of doctrine can be explored via John Young, *Confucianism and Christianity*, pp. 28–39; see also the detailed exegesis by Hu Guozhen (Peter Hu), "Jianjie tianzhu shiyi," pp. 255–66. Peter Hu and Douglas Lancashire are currently preparing an English translation of the entire *Tianzhu shiyi*.

76. Conway, *Vita Christi*, pp. 83 and 90; on the power of the Incarnation as a theme in Renaissance theology, see O'Malley, *Praise and Blame*, pp. 140–42.

77. Conway, *Vita Christi*, p. 83 on the monks. The fact that Ricci had little time for contemplation was accepted and understood by his teachers, who felt that though some contemplation was good, too much time for contemplation was not necessary in the Jesuit's busy life of action; as they put it, *"Vita mixta, tanto nobilior est et utilior."* See Iparraguirre, "Para la historia de la oración," pp. 83 and 124. Ibid., p. 88, shows that Fabio de Fabi, to whom Ricci often wrote from China, wrote a 200-page

manuscript on prayer and contemplation. Ibid., pp. 94–95, presents Acquaviva's thoughts on the "pure affection and peace of the soul."

78. Ignatius of Loyola, *Spiritual Exercises,* tr. Puhl, p. 52, nos. 111–14. Barthes comments cleverly on this passage in *Sade, Fourier, Loyola,* p. 64.

79. Ignatius of Loyola, *Exercitia Spiritualia* (Madrid, 1919), annotated ed., pp. 65–66 for parallel textual examples. On the pseudo-Matthew infancy gospels, see *New Testament Apocrypha,* ed. Wilson and Schneemelcher, 1/406–8.

80. Ignatius, *Exercitia Spiritualia* (Madrid, 1919), [Further notes on problems in the directory] p. 109 n. 17. Ludolfus, *Vita,* ed. Bolard, p. 39 (pt. 1, ch. 9), quotes Chrysostum. For other criticisms of "apocryphal matter, like midwives at the Nativity" see Baxandall, *Painting and Experience,* p. 43.

81. *FR,* 1/87.

82. Montaigne, *Journal de Voyage,* p. 237.

83. Martin, *Roma Sancta,* pp. 90–91.

84. Ricci describes the incident in *FR,* 1/305. On Almeida's absence, see ibid., and Dehergne, *Répertoire,* p. 8; on wax and lamp oil as crucial gifts, see *FR,* 1/195, 2/482.

85. Ricci, *Jifa,* p. 5 (reprint p. 17).

86. Ricci, *Li Madou ti baoxiang tu,* p. 6b. The identification of the Sevillian original for the Wierix print was made by Berthold Laufer in 1910, and published in his "Christian Art in China," pp. 110–11, but a number of baffling problems remain. The print seems clearly identifiable, via its caption, to Wierix n. 546 on p. 98 of Louis Alvin, *Catalogue raisonné de l'oeuvre des trois frères Jean, Jérome et Antoine Wierix* (Brussels, 1866); but the Riccian and Japanese versions are only partially similar to that Wierix print (reproduced in Mauquoy-Hendrickx, *Les Estampes de Wierix,* 1/114) or to the Seville original (reproduced in C. R. Post, *A History of Spanish Painting* [Harvard University Press, 1930], 3/298). Nagayama Tokihiko, *Taigwai shiryō,* confirms the Nagasaki origins, and the difference from the China version, as does Nishimura Tei in his detailed article "Nihon yasokai": but neither scholar can provide the connecting link in the chain of transmission. To make things more difficult, the copy of Cheng Dayue's *Chengshi moyuan* in the Peking rare book library (of which microfilms are available in the Harvard and Yale libraries) is missing the picture altogether, which has clearly been cut out, as can be seen by the jagged page edge in ibid., juan 6 (xia), p.

43: the Mary picture should have been on the obverse of the Lot and Sodom picture, just as Emmaus is on the obverse of Peter in the waves (ibid., pp. 38a and b). That the Mary print *should* be there is shown by the *mu-lu* to that juan (rather confusingly printed as juan 12 on the *mu-lu* page itself) where a solitary *tu* (picture) without any *wen* (essay) is listed as following the first three picture-essay combinations. Therefore I have been restricted to the version printed in Ricci's *Li Madou ti baoxiang tu.*

87. For an immensely detailed account of Seville's role in the overseas trade of this time, see Huguette and Pierre Chaunu, *Seville et l'Atlantique (1504–1650)*, 8 vols. (Paris, 1955), especially vol. 3, "Le trafic de 1561 à 1595."

NINE

INSIDE THE PALACE

1. *OS,* p. 214, letter of Oct. 12, 1596, quotation identified by Tacchi Venturi. The translation is Robert Fitzgerald's, *The Aeneid* (Random House, 1983), p. 164.
2. *FR,* 1/5. These are the opening sentences of Ricci's own introduction to his *Historia.*
3. *OS,* p. 26, letter of Dec. 1, 1581: *"mas ja em mansebo tenho a naturesa dos velhos que sempre louvo o tempo passado."* Mansebo, youth, would now be written *mancebo* in standard Portuguese.

BIBLIOGRAPHY

ACQUAVIVA, CLAUDIO. *The Directory to the Spiritual Exercises* (1599), in *The Spiritual Exercises of Saint Ignatius of Loyola.* Tr. W. H. Longridge. London: A. R. Mowbray, 1950, pp. 273–351.

——————. *Letters* (*29 Sept. 1583*), in *Renovation Reading,* pp. 47–69. Woodstock College, 1886.

——————. *Letters* (*19 May 1586*), in *Renovation Reading,* pp. 78–95. Woodstock College, 1886.

——————. *Letters* (*12 Jan. 1590*), in *Lettres choisies des Généraux aux pères et frères de la compagnie de Jésus,* vol. 1, pp. 109–13. Lyon, 1878.

——————. *Letters* (*1 Aug. 1594*), in *Lettres choisies des Généraux aux pères et frères de la compagnie de Jésus,* vol. 1, pp. 118–30. Lyon, 1878.

——————. *Letters* (*14 Aug. 1601*), in *Select Letters of Our Very Reverend Fathers General to the Fathers and Brothers of the Society of Jesus,* pp. 47–49. Woodstock College, 1900.

Ad Herennium. Tr. Harry Caplan. New York: Loeb Classical Library, 1968.

ADVERSI, ALDO. "Ricci, Matteo," in Vincenzo Brocco, comp., *Dizionario Bio-Bibliografico dei Maceratesi,* pp. 357–95, vol. 2 of *Storia di Macerata.* Macerata, 1972.

AGRIPPA, CORNELIUS. *Of the Vanitie and Uncertaintie of Artes and Sciences.* Tr. James Sanford. London: Henry Wykes, 1569.

BIBLIOGRAPHY

ANCEL, RENÉ. "La disgrâce et le procès des Carafa, d'après des documents inédits (1559–1567)," *Revue Bénédictine* 24 (1907): 224–53, 479–509; 25 (1908): 194–224; 26 (1909): 52–80, 189–220, 301–24.

ANGELES, F. DELOR. "The Philippine Inquisition: A Survey," *Philippine Studies* 28 (1980): 253–83.

AQUINAS, THOMAS. *The Pocket Aquinas.* Ed. and intro. Vernon J. Bourke. New York, 1960.

—————, comp. *Catena Aurea: Commentary on the Four Gospels Collected out of the Works of the Fathers by S. Thomas Aquinas.* Tr. M. Pattison et al. 6 vols. Oxford: Parker, 1874.

ATWELL, WILLIAM S. "International Bullion Flows and the Chinese Economy circa 1530–1650," *Past and Present* 95 (1982): 68–90.

AUGUSTINE. *The Confessions of St. Augustine.* Tr. E. B. Pusey. London: Everyman's Library, 1957.

AZEVEDO, J. LUCIO D'. *Historia dos Christãos Novos Portugueses.* Lisbon, 1921.

BACON, FRANCIS. *Selected Writings.* Ed. Hugh G. Dick. New York: Modern Library, 1955.

BAIÃO, ANTÓNIO. *A Inquisição de Goa.* 2 vols. Lisbon, 1930, 1945.

BARTHES, ROLAND. *Sade, Fourier, Loyola.* Tr. Richard Miller. New York, 1976.

BAXANDALL, MICHAEL. *Painting and Experience in Fifteenth Century Italy.* Oxford: Clarendon Press, 1972.

BECKMANN, JOHANNES. *China im Blickfeld der mexikanischen Bettelorden im 16. Jahrhundert.* Schöneck/Beckenried, Schweiz, 1964.

BEISSEL, STEPHAN, S.J. *Geschichte der Verehrung Marias im 16. und 17. Jahrhundert.* Freiburg, 1910.

BELLAY, JOACHIM DU. *Les Regrets et autres oeuvres poëtiques, suivis de Antiquitez de Rome.* Geneva: Droz, 1966.

BERLING, JUDITH A. *The Syncretic Religion of Lin Chao-en.* New York: Columbia University Press, 1980.

BERNARD, HENRI, S.J. *Aux Portes de la Chine: Les Missionaires du Seizième Siècle, 1514–1588.* Tientsin, 1933.

—————. *La Découverte de Nestoriens Mongols aux Ordos et l'histoire ancienne du Christianisme en Extrême-Orient.* Tientsin, 1935.

—————. *Le Frère Bento de Goes chez les Musulmans de la Haute Asie (1603–1651).* Tientsin, 1934.

—————. *Le Père Matthieu Ricci et la Société Chinoise de son temps (1552–1610).* 2 vols. Tientsin, 1937.

—————. *Les Iles Philippines du Grand Archipel de la Chine: Un essai de la conquête spirituelle de l'Extrême-Orient, 1571–1641.* Tientsin, 1936.

—————. *Matteo Ricci's Scientific Contribution to China.* Tr. E. C. Werner. Peiping, 1935.

BERTUCCIOLI, GIULIANO. *A Florentine in Manila.* Manila: Philippine-Italian Association, 1979.

BETTRAY, JOHANNES, S.V.D. *Die Akkommodationsmethode des P. Matteo Ricci S.I. in China.* Rome: Analecta Gregoriana, 1955.

BOCCACCIO, GIOVANNI. *The Decameron.* Tr. G. H. McWilliam. Harmondsworth: Penguin Books, 1972.

BODENSTEDT, MARY IMMACULATE. *The Vita Christi of Ludolphus the Carthusian.* Washington, D.C.: Catholic University of America Press, 1944.

BORTONE, FERNANDO, S.J. *P. Matteo Ricci S.J.: Il "Saggio d'Occidente."* Rome: Editori Pontifici, 1965.

BOSWELL, JOHN. *Christianity, Social Tolerance and Homosexuality.* Chicago: University of Chicago Press, 1980.

BOVILL, E. W. *The Battle of Alcazar: An Account of the Defeat of Don Sebastian of Portugal at El-Ksar el-Kebir.* London: Batchworth, 1952.

BOXER, C. R. *The Christian Century in Japan, 1549–1650.* Berkeley: University of California Press, 1967.

—————. *Fidalgos in the Far East, 1550–1770.* London: Oxford University Press, 1968.

—————. "Macao as a Religious and Commercial Entrepôt in the Sixteenth and Seventeenth Centuries," *Acta Asiatica* 26 (1974): 64–90.

—————. "Moçambique Island as a Way-station for Portuguese East-Indiamen, *Mariners' Mirror* 48 (1962): 3–18.

—————. *Portuguese Society in the Tropics: The Municipal Councils of Goa, Macao, Bahia and Luanda, 1510–1800.* Madison: University of Wisconsin Press, 1965.

—————, ed. *South China in the Sixteenth Century: Being the narratives of Galeote Pereira, Fr. Gaspar da Cruz, O.P., Fr. Martín de Rada, O.E.S.A. (1550–1575).* London: Hakluyt Society, 1953.

—————. *The Great Ship from Amacon: Annals of Macao and the Old Japan Trade, 1555–1640.* Lisbon, 1959.

BRADING, D. A., and HARRY E. CROSS. "Colonial Silver Mining: Mexico and Peru," *Hispanic American Historical Review* 52 (1972): 545–79.

BRAUDEL, FERNAND. *The Wheels of Commerce (Civilization and Capitalism, 15th–18th Century,* vol. 2). Tr. Siân Reynolds. New York, 1982.

BROOK, TIMOTHY. "The Merchant Network in 16th Century China," *Journal of the Economic and Social History of the Orient* 24:2 (May 1981): 165–214.

BROOKS, MARY ELIZABETH. *A King for Portugal: The Madrigal Conspiracy, 1594–95.* Madison and Milwaukee: University of Wisconsin Press, 1964.

BROWN, L. W. *The Indian Christians of St. Thomas: An Account of the Ancient Syrian Church of Malabar.* Cambridge: Cambridge University Press, 1956.

Cambridge History of Islam. Ed. P. M. Holt, Ann Lambton, Bernard Lewis. Vol. 1A, *The Central Islamic Lands;* vol. 2A, *The Indian Sub-Continent.* Cambridge: Cambridge University Press, 1977.

CANISIUS, PETER. *Ane Cathechisme, 1588.* English Recusant Literature, vol. 32. Menston, Yorkshire: Scolar Press, 1970.

CARLETTI, FRANCESCO. *My Voyage around the World: A 16th Century Florentine Merchant.* Tr. Herbert Weinstock. London: Methuen, 1963.

CARRUTHERS, DOUGLAS. "The Great Desert Caravan Route, Aleppo to Basra," *Geographical Journal* 52 (July–December 1918): 157–84, map facing p. 204.

CASTELLANI, GIUSEPPE, S.J. "La Tipografia del Collegio Romano," *Archivum Historicum Societatis Iesu* 2 (1933): 11–16.

CERVANTES, MIGUEL. *Don Quixote.* Tr. J. M. Cohen. Penguin Books, 1982.

CHAN, ALBERT, S.J. "Chinese-Philippine Relations in the Late Sixteenth Century and to 1603," *Philippine Studies* 26 (1978): 51–82.

——————. *The Glory and Fall of the Ming Dynasty.* Norman: University of Oklahoma Press, 1982.

——————. "Peking at the Time of the Wanli Emperor (1572–1619)," in *Proceedings of the International Association of Historians of Asia,* Second Biennial Conference, Taipei, Taiwan, 1962, pp. 119–47.

CHAUNU, PIERRE. *Les Philippines et le Pacifique des Ibériques (XVIe, XVIIe, XVIIIe siècles).* Paris: S.E.V.P.E.N., 1960.

CH'EN, KENNETH. "A Possible Source for Ricci's Notices on Regions near China," *T'oung Pao* 34 (1938): 179–90.

CHENG DAYUE 程大約 . *Chengshi moyuan* 程氏墨苑 [The Ink Garden of Mr. Cheng]. 13 + 9 juan, 1609.

CHENG PEI-KAI. "Reality and Imagination: Li Chih and T'ang Hsien-tsu in Search of Authenticity." Ph.D. dissertation, Yale University, 1980.

CICERO, TULLIUS. *De Senectute.* Tr. W. A. Falconer. New York: Loeb Classical Library, 1923.

CIPOLLA, CARLO M., ed. *The Fontana Economic History of Europe: The Sixteenth and Seventeenth Centuries.* Glasgow: Collins, 1981.

322

CLAIR, COLIN. *Christopher Plantin.* London: Cassell, 1960.

CLAVIUS, CHRISTOPHER. *Astrolabium.* Rome: Bartholomo Grasso, 1593.

CLERCQ, CARLO DE. "Les éditions bibliques, liturgiques et canoniques de Plantin," in *Gedenkboek der Plantin-Dagen,* pp. 283–318. Antwerp, 1956.

CONWAY, CHARLES ABBOTT, JR. *The* Vita Christi *of Ludolph of Saxony and Late Medieval Devotion Centred on the Incarnation: A Descriptive Analysis.* Salzburg: Analecta Cartusiana, 1976.

COOPER, MICHAEL, S.J. "The Mechanics of the Macao-Nagasaki Silk Trade," *Monumenta Nipponica* 27 (1972): 423–33.

CORREIA-AFONSO, JOHN, S.J. *Jesuit Letters and Indian History, 1542–1773,* 2d ed. London: Oxford University Press, 1969.

——————. *Letters from the Mughal Court: The First Jesuit Mission to Akbar (1580–1583).* St. Louis: Institute of Jesuit Sources, 1981.

——————. "More about Akbar and the Jesuits," *Indica* 14:1 (March 1977): 57–62.

COSTA, ANTHONY D'. *The Christianisation of the Goa Islands, 1510–1567.* Bombay, 1965.

COUTO, DIOGO DO. *Decada Decima da Asia.* Lisbon, 1788.

CRONIN, VINCENT. *The Wise Man from the West.* London, 1955.

CROS, JOSEPH-MARIE, S.J. *Saint François de Xavier, sa vie et ses lettres.* 2 vols. Toulouse and Paris, 1900.

CULLEY, THOMAS, S.J., and CLEMENT MCNASPY, S.J. "Music and the Early Jesuits (1540–1565)," *Archivum Historicum Societatis Iesu* 40 (1971): 213–45.

CUSHNER, NICHOLAS P. "Merchants and Missionaries: A Theologian's View of Clerical Involvement in the Galleon Trade," *Hispanic American Historical Review* 47 (1967): 360–69.

DAINVILLE, FRANÇOIS DE, S.J. *La Géographie des humanistes.* Paris: Beauchesne, 1940.

——————. *L'Education des Jésuites (XVIᵉ–XVIIIᵉ siècles).* Comp. Marie-Madeleine Compère. Paris: Editions de Minuit, 1978.

DANIEL, NORMAN. *Islam and the West: The Making of an Image.* Edinburgh: University of Edinburgh Press, 1960.

DAVIS, NATALIE ZEMON. *The Return of Martin Guerre.* Cambridge: Harvard University Press, 1983.

DEE, JOHN. "Mathematicall Praeface," in H. Billingsley, tr., *The Elements of Geometrie of the most auncient Philosopher Euclide of Megara.* London: John Daye, 1570.

DEHERGNE, JOSEPH, S.J. *Répertoire des Jésuites de Chine, de 1552 à 1800*. Rome and Paris, 1973.

——————, and DONALD LESLIE. *Juifs de Chine, à travers la correspondance inédite des Jésuites du dix-huitième siècle*. Rome and Paris, 1980.

D'ELIA, PASQUALE M., S.J. *Fonti Ricciane*. See *FR*.

——————. "Further Notes on Matteo Ricci's *De Amicitia*," *Monumenta Serica* 15:2 (1956): 356–77.

——————. *Il Mappamondo Cinese del P. Matteo Ricci S.I. (Terza Edizione, Pechino, 1602) Conservato presso la Biblioteca Vaticana*. Rome: Vatican City, 1938.

——————. "Il trattato sull' Amicizia, Primo Libro Scritto in Cinese de Matteo Ricci S.I. (1595)," *Studia Missionalia* 7 (1952): 425–515.

——————. "Musica e canti Italiani a Pechino," *Revista degli Studi Orientali* 30 (1955): 131–45.

——————. "Presentazione della prima traduzione Cinese di Euclide," *Monumenta Serica* 15:1 (1956): 161–202.

DELUMEAU, JEAN. *Vie économique et sociale de Rome dans la seconde moitié du XVIᵉ siècle*. 2 vols. Paris: E. de Boccard, 1957.

Dictionary of Mnemonics. London: Eyre Methuen, 1972.

DIFFIE, BAILEY W., and GEORGE D. WINIUS. *Foundations of the Portuguese Empire, 1415–1580*. Minneapolis: University of Minnesota Press, 1977.

DMB, Dictionary of Ming Biography. Ed. L. Carrington Goodrich and Chao-ying Fang. 2 vols. New York: Columbia University Press, 1976.

Doc. Ind., Documenta Indica. Ed. Joseph Wicki, S.J. *Monumenta Missionum Societatis Jesu, Missiones Orientales*, vol. 10 (1575–1577), Rome, 1968; vol. 11 (1577–1580), Rome, 1970; vol. 12 (1580–1583), Rome, 1972.

DUFFY, JAMES. *Shipwreck and Empire, Being an Account of Portuguese Maritime Disasters in a Century of Decline*. Cambridge: Harvard University Press, 1955.

DUNNE, GEORGE H., S.J. *Generation of Giants: The Story of the Jesuits in China in the Last Decades of the Ming Dynasty*. London, 1962.

DURUY, GEORGE. *Le Cardinal Carlo Carafa (1519–1561): Etude sur le pontificat de Paul IV*. Paris: Hachette, 1882.

DUYVENDAK, J. J. L. "Review of Pasquale d'Elia, *Le Origini Dell' Arte Christiana Cinese (1583–1640)*," *T'oung Pao* 35 (1940): 385–98.

ELISON, GEORGE. *Deus Destroyed: The Image of Christianity in Early Modern Japan*. Cambridge: Harvard University Press, 1973.

Eminent Chinese of the Ch'ing Period. Ed. Arthur W. Hummel. 2 vols. Washington, D.C., 1944.

EPICTETUS. *Encheiridion,* in *The Discourses as Reported by Arrian, the Manual and Fragments.* Ed. and tr. W. A. Oldfather. 2 vols. New York: Loeb Classical Library, 1926.

ESSEN, L. VAN DER. *Alexandre Farnèse, Prince de Parme.* Vols. 3 and 4. Brussels, 1934–35.

ESTOILE, PIERRE DE L'. *The Paris of Henry of Navarre.* Ed. and tr. Nancy L. Roelker. Cambridge: Harvard University Press, 1958.

FANG HAO 方豪 . "Li Madou *Jiaoyou lun* xinyan" 利 瑪 竇 交 友 論 新 研 [New Study of Ricci's Work on Friendship]. In *Fang Hao liushi ziding gao,* pp. 1847–70.

————. *Liushi ziding gao* 六 十 自 定 稿 [Collected Essays at Sixty]. 2 vols. Taipei, 1969.

————. "Notes on Matteo Ricci's *De Amicitia*," *Monumenta Serica* 14 (1949–55); 574–83.

————. "Tianzhu shiyi zhi gaicuan" 天 主 實 義 之 改 竄 [Variant editions of the *True Doctrine of the Lord of Heaven*]. In *Fang Hao liushi ziding gao,* pp. 1593–1603.

FEDRICI, CESARE (Cesar Frederick). *Voyages and Travels* (*1563–1581*). In Hakluyt, *Second Volume,* pp. 339–375, and in Kerr, *General History,* vol. 7, pp. 142–211.

FITCH, RALPH. "Journey to India over-land in 1583." In Kerr, *General History,* vol. 7, pp. 470–505.

————. *Letters.* In Kerr, *General History,* vol. 7, pp. 513–515.

FITZPATRICK, MERRILYN. "Local Interests and the Anti-Pirate Administration in China's Southeast, 1555–1565," *Ch'ing-shih wen-t'i* 4:2 (December 1979): 1–50.

FLORUS, LUCIUS ANNAEUS. *Epitome of Roman History.* Tr. E. S. Forster. New York: Loeb Classical Library, 1929.

FOK KAI CHEONG. "The Macao Formula: A Study of Chinese Management of Westerners from the Mid-Sixteenth Century to the Opium War Period." Ph.D. dissertation, University of Hawaii, 1978.

FORKE, A. "Ein islamitisches Traktat aus Turkistan: Chinesisch in Arabischer Schrift," *T'oung Pao,* n.s. 8 (1907): 1–76.

FR, Fonti Ricciane. Pasquale M. d'Elia, S.J., ed., *Storia dell' Introduzione del Christianesimo in Cina.* [The annotated version of Ricci's original manuscript of the *Historia.*] 3 vols. Rome, 1942–49.

FRANKE, OTTO. "Li Tschi und Matteo Ricci." In *Abhandlungen der Preussischen Akademie der Wissenschaften,* Jahrgang 1938, Phil-Hist, no. 5. Berlin, 1939.

FRANKEN, DANIEL. *L'Oeuvre gravé des van de Passe.* Amsterdam and Paris, 1881.

FRECCERO, JOHN. "Dante's Firm Foot and the Journey without a Guide," *Harvard Theological Review* 52 (1959): 245-81.

FROIS, LUIS. *Tratado dos Embaixadores Japões que forão de Japão à Roma no anno de 1582.* Ed. J. A. Abranches Pinto, Yoshitomo Okamoto, and Henri Bernard, S.J. Tokyo: Sophia University, 1942.

FURBER, HOLDEN. *Rival Empires of Trade in the Orient, 1600-1800.* Minneapolis: University of Minnesota Press, 1976.

GANSS, GEORGE E., S.J. "The Christian Life Communities as Sprung from the Sodalities of Our Lady," *Studies in the Spirituality of Jesus,* 7:2 (March 1975): 46-58.

——————. *Saint Ignatius' Idea of a Jesuit University.* Milwaukee, Wis.: Marquette University Press, 1954.

GEISS, JAMES PETER. "Peking under the Ming (1368-1644)." Ph.D. dissertation, Princeton University, 1979.

GENTILI, OTELLO, and ALDO ADVERSI. "La Religione." In Aldo Adversi et al., eds., *Storia di Macerata,* vol. 5, pp. 5-107.

GILES, LIONEL. "Translations from the Chinese World Map of Father Ricci," *Geographical Journal* 52 (July-December 1918): 367-85, and 53 (January-June 1919): 19-30.

GINZBURG, CARLO. *The Cheese and the Worms: The Cosmos of a Sixteenth-Century Miller.* Tr. John and Anne Tedeschi. Baltimore: Johns Hopkins University Press, 1980.

GOMES DE BRITO, BERNADO. *The Tragic History of the Sea: 1559-1565.* Ed. and tr. C. R. Boxer. Cambridge: Hakluyt Society, 1968.

——————. *The Tragic History of the Sea: 1589-1622.* Ed. and tr. C. R. Boxer. Cambridge: Hakluyt Society, 1959.

GOMEZ, DUARTE. *Discursos sobre los comercios de las dos Indias.* Madrid, 1622.

GRATAROLI, GUGLIELMO (Medico Bergomante). *De Memoria Reparanda, Augenda, Servandaque, liber unus; De locali vel artificiosa memoria, liber alter.* Rome, 1555.

——————. *The Castel of Memorie.* Tr. William Fulwood. London: William How, 1573.

GREENBLATT, STEPHEN. *Renaissance Self-Fashioning: From More to Shakespeare.* Chicago: University of Chicago Press, 1980.

GREENE, THOMAS M. *The Light in Troy: Imitation and Discovery in Renaissance Poetry.* New Haven: Yale University Press, 1982.

GROTO, LUIGI. *Troffeo della Vittoria Sacra Ottenuta dalla Christianiss. Lega contra Turchi nell' anno MDLXXI.* Venice: Sigismondo Bordogna, 1572.

GU BAOGU 顧 保 鵠 (Ignatius Ku, S.J.). "Li Madou di zhong-wen zhushu" 利 馬 竇 的 中 文 著 述 [Matteo Ricci's Writings in Chinese]. In *Shenxue lunji* (*Collectanea Theologica*), no. 56 (Summer 1983): 239–54.

GUIBERT, JOSEPH DE, S.J. "Le Généralat de Claude Acquaviva (1581–1615)," *Archivum Historicum Societatis Iesu* 10 (1941): 59–93.

—————. *The Jesuits: Their Spiritual Doctrine and Practice.* Tr. William J. Young, S.J. St. Louis: Institute of Jesuit Sources, 1972.

Gujin tushu jicheng 古 今 圖 書 集 成 , comp. Chen Menglei 陳 夢 雷 et al. 800 vols. Shanghai: Zhonghua shuju, 1934.

GULIK, ROBERT H. VAN. *Erotic Colour Prints of the Ming Period.* 3 vols. Tokyo: privately printed, 1951.

GUO TINGXUN 過 庭 訓 comp. *Guochao jingsheng fenjun renwu kao* 國 朝 京 省 分 郡 人 物 攷 [Biographies of Ming Dynasty Worthies]. 115 juan. Taiwan, 1971 reprint.

HAKLUYT, RICHARD. *The Second Volume of the Principal Navigations, Voyages, Traffiques and Discoveries of the English Nation.* London, 1599. *The Third and Last Volume. . . .* London, 1600.

HANSON, CARL A. *Economy and Society in Baroque Portugal, 1668–1703.* Minneapolis: Minnesota University Press, 1981.

HARRIS, GEORGE, S.J. "The Mission of Matteo Ricci, S.J.: A Case Study of an Effort at Guided Cultural Change in the Sixteenth Century," *Monumenta Serica* 25 (1966): 1–168.

HEATH, THOMAS L. *The Thirteen Books of Euclid's Elements.* 3 vols. Cambridge: Cambridge University Press, 1926.

HEAWOOD, E. "The Relationships of the Ricci Maps," *Geographical Journal* 50:4 (October 1917): 271–76.

HERSEY, G. L. *Pythagorean Palaces: Magic and Architecture in the Italian Renaissance.* Ithaca: Cornell University Press, 1976.

HICKS, LEO, S.J. "The English College, Rome and Vocations to the Society of Jesus, March, 1579–July, 1595," *Archivum Historicum Societatis Iesu* 3 (1934): 1–36.

HILLGARTH, J. N. *Ramon Lull and Lullism in Fourteenth-Century France.* London: Oxford University Press, 1971.

HO PENG-YOKE and ANG TIAN-SE. "Chinese Astronomical Records on Comets and 'Guest Stars,'" *Oriens Extremus* 17 (1970): 63–99.

HODGSON, MARSHALL G. *The Venture of Islam,* vol. 3, *The Gunpowder Empires and Modern Times.* Chicago: University of Chicago Press, 1974.

HOSHI AYAO. "Transportation in the Ming Period," *Acta Asiatica* 38 (1980): 1–30.

HU GUOZHEN 胡 國 楨 (Peter Hu), S.J. *Jianjie Tianzhu shiyi* 簡 介 天 主 實 義 [Topical Outline of the *True Meaning of the Lord of Heaven*]. *Shenxue lunji (Collectanea Theologica)*, no. 56 (Summer 1983): 255–66.

HUANG, RAY. *1587, a Year of No Significance: The Ming Dynasty in Decline*. New Haven: Yale University Press, 1981.

—————. "Military Expenditures in Sixteenth Century Ming China," *Oriens Extremus* 17 (1970): 39–62.

HUCKER, CHARLES O. *The Censorial System of Ming China*. Stanford: Stanford University Press, 1966.

HUNG MING-SHUI. "Yüan Hung-tao and the Late Ming Literary and Intellectual Movement." Ph.D. dissertation, University of Wisconsin at Madison, 1974.

HUNG YEH 洪 業 (William Hung). "Kao Li Madou di shijie ditu" 考 利 馬 實 的 世 界 地 圖 [A Study of Ricci's World Map]. First published in *Yugong* 禹貢 , April 11, 1936; reprinted in *Hung Yeh lunxue ji* 洪 業 論 學 集 [Collected Essays by William Hung], Peking, 1981, pp. 150–92.

IGNATIUS OF LOYOLA. *The Constitutions of the Society of Jesus*. Translation and Commentary by George E. Ganss, S. J. St. Louis: Institute of Jesuit Sources, 1970.

—————. *Exercitia Spiritualia Sancti Ignatii de Loyola et eorum directoria— ex autographis vel ex antiquioribus exemplis collecta*. Madrid, 1919.

—————. *Exercitia Spiritualia: Textum Antiquissimorum nova editio lexicon textus hispani*. Monumenta Historica Societatis Iesu, vol. 100. Rome, 1969.

—————. *The Spiritual Exercises*. Tr. Thomas Corbishley, S.J. London: Burns & Oates, 1963.

—————. *The Spiritual Exercises*. Tr. Louis J. Puhl, S.J. Chicago: Loyola University Press, 1952.

IPARRAGUIRRE, IGNACIO, S.J. "Para la Historia de la Oración en el Collegio Romano durante la secunda mitad del siglo XVI," *Archivum Historicum Societatis Iesu* 15 (1946): 77–126.

ISRAELI, RAPHAEL. *Muslims in China: A Study in Cultural Confrontation*. Copenhagen: Scandinavian Institute of Asian Studies, 1980.

IWAO SEIICHI. "Japanese Foreign Trade in the 16th and 17th Centuries," *Acta Asiatica* 30 (1976): 1–18.

JACOBS, HUBERT TH. TH. M., S.J., ed. *A Treatise on the Moluccas* (*c. 1544*). [Attr. to António Galvão]. St. Louis, Mo., 1971.

Jiangzhou zhi 絳 州 志 [Gazetteer of Jiangzhou, Shanxi]. 20 juan. 1766 ed.

JIAO HONG 焦 竑 *Dan yuan ji* 澹 園 集 [Collected Writings]. Jinling congshu ed., 1916.

Jiaxing fuzhi 嘉 興 府 志 [Gazetteer of Jiaxing Prefecture]. 88 juan. (1879); Ch'eng-wen reprint, 1970.

KERR, ROBERT, comp. *General History and Collection of Voyages and Travels, Arranged in Systematic Order,* vol. 7. Edinburgh, 1812.

KOBATA A[TSUSHI]. "The Production and Uses of Gold and Silver in Sixteenth- and Seventeenth-Century Japan," *Economic History Review,* 2d ser. 18 (1965): 245–66.

KU, JOSEPH KING-HAP. "Hsü Kuang-ch'i: Chinese Scientist and Christian (1562–1633)." Ph.D. thesis, St. John's University, New York, 1973.

LACH, DONALD. *Asia in the Making of Europe.* Vol. 1 (in two books), *The Century of Discovery.* Chicago: University of Chicago Press, 1965.

LANCASHIRE, D[OUGLAS]. "Buddhist Reaction to Christianity in Late Ming China," *Journal of the Oriental Society of Australia* 6:1, 2 (1968–69): 82–103.

LANDES, DAVID S. *Revolution in Time: Clocks and the Making of the Modern World.* Cambridge: Harvard University Press, 1983.

LAUFER, BERTHOLD. "Christian Art in China," *Mitteilungen des Seminars für Orientalische Sprachen,* 1910, pp. 100–118 plus plates.

LI ZHI 李 贄 . *Fenshu* 焚 書 , and *Xu fenshu* 續 焚 書 . 2 vols. Peking, 1975.

LIEBMAN, SEYMOUR. "The Jews of Colonial Mexico," *Hispanic American Historical Review* 43 (1963): 95–108.

LIN JINSHUI 林 金 水 . "Li Madou zai Zhongguo di huodong yu yingxiang" 利 玛 窦 在 中 国 的 活 动 与 影 响 [Matteo Ricci's Activities and Influence in China]. *Lishi yanjiu* 1983, issue 1: 25–36.

LINSCHOTEN, JOHN HUIGHEN VON. "Report ... concerning the imprisonment of Newbery and Fitch." In Kerr, *General History,* vol. 7, pp. 515–20.

LUBAC, HENRI DE. *La rencontre du Bouddisme et de l'Occident.* Paris: Aubier, 1952.

LUDOLFUS OF SAXONY. *The Hours of the Passion from The Life of Christ.* Tr. H. J. C[oleridge]. Quarterly Series, vol. 59. London: Burns & Oates, 1887.

—————. *Vita Jesu Christi.* Ed. A.-C. Bolard, L.-M. Rigollot, and J. Carnandet. Paris and Rome, 1865.

LULL, RAMON. *Le Livre du Gentil et des trois Sages.* Ed. and part tr. Armand Llinarès. Paris: Presses Universitaires de France, 1966.

LUTHER, MARTIN. *Letters of Spiritual Counsel.* Tr. and ed. Theodore Tappert. Library of Christian Classics, vol. 18. Philadelphia, 1955.

Lyra Graeca. Tr. J. M. Edmonds. New York: Loeb Classical Library, 1931.

MAFFEI, GIAN PIETRO. *L'Histoire des Indes Orientales et Occidentales.* Tr. M. M. D. P. Paris, 1665.

MARGIOTTI, FORTUNATO, O.F.M. "Congregazioni laiche gesuitiche della antica missione cinese," *Neue Zeitschrift für Missionwissenschaft* 18 (1962): 255–74 and 19 (1963): 50–65.

—————. "Congregazioni Mariane della antica missione cinese." In Johann Specker and P. Walbert Bühlmann, eds., *Das Laienapostolat in den Missionen* (Supplement 10 to the *Neue Zeitschrift für Missionwissenschaft*). Schöneck-Beckenried, Switzerland, 1961.

MARTIN, GREGORY. *Roma Sancta (1581).* Ed. George Bruner Parks. Rome, 1969.

MATHEW, C. P., and M. M. THOMAS. *The Indian Churches of Saint Thomas.* Delhi, 1967.

MAUQUOY-HENDRICKX. *Les estampes des Wierix conservées au cabinet des estampes de la bibliothèque royale Albert 1ᵉʳ.* 3 vols. Brussels: Bibliothèque Royale Albert 1ᵉʳ, 1978.

METLITZKI, DOROTHEE. *The Matter of Araby in Medieval England.* New Haven: Yale University Press, 1977.

MILLER, JOSEF, S.J. "Die Marianischen Kongregationen vor der Bulle 'Omnipotentis Dei': Ein Beitrag zu ihrer Charakteristik," *Archivum Historicum Societatis Iesu* 4 (1935): 252–67.

MILLINGER, JAMES. "Ch'i Chi-kuang—A Military Official as Viewed by his Contemporary Civil Officials," *Oriens Extremus* 20 (1973): 103–17.

MOCQUET, JEAN. *Voyages en Afrique, Asie, Indes Orientales et Occidentales.* Paris: Jean de Heuqueville, 1617.

MONTAIGNE, MICHEL DE. *Journal de Voyage en Italie, par la Suisse et l'Allemagne en 1580 et 1581.* Ed. Charles Dédéyan. Paris: Société des belles lettres, 1946.

Monumenta Paedagogica Societatis Iesu quae primam rationem studiorum anno 1586 editam praecessere. Ed. Caecilius Gomes Rodeles et al. Madrid, 1901.

MOULE, G. E. "The Obligations of China to Europe in the Matter of Physical Science Acknowledged by Eminent Chinese," *Journal of the North-China Branch of the Royal Asiatic Society,* n.s. 7 (1871): 147–64.

MULLAN, ELDER, S.J., and FRANCIS BERINGER, S.J. *The Sodality of Our Lady Studied in the Documents.* New York, 1912.

NADAL, JERONIMO (Hieronymo Natali). *Adnotationes et Meditationes in Evangelia quae in sacrosancto missae sacrificio toto anno leguntur.* Antwerp: Martinus Nutius, 1595.

—————. *Evangelicae Historiae Imagines, ex ordine Evangeliorum.* Antwerp, 1596.

NAGAYAMA TOKIHIKO (Tokihide) 永 山 時 英 . *Taigwai shiryō biz-hutsu taikwan* 對 外 史 料 美 術 大 觀 . [An Album of Historical Materials Connected with Foreign Intercourse]. Nagasaki, 1919.

NEEDHAM, JOSEPH. *Science and Civilisation in China.* Cambridge: Cambridge University Press, 1954–.

New Cambridge Modern History. Vol. 3, *The Counter-Reformation and the Price Revolution, 1559–1610.* Ed. R. B. Wernham. Cambridge: Cambridge University Press, 1971.

NEWBERY, JOHN. *Letters.* In Kerr, *General History,* vol. 7, pp. 505–13.

NISHIMURA TEI 西 村 貞 . "Nihon yasokaihan dōban seibo zu ni tsuite" 日 本 耶 穌 會 板 銅 版 聖 母 圖 に 就 い て . [The Mother and Child (Etching) issued by the Society of Jesus of Japan]. *Bijutsu kenkyu* 美 術 研 究 , 69 (September 1937): 371–82.

O'CONNELL, MARVIN. *The Counter Reformation, 1559–1610.* New York, 1974.

O'MALLEY, JOHN W. *Praise and Blame in Renaissance Rome: Rhetoric, Doctrine, and Reform in the Sacred Orators of the Papal Court, c. 1450–1521.* Durham, N.C.: Duke University Press, 1979.

OS. The Letters of Matteo Ricci, in *Opere Storiche.* Ed. Pietro Tacchi Venturi, S.J. Vol. 2, *Le Lettere dalla China.* Macerata, 1913.

PACHTLER, G. M., S.J. *Ratio Studiorum et Institutiones Scholasticae Societatis Jesu.* Vol. 1, *1541–1599.* Berlin, 1887.

PACI, LIBERO. "La Decadenza Religiosa e la Controriforma." In *Storia di Macerata,* vol. 5, pp. 108–246. Comune di Macerata, 1977.

—————. "Le Vicende Politiche." In *Storia di Macerata,* vol. 1, pp. 27–419. Comune di Macerata, 1971.

PALMER, ROBERT E. A. "Martial." In T. J. Luce, ed., *Ancient Writers: Greece and Rome.* 2 vols. New York, 1982.

PANIGAROLA, FRANCESCO. *Trattato della Memoria Locale*. Approx. 1572. *MS* no. 137 in Biblioteca Communale, Macerata.

PARRY, J. H. *The Age of Reconnaissance: Discovery, Exploration and Settlement, 1450 to 1650*. Berkeley: University of California Press, 1981.

PASTOR, LUDWIG, FREIHERR VON. *The History of the Popes from the Close of the Middle Ages*. Tr. Ralph Francis Kerr. Vol. 14, *Marcellus II (1555) and Paul IV (1555-1559)*; vol. 18, *Pius V (1566-1572)*. London: Kegan, Paul, 1924, 1929.

PELLIOT, PAUL. "Les Franciscains en Chine au XVIe et au XVIIe siècle," *T'oung Pao*, n.s. 34 (1938): 191-222.

PFISTER, LOUIS, S.J. *Notices Biographiques et Bibliographiques sur les Jésuites de l'ancienne mission de Chine, 1552-1773. Variétés Sinologiques*, 59. 2 vols. Shanghai, 1932.

PHILLIPS, EDWARD C., S.J. "The Correspondence of Father Christopher Clavius S.I. preserved in the archives of the Pont. Gregorian University," *Archivum Historicum Societatis Iesu* 8 (1939): 193-222.

PILLSBURY, BARBARA. "Muslim History in China: A 1300-year Chronology," *Journal of the Institute of Muslim Minority Affairs* 3:2 (1981): 10-29.

Pinghu xianzhi 平 湖 縣 志 . [Gazetteer of Pinghu County]. 26 juan. 1886; reprint of 1975.

PIRRI, PIETRO, S.J. "Sultan Yahya e il P. Acquaviva," *Archivum Historicum Societatis Iesu* 13 (1944): 62-76.

PLANCIUS, PETRUS. *A Plaine and Full Description of Petrus Plancius his Universall Map*. Tr. M. Blundevile. London: John Windet, 1594.

PLANTIN, CHRISTOPHE. *Correspondance de Christophe Plantin*. Ed. J. Denucé Vols. 8 and 9. Antwerp, 1918.

PLINY. *Natural History*. Tr. H. Rackham. New York: Loeb Classical Library, 1942.

PTAK, RODERICK. "The Demography of Old Macao, 1555-1640," in *Ming Studies*, 15 (Fall 1982): 27-35.

PYRARD DE LAVAL, FRANÇOIS. *The Voyage of François Pyrard of Laval to the East Indies, the Maldives, the Moluccas and Brazil (1601-1611)*. Tr. Albert Gray and H. C. P. Bell. 2 vols. in 3. Hakluyt Society, 1888; reprinted New York: Burt Franklin, n.d.

QUINTILIAN. *Institutio Oratoria*, vol. 4. Tr. H. E. Butler. New York: Loeb Classical Library, 1936.

RABELAIS, FRANÇOIS. *The Histories of Gargantua and Pantagruel*. Tr. J. M. Cohen. Penguin Books, 1970.

RAHNER, HUGO, S.J. *Ignatius the Theologian*. London: Chapman, 1968.

RANKE, LEOPOLD. *The History of the Popes, Their Church and State, in the Sixteenth and Seventeenth Centuries*. Tr. Walter Keating Kelly. New York: Colyer, 1845.

RENICK, M. S. "Akbar's First Embassy to Goa: Its Diplomatic and Religious Aspects," *Indica* 7 (1970): 33–47.

RICCI, MATTEO, S.J. *Collected Letters*. See *OS*.

————. *Ershiwu yan* 二 十 五 言 [Twenty-five Sayings from Epictetus]. In *Tianxue chuhan*, vol. 1, pp. 331–49.

————. *Historia*. See *FR*.

————. *Jiaoyou lun* 交 友 論 [Treatise on Friendship]. In *Tianxue chuhan*, vol. 1, pp. 299–320.

————. *Jifa* 記 法 [Treatise on Mnemonic Arts]. Revised Zhu Dinghan 朱 鼎 瀚 , in Wu Xiangxiang ed. 吳 相 湘 , *Tianzhujiao dongchuan wenxian* 天 主 教 東 傳 文 獻 [Source Materials on Christianity in Asia]. Taipei, 1964.

————. *Jiren Shipian* 畸 人 十 篇 (1608) [Ten Discourses by a Paradoxical Man]. In *Tianxue chuhan*, vol. 1, pp. 117–281.

————. *Li Madou ti baoxiang tu* 利 瑪 竇 題 寶 像 圖 [Ricci's Commentaries on the Sacred Pictures], 8 + 6 pp. In Tao Xiang 陶 湘 ed., *Sheyuan mocui* 涉 園 墨 萃 (1929).

————. *Tianzhu shiyi* 天 主 實 義 . [The True Meaning of the Lord of Heaven]. In *Tianxue chuhan*, vol. 1, pp. 351–635.

————. *Tianzhu shiyi*, ch. 1, "The True Meaning of the Lord of Heaven." Tr. Douglas Lancashire. *China Mission Studies (1550–1800) Bulletin* 4 (1982): 1–11.

————. *Entretiens d'un lettré chinois et d'un docteur européen, sur la vraie idée de Dieu*. (Anon. tr. into French of *Tianzhu shiyi*.) In *Lettres édifiantes et curieuses*, vol. 25, pp. 143–385. Toulouse, 1811.

————. *Xiqin quyi bazhang* 西 琴 曲 意 八 章 [Eight Songs for the Western Instruments]. In *Tianxue chuhan*, vol. 1, pp. 283–291.

————, and XU GUANGQI. *Jihe yuanben* 幾 何 原 本 , [The Elements of Euclid]. In *Tianxue chuhan*, vol. 4, pp. 1921–2522.

————, and others. *Bianxue yidu* 辯 學 遺 牘 [Letters on Buddhism and Christianity]. In *Tianxue chuhan*, vol. 2, pp. 637–87.

ROMBERCH, JOHANN HOST VON. *Longestorium Artificiose Memorie*. Venice: Melchior Sessa, 1533.

ROOSES, MAX. *Christophe Plantin, Imprimeur Anversois.* Antwerp, 1883.

ROOVER, RAYMOND DE. "The Business Organization of the Plantin Press in the Setting of Sixteenth Century Antwerp." In *Gedenkboek der Plantin-Dagen,* pp. 230–46. Antwerp, 1956.

ROSSABI, MORRIS. "Muslim and Central Asian Revolts." In Jonathan Spence and John E. Wills, Jr., eds., *From Ming to Ch'ing,* New Haven: Yale University Press, 1979.

ROSSI, PAOLO. *Francis Bacon, from Magic to Science.* Tr. Sacha Rabinovitch. London, 1968.

ROTH, CECIL. *The House of Nasi: Doña Gracia.* Philadelphia, 1948.

SAKAMOTO MITSURU 坂 本 満 . "Lepanto sentōzu byōbu ni tsuite." レ パ ン ト 戦 闘 図 屏 風 に つ い て (Screen painting of the battle of Lepanto—A Study of early Western style painting in Japan and its background in Europe). *Bijutsu kenkyu* 246 (May 1966): 30–44, plates 3–6.

SASSETTI, FILIPPO. *Lettere edite e inedite.* Ed. Ettore Marcucci. Florence, 1855.

SCHILLING, DOROTHEUS, O.F.M. "Zur Geschichte des Martyrerberichtes des P. Luis Frois, S.I.," *Archivum Historicum Societatis Iesu* 6 (1937): 107–13.

SCHIMBERG, ANDRÉ. *L'Education Morale dans les collèges de la Compagnie de Jésus en France (16e, 17e, 18e siècles).* Paris, 1913.

SCHURZ, WILLIAM LYTLE. *The Manila Galleon.* New York, 1939, 1959.

SCHÜTTE, JOSEF FRANZ S.J. *Valignano's Mission Principles for Japan.* Tr. John J. Coyne, S.J. Vol. 1, *From His Appointment as Visitor until His First Departure from Japan (1573–1582),* pt. I, *The Problem (1573–1580).* St. Louis: Institute of Jesuit Sources, 1980.

SCHWICKERATH, ROBERT. *Jesuit Education, Its History and Principles, Viewed in the Light of Modern Educational Problems.* St. Louis, 1903.

SENECA. *The Controversiae.* Tr. M. Winterbottom. New York: Loeb Classical Library, 1974.

Shaozhou fuzhi 韶 州 府 志 . [Gazetteer of Shaozhou Prefecture]. 40 juan (1874). 1966 reprint.

SHEN DEFU 沈 德 符 . *Bizhou zhai yutan* 敝 帚 齋 餘 談 (譚) [Casual writings from the "Worn Brush" Studio]. 52 leaves, 1880.

————. *Wanli yehubian* 萬 曆 野 獲 編 [Gleanings from the Wanli Reign]. (34 ch. 1619) Peking reprint, 1959.

SMALLEY, BERYL. *English Friars and Antiquity in the Early Fourteenth Century.* New York, 1960.

SMITH, VINCENT EDWARD. *St. Thomas on the Object of Geometry*. Milwaukee: Marquette University Press, 1954.

SO, KWAN-WAI. *Japanese Piracy in Ming China During the 16th Century*. Lansing: Michigan State University Press, 1975.

SOAREZ, CYPRIANO. *De Arte Rhetorica*. Paris, 1573.

SORABJI, RICHARD. *Aristotle on Memory*. London: Duckworth, 1972.

SPALATIN, CHRISTOPHER, S.J. "Matteo Ricci's Use of Epictetus' Encheiridion," *Gregorianum* 56:3 (1975): 551–57.

SPATE, O. H. K. *The Spanish Lake*. Vol. 1 of *The Pacific since Magellan*. London: Croom Helm, 1979.

STAHL, WILLIAM HARRIS, and RICHARD JOHNSON, with E. L. BURGE. *Martianus Capella and the Seven Liberal Arts*. 2 vols. Vol. 1, *The Quadrivium of Martianus Capella;* vol. 2, *The Marriage of Philology and Mercury*. New York: Columbia University Press, 1971, 1977.

STEVENS, THOMAS. "Voyage to Goa in 1579, in the Portuguese Fleet." In Kerr, *General History,* vol. 7, pp. 462–70.

Storia di Macerata [The History of Macerata]. Eds. Aldo Adversi, Dante Cecchi, and Libero Paci. 5 vols. Comune di Macerata, 1971–77.

TACCHI VENTURI, PIETRO S.J.. *Opere Storiche*. See *OS*.

————. *Storia della compagnia di Gesù in Italia*. 3 vols. Rome, 1922–38.

TAKASE KŌICHIRŌ. "Unauthorized Commercial Activities by Jesuit Missionaries in Japan," *Acta Asiatica* 30 (1976): 19–33.

TAO GU 陶 榖 , *Qing yi lu* 清 異 錄 [Collected Observations]. 2 juan. Xiyin gan congshu ed., 1840.

THIERSANT, P. DABRY DE. *Le Mahométisme en Chine et dans le Turkestan Oriental*. 2 vols. Paris, 1878.

THOMAS, KEITH. *Religion and the Decline of Magic*. New York, 1974.

THORNDIKE, LYNN. *History of Magic and Experimental Science*. Vols. 5 and 6, *The Sixteenth Century*. New York: Columbia University Press, 1941.

Tianxue chuhan 天 學 初 函 [Early writings on Christianity in China]. Ed. Li Zhizao 李 之 藻 . Taipei, 1965 reprint in 6 vols.

TRIGAULT, NICOLA, S.J. *China in the Sixteenth Century: The Journals of Matthew Ricci, 1583–1610*. Tr. Louis J. Gallagher, S.J. New York, 1953.

UBELHÖR, MONIKA. "Hsü Kuang-ch'i (1562–1633) und seine Einstellung zum Christentum," *Oriens Extremus* 15:2 (December 1968): 191–257 and 16:1 (June 1969): 41–74.

VERBEEK, J. and ILJA M. VELDMAN, comps. *Hollstein's Dutch and Flemish Etchings, Engravings and Woodcuts, ca. 1450–1700*. Vol. 16, "De Passe (Continued)." Amsterdam: Van Gendt, 1974.

VILLARET, EMILE, S.J. *Les Congrégations Mariales*. Vol. 1, *Des origines à la suppression de la compagnie de Jésus (1540-1773)*. Paris, 1947.

——————. "Les premières origines des congrégations Mariales dans la compagnie de Jésus," *Archivum Historicum Societatis Iesu* 6 (1937): 25-57.

VILLOSLADA, RICCARDO G. *Storia del Collegio Romano dal suo inizio (1551) alla soppressione della Compagnia di Gesù (1773)*. Rome: Gregorian University, 1954.

VOET, LEON. *The Golden Compasses: A History and Evaluation of the Printing and Publishing Activities of the Officina Plantiniana at Antwerp*. 2 vols. Amsterdam and London, 1969.

WALKER, D. P. *The Ancient Theology: Studies in Christian Platonism from the Fifteenth to the Eighteenth Century*. London, 1972.

——————. *Spiritual and Demonic Magic, from Ficino to Campanella*. London: Warburg Institute, 1958.

——————. *Studies in Musical Science in the Late Renaissance*. Leiden: Brill, 1978.

WICKI, JOSEF, S.J. "The Spanish Language in XVI-Century Portuguese India," *Indica* 14:1 (March 1977): 13-19.

WIEGER, LÉON, S.J. "Notes sur la première catéchèse écrite en chinois 1582-1584," *Archivum Historicum Societatis Iesu* 1 (1932): 72-84.

WILHELM, RICHARD. *The I Ching or Book of Changes*. Tr. Cary F. Baynes. Princeton: Princeton University Press, 1967.

WINN, JAMES ANDERSON. *Unsuspected Eloquence: A History of the Relations Between Poetry and Music*. New Haven: Yale University Press, 1981.

WRIGHT, A. D. *The Counter-Reformation: Catholic Europe and the Non-Christian World*. New York, 1982.

XIE ZHAOZHE (Hsieh Chao-che) 謝肇淛. *Wu za zu* 五雜俎 16 juan. 1795 ed., and Peking reprint, 1959.

XU SHUOFANG 徐朔方. "Tang Xianzu he Li Madou" 汤显祖和利玛窦 [Tang Xianzu and Matteo Ricci], *Wenshi* 文史 12 (September 1981): 273-81.

YANG LIEN-SHENG. "Historical Notes on the Chinese World Order." In John K. Fairbank, ed., *The Chinese World Order*. Cambridge: Harvard University Press, 1968.

YATES, FRANCES A. *The Art of Memory*. Penguin Books, 1969.

YERUSHALMI, YOSEF HAYIM. *Zakhor, Jewish History and Jewish Memory*. Seattle: University of Washington Press, 1982.

YIN FALU 阴 法 曾 . "Li Madou yu Ouzhou jiaohui yinyue di dongchuan" 利 玛 窦 与 欧 洲 教 会 音 乐 的 东 传 [Matteo Ricci and the transmission of European music to the East], *Yinyue Yanjiu* 音 乐 研 究 , no. 2, 1982, pp. 87–90 and 103.

YOUNG, JOHN D. *Confucianism and Christianity, the First Encounter.* Hong Kong: Hong Kong University Press, 1983.

————. *East-West Synthesis: Matteo Ricci and Confucianism.* Hong Kong: University of Hong Kong, 1980.

YÜ CHÜN-FANG. *The Renewal of Buddhism in China: Chu-hung and the Late Ming Synthesis.* New York: Columbia University Press, 1981.

YUAN TSING. "Urban Riots and Disturbances." In Jonathan D. Spence and John E. Wills, eds., *From Ming to Ch'ing: Conquest, Region and Continuity in Seventeenth-Century China.* New Haven: Yale University Press, 1979.

ZANTA, LÉONTINE. *La renaissance du stoïcisme au XVIe siècle.* Paris, 1914.

ZHANG XIE 張 燮 . *Dongxiyang kao* 東 西 洋 考 [Study of the Eastern and Western Oceans]. 12 juan. 1617–18. Taipei, 1962 reprint.

ZHANG XUAN 張 萱 . *Xiyuan wenjian lu* 西 園 聞 見 錄 [Notes on Ming History]. Prefaces 1627 and 1632. 106 juan. Peking, 1940.

Zhaoqing fuzhi 肇 慶 府 志 . [Gazetteer of Zhaoqing Prefecture]. 22 juan. 1833; 1967 reprint.

ZHUANGZI. *The Complete Works of Chuang Tzu.* Tr. Burton Watson. New York: Columbia University Press, 1968.

ZOU YUANBIAO 鄒 元 標 . "Da Xiguo Li Madou" 答 西 國 利 瑪 竇 [A reply to Ricci letter] in *Yuan xue ji* 願 學 集 , *Siku quanshu* ed., juan 3, p. 39.

INDEX

CHINESE NAMES, WITH THE OLDER WADE-GILES ROMANIZATION FORMS IN PARENTHESES

Akbar, Muslim emperor, 86, 105–06
Albuquerque, Afonso de, 103, 173
Alcazarquivir, battle of, 33, 36–38, 106
alchemy, 17–21, 152; in late Ming
   China, 185, 188; Ricci and, 185–88
allegory, 5
Almeida, Antonio, 49, 260
Almeida, Luis de, 175–76
Alva, duke of, 28–29, 205
Alvarez, Emmanuel, 62, 170
ambergris, 187
Analects, The, 138
ancient mnemonics, 5–6, 8, 11, 14, 18,
   22–23, 156, 157. *See also* Classical
   Western texts; *specific authors; works*
Ancona, 29, 30; Jews in, 108, 110, 205
Anes, Gonçalo, 107
Annunciation, 78
Anthony of Padua, 77
Antonio, Don, 107
Antwerp, 87, 201; 1585 Spanish siege
   of, 33, 165
appearance, religious, 114–16
Aquinas, Thomas, 14, 69–70, 99, 135;
   on mathematics, 144–45; mnemonic
   theory of, 13, 16; *The Perfection of
   Spiritual Life,* 55; *Summa Against the
   Gentiles,* 222
Arabic, 103, 119, 134
architecture: Chinese, 212–13; Western,
   21, 213
Aristophanes, 141
Aristotle, 13, 41, 143
Armenia, 119
art: Chinese, 11, 210; Western, 11, 13,
   34, 63, 131–32, 147, 171–73, 201,
   245–47, 262
Arte Rhetorica, De (Soarez), 5
Art of Memory, The (Yates), 10
Ascension, 63
Assumption of the Virgin, 78
astrolabe, 73, 143, 148
astrology, 18, 19, 20
astronomy: Chinese, 146; Western, 21,
   66, 142–43, 145–48
Augustine, 16
Augustinian missionaries, 51, 52
autos-da-fé, 111

Bacon, Francis, 12–13
banditry, 45, 46, 57
Barbosa, Pero, 71–72
Barradas, João, 91–92, 266
Bassein, 41
beating procedures, Chinese, 48–49
beggary: Chinese, 218; Italian, 206–208
Bei River, 88, 90
Bencivegni, Nicolo, 232
Bengal, 174
Berwouts, Roger, 170
Bible, 11, 214; in Christian mnemonic
   tradition, 14–16; Plantin, 86–89, 105,
   121, 179; road to Emmaus episode,
   128–32; Sodom and Gomorrah epi-
   sode, 201–204, 221, 223; walking-on-
   water episode, 59–64
Bijapur, 104, 173
black slaves, 79, 208, 209
Board of Rites, 152, 195, 257
Boccaccio, Giovanni, 102
bookbinding, Chinese, 154
Book of Changes, 151
*Book of the Gentile and the Three Sages,
   The* (Lull), 101
Borgia, Francis, 170
Bramante, 233, 234
Brazil, 37, 65, 68, 71, 79, 107
Bridget of Sweden, 14
Buddhism, 21, 85–86, 95, 102, 116, 210,
   224, 249; Christian criticism of,
   250–59; and Christianity, paralleled,
   114–15, 252; importance of appear-
   ance in, 114–15; Ricci on, 216, 217,
   250–59
Burma, 225

calendars, 144, 181
calligraphy, 9, 11, 154, 155, 210
canal travel, Chinese, 83–84
Canary Islands, 68
Canisius, Peter, 223
Canton, 43, 49, 118, 174, 178, 187
Capella, Martianus, 8
Cape of Good Hope, 19, 40, 64, 65, 70
Carafa, Carlo, 205
Carafa, Gian Pietro, 40. *See also* Paul
   IV, Pope